Luminos is the Open Access monograph publishing program from UC Press. Luminos provides a framework for preserving and reinvigorating monograph publishing for the future and increases the reach and visibility of important scholarly work. Titles published in the UC Press Luminos model are published with the same high standards for selection, peer review, production, and marketing as those in our traditional program. www.luminosoa.org

Feeling Like Lovers

Feeling Like Lovers

Affect in Medieval Sufism

Matthew Thomas Miller

UNIVERSITY OF CALIFORNIA PRESS

University of California Press
Oakland, California

Suggested citation: Miller, M. T. *Feeling Like Lovers: Affect in Medieval Sufism*. Oakland: University of California Press, 2026. DOI: https://doi.org/10.1525/luminos.265

Library of Congress Cataloging-in-Publication Data

Names: Miller, Matthew Thomas author.
Title: Feeling like lovers : affect in medieval Sufism / Matthew Thomas Miller.
Description: Oakland, California : University of California Press, [2026] | Includes bibliographical references and index.
Identifiers: LCCN 2025026771 (print) | LCCN 2025026772 (ebook) | ISBN 9780520426337 (hardcover) | ISBN 9780520426344 (paperback) | ISBN 9780520426351 (ebook)
Subjects: LCSH: God (Islam)—Worship and love. | Affect (Psychology)—Religious aspects—Sufism.
Classification: LCC BP189.65.L68 M55 2026 (print) | LCC BP189.65.L68 (ebook)

LC record available at https://lccn.loc.gov/2025026771
LC ebook record available at https://lccn.loc.gov/2025026772

GPSR Authorized Representative: Easy Access System Europe,
Mustamäe tee 50, 10621 Tallinn, Estonia, gpsr.requests@easproject.com

35 34 33 32 31 30 29 28 27 26
10 9 8 7 6 5 4 3 2 1

Dedicated to my mother and first best friend, Donna Marie Conrady-Miller. Mom, you taught me to read (with some help from Grandma Laura Conrady) and to love learning. If I know anything of what love feels like, it is because you first loved me so much. You passed away much too young, shortly before I began the journey that led to this book, but I know you were with me the entire time, helping me finish it. I love you, Mom, and I miss you dearly every day.

CONTENTS

Acknowledgments — *ix*
Technical Notes — *xv*

Introduction: "Begin a Love Affair!" — *1*

1. "Passionate Desire Conquered Him": The Felt Life of a Sufi Lover — *39*
2. "An Internal Turmoil Overtook the Shaykh": The Æffects of Music and Place in *Samāʿ* — *74*
3. Getting into the Habit(us) of Being a Lover: Æffective Hermeneutics and the Formation of Sufi Feeling Subjects in *Samāʿ* — *100*
4. "Expressing Meanings (*Maʿānī*) in the Clothing of Forms": Sufism's Æffective Poetics — *130*
5. "When the Wine of Love Started Taking Its Æffect": Self-Annihilation (*Fanāʾ*) and the Force Dynamics of Sufi Poetry — *161*

Conclusion: Restoring the Sufi Mind-Body — *189*

Bibliography — *197*
Index — *213*

ACKNOWLEDGMENTS

The journey to completing this book was a long one, and it came to fruition only because I received the help and support of many people and institutions along the way.

Let me begin what will certainly be my insufficiently detailed expressions of gratitude by thanking those institutions who have supported me along the way. This book developed out of ideas that I started grappling with in the last chapter I wrote for my dissertation (chapter 3) (which appears in the present work in revised and expanded form in chapter 5). My dissertation research was generously supported by a Roshan Cultural Heritage Institute Fellowship for Excellence in Persian Studies and a dissertation fellowship from Washington University in St. Louis (Wash U).

My ability to take the risk of developing that set of ideas from that final dissertation chapter into a whole new project is largely due to the fact that the Roshan Institute for Persian Studies at the University of Maryland (UMD) gave me a job after I completed my PhD and has supported me in myriad ways since, from awarding me an Independent Scholarship, Research and Creativity Award for course release time to providing all of those essential—though often uncredited—forms of intellectual support, such as library services, office space, etc., that made it possible to research and write this book. Special thanks to the team in UMD's Interlibrary Loan office who fielded innumerable requests for books and articles, even in the depths of the COVID-19 pandemic. It is not an exaggeration to say that I never could have written this book without UMD Library's ILL team.

Research in the humanities is often portrayed as an individual sport. The humanities scholar works alone in the depths of the library or at a book-stacked and paper-cluttered desk in their office or study. This portrayal is true up to a point: humanists do often research solo and publish their findings in single-authored articles and monographs. But this is only part of the story. The contributions of many teachers and intellectual interlocutors are obscured in this highly individualized and simplistic rendering of the production process for humanistic scholarship. We can only come to the point where we are capable of conducting research alone at our desks because we have been trained to do so by many teachers in the past, from our first teachers who taught us to read up to those professors who helped us polish our advanced research language skills and learn to make scholarly arguments in our dissertations. Even after our PhD years, our scholarship develops and improves through an iterative process of revising in response to the feedback our colleagues provide in conferences, workshops, peer review, and personal conversations. I want to be sure to highlight here some of the individuals who played these roles in my intellectual formation and the development of this book.

I am deeply indebted to many teachers along the way for patiently nurturing me intellectually and providing the training necessary to complete this work: to Pamela Vollman and Randy Moning for awakening my interest in learning in grade school; to Robert Sauerbrey, Christopher Winiarski, and Andrew Bensman for pushing me to expand my intellectual and moral horizons in high school; to Frank Flinn, Pamela Parmash, Mark Chmiel, and John Kavanaugh for helping me see religion and religious studies in new ways in my undergraduate years; to Nesrine Basheer, Mohamed-Salah Omri, and Hayrettin Yücesoy for training me up in Arabic; to Asad Ahmed for encouraging my intellectual curiosity and giving me confidence to engage classical Arabic by unapologetically throwing me into Abū Ḥāmid al-Ghazālī's original texts early in my Arabic training; to Tina Rahimi, my long-time Persian conversation teacher, for keeping my spoken Persian alive while I spent the last twelve years reading almost exclusively medieval Persian texts; and to Lynne Tatlock for her tireless support of me in her role of director of Comparative Literature at Wash U.

I also want to thank numerous colleagues who patiently listened to or read parts of this work at different stages of its development and provided helpful feedback. I am likely forgetting as many as I am remembering to mention here, but I am especially grateful to the following scholars for their feedback at different points over the preceding eight years: Samuel Hodgkin, Domenico Ingenito, Ahmad Karimi-Hakkak, Franklin Lewis, Leonard Lewisohn, Jane Mikkelson, Arjun Nair, Fatemeh Shams, Sunil Sharma, Axel Takacs, and Claudia Yaghoobi. Alexander Jabbari gave insightful feedback on several of this work's early chapters too, in addition to providing constant moral support during the always trying graduate school and early career years. My highest appreciation goes to Cameron Cross and Austin O'Malley. We all happened to be in Chicago right as we all began writing our dissertations on "classical" Persian literature topics, so we formed a dissertation workshop to provide a first round of feedback to each other before we submitted our chapter drafts to our advisors. Over the ensuing years we loyally read and provided feedback on each and every chapter each of us wrote. These workshop sessions would sometimes stretch over several hours in cafes or bars around Hyde Park and, later, online. We kept this writing workshop going after we finished our PhDs and, with the addition of Michael Pifer, have continued workshopping (most) of our subsequent articles and book chapters until today. I am equally grateful for all I have learned from these accomplished scholars in the decade-plus of our writing workshops and for their friendship and support along the (very long) way.

There are also a number of colleagues that played pivotal roles at different points. Anca Parvulescu first suggested to me, while reviewing my job application materials in 2014, that I should use affect theory as a framing for what became this book. Maxim Romanov and Sarah Bowen Savant have been boon intellectual companions and collaborators in the Islamic digital humanities (DH) work that occupied my research time when I was not working on this book. While the rapidly increasing load of our joint Islamic DH projects led to several years' worth of delays in finishing this book, the time spent working with them on these projects was always a joy. I am grateful to Savant, too, for strongly encouraging me to not be afraid to write a first book that is not a revision of my dissertation. I would be remiss if I did not also thank my digital humanities lab team members at the University of Maryland, especially Osama Eshera, John Mullan, Jonathan Allen, and Taimoor Shahid Khan, for holding down the fort for me in late 2023 and early 2024 while I avoided most grant-related administrative duties to put the final touches on this manuscript. Lastly, I owe a huge debt to Lorenz Nigst for meticulously and eruditely reviewing my Arabic translations, offering both several corrections and some stylistic suggestions for revising my at times overly literal English renderings.

Without a doubt, I owe my greatest intellectual debt to Fatemeh Keshavarz and Ahmet T. Karamustafa. My debt to these mentors goes far beyond what I am able to put into words. Since that day I walked into Keshavarz's office in my senior year of undergrad asking—probably annoyingly—a million questions about Rūmī, and she made what seemed to me an incredible offer—"If you are serious about studying Rūmī, I will start teaching you Persian right now"—she has indefatigably taught me not only Persian, but also so much about literature, life, and how to be a good person and innovative scholar. She has faithfully guided me since and spent untold numbers of hours helping form me into the scholar and person I am today. Karamustafa likewise has been a consummate mentor on intellectual and personal matters since the day I timidly stumbled into one of his Islamic history survey courses as an undergrad. His fierce intellect and seemingly encyclopedic knowledge of everything Islamic-studies related is perfectly balanced by the tremendous kindness and calming presence he exudes. He always seems to know just what to say and when to his students, friends, and family. Both Keshavarz and

Karamustafa are models for the scholar-teacher-mentor-public intellectual that I aspire to become now as I cross into the "mid-career scholar" zone. I feel blessed to have been able to train under both of them and to now call them colleagues and friends. Thank you, my *ustādān* (professors), for everything over the last nearly two decades.

Another special thanks is due to Paul Losensky. Exceedingly kind, he graciously accepted the desperate plea of this then young graduate student from another university at the 2012 Middle East Studies Conference to serve as the outside committee member on what I thought was going to be a dissertation focused on Fakhr al-Dīn ʿIrāqī. He not only served on that committee but also sent me *extensive* feedback on each dissertation chapter draft, including the large appendix of translations of nearly one hundred poems, incredibly correcting even the smallest errors of grammar, spelling, and punctuation throughout.[1] I still remember my excitement, mixed with not a little fear, when he would send his handwritten comments on each chapter, snail mail in one of those big US Priority Mail envelopes. He has remained since an incredible intellectual interlocutor, always willing to dedicate unrewarded and unrecognized time to give his incisive constructive feedback to not only me, but many other junior scholars in the field of Persian studies.

My last intellectual expression of gratitude goes to the many scholars cited throughout this work. I have learned immeasurable amounts from all of them, even ones that I disagree with at points in the present study. I try, as much as possible throughout this work, to engage in a citational practice of generosity, in the sense that I want to highlight what I have learned from all these different scholars rather than citing just to critique (though this obviously is not completely avoidable in a scholarly work). We do not have to agree with everything another scholar says to recognize and value their work.

Before concluding my intellectual acknowledgements, I want to take a page from the prefaces of two towering scholars of Persian, Arabic, and Islamic studies—Julie Scott Meisami and Shahab Ahmad—and apologize to those scholars whose recent work I have missed or whose arguments I have not fully integrated or responded to in the depth they deserve.[2] When I began working on the ideas that became this book in the latter half of my dissertation way back in 2014–15, very little had been written on Sufism and the body, embodiment, sense, and, especially, emotion/affect. This book and its theoretical framework have benefited tremendously from the significant rise in new publications touching on these issues in the domain of Sufi and Islamic studies more broadly, which has grown steadily since the mid-2010s and exploded in particular after 2020. These works have substantially enriched this project while also presenting some difficulties. Incorporating many

1. These translations are under contract with University of California Press. See Miller, *God's Wild Lovers*.

2. Meisami, *Structure and Meaning*, xii–xiii; Shahab Ahmed, *What Is Islam?*, xiii.

new germane studies in the late stages of a project is always difficult. While I have tried to integrate as many studies from 2022 and 2023 as I could, I am sure that I have missed some as I focused on finishing the final drafts of this book's chapters from the latter half of 2022 to the first few months of 2024. It is likely too that I have missed some others from 2021 or even a bit earlier that were "slow to come to hand," as Shahab Ahmad aptly remarks in the preface to his work.[3] To all of these scholars, I deeply apologize.

I could not have asked for a better press and set of editors (Eric Schmidt, Jyoti Arvey, and Margo Irvin) to help bring *Feeling Like Lovers* into the world. I am grateful to Schmidt and Arvey for immediately believing in the promise of the book when I sent them the proposal and to Irvin for shepherding this work to completion and helping me—a nervous, first-time manuscript author—navigate the publication process. I am also deeply grateful to Anitra Grisales and Catherine Osborne for their superb editing work on this manuscript and to I. S. Bosschieter (Pierke) for its thorough index.

Finally, I will end by expressing my utter and complete appreciation and love to all my family members. I am fortunate to have a wonderful family who always reminds me that there is much more to life than the academic game. My parents, Donna Conrady-Miller and Richard Miller, raised me in a home full of love and sacrificed a great deal in order to always put their children's needs first. It sounds like a cliché, but I really do owe them everything, and I know that I would never be the person I am today without them. To my siblings—Mitchell Miller, Megan Miller, and now Megan's husband Dusty Israel—thank you for being exactly who you are. There are few things I enjoy more than spending time with you on holidays or on your visits to D.C. I hope it does not sound too patronizing to say, as your older brother, that I am so proud of you.

Almost at the exact same time as I met Rūmī in undergrad, I had the fortune of meeting Nima Sheth through a social justice magazine we worked on together. As soon as we got together, her family adopted me into their family as well. Chaturbhuj and Smita Sheth and Mansi and Sunny Chaudhry—thank you for welcoming me with open arms. I cannot tell you how much it has meant to me to become part of your family over the last two decades. Your home became a second home right when I needed it most. To all my family, Millers and Sheths alike, I love you all, and please know that none of this would have been possible without your constant love and support.

Above all else, I would like to thank Nima Sheth, my partner in life, best friend, and soulmate. She has been by my side for the last two decades, constantly supporting, challenging, and encouraging me in more ways than I could ever list. Words, as the Sufi poets this book discusses know so well, cannot express the depth of my love for you, Nima. This is a book about feeling, especially the diverse

3. Shahab Ahmed, *What Is Islam?*, xiii.

somatic-affective manifestations of love on the Sufi path to their Beloved. If I myself have any level of experiential understanding of the intense feeling of love Sufi masters have for their Beloved, it is because you came into my life and ignited that in me. I will never in my life forget that moment when we were talking late into the night a few months after we met and you, with your admirable courage and frankness, finally just came out and asked me what we both had been circling around for a while: "So what are we? Do you like me or not?" As soon as you said this, I felt like I had been rocketed into the sky with joy. I felt like I was flying. It was a very visceral feeling that took over my whole body. I had fallen in love, and my beloved loved me back. Later, when I read Rūmī's famous *ghazal* that begins *ʿishq ast dar* [or, *bar*] *āsimān parīdan* ("Love is: flying in (or upon or to) the sky"), I instantly understood what he meant—not just in a linguistic sense but also the feeling he was aiming to capture and convey.[4] Then, when I thought I could never love anyone else as much as you, we brought two little wild bundles of joy and sass, Moksh and Samudr, into the world. Truly, all words fail when I try to articulate what you two mean to me. I used to think it unbearably corny when I would hear people address their children as "my soul" or "soul of my soul." Then you two came along, and suddenly I immediately understood—that is, I felt what these words *mean*. In the final analysis, while I am deeply grateful for all the intellectual gifts I have been given by all those colleagues mentioned above, what I am most grateful for in this world is the deep and powerful feeling of love that I feel every day because of you three, Nima, Moksh, and Samudr.

4. Rūmī, *Kulliyyāt-i Shams*, 4:177–78.

TECHNICAL NOTES

Feeling Like Lovers attempts to walk the tightrope of addressing both diverse specialists (in Islamic, Sufi, and religious studies, comparative literature, affect theory, history of emotions, potentially even others) and general readers. In an effort to speak to all these audiences, I have tried to declutter the text when possible but preserve technical aspects where I felt them to be important. So, while, for example, I opt for the more simplified version of rendering dates only in the Common Era (CE), I do fully transliterate Arabic and Persian words and names according to the *International Journal of Middle Eastern Studies (IJMES)* system. When rendering words and names into the *IJMES* transliteration system, I do so according to the language of the original text or the language of writing the subject is more typically associated with. For example, Abū Ḥāmid al-Ghazālī—one of this work's central figures—is ethnically Persian by birth and wrote both in Persian and Arabic, but he is better known for his Arabic works, so I render his name according to the *IJMES* Arabic transliteration system and Arabic naming conventions. His brother, Aḥmad Ghazālī, however, wrote all of his major works in Persian, so I render his name according to Persian conventions. Lastly, in an effort to adopt and normalize as far as possible more inclusive language patterns, I use "they/them/theirs" pronouns to refer to a singular subject in contexts where gender is not specified in the text.

Introduction

"Begin a Love Affair!"

"BRING ME ḤASAN THE [BEAUTIFUL] SINGER"

The scene: mid-thirteenth-century Anatolia, in a city named Tūqāt. The world-famous Persian Sufi poet and mystic Fakhr al-Dīn ʿIrāqī (d. 1289) sits in the courtyard of his well-appointed lodge, staring intently across the way at a beautiful young man. His name is Ḥasan. He is a musician whose physical beauty is matched only by the equally legendary beauty of his voice.[1] The local governor, Amīr Parvānah (d. 1277), who generously built ʿIrāqī's lodge, has brought him to ʿIrāqī at his specific request. Amīr Parvānah had originally offered ʿIrāqī a substantial donation of gold to support his new lodge and its growing number of disciples, but ʿIrāqī flatly rejected it, saying that Amīr Parvānah could not "deceive [him] with gold." Instead, he insisted that Amīr Parvānah should bring to him "Ḥasan the singer" (*qavvāl*).

1. This anecdote is a contextualized and elaborated version of the one that appears in the anonymous biography appended to several early manuscripts of ʿIrāqī's *dīvān*. Nafīsī includes this document in his edition of ʿIrāqī's *Kulliyyāt* (Anonymous, "Muqaddimah-yi dīvān," 46–65). This biography of ʿIrāqī was written quite early, possibly even in the fourteenth century, and subsequently became the primary basis for almost all his future biographies in the premodern period. See Chittick and Wilson, "Introduction," 62n1. For an overview and critical assessment of ʿIrāqī's biography, see Miller, "Ocean of the Persians." Chittick and Wilson provide a full translation of this anonymous biography in Chittick and Wilson, "Introduction." They do, however, add a few components (e.g., purported letters of ʿIrāqī, some historical contextualizing information) that do not appear in the original biography, and they also make a number of problematic translation decisions aimed at heteronormativizing ʿIrāqī's love interests (on this last point, see following footnote). I have, therefore, decided to provide my own translations of ʿIrāqī's biographical account throughout this book. For earlier iterations of many of these passages, see my translations in "Embodying the Beloved" and "Ocean of the Persians."

Some onlookers may have been surprised by ʿIrāqī's categorical rejection of the generous financial donation, but these responses just show their ignorance of Ḥasan's true inestimable worth. He is not any old singer. The accounts describe him as "without peer in beauty and pleasing in elegance" and report that "people had placed the seal of his love on their hearts and tossed their souls to the wind out of love for him." Such was their love for this premodern heartthrob that when Amīr Parvānah's messenger arrived to take Ḥasan to ʿIrāqī's lodge, "ten thousand men from among Ḥasan's lovers gathered and forbid it." Ḥasan was only successfully dispatched to Tūqāt after the local governor began hanging the members of Ḥasan's entourage who were defying Amīr Parvānah's orders.[2]

The environment in Tūqāt is electric in anticipation of Ḥasan's musical-poetic performance—what Sufis call a *samāʿ* session.[3] Crowds of disciples throng around the legendary Sufi and the beautiful youth in the lodge's courtyard. Some look at the former, awed by his spiritual reputation for achieving the highest levels of mystic experience. Others look at the latter, befuddled by his beauty and eagerly anticipating his famously melodious voice. ʿIrāqī gazes at Ḥasan with an intensity that can only be described as deeply meditative. As the appointed time grows near, the crowd gradually quiets in anticipation. Then the silence is broken by the angelic voice of Ḥasan, singing: "Love is a phoenix for whom there is no trap / In both worlds there is no sign or name for it"—the opening lines of a trio of poems inspired by Ḥasan that ʿIrāqī composed especially for this occasion, according to his biography. Ḥasan continues:

2 Indeed no one has found its quarter,
for there are no footprints in its field.
3 In its heaven of soul-enlivening union,
there are no pure wine-drinkers except from its lips.
4 The entire world drinks its cup to the bottom,
although the world is not outside the cup.

2. Contrary to Chittick and Wilson's rendering of this scene ("Introduction"), the focus in the original story is squarely on Ḥasan's peerless beauty and the fervent love he has evoked in the men of his town. While his musical skills and melodious voice are part of his powerful allure, his effect on his army of lovers—and ʿIrāqī—cannot be reduced to the impact of these technical skills alone. The anonymous biographer's passing mention that most of the men in love with Ḥasan are not true lovers (*ʿāshiq*), but rather only fornicators (*fāsiq*), reinforces the point that the extraordinary interest in Ḥasan is a product of his physical beauty and sexual allure as much as anything else.

3. Translated variously as "spiritual concert," "(spiritual) audition," or, as Ingenito has recently suggested, "lyrical ritual," *samāʿ* sessions are spiritual rituals in which Sufis meditate on poetry recited to musical accompaniment. They sometimes include dancing as well. Ingenito has questioned whether ʿIrāqī himself was such a high profile proponent of *samāʿ* or only later came to be regarded as such (*Beholding Beauty*, 446n9). For my purposes here, this distinction is not important because what I am concerned with is the reception history of Sufi biographical works and how they were understood by and shaped Sufi communities. For more on my approach to Sufi biographies and how I use them in this study, see the Introduction.

5 My morning and night are its cheeks and tresses,
although where it is there is not morning or night.
6 If it casts off the veil from its face suddenly,
the world from end to end will become unfulfilled, [and] become nonexistent.
7 O morning breeze, if you pass by Love's quarter
we only have this message for it:
8 O beloved—our very soul is you—
not even one moment is tranquil without you.
9 Everyone in this world is desirous of something,
[but] there is no other aim or desire for us save your lips.
10 Everyone who has a beloved carries his name on his lips,
[but] our beloved does not have a name.
11 Since your lips and eyes intoxicated us
our sweetmeats have been nothing but your sugar and almonds.
12 Since our hearts became entangled in your tresses
our work has been nothing but lassos and traps.
13 The fortunate one in both worlds is your lover—
he has no ill-wisher!
14 Begin a love affair with ʿIrāqī!
Even though he is not worthy of such a blessing.[4]

The poem asserts the most fundamental of realities for followers of the "Path of Love" (*rāh-i ʿishq*) school of Sufism: The grounding of all being is love.[5] Nothing exists apart from it (lines 4, 6). It is beyond words, signs, and names (lines 1, 10). It has no quarter and any attempts to trap it are useless (lines 1–2). Such cryptic symbolic allusions can easily be fleshed out with reference to Sufi theoretical and hermeneutic works. Drawing on the Neoplatonic tradition in Sufism, they would tell us that Love is the ultimate reality—absolute being (*vujūd*) itself—that

4. Persian text taken from ʿIrāqī, *Kulliyyāt-i ʿIrāqī (Muḥtasham)*, 234–35. Another version can be found in ʿIrāqī, *Kulliyyāt-i ʿIrāqī (Nafīsī)*, 159–60. The translations in this book are my own, unless otherwise noted.

5. For the development of this "school," "religion," or "path," see Lumbard, "From *Hubb* to *ʿIshq*"; Zargar, *Sufi Aesthetics*, 63–119. Lewisohn, in particular, in "Sufism's Religion of Love," provides a masterful and concise overview. This "school" is not monolithic, however; there are different trends within it, with some tending more toward an interest in love as a metaphysical concept and others more toward its ecstatic practice. Ingenito makes this helpful distinction in his study of Saʿdī. He argues that there is an important difference between "mysticism-inclined" Sufis such as Rūmī or ʿIrāqī, who he associates with "intoxicating amatory ecstasy," "ecstatically metaphysical poetry," and "an intoxicating religion of love and its aesthetic component, which stresses the role of the human beloved as a physical bridge to experience a taste of divine beauty," and Saʿdī, whose "true core of . . . lyrical output is the contemplation of beauty at the intersection of multiple philosophical, physiological, and spiritual experiences of the world" (*Beholding Beauty* 309–12; see also 335, 353, 380–83, 394–95). My focus in this study is more on the "intoxicating amatory ecstasy"-type manifestations of the Sufi Path of Love. I see this distinction not so much as one we can make Sufi figure by Sufi figure but more one of modality, with all figures oscillating between these poles in different contexts even while they may have a proclivity for one or the other.

is beyond any entification, without "name or sign." Yet at the same time, it "flows in everything," as ʿIrāqī says in his own theoretical treatise on love, the *Lamaʿāt*: "Love flows in everything, so necessarily it is all things. . . . There is nothing in existence except it. And if not for it, that which was manifested into existence would not have manifested. That which has manifested was manifested from love and love flows in it—it is all love."[6]

Love created the world, manifesting itself into the forms of the Beloved and the lover—that is, God and humanity, respectively—so that it might come to know itself. We see this reflected in the poem in the gradual "belovedification" of the more abstract, distant, and unknowable figure of Love in the opening lines. By line 6, Love "casts off the veil from its face"—an act that has paradoxical results for those who witness this spectacular occurrence. On the one hand, the untrappable phoenix of Love, without "sign or name," now becomes a beloved whose lips, eyes, and tresses intoxicate and are pined for (lines 9–12) and to whom the love letter that forms the remainder of the poem (lines 8–14) is written. On the other, this act of Love unveiling itself to the world reveals the world itself to be nothing (line 6).[7]

We could continue in this manner for many pages, going into great depth about how this poem versifies aspects of Sufism's complex amatory metaphysics and the way its poetic symbols represent or refer to concepts in this voluminous theoretical tradition. Many have done so magisterially.[8] And these symbolist hermeneutic readings are a crucial step for intellectual comprehension of these texts. But a philosophical understanding is ultimately not what this poem—or any of the thousands of other amatory texts, poetic or otherwise, in the long tradition of the Sufi Path of Love—primarily prescribes for its spiritual audience members. It suggests, rather, that true understanding of these divine mysteries can only come through experience of a specific type: loving. One must make God—the knowable form of ultimate reality—one's beloved (line 10, 13–14), become intoxicated by His lips and eyes, entangled in His tresses (lines 9, 11–12). One must, in short, have a "love affair" with God (line 14). Or, if one is still not yet capable of loving God, one should at least have a love affair with one of his earthly beauties, the "tresses" that

6. ʿIrāqī, *Kulliyyāt-i ʿIrāqī (Muḥtasham)*, 473; ʿIraqi, *Divine Flashes*, 84–85. For a full English translation of ʿIrāqī's *Lamaʿāt*, see ʿIraqi, *Divine Flashes.*

7. For a full account of ʿIrāqī's love theory in the *Lamaʿāt*, see Chittick and Wilson, "Introduction"; Miller, "Ocean of the Persians"; Feuillebois-Pierunek, *A la croisée des voies célestes*. For the important differences between earlier theories of love, especially Aḥmad Ghazālī's (whose tradition ʿIrāqī claims he is following), and ʿIrāqī's, see Pourjavady, "The Concept of Love in ʿErāqi and Ahmad Ghazzāli."

8. For noteworthy examples of the Sufi symbolist hermeneutic approach to interpreting poetry, see Chittick, *The Sufi Path of Love*; Lewisohn, *Beyond Faith and Infidelity*; Nurbakhsh, *Sufi Symbolism (I–XVI)*; Lewisohn, "Sufi Symbolism"; Ilahi-Ghomshei, "Principles"; Lewisohn, "Prolegomenon to the Study of Hafiz," 31–73. For broader overviews of the stock poetic imagery found in Persian, especially Sufi, poetry, see Schimmel, *A Two-Colored Brocade*; de Bruijn, *Persian Sufi Poetry*; Seyed-Gohrab, *Laylī and Majnūn.*

he sets up as "lassos and traps" on Earth to snare the hearts of all the lovers who have not yet realized that the ultimate object of their love is Him (line 12).

This poem is not unique in its advocacy for a Sufi amatory cosmology and piety. Indeed, its central point—that ultimate reality/God is love/a beloved who engages humanity through "love affairs," as ʿIrāqī terms it above—is the inspiration for not only tens of thousands of Sufi poems and theoretical treatises but also a large number of works of modern scholarship and popular literature. No one in Islamic studies would contest this basic assertion.[9] Yet, despite this seeming thematic ubiquity and scholarly consensus, I will argue in this book that we have not fully appreciated the analytical implications of these radical ideas about the nature of God and his relationship to humanity.[10] We have mapped the theoretical landscapes of this amatory metaphysics. We have historically studied the lives of many of its Sufi proponents. We have traced its discursive and symbolic ramifications in Sufi poetry and prose.[11] But we have not let these astonishing claims fully guide our approach to studying Sufi meaning creation, subject formation, and epistemology.

Feeling Like Lovers approaches the study of Sufism differently. Focusing especially on its later dominant Path of Love school, this book analytically centers the foundational Sufi ontological and epistemological claims that God is love and that God communicates, most effectively at least, with humanity through the "language of love"—through, that is, effecting *in human bodies* dizzyingly complex somato-affective experiences composed of often nearly indescribable panoplies of

9. As Shahzad Bashir says, "In Persianate societies during the centuries that concern me [and us here], being a Sufi implied that one had come under the spell of love" (Bashir, *Sufi Bodies,* 107). Chittick goes even further, arguing that "if a single word can sum up Islamic spirituality—by which I mean the very heart of the Quranic message—it should surely be *love*" (not the alternative, "knowledge") (*Divine Love*, xi, emphasis original). See also Lewisohn's conclusion in "Sufism's Religion of Love," 178–80. And it is not just modern scholars who hold this view. As Chittick points out, early Sufis, such as Hujwīrī and Anṣarī, maintain that the path of Sufism is nothing other than the "path of love" (*Divine Love*, 292–93). For examples of the importance of love in Sufism in the popular imagination, see the (problematic) popularization of Rūmī as the Sufi love poet *par excellence* in Europe and America. See Arjana, *Buying Buddha.*

10. The title of this book, *Feeling Like Lovers: Affect in Medieval Sufism*, attempts to play off of the titles of the books that have most influenced my approach, at the analytical level at least, in this current study. See, for example, Bashir, *Sufi Bodies*; Kugle, *Sufis and Saints' Bodies*; Schaefer, *Religious Affects*; Somerset, *Feeling Like Saints*; McNamer, *Affective Meditation*; Burger and Crocker, *Medieval Affect, Feeling, and Emotion.*

11. For some exemplary treatments that approach the study of Sufism's amatory metaphysics from the perspective of intellectual history or primarily as a philosophical system, see Ritter, *The Ocean of the Soul*; Chittick, *The Sufi Path of Love*; Ernst, "The Stages of Love"; Sattārī, *ʿIshq-i Ṣūfiyānah*; Zargar, *Sufi Aesthetics*; Lewisohn, "Prolegomenon to the Study of Hafiz"; Chittick, *Divine Love*; Bell and Al Shafie's introduction to Daylamī, *A Treatise on Mystical Love*; Lumbard, "From *Hubb* to *ʿIshq*"; Lewisohn, "Sufism's Religion of Love"; Lumbard, *Aḥmad Al-Ghazālī*; Murata, *Beauty in Sufism*; Rustom, *Inrushes of the Heart.* Compare, for example, to Giffen, *Theory of Profane Love*, and Bell, *Love Theory*, to understand how Sufi theories of love both contrast with and adapt love theories drawn from the non-Sufi Islamic literary and intellectual domains.

feelings. It explores how love's path was experienced as a *felt* reality in Sufi life and how the diverse ways it *felt* to be a lover played a central role in Sufi subject formation and knowledge acquisition about God. If the best way to get to know God is to "begin a love affair," as ʿIrāqī encourages us to do in his poem, what is it about the experience of love that is so incomparably instructive? Why are the metaphysical treatises on divine love not enough? What does God convey by *affecting* us that we cannot learn discursively? Why, in short, must we *feel* to truly *know* God?[12]

DOING THE WORK OF RELIGION RIGHT: STANDING ON THE SHORELINE OF KNOWLEDGE OR DROWNING IN THE OCEAN OF LOVE?

Abū Ḥāmid al-Ghazālī (d. 1111 CE) is most prominently remembered as one of the great theorists of the medieval Sufi tradition. He was a voluminous writer in Arabic and his native Persian. Famously erudite, he was appointed in his early thirties to teach at the most important educational institution of his time, the Niẓāmiyya *Madrasa* of Baghdad, by the powerful Saljūq vizier Niẓām al-Mulk (d. 1092). He taught the traditional Islamic sciences for many years before a crisis of faith led him to abandon his prestigious teaching post and adopt the Sufi mode of piety. His embrace of Sufism, however, did not stop his intellectual production. In fact, it seems to have made his works all the more urgent and sophisticated in their engagement with the full range of Islamic knowledge. They consistently display not only a strong tendency toward intellectual systemization of past Sufi thought but also an affinity with Islamic philosophy.[13] He was, in short, a consummate Sufi intellectual. He believed in the power of the intellect and ideas to move people and change the world. He was not—or, at least, is not remembered as—one of the "intoxicated," love-mad Sufis who shunned intellectual life and its ideas for the merry, drunken world of the Sufi winehouse and its poetic ditties.

Yet this portrayal of Abū Ḥāmid al-Ghazālī as a stuffy and sober intellectual, wrapped up exclusively in the rarefied realm of abstract ideas, is a bit unfair. As we will see in multiple places throughout this book, he was deeply sensitive to the nondiscursive aspects of meaning and knowledge production and readily admitted the limited utility of language and intellectual forms of knowledge for revealing divine realities. He makes this dual point quite pithily in his Persian work *Kīmiyā al-saʿādat* when discussing how Sufis interpret the nearly ubiquitous imagery of wine and love in their poetic tradition:

12. The different somato-affective experiences—e.g., longing, burning with desire, joy—experienced on the Sufi Path of Love are, of course, often mentioned in the previously cited Sufi-studies scholarship. But these studies, which tend primarily towards intellectual history, do not see feeling or affect as primary constituents of Sufi knowledge or subject formation.

13. On al-Ghazālī's thought and its relation to Islamic philosophy (especially Ibn Sīnā), see Griffel, *Al-Ghazali's Philosophical Theology*; Treiger, *Inspired Knowledge in Islamic Thought*. For a counterpoint to the reading of al-Ghazālī as heavily indebted to philosophical tradition, see Dagli, *Ibn Al-ʿArabi and Islamic Intellectual Culture*, 7–59.

They understand from "the tress" the chain of forms of the divine presence, for one who wants to get a scent [of it] with the application of the intellect (*ʿaql*)—although they know the tip of a hair is among the wonders of the divine presence—when just one twist [of the tress] befalls them, all the numbers become wrong and the intellects are stupefied. When there is discussion of wine and drunkenness in poetry, they do not understand the external [meaning], like the poet said: "Even if you pour two thousand goblets of wine / you will not go mad with love until you drink the wine!" They understand from this that the work of religion does not get done right with discussion (*ḥadīs̱*) or learning (*taʿallum*). It gets done correctly with "tasting" (*ẕawq*). If you talk (*ḥadīs̱*) a lot about love and passionate desire (*maḥabbat va ʿishq*), asceticism, trust in God, and other spiritual ideas, write [about them] in books and all over many pages, no benefit will accrue to you until you become that way of being (*ṣifat*).[14] They understand something different from what is said in the verses on the dilapidated winehouse (*kharābāt*), like when they say:

Whoever has not gone to the dilapidated winehouse (*kharābāt*) is without religion
Because the dilapidated winehouse (*kharābāt*) is the very root of religion.

They understand the dilapidated winehouse (*kharābāt*) as the destruction of the ways of being (*ṣifāt*) of humanity.[15] For the roots of religion are that what is living be destroyed so that what is not manifest in the innermost part of a human becomes manifest and living.[16]

In this passage, al-Ghazālī links a familiar set of epistemological tools and aids that we will often see Sufi authors associate with one another in this book: intellect (*ʿaql*), learning (*taʿallum*), and language, in both its written (e.g., in books and pages) and spoken forms (*ḥadīs̱*). The common feature of this constellation is their roots in the traditional Islamic sciences, both of the rational (*maʿqūl*) and transmitted (*manqūl*) (in writing or speech) varieties.[17] As we will see in a striking anecdote in chapter 1, they are what constitute traditional Islamic "learning" (*taʿallum*) in the *madrasa* context. They are the principal ways that non-Sufis learn about God and what it means to be a good Muslim: through the intellectual knowledge (i.e., the propositional content), conveyed by language, in books or uttered by a teacher and through the application of reason wielded by a well-trained intellect.

14. On the complicated history of the two forms of love mentioned here—*maḥabbat* and *ʿishq*—see Lumbard, "From *Hubb* to *ʿIshq*." But also see ʿIrāqī's dismissal of the distinction between these two terms below.

15. *Kharābāt* is a place name, literally meaning "ruins," that is commonly used in Persian to refer to the carnivalesque space of the "winehouse." It is built on the adjective *kharāb*, meaning "ruined" or "drunk." On the significance and interrelation of the terms for "ruined"/"drunk" (*kharāb*) and "winehouse"/"ruins" (*kharābāt*), see chapter 4.

16. al-Ghazālī, *Kīmiyā*, 364–65. All translations from al-Ghazālī's *Kīmiyā* are mine. There is a full English translation of this work (al-Ghazzali, *The Alchemy of Happiness*), though it suffers from a few issues.

17. The term here for "rational" (*maʿqūl*) is from the same Arabic trilateral root as "intellect" (*ʿaql*). The Arabic language is (mostly) based on a trilateral root system, which means that words that share a base set of three letters (occasionally four), though they may look dissimilar on the surface, are semantically related. Although Persian is not based on this system of trilateral roots, it uses many such Arabic words with (usually) similar or related meanings.

Against this logo-ratiocentric epistemological team, al-Ghazālī sets another that gains knowledge about God through "drinking," "tasting" (Persian *ẕawq*, or Arabic *dhawq*), "becoming," and "going."[18] "The work of religion," he says, "does not get done right" when we try to do it through language and learning alone. Reading books about the dilapidated winehouse of the Sufis (*kharābāt*) is not the same as getting oneself "destroyed" with its love-intoxicating wine. One must, as the poems he cites suggest, go to the winehouse and drink the wine to experience Sufism's highest reality: the destruction of the human self (*fanāʾ*) in a bewildering and frenzied stupor that Sufis describe alternately as drunkenness, illness, madness, drowning, burning, and even assault, as we will see in examples throughout this book. One must *taste* this reality. One must *become* it to know it. This is how "the work of religion . . . gets done correctly."

al-Ghazālī's passage suggests two interlocking points about Sufi epistemology that form the foundation for *Feeling Like Lovers*. First, he uncompromisingly asserts that Sufi epistemology is fundamentally experiential, at least when it comes to the highest levels of spiritual knowledge. Its spiritual pedagogy and formation require one to engage in a mode of being, even if only initially in "play" form (as we will see in an example from Rūmī below), to embody it, to even "become" it, as al-Ghazālī says. Knowing God and God's essence—love—requires one to "taste" (*ẕawq*) and drink of them.

Second, al-Ghazālī quite explicitly demarcates strict limits for the ability of intellectually based forms of knowledge to communicate the highest divine realities about God to human beings. He is not against them, and they are powerful tools—he was a voluminous writer and famous teacher, after all. But as epistemological modes/tools, they have limited utility. To put this another way, the ultimate Sufi knowledge basin is the "[ocean] of love," and the "furthest end of intellectual knowledge" is the "shore" of this ocean, as Abū Ḥāmid al-Ghazālī's brother, the famously profligate Sufi lover Aḥmad Ghazālī (d. 1123 or 1126), puts it in his treatise on love, the *Savānah:*

> The furthest end of intellectual knowledge is the shore of love. If one is on the shore, they have news of a portion of it. And if one steps forward, they will drown. Then, how will they discover [anything] and give news [of it]? For one who is drowned what is intellectual knowledge? . . . No! Intellectual knowledge is the moth of [the candle of] love. One's knowledge is the outer part of the work [of love]. Inside it, first their intellectual knowledge burns. Then, how could they bring news out [of love's fire]?[19]

Neither of these points, to be clear, are ground-shaking observations for veterans of Sufi studies. They are stock motifs, replete throughout Sufi sources and modern scholarly accounts alike. But what existing literature has not done is to draw out

18. For more on Sufi notion of *dhawq* or *ẕawq*, see later chapters. As both Kueny and Hoffman point out, *dhawq* was also used outside of Sufism in an epistemic sense too, e.g., in the Qurʾān as humanity coming to "taste" or "know" a variety of different somato-affective (my phrasing) punishments and God's "mercy." See Kueny, "Tasting Fire"; T. Hoffmann, "Taste My Punishment."

19. Ghazālī, "Savānah," 9.

the analytical implications of these epistemological claims. If intellectual forms of knowledge—broadly defined—do not cut it, if "no benefit will accrue to you" from book learning alone, then why do most studies in our field approach the textual tradition of premodern Sufism so *intellectually?*[20] That is, why do most studies of medieval Sufism analyze Sufi texts primarily as bearers of intellectual ideas, concepts, or symbolic meaning, as containers of propositional content, as vehicles for the dissemination of discursive constructs?

Using our philological and historical methods, we have perused Sufism's textual record: mapping its metaphysical system, identifying its intertextual and historical references, cataloging the allegorical meaning of each of its metaphoric symbols, and writing detailed accounts of Sufism's historical development. Recent studies have approached medieval Sufism's textual record with considerable theoretical sophistication, using new critical methodologies to study its discursive constructions of power, gender, sexuality, etc.[21] All these efforts represent crucial advances in our knowledge of medieval Sufism. But these approaches do leave critical gaps in their (often implicit) assumption that the intellectual, "factual," and/or discursive content of language is the primary prism through which to understand culture. This "logocentrism," as affect theorists term it, inadvertently marginalizes—even occludes—the non-, pre-, and paralinguistic elements of human experience and culture. As Michael Beard relatedly observes in a recent piece dealing with sensory history in Persian literature:

> It's odd that we would have to defend the sensory world, but we have the ability to ignore it. As analysts and critics, we are more comfortable with meanings. They're always easy to find, and they can be important: historical background, biography, patterns of imagery, moral advice, etc. But we've learned to look past the world of the sensory. It's become the thing right in front of us that we don't quite see any longer, like the purloined letter in Edgar Allan Poe's influential story by the same name, the elephant in the room.[22]

In response to this oversight, scholars of Sufism in recent years have increasingly been focusing on the study of Sufi embodiment, material culture, and sensory history.[23] While these studies have made impressive strides in the exploration of

20. Osborne makes the related observation that "scholarship about the Qur'an has historically been dominated by textually driven approaches" ("The Qur'an and Affect," 1).

21. For some prominent examples of these approaches, see Safi, *Politics of Knowledge*; Mojaddedi, *The Biographical Tradition in Sufism*; Cornell, *Realm of the Saint*; Ruffle, *Gender, Sainthood, & Everyday Practice in South Asian Shi'ism*; Shaikh, *Sufi Narratives of Intimacy*; Yaghoobi, *Subjectivity*; Yaghoobi, "Yusuf's 'Queer' Beauty"; Kugle, *Homosexuality in Islam*; Kugle, "Sultan Mahmud's Makeover"; Bashir, *Sufi Bodies*; Kugle, *Sufis and Saints' Bodies*; Tourage, *Rūmī and the Hermeneutics of Eroticism*; Miller, "Embodying the Beloved."

22. Beard, "Introduction: Minds/Senses," 13.

23. See, for example, Kugle, *Sufis and Saints' Bodies*; Bashir, *Sufi Bodies*; Zargar, *Sufi Aesthetics*; Elias, *Aisha's Cushion*; Bashir, "Narrating Sight"; Alexandrin, "Witnessing the Lights"; Alexandrin, "Minding the Body"; Papas, "Creating a Sufi Soundscape"; Bashir, "World as a Hat"; Abuali, "Visualizing the Soul";

the nonintellectual/nondiscursive dimensions of Sufi life, they have really only scratched the surface. Large chronological, geographic, and group-specific gaps remain in our knowledge of these related, though diverse, dimensions of pre-modern Sufi embodied and material life—to say nothing of the overlapping and interlocking intellectual and ritual worlds Sufis would have daily traversed in the broader Islamicate social contexts they inhabited.[24]

Feeling Like Lovers extends this growing body of literature by focusing on another embodied, sensory, and even in a certain sense material aspect of the spiritual life of Sufis: their experience of affect/emotion. Joining a small but growing literature on affect and emotion in the Islamicate world, I ask here what the *felt* dimension of Sufi practices and formation on the Path of Love can tell us about Sufism as a mode of piety and epistemology.[25] Why is the Sufi answer to the limits

---

Abuali, "'I Tasted Sweetness'"; Ingenito, *Beholding Beauty*; Kugle, "Caps, Heads, and Hearts"; Miller, "Embodying the Beloved"; Hotham, "Sensing the Ascent"; Bigelow, "Senses of Belonging"; Hofer, "On the Material and Social Conditions of Khalwa in Medieval Sufism"; Seyed-Gohrab, "Beyond Senses." I will discuss and cite these studies as relevant throughout the book, since many touch on affect/emotion.

24. In his introduction to the special issue on Islamic sensory history that he organized, Lange also comments that "studies that explicitly address sensation in Sufi contexts are rare," despite it being a "fertile arena for research on the senses" ("Introduction," 3). He repeats this point about Islamic studies more broadly too in "Al-Jāḥiẓ on the Senses," 22. For other notable studies of body/embodiment, material culture, and sensory history in the broader Islamicate world, see King, *Scent from the Garden of Paradise*; Patel, "Their Fires Shall Not Be Visible"; McGregor, *Islam and the Devotional Object*; Knight, *Muhammad's Body*; Alharthi, *The Body in Arabic Love Poetry*; Bursi, "You Were Not Commanded"; King, "Medieval Islamicate Aromatherapy"; and the studies in Khorrami and Moosavi, *Losing Our Minds.*

25. There are a handful of studies that engage the topic of affect/emotion and Sufism (some more directly than others): Schofield, "Learning to Taste the Emotions"; Gill, *Melancholic Modalities*; Elias, "Mevlevi Sufis"; Lunn and Schofield, "Delight"; M. S. Rizvi, "Music, Emotions and Reform in South Asian Islam"; Werbner, "The Abstraction of Love"; Knysh, "Tasting, Drinking and Quenching Thirst"; Gondos, "Seekers of Love"; Yep, "Emotion and Islamic Hagiology"; Shahid, "Saif Al-Mulūk," 235–97. Most of the existing studies on emotions/affect in the Islamicate world treat a wide range of disparate topics and periods, with the most developed areas being emotions/affect and the Qur᾿ān (as a text and in recited form), music, and anthropological studies of Muslim communities: Abu-Lughod, *Veiled Sentiments*; Mahmood, *Politics of Piety*; Ohlander, "Fear of God (*Taqwā*) in the Qur'ān"; Hirschkind, *The Ethical Soundscape*; Marranci, *The Anthropology of Islam*; Melchert, "Exaggerated Fear"; Myrne, "Discussing Ghayra in Abbasid Literature"; Schofield, "Music, Art and Power"; Schofield, "Emotions in Indian Music History"; Gade, *Perfection Makes Practice*; Elias *Aisha's Cushion*, 139–74; Ben-Ami, "Wonder in Early Modern Ottoman Society"; Keshavmurthy, "Translating Rāma"; Moukheiber, "Gendering Emotions"; Katz, "Beyond Ḥalāl and Ḥarām"; Bray, "Codes of Emotion"; Bray, "Ya῾qūb b. al-Rabī῾ Read by al-Mutanabbī and al-Mubarrad"; Khalek, "Al-Dāraquṭnī's (d. 385 AH) *Faḍā᾿il Al-Ṣaḥāba*"; Bauer, "Emotion in the Qur'an"; Bauer, "Emotions of Conversion"; Blatherwick, "'And the Light in His Eyes Grew Dark'"; Hoffmann, "Taste My Punishment"; Mian, "Muslim Political Philosophy"; Ruffle, *Gender, Sainthood, & Everyday Practice in South Asian Shi'ism*, 85–120; Wolf, *The Voice in the Drum*; Hotham, "Affect, Animality, and Islamophobia"; Gruber, "In Defense and Devotion"; K. Rizvi, "Introduction," 3–5; Key, *Language*, 196–240; Osborne, "Aural Epistemology"; Osborne, "The Qur'an and Affect"; Osborne, "The Experience of the Recited Qur᾿an"; Robinson, "The Great Mughals"; Kueny, "Tasting Fire"; Houghteling, "Sentiment in Silks"; Tourage, "Affective Entanglements"; Vignone, "Fear and Learning in Medieval Islam"; Elias, *Alef Is for Allah*; Khoja-Moolji, *Sovereign Attachments*; Osborne, "Feeling the Words"; Ghazzal, "From Anger on Behalf of God"; A. Hoffmann,

of our ability to understand divine realities a deceptively simple—and to some even preposterous and illicit—recommendation to go fall in love?[26] What would it mean to try to understand this amatory pedagogy and the *felt* experiences of what the al-Ghazālī brothers describe as burning in the candle or drowning in the ocean of love or getting drunk, destroyed, and lovesick in the Sufi winehouse (experiences of *z̲awq* and "states," *aḥvāl*, s. *ḥāl*) as epistemological? To answer these questions, we need to affectively orient our mode of analysis and reframe discussions of meaning, epistemology, and subject formation more capaciously to include nonintellectual/nondiscursive, *felt* forms of knowledge.[27]

FEELING OUR WAY TO GOD: THE PRACTICE OF LOVE AND AFFECTIVE ENTRAINMENT

In the final line of his poem, ʿIrāqī pleads that someone "Begin a love affair with ʿIrāqī!" In an ultimate sense, ʿIrāqī is petitioning God to ignite the love affair. God is Love—the origin and end of all love. But the poem's imaginary performance context at the legendary *samāʿ* session in Tūqāt, and the lines that precede this entreaty, make the identity of the longed-for beloved more complex. And productively so. The

"Angry Men"; and the studies collected in Rajamani, Pernau, and Butler Schofield, *Monsoon Feelings*. We should not exaggerate, however, the amount of research done in this area: even in perhaps the most studied nexus of emotion/affect and Islamicate studies, i.e., of the Qurʾān, Osborne observes that the existing literature is still "scant but developing" ("The Qur'an and Affect," 1). Gade's introduction to affect and emotions in Islam ("Islam") deserves special mention here for presenting many cogent general framing observations on emotions/affect in the Islamic tradition and a fertile range of potential future avenues of research (including noting the important role of emotions in Sufism).

26. The centrality of specific affective dispositions to different modes of piety is not exclusive to Sufism. It would be useful to compare Sufism's focus on love to the "cultivation" of what Christopher Melchert describes as "anxious" or "exaggerated fear" in early Islamic ascetic-renunciant communities ("Exaggerated Fear") or the "dread" Vignone sees as central to the piety of medieval Islamic scholarly (*ʿulamāʾ*) classes ("Fear and Learning in Medieval Islam").

27. It is on this point that this current study parts ways with most of the existing scholarship on emotions/affects in the Islamic world, which tends to catalog and describe these assemblages of feeling without understanding them as one of the most important epistemological modes of knowledge acquisition and subject formation, especially in Sufism. For some important exceptions to this generalization, see the following studies, which all treat emotion/affect/feeling in some way as a constituent element of meaning/knowledge (and thus subject or identity formation, even if they do not explicitly state it in these terms): Abu-Lughod, *Veiled Sentiments*; Nelson, *The Art of Reciting the Qur'an*; Gade, *Perfection Makes Practice*; Hirschkind, *The Ethical Soundscape*; Marranci, *The Anthropology of Islam*; Osborne, "The Experience of the Recited Qurʾan"; Schofield, "Learning to Taste the Emotions"; Bauer, "Emotion in the Qur'an," 10–15; Key, *Language*, 196–240; Bauer, "Emotions of Conversion"; Harb, *Arabic Poetics*; Schofield, "Music, Art and Power"; Osborne, "Aural Epistemology"; Lunn and Schofield, "Delight"; Gill, *Melancholic Modalities*; Elias, *Alef Is for Allah*; Osborne, "Feeling the Words"; Osborne, "The Qur'an and Affect"; Vignone, "Fear and Learning in Medieval Islam"; Hoffmann, "Angry Men"; Abuali, "Visualizing the Soul"; Abuali, "Words Clothed in Light"; Hofer, "On the Material and Social Conditions of Khalwa in Medieval Sufism"; Schofield, "Emotions in Indian Music History"; Shahid, "Saif Al-Mulūk," 235–97. See also Yaghoobi, *Subjectivity* (especially chapters 4–5), for another perspective on how love can shape subjectivities.

poem makes clear that ʿIrāqī longs for the divine Beloved, but at the same time he is "entangled in [His] tresses," those earthly "lassos and traps." While the majority of the poem focuses on the divine and metaphysical side of God-Love's machinations in the universe, the final lines present the possibility of coming to know God the Beloved through earthly love. The poem's comparatively lesser focus on this dimension of God/Love's modus operandi seems to suggest its lack of importance in the face of the soaring heights of Sufi metaphysics, represented in this poem by the "phoenix" who traverses both worlds and the heavens and is the source of the whole universe. One could be forgiven for missing line 12's gesture toward its earthly embodiments.

But it is highly unlikely that anyone in the *samāʿ* session that day in Tūqāt would have missed this line and its radical implications, because arrayed before them was one of the paragons of these "lassos and traps": Ḥasan. And this poem, composed by ʿIrāqī and being sung to him by this beautiful "tress" of God dangling down to Earth right before him, was the opening of one of the Sufi Path of Love's central rituals, *samāʿ*, which, as we will see, was one of the principal Sufi sites for the cultivation and practice of embodied love. These contextual factors decisively shift this poem's center of gravity. In this performance context, at least, the poem's metaphysical focus is mostly prelude to the main feature. It is background information—a theoretical pedestal that in a certain sense aggrandizes Ḥasan even more. He is not just dashingly beautiful and musically talented; he is also a perfect embodiment of God's beauty on Earth, and he has a divinely sanctioned role to play. He is there to make people fall in love—with him, with God; the difference is no longer as clear. ʿIrāqī is imploring God *and* Ḥasan to begin a love affair in this storied *samāʿ* session (which I discuss further in chapter 1).

But why encourage such flirtations with earthly love entanglements, especially with their equally great potential for imperiling young Sufi seekers' spiritual advancement if they get a little too wrapped up in the "tresses" of earthly beauties? Because, in short, there is no other way to truly learn how to be God's lover than to train to become one, as Jalāl al-Dīn Rūmī (d. 1273) suggests in the poem below:

1 Consider it a gift from God that afflictions have come to you from love's quarters!
Love of embodied forms (*majāzī*) in the end passes onto love for God.
2 The fighter gives his son a toy sword
So he will become a master of it and then take a real sword into battle.
3 Loving another human being is the toy sword—
When you become entangled at the end of love's path, that love will be transformed into love for God.
4 In the beginning, for years, Zulaykhā's love was for Yūsuf,
but in the end it became love for God, and it made her turn away from Yūsuf.[28]

Most scholars have taken lines such as these as testaments to the ultimate triviality of embodied (*majāzī*) love in Sufism. *Majāzī* love, they tell us, is "derivative"

28. Rūmī, *Kulliyyāt-i Shams*, 1:22–23.

or "cold and unreal."[29] More often this neglect occurs through de-emphasis, through the almost invisible process by which one decides what to prioritize and what to relegate to the footnotes or the proverbial "another study." Why focus on the earthly love practices of some "intoxicated" Sufis and the flesh-and-blood beloveds that ignite them when the real prize is divine love and the esoteric mystical secrets revealed by God, the ultimate Beloved, to his earthly lovers and conveniently elaborated in Sufi metaphysical treatises? Sufis themselves even seem at times to dismiss the role of earthly love. Rūmī, in this same poem, appears to lend credence to this interpretation, advising his listeners that "love of embodied forms (*majāzī*) in the end passes on to love for God."

Rūmī's primary intent in these lines, however, is not to devalue the "toy sword[s]"—the earthly beloveds—of Sufi amatory spiritual practices as just toys. Rather, he is highlighting how the embodied experience of playing with them—of being in love—prepares the novice for the real thing. As he explains, "The fighter gives his son a toy sword / So he will become a master of it and then take a real sword into battle." This point about the pedagogical potential of embodied play is so key that he returns to illustrate it through the example of the famous lovers of medieval Islam, Yūsuf and Zulaykhā, a couple lines later: "In the beginning, for years, Zulaykhā's love was for Yūsuf, / but in the end it became love for God, and it made her turn away from Yūsuf." Zulaykhā's earthly love play (*ʿishq-bāzī*) was not a momentary affair or just the tiny spark that was needed to ignite the fires of divine love. It went on "for years." Rūmī and, apparently, God himself, see quite a bit of pedagogical potential in this process of earthly love. But why?

The mode of learning that Rūmī suggests here is not an intellectual or rational form of knowledge (*ʿilm, maʿqūl, manqūl*). It is a type of experiential knowledge that harnesses embodied experience to teach the Sufi how to better love God. Playing with a toy sword—manipulating it, feeling how it responds in pretend live action, even how being struck by one feels—teaches a youth how to better wield a real sword and avoid the blows of one's armed opponent in war. Just so, experiencing the overwhelming affective and sensorial symphony one feels when playing with a "toy" earthly beloved instructs the Sufi on how one must feel and act to become a lover of God. The quickening of the lover's heart when they first fall in love with the beloved, the seemingly endless nights of overwhelming longing and burning with desire, the full-body surge of excitement and loss of self during even the most fleeting moments of union, and the impossibly desolate feeling of incompleteness when the beloved is gone: "This is love," as Rūmī asserts in the opening of one of his most famous poems.[30] How could one love God if one has never experienced

29. Chittick, *The Sufi Path of Love*, 200–201. I discuss how this framing of *majāzī* forms of love as "derivative" distorts—whether intentionally or not—the study of Sufi earthly forms of love play in chapter 1 and, previously, in Miller, "Embodying the Beloved." Compare to Chittick's discussion of this same set of verses in the opening pages of *Divine Love*, xi–xii.

30. Rūmī, *Kulliyyāt-i Shams*, 4:177–78.

this? How would one even know that what one feels toward God is love and not pious posturing and intellectual self-delusion? Love is an experiential reality that one must feel to know and practice to properly perform. No one would ever suggest sending young soldiers into war who had only read about swordplay in books. Nor, Rūmī emphasizes here, should we expect Sufis to enter God's arena of divine love without having first practiced their "love play" (*ʿishq-bāzī*) with an earthly beloved or two.

God may be the ultimate teacher in this amatory form of Sufi love training, but he sets up the learning environment in an almost Montessorian manner to allow his pupils to learn through their play with beautiful earthly beloveds, such as Yūsuf or Ḥasan. These figures are not ends in themselves, but it is their unique bodily capacity to most fully reflect the beauty of God that enables God to communicate through them, to affectively educate and act upon His chosen earthly lovers. Remember, Rūmī opens his comparison of embodied love and toy-sword play by telling the reader that we should count ourselves fortunate if we have experienced "afflictions [that] have come from love's quarters" (*żarar āmad*). The bodies of the earthly beloveds and their divinely sourced beauty are certainly critical supporting players in "love's [classroom] quarters," but they are instructional aids in the educational process, *not* the skill or content to be learned. That role belongs to the experience of love and its myriad associated somato-affective sequelae ("affliction" is only one of many such related examples), which instruct and train the Sufi lover not just through calling to mind an abstract emotional state but rather by making them *feel* in diverse and sometimes conflicting ways. It is these affects' effects on the body of the Sufi that forms them into lovers—that is, into a specific type of *feeling* subject.

"Teaching" may not be the best framing for this process. It may be better to compare it to the process of entrainment, in the sense that scientific literature uses this term to mean the gradual bringing into alignment of two processes, such as phases of light/dark and our circadian rhythms, brain waves and various external stimuli, or, perhaps most relevant here, our bodies and the rhythms of music. Entrainment is an educational process in the broadest sense. But it does not have the strong association with the conveyance of intellectual knowledge that "teaching" or "pedagogy" does. It is a mode of educating the somato-affective body, disciplining it, and inculcating in it a certain rhythm or set of responses. It trains the body to act in certain ways by acting upon it and gradually coaxing it to follow certain patterns in certain situations.[31]

Rereading Rūmī's verses from this perspective, what the toy-sword image captures is better understood as a type of affective entrainment. God/Love uses the earthly embodied experience of love to entrain the Sufi lovers, with the diverse

31. See also Bigelow's interesting use of the notion of "social entrainment," which underlines the importance of sense experience for community formation ("Senses of Belonging," 23–24).

rhythms of love progressively bringing the aspiring lover's affective system into sync with Him—that is, Love with a capital L. The rhythms, the beat, of this amorous affective entrainment are those patterns of bodily responses and sensations, those assemblages of feelings, that we experience when love "conquers" us, from lovesickness's "afflictions" and palpable loss of control to the soaring feeling of elation in those intoxicating moments of union and, ultimately, loss of self (*fanā'*). Like learning to wield a sword in battle, this process—generically glossed as "falling in love"—is a type of muscle-memory training in how one must act and feel to have a chance at achieving proximity to God and learning His divine realities. The affective muscle of love needs practice to learn how to respond to God's invitation to be His lover.[32] The Sufi body and its somato-affective system—*not* just the intellectual mind—very much needs to learn too on the Sufi Path of Love because becoming a Sufi lover meant learning to *feel* in certain specific ways.[33] Sufi lover subjectivity, in other words, was characterized by and constructed through the mobilization of complex amalgamations of *feeling* as much as, or perhaps even more than, the discursive or intellectual components of the Sufi tradition.[34]

WHAT/HOW DOES LOVE MEAN: THEORETICAL STARTING POINTS FOR THE STUDY OF SUFI LOVERS

Love's permutations in medieval Sufism are diverse. At the most basic level, there are multiple terms for love in medieval Persian and Arabic, but, as ʿIrāqī says in the opening of the *Lamaʿāt*, "whether you term it *maḥabba* or *ʿishq*, the terminology

32. Abuali and Hofer's recent works are particularly resonant with my concern to demonstrate how affect forms Sufi subjects. While they do include discussions of emotions/affects at times in their discussions (e.g., Abuali, "Visualizing the Soul," 171; Abuali, "'I Tasted Sweetness,'" 55–57, 66), their studies focus more on the role of the physical senses and material objects in the "psycho-somatic training" of the Sufi "habitus," as Abuali terms it ("Words Clothed in Light," 281), or the "disciplin[ing]" of the Sufi body, as Hofer often frames it ("On the Material and Social Conditions of Khalwa in Medieval Sufism," 5). Also see Gade's ethnographic study, *Perfection Makes Practice*, on the diverse ways in which affect suffuses the processes of learning, teaching, and performing Qur'ānic recitation in Indonesia.

33. Relatedly, see Marranci's study of the "emotional component" of Muslim identity formations—i.e., "the different ways of feeling to be Muslim"—and reconceptualization of the Islamic *ummah* as a "community of feelings" (*The Anthropology of Islam*, 8, 95–114, 146).

34. Shahab Ahmed understands the role of love in the Path of Love in a similar way, remarking, "Love functions as an elevating experience for the realization, apprehension, and experience of the values and higher Truth. . . . It functions, in other words . . . as a mode of knowing, of valorizing and meaning-making. . . . I suggest, however, [*pace* Chittick] that rather than draw a sharp distinguishing line between 'love' and 'knowledge,' it is more accurate to conceive of love as construed and practiced by *madhhab-i ʿishq* precisely as a register or *type of knowing*: the *experience* of love is a learning experience (or an experience of learning) that *teaches* the lover how to identify value . . . and to constitute the human being—both as individual and society—accordingly, in terms of those value" (emphasis original) (*What Is Islam?*, 42).

is not contestable."[35] The more significant differences for the purposes of this study can be seen in what we might call love's different functional modalities in culture: love as a philosophical/metaphysical concept or symbol, love as a discursive construction, and love as an affect/feeling/emotion. Although they share the linguistic appellation "love," they all play different roles in Islamicate cultures. They operate along different wavelengths or vectors, each shaping culture, mind, and bodies in distinct ways. In differentiating these cultural modalities of love, however, I do not mean to suggest an absolute division between them. They also co-construct one another to a degree, even if they are not fully collapsible—a productive tension we will see throughout this book.

Without denying the validity and importances of love's other modalities, *Feeling Like Lovers* aims to investigate the last constellation of these terms, love in its affective/emotional modality—that is, the machinations of love as a felt reality in the lives of medieval Sufis. This is the modality of love that Sufi biographies and poems show acting upon individuals, transforming them and inducing in them wide-ranging somato-affective sequelae. It is not the intellected or systematizable form of Sufi metaphysics.[36] As we saw in the examples from the al-Ghazālī brothers, it seeks to destroy the rational mind and its cogitated castles as it brings the body of its (un)lucky victim under its control. It is not the discourse or script of love that seeks to structure social relations or gender and sexuality along its amorous lines.[37] It is what love *feels* like, which is evasive of, even if partially constructed by and imbricated with, language and intellectual and discursive formations. (Language, as all the Sufi poets admit, fails to ever fully capture it, even as its linguistic ramifications suffuse their works.) It is above all *felt* as a force in the bodies and lives of Sufis that, as Bashir remarks, is "known through its causes and effects."[38] It affects individuals by effecting certain types of experiences in the feelingscapes of their bodies. It, in short, is an æffect—a term I use throughout this book to capture love's potential to be experienced as a wide range of somative-

35. ʿIrāqī, *Kulliyyāt-i ʿIrāqī (Muḥtasham)*, 455.

36. Most studies of love in medieval Sufism focus on love as a philosophical or metaphysical concept, including what I will term the cogno-spiritual approach to poetry in chapter 2, which studies the symbolism of love in poetry as signs pointing to the supernal realm of divine meanings (*maʿānī*). See studies cited there and others in footnote 8 of this chapter.

37. Andrews and Kalpakli (*The Age of Beloveds*), Bashir (*Sufi Bodies*, 107–63), Kugle (*Sufis and Saints' Bodies*, 181–220), and my own earlier study ("Embodying the Beloved") primarily look at the discourse ("script," as Bashir and Andrews and Kalpakli term it) of love and how it structures social relations and norms of gender and sexuality in the Islamicate world.

38. Bashir, in the larger quote from which this phrase is drawn, gestures towards love as a "force" and felt reality too, remarking that "Love in medieval Islamic literatures is considered a force known through its causes and effects. . . . [It] stirs up human beings in a way more potent than any other force that can act upon their bodies and minds" (*Sufi Bodies*, 109–10). His treatment of love in his influential work, however, focuses primarily on love as a discourse, not a felt reality.

affective transformations (affects/effects) and its key role in forming (i.e., *effecting*) Sufi lover feeling subjects.[39] It *æffects* them.

In attempting to study the æffective life of medieval Sufis, *Feeling Like Lovers* draws inspiration from a large body of other works with varying chronological foci that have similarly sought to understand the role of affect, feelings, and emotions in cultural formations. This work has generally been done either under the banner of affect theory or history of emotions. Both categories of scholarship cover a wide range of studies. Affect theory, in particular, is a diverse intellectual enterprise and has been used to subsume research programs with important differences between them.[40] The varying trajectories of the branches of affect theory and the history of emotions revolve largely around how they define the "feelings" that they study—affect vs. emotion, or a spectrum of both—and how they define each of these terms.

Historians of emotions concentrate primarily on what Burger and Crocker term "scripted norms" or "socially legible" forms of feeling.[41] These are the culturally recognized constructions or discursive categories of feelings that structure and are structured by the felt realities of a subject.[42] They are the "voluntarily involuntary" patterns of bodily response that are inculcated in us through seemingly endless "repetitions ('overlearning')" and closely linked with associated social and material contexts, specific experiences (e.g., dogs growl and then bite), institutions (e.g., church), and ways of life (e.g., monastic).[43] They are the assemblages of somato-affective responses consciously "processed, described, and performed."[44]

Affect theory does not reject the history of emotions, but it begins from the premise that the study of the culturally defined set of emotional categories is not enough. It holds that the "bodily feelings" prior to, outside of, and around fixed, culturally sanctioned emotions cannot all be collapsed so easily into these discursive categories.[45] There is something more there. These "intensities of feeling" or "bodily intensities," as Burger and Crocker term them, are pre-, or at least para-, linguistic and thus pre-/parasocial to varying extents as well.[46] They are those "irruptions" or "outbreaks" of feeling that "cannot adequately be rendered using the expressivist, intentionalist idiom of emotion" and that only become socially intelligible when a subject consciously organizes them into the "recognizable contours"

39. I am indebted to Cameron Cross for suggesting this linguistic means for representing the multifaceted nature and power of love.

40. For varying perspectives on the complex genealogy of affect theory and its markedly dissimilar schools of thought, see Schaefer, *Religious Affects*, 23–35; Bray and Moore, "Introduction," 1–6; Schaefer, *The Evolution of Affect Theory*.

41. Burger and Crocker, "Introduction," 2, 11.

42. Scheer, "Are Emotions a Kind of Practice," 195–96.

43. Reddy, "The Unavoidable Intentionality of Affect," 175.

44. Trigg, "Introduction," 5–7; Burger and Crocker, "Introduction," 9.

45. Burger and Crocker, "Introduction," 5–9; Trigg, "Introduction," 5–7; Schaefer, *Religious Affects*, 4.

46. Burger and Crocker, "Introduction," 1, 8.

of a discursively defined emotional script.[47] Affects are, as Schaefer argues, the *felt* "lattice" of "propulsive" forces of "experience, thought, sensation, feeling, and action that are not necessarily captured or capturable by language or self-sovereign 'consciousness,'" that is, "the shapes and textures that inform and structure our embodied experience at or beneath the threshold of cognition."[48] They may "register in awareness as feelings, emotions, and moods," but they ultimately are not ever completely reducible to socially defined categories of experience.[49] In more concrete terms, what they are talking about here are felt experiences like "a tug of longing, a pinprick of annoyance, a pang of grief"; "the beat of the heart; the rush of blood to the face; the flow of tears from the eyes"; "the incipient, ineffable moment of disquiet that arises when you sense that something is off in your environment," or "the spark, the electric tingle of expectation, before a first kiss," to list some specific examples given in the literature on affect.[50] Affect theory's stance is that the history-of-emotions approach does not pay adequate attention to, nor does it possess an analytical or terminological apparatus for, the study of these and "innumerable other similar sensations" that fall short of the full label of an "emotion," yet give fullness, texture, and power to the felt dimension of embodied human lived experience.[51]

Within affect theory, however, there is disagreement on the exact nature of affect and the bounds of what constitutes its research ambit. There are at least two important schools of thought.[52] The Deleuzian branch of affect theory, practiced prominently by Brian Massumi, Erin Manning, and Patricia Clough, for example, sees affect as "prediscursive compulsions" or a "prepersonal," "preprocessed force, intensity, or physiological shift" that are *distinct from emotions*. Emotions, in their view, are something wholly different.[53]

The phenomenological branch of affect theory, however, takes a more flexible approach on this point. Exemplified in the works of Eve Kosofsky Sedgwick, Sara Ahmed, Lauren Berlant, Jasbir Puar, Ann Cvetkovich, and Sianne Ngai, phenomenologically inclined affect theorists concur with their Deleuzian partners in theory that there are felt forces outside the purview of the emotional catego-

47. Burger and Crocker, "Introduction," 6, 10.

48. Schaefer, *Religious Affects*, 4, 23–24.

49. Schaefer, *Wild Experiment*, 19.

50. Trigg, "Introduction," 5–6; Schaefer, *Wild Experiment*, 19; Bray and Moore, "Introduction," 2.

51. Bray and Moore, "Introduction," 2. Scheer, although not coming from the affect theory camp, also criticizes the history of emotions approach for "detach[ing]" emotion from the human body and its "contribution . . . to emotional experience" ("Are Emotions a Kind of Practice," 195–96). For more on Scheer's Bourdieuan approach to affect/emotion, see below.

52. Bray and Moore argue that there is a third division of affect theory, which they term the "psychobiological approach." This approach, they argue, "looks at how affects, emotions, and feelings complexly intertwine to structure human experience." Examples of this work can be found in the scholarship of Silvan Tomkins, Eve Sedgwick, and Elspeth Probyn ("Introduction," 5).

53. Schaefer, *Religious Affects*, 24–28; Bray and Moore, "Introduction," 2–5.

ries and scripts of a culture. But they diverge from the Deleuzian flavor of affect theory in also including emotions in their more broadly defined scope of affective study.[54] Many scholars in this phenomenological branch adopt a big-tent approach in their deployment of the terms feeling, emotion, and affect.[55] Sianne Ngai articulates this ecumenical approach well in her argument for framing affect-emotion as a spectrum—not an irreconcilable binary—that moves from the less to the more "structured," "sociolinguistically fixed," or "organized" instances of feeling.

> While the distinction between affect and emotion is thus helpful here in a number of ways, I will not be theoretically leaning on it to the extent that others have—as may be apparent from the way in which I use the two terms more or less interchangeably. In the chapters that follow, the difference between affect and emotion is taken as a modal difference of intensity or degree, rather than a formal difference of quality or kind. My assumption is that affects are less formed and structured than emotions, but not lacking form or structure altogether; less "sociolinguistically fixed," but by no means code-free or meaningless; less "organized in response to our interpretations of situations," but by no means entirely devoid of organization or diagnostic powers. As suggested above, ambient affects may in fact be better suited to interpreting ongoing states of affairs. What the switch from formal to modal difference enables is an analysis of the transitions from one pole to the other: the passages whereby affects acquire the semantic density and narrative complexity of emotions, and emotions conversely denature into affects. At the end of the day, the difference between emotion and affect is still intended to solve the same basic and fundamentally descriptive problem it was coined in psychoanalytic practice to solve: that of distinguishing first-person from third-person feeling, and, by extension, feeling that is contained by an identity from feeling that is not. Rather than also trying to dissolve this subjective/objective problematic by creating two distinct categories of feeling, this study aims to preserve it for its aesthetic productivity.[56]

Other scholars have sought to break out of the limits of the affect theory-history of emotions binary by suggesting other terms, such as "feeling" or "emotional practice" (in the Bourdieuan sense), as more appropriate ways of referring to the felt diversity of human embodied experience.[57] Scheer's attempt to reframe this debate is especially generative. She suggests conceptualizing emotions as "emotional practices" in terms of Bourdieuan practice theory, as a way to bridge the disembodied, discursive script-focused history of emotions approach and the embodied, though ahistorical (Massumian) or present-focused uses of affect theory. "Thinking of emotion as a kind of practice," she argues, "can help historians get over the sense that the history of emotions can only be a history of changing emotional norms and expectations but not a record of change in feeling. Emotions change over time

54. Schaefer, *Religious Affects*, 24, 28; Bray and Moore, "Introduction," 3–6.

55. Schaefer, *Wild Experiment*, 61.

56. Ngai, *Ugly Feelings*, 27–28.

57. McNamer, "Feeling," 246–7; Scheer, "Are Emotions a Kind of Practice."

not only because norms, expectations, words, and concepts that shape experience are modified, but also because the practices in which they are embodied, and bodies themselves, undergo transformation."[58]

In *Feeling Like Lovers*, I pursue the study of feeling in medieval Sufism in an "intersectional" way, as Burger and Crocker term it—that is, an approach that combines key parts of the phenomenological branch of affect theory and history of emotions (with a dash of Scheer's Bourdieuan "practice" approach) to illustrate how affect and emotions worked together *historically* to produce *feeling* Sufi subjects.[59] I am not dogmatically committed to any particular theorist or theoretical orientation, and my terminological choices reflect this intersectional approach. I make use of the terms feeling, affect, and emotion throughout this book based on what feels most appropriate in the given context, even while at a general level, I tend to opt for affect, or æffect, most frequently.[60] My approach to this terminological debate is closest to Ngai, who, as she says above, does not "theoretically lean on [the distinction between affect and emotion] to the extent that others have."

Feeling Like Lovers will not seek to settle debates within affect theory or the history of emotions or to iron out any inconsistencies across their theoretical or terminological frameworks. While I find these theoretical frameworks generative as analytical inspiration for reading Sufi texts, and I will at times gesture toward possible broader theoretical implications of this study for these fields, this book is not aiming to bring about any theoretical reconciliation or new grand narrative for these fields. It is primarily a book about Sufism and the central role feeling plays within its epistemology and modes of subjective formation—a role, I note with gratitude, that these fields have helped me see and, hopefully, describe more clearly here. In the following sections, I will elaborate on what I see as these fields' key implications for this study.

FEELING/THINKING/KNOWING RELIGION: BEYOND THE MIND-BODY BINARY

Much modern scholarship, across many fields, is shaped in diverse ways by a dualistic conception of the mind and body. At the risk of oversimplification, the short version goes something like this. On one side of this binary is the mind: a separate,

58. Scheer, "Are Emotions a Kind of Practice," 220.

59. Burger and Crocker, "Introduction," 2, 10, 12. *Feeling Like Lovers* thus joins the essays in the landmark volume *Medieval Affect, Feeling, and Emotion* in pushing for a "medieval turn" in affect theory, which, until quite recently, was largely focused on studies of modern culture (Burger and Crocker, "Introduction," 3, 5). I see affect, to be clear, as a (somato-affective) historical construct and seek to understand medieval Sufi affect in its own historical and culturally defined terms, even with the limitations imposed by its representation. On the limitations of representation and critique of transcultural/transhistorical approaches to affect, see Elias, "Mevlevi Sufis."

60. On the tradition of using these terms "interchangeably," see Ngai, *Ugly Feelings*, 27–28, and also Scheer, "Are Emotions a Kind of Practice," 198.

higher organ that directs an elite team of cognitive capacities such as rationality, cognition, and language (the last of these understood in the traditional, limited sense of a tool that communicates propositional content, "facts," intellectual concepts and ideas, or discursive constructions). On the other is the body: a lower, physical entity that must be operated and controlled by the mind (via its director "I" self) and serves primarily as a container for the mind and as a tool that feeds inputs to the mind from the senses and feeling/affect/emotion. Most scholars do not present it in such a caricatured manner, obviously, but this binary Cartesian view of human perception, knowledge, and experience can shape even excellent scholarship in quite subtle and implicit ways—for example, in what modern scholars have decided to focus on and how they approach and frame their analyses.

In different ways and to different extents, affect theory and the history of emotions each begin by challenging the dominance of academic approaches to the study of culture that privilege the mind side of this binary. They urge us to move beyond the implicit assumptions that, as Schaefer says, "humans are basically thinking, reasoning beings, that what makes us tick is a sedimentation of words and ideas," and that human culture and, thus, cultural studies "starts and ends with books, ideas, and beliefs."[61] Mind-focused scholarly approaches like these, affect theory and history of emotions proponents aver, take deeply lived and felt religious traditions and reduce them to the facts, figures, and metaphysical and discursive formulations that can be mined from their textual remains—an approach that often privileges religion's metaphysical and normative dimensions at the expense of ones connected to the body or material life.

The fields of affect theory and history of emotions have helped us see the diverse ways in which religion *feels* as much, or more (depending on the theorist), as it thinks.[62] They make evident that what something *is* in a metaphysical system does not fully convey what it *means* to practitioners when these ideas or concepts are embodied, performed, and/or summoned in ritual practice. They insist that how we *feel* about God is potentially prior to, but at the minimum, constitutive of, what we think (and then write) about God. They propose that affects/emotions are fundamental epistemological stepping stones on the path to God and play a key role in forming religious subjects.

Insisting on affect/emotion's foundational role in religion does *not* mean, however, that thinking and everything typically associated with it, from reason and "the mind" to their purported rational/mental projections into metaphysics and language, are not involved in or important to religion and its practice.

61. Schaefer, *Wild Experiment*, 19; Schaefer, *Religious Affects*, 11. For a critique of approaches to metaphysics of religious traditions without attending to their "emotional" aspects, see Wynn, "Metaphysics and Emotional Experience."

62. Schaefer, *Religious Affects*, 8–9. To my knowledge, Bauer is the only scholar in Islamic studies who says something similar, asserting that "In the Qurʾan, feeling is a part of believing" (Bauer, "Emotion in the Qur'an," 16).

They are. But affect theory and history of emotions seeks to focus our attention on their eponymous felt phenomena because they have typically been neglected or relegated to markedly second-class status in much previous religious studies scholarship. Indeed, despite the polemic tone and grand claims of some affect theory and history of emotions work, the best scholarship from these fields has quite explicitly sought to militate against the mind/body binary that has cleaved, in many people's minds, these two domains and their associated implements apart.[63] Their foregrounding of affect/emotion—i.e., part of the Team Body side of the binary—is not meant to serve as fodder for feeding this binary's strength, but rather as a devastating strike against its foundational assumption that the mind/body and their team members can ever be neatly separated. Feeling, thinking, and knowing are not separate processes, nor are these seemingly subjective processes sealed off from the social sphere. "What needs to be emphasized," Scheer argues, "is the mutual embeddedness of minds, bodies, and social relations in order to historicize the body and its contributions to the learned experience of emotion."[64] What we need to study—historically and in the present—is feeling/thinking/knowing subjects.

FEELING/THINKING/KNOWING SUBJECTS: ÆFFECTING EPISTEMOLOGY AND SUBJECTIVITY IN THE SOMATO-AFFECTIVE BODY

As mentioned previously, a growing body of scholarship in Sufi studies has sought to understand how Sufi discourses on gender, sexuality, normative practice, group identity, etc. have shaped Sufi subjectivities. This model of discourse as a pseudo-agent with the power to fashion an individual's innermost self famously has its roots in Foucault's theorizations of power/knowledge. The analytical power of this theoretical framing and the importance of the subsequent avalanche of scholarship utilizing it are incontestable. It has fundamentally reshaped our understanding of culture, knowledge, and subjectivity, and how they are all co-constructed.

But for affect theorists, Foucault's theory of power/knowledge is incomplete because, they maintain, it is not just discursive forms of knowledge that shape us and our cultures. Feeling too has this power.[65] Feeling is another modality of power/knowledge. Operating through a "sensualized epistemology," it informs and forms subjects through the human body's somato-affective circuits.[66] To

63. The reader could be forgiven for thinking that affect theory "recapitulate[s] the assumption that feeling is separate from thinking" because it sometimes *does*, as Schaefer notes in *Wild Experiment* (4).

64. Scheer, "Are Emotions a Kind of Practice," 199. For an even stronger assertion of the feeling basis of thought and mind, see Schaefer, *Wild Experiment.*

65. Schaefer, *Wild Experiment*, 57–63.

66. The term "sensualized epistemolog[y]" originates in Lauren Berlant's groundbreaking work *Cruel Optimism* (64), but has since been elaborated further by Schaefer (*Wild Experiment*, 57–79). He

understand subjectivity, affect theory asserts, "we have to look past words themselves. It's the affects carried by words—as well as by all the other wordless things enfolding our bodies—that add up to make subjectivity."[67] We have to learn how to read and interpret this felt form of power/knowledge—this "power-knowledge-affect," as Schaefer terms it—that circulates around, between, and inside of bodies, texts, settings, and objects, constructing subjects, societies, and cultures through the feelings it produces.[68]

This feeling/knowledge forms subjects through its *powerful* machinations in what I will call here the somato-affective body. While this felt body often overlaps with the physical or sensory body discussed in studies of the body/embodiment, sensory history, and/or material culture, I use this more specific term to focus attention on the internal affective sensorium or feelingscape that is *æffected* in/through the human body. But while I want to highlight the somato-affective body in *Feeling Like Lovers*, I also want to be careful to spell out what this term does *not* mean. I categorically do *not* intend it to re-effect a mind-body separation. The somato-affective body is imbricated with the "mind" and its team members in complex ways, as we will see throughout this book. It is a "knowing body" or "mindful body," as Scheer says.[69] I use the somato-affective body primarily as a framing device that helps analytically center the experience of the felt body and surface how its panoply of defined and ill-defined feelings—rendered shorthand as emotions, affects, or, as I prefer, æffects—work on this feeling body to produce the feeling/knowing part of the larger aggregate feeling/thinking/knowing subject. As Scheer says when discussing the mind/body, "though in this text it is sometimes necessary to distinguish between the two in order to emphasize the contribution of the bodily organism to emotional experience," these distinctions are heuristic, *not* ontological, and should not be taken to deny the ultimate "intertwine[ment]" of the somato-affective body with the mind and its tools.[70]

Another note of caution: feeling/knowledge should not be understood as *only* an external force that descends upon subjects as a result of some external stimulus, forming their somato-affective subjectivity through its *powerful* machinations

---

captures the main thrust of this concept pithily: "Sensualized epistemology—a theory of knowledge in full communion with feeling" (26).

67. Schaefer, *Wild Experiment*, 19–20.

68. Schaefer, *Religious Affects*, 35. Crocker makes similar points in "Medieval Affects Now," 91–92. While *Feeling Like Lovers* focuses primarily on Sufi æffects as an internal felt form of meaning/knowledge, this is not to discount its sociopolitical power to effect Sufi sociopolitical identities, power relations, or projects. It would very much be doing this too: Sufism is as much a sociopolitical project as a mode of piety. I touch on the powerful æffects of the Sufi lover subjectivity in the sociopolitical sphere in a few places (see chapters 2, 4, and 5), but it is not my focus in this work. For examples of this latter sociopolitical approach to emotion/affect in premodern Islamic context, see Vignone, "Fear and Learning in Medieval Islam"; Bauer, "Emotions of Conversion."

69. Scheer, "Are Emotions a Kind of Practice," 200–201.

70. Scheer, "Are Emotions a Kind of Practice," 200.

in or upon them, as my first sentence in the previous paragraph may seem to imply. The feeling/knowing part of feeling/thinking/knowing subjects can also be æffected in another way: the subject can *affect* (that is, practice) particular emotional or affective practices until they perfect (that is, *effect*) them and the related desired subjectivity.[71] Emotions and affects, in other words, should also be understood as "practices" that "are skillful behaviors, dependent (as the term suggests) on practice until they become automatic."[72] This Bordieuan "practices" framing complicates the common portrayal of emotions and affects as only "reactions" or "triggered responses" to external stimuli.[73] It gives agency and *power* to the subject as well, as people can help forge their own feeling/knowing subjectivity and somato-affective knowledge through *practice*—a point on which proponents of practice theory approaches to emotion/affect and, as we will see in later chapters, medieval Sufis fully agree.

STUDYING THE ÆFFECTIVENESS OF LITERATURE IN HISTORY: REEMBODYING MEANING AND ACTUALIZING TEXTUAL ABSENCES

The reader of *Feeling Like Lovers* may be surprised, as the affect theorist Sara Ahmed remarks in her landmark book *The Cultural Politics of Emotions*, that "for a book on emotions, which argues that emotions cannot be separated from bodily sensations, this book may seem very oriented towards texts."[74] However, the focus on texts in a study of affect/emotion is not, as Ahmed cautions, a contradiction in terms. The fields of affect theory and history of emotions do not deny the important role of language and texts in human culture. Nor, for that matter, do they necessarily dismiss the work of generations of scholars who have focused on texts as historical documents or as bearers of intellectual or discursive constructs.

Instead, they encourage us to shift our analytical focus on texts. They ask us to see texts as more than just bearers of propositional content, repositories of information (whether intellectual ideas or historical "facts"), or—especially with the "postmodern turn" in theory—discursive constructs (e.g., power)—a tendency that some affect theorists have termed the "linguistic fallacy."[75] They ask us to expand our notion of meaning, to adopt a much more expansive and embodied

71. Building on Scheer's point in "Are Emotions a Kind of Practice" (202, 220), and gesturing towards Gade's book title, *Perfection Makes Practice*.

72. Scheer, "Are Emotions a Kind of Practice," 202.

73. Scheer, "Are Emotions a Kind of Practice," 206, 220.

74. Sara Ahmed, *Cultural Politics*, 12.

75. For a good summary of this argument, see Schaefer, *Religious Affects*, 4–7, 10–12, 17–18, 29. Affect theory, much more so than scholarship on the history of emotions, has challenged cultural studies to go beyond the study of emotions-as-discursive-constructions framing. See also Scheer's work (discussed above and below) who goes beyond the emotions-as-discursive-constructions framing in a different way.

conception of meaning, to follow meaning's full arc from its beginning in a particular (somato-affective) body into language (or other form of communication) and then all of the way through its long tail in its diverse ramifications in the (somato-affective) bodies of its audience members.

Following this full arc of meaning necessitates that we analyze texts in new ways. We need to approach them with an eye toward how they "form ligatures with pulsing flesh-and-blood creatures," as Schaefer terms it, and with acute attention to the way that feelings, emotions, and affects are framed, scripted, and reproduced in texts.[76] To explore how the "thick, embodied forces" of affect/emotion shape the language of texts in ways that are not reducible to their discursive or intellectual content alone.[77] To answer the question of, as Karen Bray and Stephen D. Moore frame it in their recent volume, "how the sensory encounter with it [the text] *felt* to particular bodies in particular places in particular moments of history."[78] To analyze language as a human tool for conveying æffective meaning—for, that is, "circulat[ing] and distribut[ing] affects"—as much as propositional content, historical facts, intellectual ideas, or power in the form of discourse.[79]

Reembodying Meaning

Feeling Like Lovers models this æffective analytical approach in its engagement with a wide range of texts. Some of these texts are theoretical in nature, but, if there is a surprising element in this work for historians of emotion and affect, it is the fact that *Feeling Like Lovers* has a special focus on the preeminent literary genre of medieval Persian Sufism: poetry. To be clear, this would only be surprising to some historians of emotion and affect because, as McNamer notes, these fields have often overlooked the importance of literary genres in their studies: "As the field has taken shape—chiefly under the leadership of scholars trained in the discipline of history, with few methodological interventions by literary specialists so far—a distinctive pattern has emerged, in which the more literary the text, the less likely it is to be regarded as a valuable source for the history of feeling."[80] This neglect of literary sources is especially problematic because not only is æffect often foregrounded in them, but indeed they serve as "scripts for the making of

76. Schaefer, "The Promise of Affect."

77. Schaefer, *Religious Affects*, 8–9; Wynn, "Metaphysics and Emotional Experience."

78. Bray and Moore, "Introduction," 7.

79. Schaefer, *Wild Experiment*, 19–20. Hirschkind makes a similar point in *The Ethical Soundscape*, where he argues that the "omnipresent" cassette sermons of 1990s Cairo are key in the construction of the "Islamic Revival" movement and its "ethical-political reasoning" *not* just because they "disseminate ideas or instill religious ideologies but [because of their] effect on the human sensorium, on the affects, sensibilities, and perceptual habits" of their listeners (2, 30). "Religious sensibilities and affects," he maintains, must be seen as having "epistemic and ethical value" in our analyses of society and politics (31).

80. McNamer, "Literariness of Literature," 1435. See also McNamer, "Feeling," 242–46; McNamer, *Affective Meditation*. Crocker makes this same point in "Medieval Affects Now," 91–92.

emotion in history."[81] Literature, from McNamer's perspective, is not a repository of emotional scripts to be mined in an exercise of historical, philosophical, or discourse analysis; it produces æffects in the audience and, as Crocker adds, in the sociopolitical world—points on which the Sufis and premodern Islamic thinkers discussed in this book would completely concur.[82]

As I will show throughout *Feeling Like Lovers*, poetry was widely regarded in the premodern Islamicate world as having particularly strong æffective qualities. It was understood to be the literary genre of the heart, of æffective states, as we will see in Abū Ḥāmid al-Ghazālī and ʿAbd al-Raḥmān Jāmī's writings. And precisely because of this special connection to æffect, it was also understood to be *the* most *powerful* literary genre—*the* genre of power. As the court litterateur Niẓāmī ʿArūżī says quite succinctly in his *Chahār maqālah* (w. 1156 CE), poetry "effects important matters in the order of the world" by exciting different affective responses in its audience members.[83] Poetry, in the premodern Islamic world, *æffected* people and the sociopolitical order of the world.

But *how* does poetry æffect people and the "order of the world," as Niẓāmī ʿArūżī says? This is a complex question.

To begin an answer, let's return to our example of ʿIrāqī and Ḥasan's *samāʿ* session. An æffective mode of textual interpretation holds that we cannot reduce the meaning of ʿIrāqī and Ḥasan's *samāʿ* session to a theoretical explanation of God's beauty reflected in earthly forms and a Sufi symbolist—what I will later term a cogno-spiritual—reading of the poems that finds their meaning primarily in the potential connections between their poetic imagery and myriad metaphysical concepts, spiritual meanings/realities (*maʿānī*), or scriptural references. We must attend to the whole experience presented in this text and incorporate into its meaning all the rich sensory and æffective elements that Ḥasan's beauty, the musical performance of the poetry, the moving ambience of its performance context (the hallowed space of the Sufi lodge), *and* the language of the poem seek to co-produce in the audience.

Taking the last of this list first: the poem. *Feeling Like Lovers* begins from the premise that meaning is multimodal. Akin to the way I describe love's different functional modalities in culture above, language similarly can operate and *mean* to audience members in different ways, along different wavelengths or vectors, simultaneously. It can convey propositional content. It can contain facts or express philosophical ideas.

81. McNamer, "Literariness of Literature," 1436. McNamer is using "script" here in a different sense than is typical in the literature. She continues, "The term 'scripts' has been used widely in emotions research across the disciplines to designate cultural templates and norms. Here, I intend something at once more literal—a conception of literary texts, that is, as literal scripts that generate a performance of feeling—and less bound to a notion of norms." On these points, see also McNamer, "Feeling," 245–46, 249.

82. Crocker expresses a similar view to McNamer, and also adds the social dimension: "What emotions did—how they were enlisted to orient subjects in accordance with intersecting nodes of identity," that is, how "they actively participate in generating the affects that might constitute different versions of gender, religion, sexuality, status, or ethnicity" ("Medieval Affects Now," 91–92).

83. Niẓāmī ʿArūżī Samarqandī, *Chahār maqālah*, 123.

It can discursively construct identities and subjects. It can use symbols, complex metaphoric imagery, and fictional narratives to refer to or represent allegorically other religious or philosophical ideas or even "spiritual realities" in other realms of existence. *And* it can convey somato-affective meaning and *æffect* audiences. These different types of meaning are not mutually exclusive. Language is often conveying all these different types of meaning—to different degrees, varying sometimes quite significantly by genre, aim, context, and the receptiveness of the individual audience member—at the same time. They work together to co-construct the whole meaning the audience member builds from instances of language.

As mentioned above, there has been no shortage of studies analyzing the historical, metaphysical, and symbolic import of Sufi poetry. Fewer have focused on the ways Sufi poetry has participated in the discursive construction of Sufi identity, gender, sexuality, etc.; these do exist, though, even if not in plenitude.[84] The modality of meaning that has received little to no attention is the main concern of *Feeling Like Lovers*: the diverse ways in which Sufis saw æffect enmeshed in their poetry and poetic hermeneutics.

Sufis, as we will see in different ways in chapters 1–4, saw æffect as playing a significant role in *how* Sufis (and non-Sufis too) make meaning out of poetry. Chapter 1 shows how Sufis understood the role of bodies in the performance context and, most importantly, how the powerful æffects they evoke in audience members allow the participants to discover higher spiritual meanings (*ma ʿānī*) in the poems that they never would have been able to arrive to in the absence of bodily induced æffect. Chapter 2 highlights Sufi perspectives on æffect's power to build (or not) meaning for the participant in the *samā ʿ* ritual through modulations in its poetic performance context and music. Chapters 3 and 4 explore Sufi hermeneutics and theories of metaphoric imagery, surfacing the overlooked centrality they assign to æffect in directing the Sufi hermeneutic process and to somato-affective experience in structuring Sufi metaphoric imagery. Long before the advent of the history of emotions or affect theory, in other words, medieval Sufis made their own arguments for the "æffectiveness of literature" and the importance of æffect to epistemology and subject formation.

Chapter 5 builds on this Sufi æffective hermeneutics, as I term it—especially Jāmī's embodied theory of metaphor, discussed in chapter 4—and attempts to extend its analytical reach by connecting it with the similarly embodied modern theory of metaphor put forward in cognitive linguistics. While I am certainly not trying to fuse these two theories of metaphor (nor am I the first to make such comparisons between premodern Islamic poetics and modern schools of thought), they both are rooted in a modal theory of language that enables us to responsibly make use of some of the linguistic tools of analysis developed in cognitive linguistics—analytical implements such as force dynamics (which I use in chapter 5) that can help us dig deeper on this question of *how* somato-affective meaning is

84. See footnote 21 in this chapter for some examples, though most do not primarily treat poetry.

produced in/by Sufi poetry.[85] I use cognitive linguistics here, thus, not to signal my commitment to its entire program or all of its claims but rather because it offers tools and concepts for fine-tooth analysis of how language creates somato-affective meaning for audiences.

At the broadest level, this is where Jāmī's implicit theory of metaphor and cognitive linguistics' overlap. They both assert, in very similar terms, that at least one major reason human beings use metaphoric language is to communicate somato-affective meaning for audience members. To be more concrete, they both propose that the association between the emotion/æffect of love and its diverse metaphoric figurations in the wine imagery of Sufi poetry is driven by the fact that their embodied human experience shares key characteristics. They are both felt and then portrayed, to take one shared aspect of one of their most common metaphoric figurations, as external agents that (1) enter, (2) overtake, and (3) induce involuntary changes in the bodies of their hosts. They are, in other words, felt and conceptualized as forces external to the individual that produce altered bodily states like "drunkenness," "love sickness," "insanity," or "bewilderment," in which the individual loses control of his body and is made to act in accordance with the "will" of the intoxicant or love. This is just one small example illustrating their shared general conclusion: The metaphors (and, really, language generally) used to describe and metaphorically represent concepts/experiences such as love are *not amodal*. That is, they are not just randomly associated mental symbols ungrounded in the actual physical object or embodied experience they purport to represent in language. The relationship is *modal*, it is "motivated." There are sensorimotor and æffective sinews connecting the mental and linguistic representation of symbols and concepts such as love with their embodied experience, and these structure the nature of this language/imagery. Cognitive linguistics can help us see how this "motivation" structures Sufi metaphoric imagery. It can help us see at a detailed mechanical level how language and meaning are embodied.[86]

My focus on this somato-affective dimension of meaning creation in *Feeling Like Lovers* should not, however, be taken as indicating that the other modalities of meaning more typically associated with the "mind"—the propositional,

85. Claiming similarities between medieval and contemporary theories of language and metaphor obviously runs the significant risk of anachronistic projection. However, Abu Deeb and Key have pointed out many other ways in which medieval Arabic poetics, particularly as represented in al-Jurjānī, prefigures aspects of much later Euro-American discussions of imagery and metaphor (Abu Deeb, *Al-Jurjānī's Theory of Poetic Imagery*; Key, *Language*, 203–204). Harb also briefly comments on some similarities between medieval Arabic and European theories of aesthetics (*Arabic Poetics*, 263–64), and Shahab Ahmed even gestures towards the overlap with premodern Islamicate theories of metaphor and those of modern cognitive linguistics (*What Is Islam?*, 394).

86. For overviews of cognitive linguistics' embodied theory of language and metaphor, see Lakoff, "The Neural Theory of Metaphor"; Lakoff and Johnson, *Philosophy in the Flesh*; Lakoff and Johnson, *Metaphors We Live By*; Johnson, *The Meaning of the Body*; Bergen, *Louder Than Words*. For studies that analyze the metaphoric expression of emotion with this framework, see Kövecses, *Metaphor and Emotion*; Kövecses, "Metaphor and Emotion."

intellectual, allegorical/symbolist, discursive—aren't operative too in Sufi hermeneutics. I am, as Scheer insists above in a related context, "distinguish[ing] between" these different linguistic modalities of meaning conveyance and focusing on the somato-affective one in this book "to emphasize [its] contribution." This is a tactical distinction to surface a type of Sufi meaning that has been largely ignored. But ultimately part of my goal in concluding this book with chapters on Sufi language and metaphor is precisely to militate against readings that would see a new mind-body binary implied in my focus on Sufi æffect.[87] Metaphoric imagery, especially in poetry, is where mind, in the form of language, and the body, in the form of somato-affective experience, most clearly come together—a point on which scholars of affect theory and history of emotions, cognitive linguists, and Sufis, such as al-Ghazālī and Jāmī, would agree.[88]

Actualizing Textual Absences

Now—without denying the power and importance of the words of the poem—we must also say that they also are not the whole show in Ḥasan's performance of ʿIrāqī's poem that night in Tūqāt. There are many more elements that would structure a participant's experience of this scene and the meaning they derive from it cumulatively as a performance: the spiritually rarefied and grandiose material environment of the lodge, the care given to the arrangement of people and choreography, the palpable anticipation that the audience members/participants must have felt as they waited for the legendarily talented and dashingly beautiful performer Ḥasan to sing, the way bodies and texts commingle in performance, the spiritual weight the presence of a spiritual master of ʿIrāqī's renown lent to the ritual, the electricity that must have permeated the scene as the crowd collectively stilled, the music commenced, and the much anticipated recitation of the first poem began, opening the ritual.

If the reader is familiar with ʿIrāqī's traditional biography, they may object that many details in my account do not appear explicitly in the original document. The anecdote of this performance in ʿIrāqī's biography gets us started, but it is not descriptively detailed. (This is not its aim or concern.) We do not have real thick historical documentation in the positivistic sense of *this* exact performance venue, *this* performance's features, and the audience responses in *this* particular performance—nor do we have these for most other historical performances of poems.[89]

87. I am grateful to an anonymous reviewer for pushing me to clarify my stance here.

88. In addition to the foregoing discussion and citations, see also Scheer, "Are Emotions a Kind of Practice," 218, where she also seems to suggest something similar, pointing scholars of affect and emotions to the fact that it is in metaphoric language—though not the exact term she uses—dealing with emotion that we see the "merging of body and mind . . . a physical involvement in thought."

89. While we have a limited number of truly straightforward (i.e., nonstylized, nonconventional) accounts of audience responses to particular texts or other objects of material culture, there are some other interesting ways to study the history of audience (affective) reception. In addition to the "actualizing absences" approach discussed here, Gruber, for example, has shown in a detailed study of the affective reception of illustrated manuscript images the various ways in which premodern Muslims

What I have provided here is an amplified version of the anonymous biographer's account. I have attempted to reconstruct it according to the historical data we have for such scenes so we can get a sense of what it would have looked like to this account's intended audience members in its full live glory.[90] This is important because, as we will see in the chapters that follow, all these textual absences partially represented, if at all, in the texts themselves played powerful roles in what it *felt* like to be a Sufi participating in this ritual of *samāʿ*. Counterintuitively, to get a more historical picture of what ʿIrāqī's poem would have meant to the audience members that night, we need to "actualiz[e] [these] absences."[91]

Some readers may bristle at the intellectual license such an act entails. But here I join historians of emotion and affect in arguing that the risk of not doing this historically informed reconstruction work is far greater and will lead to an even more distorted sense of the full scope of what these events *historically* meant for their audiences. We need, as Sarah McNamer has argued, to "combine the usual forms of textual research with considerations of what is likely to have been seen, heard, touched, even tasted at the moment of a text's performance." In refusing to engage in this work out of a well-meaning sense of intellectual modesty, as McNamer argues,

> we are continuing to prop up the manifest fiction that what we cannot decisively document did not exist or was not operative, in any essential way, in the production of affect. In disregarding what is left to the imagination, in other words, we risk throwing the proverbial baby out with the bathwater. Indeed real babies have been thrown out with the bathwater in our text-centred assessment of medieval lyrics. Certain lullabies and laments of the Virgin, for instance, are highly likely to have been performed with real babes in arms, and this surely must be factored into any assessment of the historical questions such lullabies and laments prompt.[92]

This approach to historical performance contexts has been used to great effect in historical performance studies.[93] Its origin in performance studies should not

---

felt compelled to engage in a range of "ethico-emotive responses" to manuscript images ("In Defense and Devotion").

90. On the historical context for *samāʿ* and other poetic performance contexts in the premodern Islamicate world, see Ingenito, *Beholding Beauty*, 443–518; Brookshaw, "Palaces, Pavilions, and Pleasure-Gardens"; Lewisohn, "The Sacred Music of Islam"; Avery, *A Psychology of Early Sufi Samāʿ*; Lewis, "Reading, Writing and Recitation," 69–103, 228–39; Ali, *Arabic Literary Salons*. See also chapter 2. Also see O'Malley, *The Poetics of Spiritual Instruction* for a study of how readers/listeners' experience of texts is imagined in ʿAṭṭār's didactic works. Blatherwick comments on the importance of emotion for the performance and reception of modern popular Arabic epic (*sīra*) stories in Egypt ("'And the Light in His Eyes Grew Dark,'" 227), and Moukheiber discusses emotions in musical performance contexts ("Gendering Emotions").

91. For more on "actualizing absences" as a technique, see Franko and Richards, "Actualizing Absences," and the other essays in *Acting on the Past*.

92. McNamer, "Feeling," 247–48.

93. McNamer points this out in multiple studies: McNamer, "Feeling," 247–48; McNamer, *Affective Meditation*, 146.

surprise us. As a field, performance studies understands that the meaning of a play is produced as much or more in all the minute details of its performance (from the second-to-second nature of its enactment and costuming to the design of its performance location) as in the words of the script, leaving them no choice but to reconstruct. They are not as tempted by the linguistic fallacy—the "manifest fiction," as McNamer boldly terms it—that the basic linguistic or symbolic meaning of words alone are enough to understand what a work means to audiences.

As I will argue in different ways throughout this book, the "words alone" approach to medieval Sufism is a lot like reading a script of an acclaimed play or movie silently to oneself. The reader can understand the literal meaning of the text, what happens, what themes are involved, what extratextual allusions it may be gesturing toward, etc. But how much is missed! How flat the script will seem in comparison to an award-winning performance of it in the hands of expert actors. The text of the script itself only contains vague hints, if that, of some of the most "meaningful" elements of a performance: set design; the actors' stage presence; the way the lines are brought to life by infusing them with gestures, affect, and facial expressions; the right musical accompaniment to calibrate the audience's mood; sound effects; and much more. Add to this the unpredictable variable of the myriad internal dispositions and histories each audience member brings that impinge powerfully on how they each make meaning of this complex array of vectors.[94] There is a world of difference between the script and the performance. In many ways, they do not *mean* the same thing. The latter is so much richer in what it evokes for audience members, in how it can *æffect* them—that is, ultimately, in what it comes to *mean* to them.[95]

In *Feeling Like Lovers*, I approach the interpretation of Sufi poetry and ritual from this historical performance studies–inspired perspective. I seek, where appropriate and within the bounds of existing scholarship, to "actualize absences" with the goal of highlighting for readers the potential depth and profundity of meaning that medieval Sufis derived from these performances of meaning. I do not believe nor claim that these audience experiences were uniform. As we will see in chapters 2 and 3, what I term Sufism's "æffective hermeneutics" allows for highly variegated audience responses, inflected and directed by their own internal dispositions at the moment of meaning creation. But to not venture informed conjectures at how textual absences may have powerfully shaped the ways audiences made meaning can also be a form of intellectual irresponsibility. It would be, as McNamer says, like "throwing the proverbial baby out with the bathwater." The diverse array of meaningful elements that are *not* explicitly documented in

94. The comparison between the flatness of a play or movie script and the rich sensory and affective experience of it performed is a nod to one of the progenitors of affect theory, Silvan Tomkins, and his early interest in theater. On this, see Schaefer, *Religious Affects*, 28–30.

95. The limited work on the performance context of medieval Persian poetry has made some of these points too, though, it is concerned with different issues than I am here. See studies cited in footnote 90 in present chapter and discussion in chapter 1.

the text are as important as what is in the words of the texts themselves, from features of the material performance context to aspects of the musical-poetic performance and the individual æffective states of its audience members. They decisively shape how and what the words of a text mean—which, as I will argue throughout this book, very much includes how they *feel*—to the audience.

RECONSTRUCTING SUFI WORLDS, REEMBODYING SUFI THEORY: TEXTS, GENRES, AND THE SEARCH FOR SUFI ÆFFECTS

Throughout this book I have sought to bring together my discussions of poetry with Sufi theoretical and biographical texts.[96] But my weaving together of these different genres is not just a structuring mechanism for my prose. It is intended to implicitly make a theoretical point as well. Each genre gives us a different window into the historical world of medieval Sufism. Genre distinctions are important, but Sufis did not experience these as wholly separate textual worlds—not from each other and not from their lived experience either.

Our view of these texts, and of medieval Sufism more broadly as a lived cultural formation, can become distorted if we overemphasize texts from one or the other type of genre in our analyses. To take a specific example, as I will argue in this book, Sufi studies has placed far too much emphasis on the analysis of Sufism as a metaphysical or philosophical system. This approach, rooted largely in Sufi theoretical texts and the closely aligned traditions of poetic lexicons (*iṣṭilāḥāt*) and hermeneutic commentaries (*sharḥ*), has had the unfortunate effect of warping interpretations of Sufi poetry by subjecting them to symbolist or philosophical readings that reduce them to versified accounts of Sufi metaphysics or just "pointers" to abstract spiritual realities (*maʿānī*) or scriptural references.[97] There is nothing inherently wrong about reading Sufi poetry with/through Sufi metaphysics. I do this quite extensively here too at times. But when this hermeneutic method is applied rigidly and *in isolation* to Sufi poetry, much is lost, as the poetry becomes little more than a versified vehicle for conveying Sufi philosophy. It becomes a static intellectual artifact that is no longer engaged with Sufi material life and the body that produced it, nor the ones it seeks to æffect in recitation. And this disembodying, metaphysicalizing effect is not limited to the case of poetry, as we will see.

What I have tried to do in the way I have structured my narrative in this book is to present a fuller picture of Sufism as a lived mode of piety by putting a wider

96. For other, more history-of-emotions-focused studies of Islamicate biographical literature, see Bray, "Yaʿqūb b. al-Rabīʿ Read by al-Mutanabbī and al-Mubarrad"; Bray, "Codes of Emotion"; Yep, "Emotion and Islamic Hagiology." For other history-of-emotions approaches to Sufi biographical literature, see Elias, "Mevlevi Sufis"; Werbner, "The Abstraction of Love."

97. There are, of course, notable exceptions to this generalization. For those and the scholarship critiquing this symbolist hermeneutics, see chapter 4 and 5.

range of genres in conversation to help think through Sufi amatory piety, metaphysics, and ritual practice and how they may have felt to their adherents.[98] There is no shortage of engagement with Sufi theoretical works or of philosophical readings of poetry in this study, but I try to balance this interpretative perspective—this window on medieval Sufism—by giving equal stage time to other approaches. Some of these additional windows onto the Sufi past are created with the aid of modern theoretical or analytical approaches (e.g., affect theory, different schools of poetic/literary analysis), but the most important is the genre of Sufi biography.

Reading Sufi poetry and theoretical works with/through/in Sufi biography provides a unique perspective on these other genres. In a sense, it embodies them, because these biographic documents bring together Sufi bodies, poetry, and theory in a performative crucible. They illustrate—even if in a scripted, stylized, and idealized manner—what Sufi rituals and texts meant or were *meant to mean* for Sufi bodies. They provide a window into dimensions of meaning that are not centered exclusively on the philosophical and discursive import of sources.[99] They give us a glimpse into how these texts and rituals—these tools—of spiritual formation æffected Sufis and moved their bodies. Sufi subjectivity is not just discursively or intellectually formed in these documents. It is performed and felt, and it seeks to construct their audience's subjectivity as much through the evocation of æffects as the conveyance of intellectual concepts or discursive formations.[100]

My reading of Sufi biography does not pretend to be positivistic. As noted, I often seek to reconstruct and elaborate scenes in a historically informed manner that goes beyond the "facts" as strictly presented in these texts. More positivistically inclined scholars may also object that even the details contained in these Sufi biographical accounts are often not historically accurate. I am *not* looking to these sources, however, to construct a factual history of particular medieval Sufi figures. I am interested in these biographical accounts as glimpses into how their authors understood the saintly lives they recorded, how they imagined them experiencing

98. I am partially inspired here by Cristina Maria Cervone's call to use poetry and its metaphors as an equally valid way of "thinking through" complex concepts, such as the incarnation (*Poetics of Incarnation*, 1).

99. As Bashir says in "Narrating Sight," "I believe that Sufi hagiography needs to be taken more seriously as a kind of foundational premodern Islamic literature because it constitutes our major access to social contexts for which, otherwise, we have little more than highly theoretical treatises" (233).

100. Julia Bray also cautions us not to reduce biographical anecdotes to just mines for cataloging the history of emotions in the Islamic world in a descriptive way. She argues that we should see these stories as encouraging their audiences to "problematize and probe emotions, and to make readers exercise their sympathies and ask where they might lead" ("Codes of Emotion," 196); "to shape their emotional imagination, if not their lived emotional practice" ("Yaʿqūb b. al-Rabīʿ Read by al-Mutanabbī and al-Mubarrad," 4); and to "create and circulate" "emotional values" (21). Similarly, Hoffman, looking at *Sindbād-nāmah*, writes that texts can "provide an emotional education by serving as a manual for the governance of the self" and points especially to the role that a certain emotional disposition plays in the construction of the text's ideal Islamicate masculinity ("Angry Men," 146). Yep argues for a similar approach as well ("Emotion and Islamic Hagiology").

Sufi rituals and the theoretical and poetic texts that structure and animate them, how they believed it felt to be a saint, and, thus too, how they sought to shape the felt life of the Sufi (affective) communities for which they were writing. We must always remember, as Zargar points out, "The plenitude of hagiographies within the Sufi tradition indicates that the remembered example of any saint was of no less significance than his written legacy," or, I would add, than his actual historical life.[101] I do not, in other words, treat Sufi biographies as historical documents of the saintly lives they portray, but rather as historical documents of the Sufi communities that produced them and the later generations of Sufi communities that read them and sought to emulate the behaviors of their saintly subjects.[102] In *Feeling Like Lovers*, I am interested in what they can tell us about the affective communities of medieval Sufism.[103] And these accounts are ideal documents for such an investigation because they are, as Bashir argues, "embed[ded] in epistemological paradigms particular to the historical setting in which they were produced."[104]

FLESHING OUT THE BODY OF THIS PROJECT: THE PATH FORWARD

The goal of *Feeling Like Lovers* is to surface and highlight the central role that feeling/æffect/emotion play in Sufi epistemology and subject formation. My focus on æffect in this study should *not* be read as asserting that the other modes of knowledge and meaning production—e.g., those traditionally associated with the "mind," intellect, or rationality—are not involved in Sufism. Rather, this monograph (primarily) centers æffect's role because it has not been properly foregrounded in our accounts of the diverse ways Sufis make meaning from the world (and its phenomena) and ritual practices. The goal of this work, in other words, could also be more conservatively understood as restoring æffect/feeling/emotion to the status of a partner with the other (purportedly) rationally mediated forms

101. Zargar, *Sufi Aesthetics*, 89–90. Much work has been done in recent decades on Sufi biographical works and the rich ways in which they can be read as discursively constructing Sufi identities, orthodoxy/praxis, gender, sexuality, etc. See, for example, Mojaddedi, *The Biographical Tradition in Sufism*; Hermansen, "Religious Literature"; Hermansen and Lawrence, "Indo-Persian Tazkiras"; Steinfels, "His Master's Voice"; Ohlander, "Between Historiography, Hagiography and Polemic"; Cornell, *Realm of the Saint*, 63–64; Stewart, "The Subject and the Ostensible Subject"; Miller, "Embodying the Beloved"; Pourjavady, "Stories of Ahmad Al-Ghazālī"; Kugle, "Sultan Mahmud's Makeover"; Kugle, *Sufis and Saints' Bodies*; Bashir, *Sufi Bodies*. My approach shares some overlap with these new approaches to Sufi biographical materials that read them as discursive constructs, but it privileges the nondiscursive aspects treated by the text.

102. It is worth noting, though, that many within the intended audiences of these works would likely have assumed these accounts to be historically accurate and would have read them as such.

103. For a similar reading of the idealized biographical materials contained in *Kitāb al-Aghānī* for what they can tell us about "emotional communities" and emotional reception history, see Moukheiber, "Gendering Emotions."

104. Bashir, *Sufi Bodies*, 4.

of knowledge in the co-construction of Sufi epistemology and subjectivity. Each chapter of *Feeling Like Lovers* contributes to this overarching intellectual project by opening a new window onto æffects' role in Sufism by working through different components of the "Ḥasan the Singer" anecdote discussed in brief here, progressing from the role of the physical body of earthly beloveds in exciting æffective meaning in poetic performance contexts and the Sufi amatory ritual of *shāhid-bāzī*, to the various ways in which somato-affective meaning/knowledge is produced through performance context, music, and language, especially poetry.

Chapter 1, "'Passionate Desire Conquered Him': The Felt Life of a Sufi Lover," functions as an introduction of sorts to the Sufi Path of Love and its use of physical bodies in ritual contexts to produce æffective meaning. It presents a case study of the spiritual initiation and formation of the Sufi lover *par excellence*, ʿIrāqī, through a close reading of his famous biographical account and its poetic and theoretical touchstones. Such accounts have often been dismissed in the past as inaccurate in a positivistic sense, filled as they often are with hagiographic and literary flourishes and ahistorical localizations of poems, as mentioned previously. In this chapter, I approach the account of ʿIrāqī's biography in a different way: not as a straightforward historical document, but rather as a textual embodied performance of the training of a Sufi lover's (æffective) habitus. Tracing the movements and machinations of love in ʿIrāqī's practices of embodied (*majāzī*) "love play" (*ʿishq-bāzī*), this chapter shows how Sufi lovers harness the erotogenic potential of poetry, human bodies—both others' and their own—and the epistemological potential of *feeling* to shape Sufi neophytes into genuine "lovers." The felt sense of these encounters and the æffective sequelae evoked in the lovers instruct their bodies in the necessary somato-affective dispositions for a Sufi subject and structure subsequent attempts to convey in language the nature of these experiences, as I will explore in chapters 4 and 5. This reading of ʿIrāqī's biography gives new meaning to the key Sufi ontological concept of *al-majāz qanṭarat al-ḥaqīqa*—the "metaphoric" or "figurative" world is the bridge to Reality/God—too. Often used as the theoretical explanation for why Path of Love Sufism sees nearly unparalleled pedagogical potential in physical human beauty (e.g., as mobilized in rituals such *shāhid-bāzī* or *samāʿ*, discussed in this chapter and chapters 2 and 3), this chapter closes by arguing that we need to expand the concept of the *majāz*—or, as I prefer, the "embodied" realm—as bridge to God to also include the somato-affective dimension of human experience. The diverse ways Sufis *feel* in the earthly world are foundational to the ability of the *majāz* to "bridge" Sufis to the divine.

Chapter 2, "'An Internal Turmoil Overtook the Shaykh': The Æffects of Music and Place in *Samāʿ*," and chapter 3, "Getting into the Habit(us) of Being a Lover: Æffective Hermeneutics and the Formation of Sufi Feeling Subjects in *Samāʿ*," return to the book's opening anecdote for a deep dive into how the musical-poetic ritual of *samāʿ* produces meaning for its participants. *Samāʿ* sessions, both in ʿIrāqī's biography and Sufi literature more broadly, are presented as scenes of peak spiritual advancement and knowledge acquisition about God. Past scholarship has had a pronounced tendency to attribute this spiritual efficacy primarily—if not exclusively—to the ability of the recited poetic text to prompt or facilitate the participants' realization of higher "spiritual meanings" (*maʿānī*). The ultimate meaning of *samāʿ*, in their view, is established when the listener identifies a correspondence between the imagery of the recited poem and Sufi metaphysical concepts or the *maʿānī* of the celestial realm. As I show in these chapters, however, this symbolist approach to understanding *samāʿ* elides its driving (nondiscursive) force: æffect. Putting Abū Ḥāmid al-Ghazālī's famous treatments of *samāʿ* in his *Iḥyāʾ ʿulūm al-dīn* and *Kīmiyā* in conversation with ʿIrāqī's biographical accounts of *samāʿ*, I argue across these two chapters that æffect is central to how *samāʿ*'s performance context, music, and poetry produce meaning for participants, even to the extent of structuring each participant's highly subjective process of textual interpretation itself. What we see most clearly in *samāʿ* is Sufism's æffective hermeneutics—an interpretative approach that rests on a much more deeply embodied and æffectively imbricated theory of meaning/knowledge production.

This approach to meaning is extended in a different, more textual, direction in chapter 4, "'Expressing Meanings (*Maʿānī*) in the Clothing of Forms': Sufism's Æffective Poetics," where I begin focusing on the central role æffect plays in Sufi theories of poetic imagery. Building on al-Ghazālī's theory of poetic imagery in chapter 3, I contest approaches that see Sufi meaning primarily in its "symbols" and their representation of philosophical ideas and the *maʿānī* of the supernal realm through a close reading of a key chapter of Jāmī's (d. 1492) commentary, entitled *Lavāmiʿ*, on ʿUmar ibn al-Fāriḍ's famous wine ode. Jāmī, in this otherwise highly symbolist commentary, advances another approach, which he describes as "expressing meanings in the clothing of forms." Analyzing the "complete similitude" of earthly wine and love, Jāmī presents a deeply embodied perspective on the poetic function of metaphoric imagery. Sufi poets, he argues, employ "words and phrases" drawn from what can be "sensed" (*maḥsūsāt*), such as "earthly (*ṣūrī*) wine," as metaphors for higher spiritual realities because they reproduce for the uninitiated reader somato-affective assemblages of feeling that mirror the ineffable experience of divine love and union. Jāmī's theory of metaphoric imagery sees linguistic meaning first and foremost as built upon the body's somato-affective repertoire of experience. Meaning, in this view, cannot be reduced only to the sum of the dictionary/lexicon equivalents of each word, phrase, or symbol or to their correspondences with Sufi metaphysics and the *maʿānī* of the celestial realm. Meaning *feels* like something too, and, arguably, even the supernal *maʿānī* must be *felt* to fully express what they mean, as well.

The final chapter, "'When the Wine of Love Started Taking Its Æffect': Self-Annihilation (*Fanāʾ*) and the Force Dynamics of Sufi Poetry," provides a case study of how we can apply Jāmī's embodied "æffective poetics" to how we read and analyze Sufi poetry. Focusing on a particular linguistic structure implicit in Jāmī's analysis, what modern cognitive linguists term "metaphoric force dynamics," this chapter analyzes the metaphoric structure of several portrayals of the ultimate goal of the Sufi Path of Love: *fanāʾ*, or self-annihilation in God, the Beloved. First developed by Leonard Talmy, force dynamics is an analytical framework for describing how linguistic "entities"—from concrete objects and persons to psychological and social "forces"—produce meaning through their interaction in language. Force dynamics creates meaning by enlisting our embodied sense of how objects interact within the real world and embed it within language. It thus also connects linguistic meaning to broader extratextual dimensions of individual lived experience and concept formation, productively blurring the lines between the domains of pre-textual embodied experience, imaginative formulation in texts, and readers'/audience members' textual interpretation. Using this framework, I show how the experience of *fanāʾ* flows into and structures Sufi metaphoric imagery and its most common topoi (e.g., wine, drunkenness, transgression, love sickness) in a "rogue lyric" (*qalandariyyāt*) of the great Sufi poet Farīd al-Dīn ʿAṭṭār (d. 1221). The "force" that pervades and structures the metaphoric imagery of his poem originates in God, but, I argue, is manifested linguistically—one might even say, poetically embodied—in order to model and inculcate the proper somato-affective lover habitus necessary for the radical self-less Sufi spiritual subjectivity of the "winehouse of love."

The Conclusion, "Restoring the Sufi Mind-Body," recaps some of the most important takeaways from *Feeling Like Lovers* and also returns to emphasize a point made in this Introduction and gestured at throughout the book: The traditional mind-body binary, and all its subsidary imagined binaries (e.g., sense/æffect/emotion and intellect/rational knowledge/language), are ultimately untenable. This is especially true in the Sufi context, where an emotional/æffective experience—love—is regularly elevated as the highest epistemological spiritual experience. Human knowledge exists in multiple modalities, from the somato-affective to the most rationally mediated, and there are different modes through which it is produced and circulated, but these modes/modalities of knowledge are ultimately intertwined, imbricated, and interpenetrating. Their borders are porous, and they work to co-construct our experience and understanding of everything, despite the claims of dogmatic partisans on either side of this old debate. *Feeling Like Lovers* aims to highlight the role of æffect/feeling/emotions in this process of co-constructing Sufi knowledge and feeling/thinking/knowing subjects and thereby help restore the Sufi mind-body.

1

"Passionate Desire Conquered Him"

The Felt Life of a Sufi Lover

The scene sketched in the Introduction portrays ʿIrāqī at the peak of his spiritual development. He has become a Sufi *pīr*, a spiritual master, with his own endowed Sufi lodge in Tūqāt where he would have overseen the spiritual formation of dozens of disciples.[1] In this role, he would have presided over spiritual rituals such as the *samāʿ* session depicted in that anecdote—a scene we will return to in detail in this and following chapters. But ʿIrāqī was not always the consummate Sufi lover of that opening scene. Sufi lovers are forged in the fires of love, not born.

Biographies of Sufi lovers do sometimes suggest that their saintly subjects had a certain inborn predilection to love and beauty from an early age.[2] This is the case, as we will see, with ʿIrāqī. But this inherent potential to become a Sufi lover still requires an earthly amorous initiation to be fully actualized and much practice to be refined and sustained, even surprisingly long after their purported union with the divine Beloved. The stories of these life-transforming moments, when a spark of love (*ʿishq*) cast from the beautiful face of an earthly beloved alights upon the ready kindling of a Sufi's heart, are some of the most memorable and highly cited in Sufi literature. Whole books, such as the (in)famous *Majālis al-ʿushshāq* (Assemblies of lovers), revolve around them, elaborately rereading the lives of the saints and prophets as fundamentally defined by specific amorous encounters—encounters that make them into the holy figures they are.[3] Some of these anecdotes

1. Little is known about the history of this lodge and ʿIrāqī's tenure there. For an overview of what is known, see Wolper, *Cities and Saints*, 6, 36–37.

2. Bashir, *Sufi Bodies*, 144.

3. Gāzargāhī, *Majālis al-ʿushshāq*. The historical validity of these stories is highly suspect in most cases, but, as Bashir says, *Majālis al-ʿushshāq*'s significance "lies not in being a source of information

even have long and contested afterlives into the modern period.[4] These stories have fascinated audiences throughout the centuries in large part due to the dramatic and often seemingly transgressive nature of the erotic encounters they relate. They are powerful stories. They are stories of the power of love—a power that remakes the self and spiritual practice of their Sufi subjects in ways that are often portrayed as leading them into contention with normative Islamic society even as it brings them closer to union with God.

ʿIrāqī is the subject of one of the most celebrated examples of this "lives of lovers" genre. His biography has all the hallmarks of the genre: prebirth prefiguration of his importance to the Islamic world; solid grounding in the traditional Islamic sciences as a young boy; early life as a paradigmatic practitioner of normative Islamic piety; sudden dramatic conversion to the Sufi Path of Love in a highly antinomian manner; and subsequent (controversial) practice of the amatory piety of the Sufi Path of Love. In recent years, stories of this genre have received renewed scholarly interest for their important role in discursively constructing Sufi forms of—often non-heteronormative—desire after several decades of a mixture of "denial, disavowal, and transcendentalization," as Najmabadi terms it in a different context.[5] But, as this chapter's rereading of the paradigmatic lover biography of ʿIrāqī shows, these accounts tell another story too. They narrate not just the lives of the lovers in a biographical sense or the machinations of the reigning discourses of their day. They also provide a glimpse into the affective lives of the lovers—or, at least, how the Sufi authors imagined them to have been lived *or* wanted their Sufi readers to imagine them to have been lived and thus to live their own affective lives.[6]

The bodily experience of love and its associated somato-affective entailments take center stage here. Love, in its æffective modality, is the principal pedagogical and epistemological agent in these lovers' spiritual formation and ritual practice. These accounts do, of course, attempt to discursively construct and script the emotional lives of Sufis, as historians of emotion would caution us. But they are also pulsating documents of the panoply of somato-affective experiences that exceed these categories: the rushes, the overwhelmings, the burnings, the drownings, the tears, the burstings, the subtle, what al-Ghazālī refers to as felt "impressions" and "strange wonders" that are not, he insists, the "well-known" emotions.[7] Here, it is

but in containing the most categorical presentation of a cultural topos prominent during the time it was composed" (*Sufi Bodies*, 131).

4. On the variety of ways Sufi love stories, especially homoerotic ones, have been recast, contested, and bowdlerized with the rise of heteronormative sexual mores in the modern period, see Najmabadi, "Re-Membering Amrads and Amradnumas"; Najmabadi, *Women with Mustaches and Men Without Beards*; Miller, "Embodying the Beloved"; Kugle, *Sufis and Saints' Bodies*, 181–220; Kugle, "Sultan Mahmud's Makeover."

5. Najmabadi, Women with Mustaches and Men Without Beards, 151.

6. On my approach to biographical literature, see the Introduction.

7. See the following chapter for al-Ghazālī's discussion on this point.

not primarily love's intellectual conceptualizations, philosophical systemizations, or discursive constructs that enable it to be the prime mediator of the divine-human relationship. Love *means* something to Sufis in biographical accounts like ʿIrāqī's because it *æffects* them in deeply felt ways: getting under their skin, leaving indelible somatic imprints, and unleashing seemingly uncontrollable æffective forces that purportedly made their bodies do things that contravened even the sternest commands of their rational minds and cherished modes of normative Islamic piety and law. These accounts show how love forms *feeling* Sufi subjects, entraining them in how to æffectively respond to God, instructing them in what being a lover of God means in a holistic and embodied way.

THE MAKING OF A SUFI LOVER: ÆFFECTIVE INITIATION AND SUBJUGATION ON THE SUFI PATH OF LOVE

ʿIrāqī's biography opens in a predictable manner for a legendary saint. One month prior to his birth, his father dreams that ʿAlī (the fourth caliph and the Prophet Muḥammad's son-in-law) gives him a child and says, "Take *our* ʿIrāqī and care for him well, for he will be a world conqueror" (emphasis added). The face of the child in the dream entrusted to him by ʿAlī, the father subsequently reports, exactly matches ʿIrāqī's face when he is born. ʿAlī's appearance here indicates something important. He is more than just an early caliph and member of the Prophet's family. He is particularly revered in Sufism, and Sufis believe the Prophet Muḥammad transmitted to him the deeper spiritual teachings of Islam that would become the core of Sufism's later mystical piety. In designating the baby as "*our* ʿIrāqī" and ceremonially giving him to the world as one of his own, ʿAlī marks him as a Sufi from the start.

Though destined for this fate, ʿIrāqī does not emerge from the womb as a fully formed Sufi saint on the Path of Love. He is born into an elite family of Islamic scholars in the important medieval Islamic city of Hamadān. He spends his youth learning what a son of such a prominent Islamic family would: the Qurʾān and the traditional Islamic sciences, both *manqūl* (knowledge that has been "transmitted" from Islamic authorities, e.g., reports of the Prophet, Qurʾānic commentary), and *maʿqūl* ("rational," e.g., theology, philosophy). His intellect is such that by seventeen he has emerged as a leading teacher in the Shahristān *madrasa* of Hamadān. Despite ʿIrāqī's prodigious intelligence, however, this young savant of the Islamic intellectual world is still a long way from becoming a Sufi lover, as the next event in his life brings into stark relief. He is still missing a crucial *body* of knowledge that could not be learned in a book or even transmitted directly from the head of a Sufi master to his own. It had to be felt to be learned.

One day, the anonymous author tells us, the young, intellectually proud ʿIrāqī is teaching his admiring pupils in the *madrasa* when:

> Suddenly a group of antinomian rogues (*qalandars*) arrived and entered the assembly with all their merry commotion. They started doing a poetic concert (*samāʿ*) and sang this *ghazal* with a sweet voice and perfect rhythm:
>
> We moved our belongings from the mosque to the dilapidated wine house (*kharābāt*),
> We crossed out the pages of asceticism (*zuhd*) and miracles.
> We sat in the ranks of lovers in the Magian [Zoroastrian] quarter,
> We took goblets from the hands of the dilapidated winehouse's libertines.
> It is fitting if the heart beats the drum of honor henceforth,
> For we raised the flag of fortune to the heavens.
> We have passed beyond all asceticism and spiritual stations (*maqāmāt*)—
> From asceticism and stations we only drew many goblets of toil and fatigue.
>
> When the *qalandars* had finished their melodious performance of this *ghazal*, an internal turmoil overtook the shaykh [ʿIrāqī]. Among the *qalandars* he saw a young man (*pisar*) who was without peer in beauty and was desirable to the hearts of lovers. A beauty such that if a Chinese painter saw his waving ringlets, he would have been bewildered. He saw that royal falcon again and the bird of his heart fell in the trap of love and the fire of loving desire burnt up the haystack (*khirman*) of his rationality. He took off his garments and turban, and gave them to the *qalandars*, and recited this ghazal:
>
> How wonderful it would be if you were my sweetheart!
> My intimate friend, companion, and beloved (*yār*)!
> The whole world could not contain me in this joyful state
> if for but one moment you would be my bosom buddy.
>
> After a time had passed, the *qalandars* left Hamadān and set out toward Iṣfahān. When they were gone, passionate desire (*shawq*) conquered ʿIrāqī, and his state of being (*ḥāl*) was transformed. He threw away his books. From Fakhr al-Dīn al-Rāzī's *The Great Commentary* (*al-Tafsīr al-Kabīr*) he obtained only profound forgetfulness. He obliterated grammar and announced Ibn Sīnā's book *Indications and Admonitions* (*al-Ishārāt wa-l-tanbīhāt*) was useless chatter (*fushārāt*). Abū Muḥammad al-Ḥusayn b. Masʿūd Muḥammad al-Farrāʾ al-Baghawī's *The Guideposts of Revelation* (*Maʿālim al-tanzīl*) became (*numūd*) *The Secrets of Esoteric Interpretation* (*Asrār al-taʾwīl*). He unbound (*hall sūkht*) Abū Bakr Muḥammad b. Zakariyyāʾ Rāzī's *Comprehensive Book on Medicine* (*al-Kitāb al-ḥāwī fī al-ṭibb*), and Najm al-Dīn ʿAlī b. ʿUmar al-Kātibī's "Collected Subtleties in the Uncovering of Realities" (*Jāmiʿ al-daqāʾiq fī kashf al-ḥaqāʾiq*) became "The Shining of Realities" (*Lāmiʿ al-ḥaqāʾiq*). Shahmardān b. Abū al-Khayr Rāzī's *The Garden of Astronomers* (*Rawḍat al-munajjimīn*) yielded (*bār dād*) only *The Delight of Lovers* (*Nuzhat al-ʿāshiqīn*). The language of speech was transformed into the "tongue of spiritual experience" (*zabān-i qāl bi-lisān-i ḥāl mubaddal gasht*), and the master of the sciences became a madman.[8] He then set out on the road toward his friends as a spiritually liberated man (*mujarradvār*).[9]

The anonymous author bookends this conversion narrative with references to ʿIrāqī's positionality in the premodern Islamic epistemological universe. The preconversion ʿIrāqī is a young Islamic intellectual phenom teaching the traditional

8. For a comprehensive study of *zabān-i ḥāl*, see Pourjavady, *Zabān-i ḥāl*, 148–359.
9. Anonymous, "Muqaddimah-yi dīvān," 49–50.

Islamic sciences. The anecdote begins with him in the very process of expounding this body of knowledge. But no sooner does ʿIrāqī come to function in this role of master of the traditional Islamic sciences than their mirage of true knowledge, their epistemological house of cards, comes crashing down in dramatic fashion as the *qalandar*s enter the scene. They are outsiders to the space of the *madrasa* and everything that it represents. They hail from the winehouse (*kharābāt*)—that heterotopic space where carnivalesque inversion of all mainstream Islamic values and norms is the order of the day.[10] They reject the traditional Islamic sciences, modes of asceticism (*zuhd*), and the mainstream Sufi obsessions with saintly miracles and spiritual advancement along prescribed stations. In their stead, they propose another set of spiritual practices: "wine"-fueled recitation of poetry, set to music, in the company of beautiful earthly beloveds, such as the *qalandar* youth with whom ʿIrāqī falls madly in love.[11]

The *qalandars*' argument is performative and embodied. They do not seek to engage ʿIrāqī or any of their audiences intellectually. Their pedagogy operates on a different wavelength: The rarefied knowledge of their spiritual sciences must be sensed in the physical beauty of their youths and the "perfect rhythm" of their tune. The only linguistic communication they attempt is through poetry, which, as we will see in the following chapters, seeks to convey æffective meaning as much as any form of intellectual knowledge. Not everyone in the audience would have necessarily been prepared to perceive the *qalandars*' earnest attempt to win over converts to their anacreontic mode of spirituality. But from an early age, ʿIrāqī exhibited signs of profound sensitivity to these nonintellectual forms of æffective meaning. The biography tells us that after memorizing the Qurʾān in just nine months, he would "recite the [day's portion of the Qurʾān] in a sad voice and cry" in such a moving manner that all became astonished with him (*ḥayrān-i ū*) and could hardly endure (*bī-ṭāqat shudī*) hearing the sweet melody of his voice. Such was the beauty of his sorrowful recitation that it even converted non-Muslims to Islam. He had also evinced a notable capacity for giving and receiving love since his youth. The biographer notes in passing that the companions of his youth were enamored (*shīftah*) with him, and he (*farīftah*) with them, to the point where they could not bear to be apart.

These details, which appear almost as biographical asides in his early life story, tell us something crucial about how the young ʿIrāqī perceived and acted in the world. ʿIrāqī possessed, seemingly from birth, an innate aptitude for æffective forms of knowledge. He knew how to perceive love and affect in the world, and he knew how to convey them through his voice and embodied action in the world. His acute sensitivity to the inner meaning of the Qurʾān comes out in his plaintive

10. On the wine house (*kharābāt*) as a heterotopic and carnivalesque space, see Miller, "The Qalandar King"; Miller, "The Poetics of the Sufi Carnival."

11. On the complex meaning of wine imagery in Sufism, see chapters 4 and 5.

recitations, bringing him to tears, attracting non-Muslims to Islam, and inducing astonishment and *bī-ṭāqat* in the audience.[12]

This latter experience of *bī-ṭāqat* highlights the power of this æffect on these individuals—not just in an abstract or intellectual sense, but as a felt experience and somato-affective form of meaning. Being *bī-ṭāqat*-ed implies a range of felt experiences rooted in the body's relation to the world. It can mean to lose one's strength and capacity to do something, to not be able to tolerate or bear something, to become restless from and even overpowered by something. In this particular context, what the anonymous biographer is trying to convey is that ʿIrāqī's recitation has caused that overwhelming and multifaceted feeling that engulfs you when you get lost in gripping music, a breathtaking vista, amorous union, or even a compelling story/movie and, if only for a moment, lose that sense of individual control as the æffective power of the event seems to literally penetrate your body and seize the reins of your "director self," modulating your emotional and even bodily responses. It is an experience so intense that it feels like too much to bear. This is how the Qurʾān, when properly recited, articulates itself somatically, making audience members feel by turns awestruck, remorseful, fearful, overwhelmed by the majesty of the divine word, etc. These are its effects. These are its affects. These evoked feelings, too, are what the Qurʾān means, and it takes a certain type of æffective intelligence to be able to produce these meanings in others through finely tuned modes of recitation.[13]

This brief anecdote from ʿIrāqī's youth foreshadows the importance of this form of felt meaning in his conversion to the Path of Love at the hands of the *qalandar*s. In this scene, ʿIrāqī no longer is the performer; he is the audience, he is the one *bī-ṭāqat*-ed. His aptitude in the æffective sciences enables him to perceive meaning in their performance that other audience members miss. After all, most of the audience does not go the way of ʿIrāqī and reject the normative Islamic world in the pursuit of love. But what exactly is it about the scene that so radically transforms ʿIrāqī—that is, radically *æffects* a new ʿIrāqī?

This question is complex because a lot is woven into the warp and weft of this anecdote. (It will take the rest of this chapter and the next three to fully unravel and examine all its components as we work through other examples in ʿIrāqī's biography.) The musical-poetic performance (*samāʿ*) of the *qalandar*s, with their

12. On the role and importance of affect in proper Qurʾānic recitation, and thus, conveyance of the full meaning of the Qurʾān, see Nelson, *The Art of Reciting the Qur'an*; Gade, *Perfection Makes Practice*; Gade, "Islam." On the centrality of *ḥuzn* in particular, translated adjectivally here as "plaintive," and the act of crying, see Nelson, *The Art of Reciting the Qur'an*, 89–100 and Gade, *Perfection Makes Practice*, 204–8.

13. For more on felt, non-discursive meaning and the Qurʾān, see Nelson, *The Art of Reciting the Qur'an*; Gade, *Perfection Makes Practice*; Osborne, "Aural Epistemology"; Osborne, "The Experience of the Recited Qurʾan"; Osborne, "Feeling the Words"; and al-Ghazālī's discussion of the æffects of Qurʾānic recitation in chapters 3 and 4, and the Conclusion.

"sweet voice[s] and perfect rhythm," undoubtedly has a strong impact on ʿIrāqī. Poetry and music are famous—or infamous, depending on whom you consult—in medieval Islam for their powerful æffective force on audience members. Sufis, in fact, regard poetry and music, when performed together in the ritual of *samāʿ* as a more powerful spiritual catalyst than even Qurʾānic recitation.[14] It is thus not surprising that as soon as the performance concluded, "an internal turmoil overtook the shaykh [ʿIrāqī]" (*iżṭirābī dar darūn-i shaykh mustawlī gasht*). The way the anonymous author sequences the story suggests that they see the poetry and music of *samāʿ* as playing a preparatory or activating role for ʿIrāqī's transformation—a topic I will examine in depth in the following chapters. They unsettle the previously firm foundations of ʿIrāqī the-traditional-Islamic-scholar, loosening the hold this way of life and knowledge had on him as the internal disturbance (*iżṭirābī*) they evoke overcomes him (*mustawlī gasht*). But ʿIrāqī's conversion does not happen by music and poetry alone. There is another force to be reckoned with.

In what feels like one of those obligatory scenes in every romantic story, as the music and poetry wind down, ʿIrāqī, bewildered and struck by an internal turmoil, looks into the *qalandar* troop and spies a strikingly handsome youth.[15] The anonymous biographer's praise is fulsome: He is "without peer in beauty," a "beauty such that if a Chinese painter saw his waving ringlets, he would have been bewildered." Most important of all is that he "was desirable to the hearts of lovers." He captures the heart of ʿIrāqī—a lover-to-be whose formation in the normative Islamic modes of piety and scholastic sciences just needed to be shaken up a bit for his heart to be susceptible to love's trap.

What transpires next can be thought of as a fiery baptismal initiation for the Path of Love. The "fires of loving desire" (*havā*) burn up ʿIrāqī's rationality, his *ʿaql*. This experience produces in him profound passionate desire (*shawq*) that "conquers[s] [him]," transforming "his state of being" (*ḥāl*), and leads him to engage in a series of antinomian actions. He gives his garments and turban—symbols of his high status—to the socially disreputable and disruptive *qalandar* band. He recites a love poem to the young *qalandar* who has stolen his heart. And he literally and symbolically discards texts that were the pillars of the traditional Islamic sciences—including Qurʾānic interpretation, philosophy,

14. On this point, see chapter 3, 4, and Conclusion.

15. This *qalandar* youth is described in Persian as a *pisar*, which literally means "boy." This term can be a bit misleading to translate as such in this context, however, because the figure of the beloved in medieval Persian poetry and Sufism is better understood as a "boy" in the sense of a young/adolescent man. The pinnacle of beauty in premodern Persian culture, as in the broader Late Antique world, including ancient Greece and Rome, was the teenage male who was neither a young child nor yet a full-fledged adult man. The lower and upper age limits of this status is ill-defined but could go into what might be thought of as early manhood too. On these points, see Najmabadi, *Women with Mustaches and Men Without Beards*, 15, 60; El-Rouayheb, *Before Homosexuality*, 30–32; Ingenito, *Beholding Beauty*, 199–200.

medicine, and astronomy—in a shocking display of his new appraisal of *ʿaql*'s epistemological insufficiency.

Such stories of radical spiritual transformations at the hands of love are common and celebrated in the Sufi biographical tradition.[16] The image used here of the fires of love burning up the lover's rationality is a stock motif in premodern Sufi writings. Discussion of these stories in the secondary scholarship is common enough too. But what I think has been missed in these discussions is an appreciation of the truly radical epistemological break that the *ʿaql-ʿishq* paradigm shift represents. It is not just a replacement of one intellectual approach or metaphysical system with another, which is often how Sufism's amorous spirituality is treated, explicitly or implicitly. Love is an epistemological agent that articulates itself—primarily, at least—through the body, its senses, and its æffective affordances, conveying divine knowledge through feeling rather than the ideational artifices of the intellect.

The Path of Love's somato-affective epistemology is well evidenced in this account of ʿIrāqī's youth and conversion. It is never stated directly as such, however. What language typically records of its pedagogical process is its æffects: the diverse ways it incites bodies to change after it has worked on their interior æffective levers.[17] We see glimpses of these transformations in the opening stories of ʿIrāqī's *bī-tāqat*-ing of the audiences gathered to hear him recite his daily Qurʾānic portion. The God-fearing Muslims of these accounts intellectually assent to the truth of the Qurʾānic message, no doubt. But what the Sufi biographer is most interested in relating is the æffects ʿIrāqī's recitation has on the audience: how it changes their constitution; the way it makes them feel about God and Islam; what actions it prompts them to engage in because of its alteration of their somato-affective bodies. This is a more expansive conception of meaning that presupposes intellectual comprehension but then goes beyond it or, rather, considers it as only one—and not necessarily the most important—vector of meaning and thereby, ultimately, mode of knowledge construction.

ʿIrāqī's conversion story draws out the superiority of this felt form of knowledge quite clearly. The anonymous author, as I have noted, builds the anecdote on the opposition of these two modes of epistemology by sandwiching the initiation story between incidents representing *ʿaql*-based knowledge—that is, ʿIrāqī first teaching the traditional Islamic sciences and later throwing out his library of its most important written representatives. Between these two, there is no rational argumentation that convinces ʿIrāqī to convert to the Sufi path of love. There is no debate or dispute between proponents of these camps that leads ʿIrāqī

16. See, for example, the Shaykh Ṣanʿān story in ʿAṭṭār's *Manṭiq al-ṭayr*, and, of course, as mentioned previously, Gāzargāhī's *Majālis al-ʿushshāq*, which contains elaborate stories of conversions to the Path of Love for most major Islamic figures going back to Prophet Muḥammad.

17. See Bashir's quote in the Introduction, similarly arguing that love is "known through its causes and effects."

to intellectually assent to one of their programs. There is just a performance—a poetic one, a musical one, a bodily one—and what ʿIrāqī *experiences* while viewing it that leads him to radically transform his life and spirituality.

Such æffect-based experiences will never be perfectly captured in language because they are not essentially linguistic (though language may co-construct the experience and shape its expression). To get at them we need to parse their descriptions, which are often highly metaphoric, with a view to the nature of the experience they are trying to convey in language. We need to be sensitive to how authors harness the evocative power of imagery to "generate a performance of feeling," as McNamer terms it.[18] This approach takes seriously the embodied nature of language and meaning creation, which both medieval Muslims and modern scholars have argued for in different ways, and resists the impulse to dismiss the value of such accounts as generic repetition of tired metaphoric motifs drawn from poetry that we can safely skip over in pursuit of the "actually important" historical and intellectual nuggets buried in premodern biographies. In chapters 4 and 5, I will illustrate how this æffective mode of analysis not only emerges out of medieval Islamic conceptions of poetics, but how we can also use it to great effect in our analysis of Sufi poetry to better understand how its metaphoric imagery conveys meaning in ways far more complex and embodied than the traditional Sufi symbolist approach of much modern scholarship. But first, I will apply this approach in this chapter to a prose account, with the goal of teasing out the complex constellation of felt experience the author presumes to have occurred to ʿIrāqī in this moment of conversion to the Path of Love.

The account of ʿIrāqī's experience opens with a statement that is as vague as it is revelatory: "An internal turmoil overtook the shaykh [ʿIrāqī]." This *iżṭirāb* disturbs his internal equilibrium. He no longer feels like things fit together properly. He is unsettled. His attempts to make sense of this situation with his scholastic worldview do not work. There is something else acting upon him that he cannot understand quite yet.[19] Then something clicks as he sees the beautiful *qalandar* youth. This a Janus-faced "click" that simultaneously marks an epistemological breakthrough and functions as a warning of the explosion to come, like the one you hear right before the bomb goes off in a movie or when the trap is sprung on a poor and unsuspecting animal.[20] Love invades, "trap[ping]" his heart and setting fire to his rational mind. He has lost control of the two most important organs of his body. Yet this experience is joyful: He tosses his robes and turban to

18. McNamer, "Literariness of Literature," 1436. See discussion and studies cited in the Introduction and chapters 4 and 5.

19. For a more detailed consideration of this initial phase of ʿIrāqī's conversion, see chapter 2.

20. I am gesturing here towards Schaefer's use of the idea of "click"/"clicking-into-place" (*Wild Experiments*) as that felt sense of when things suddenly come together in a highly meaningful way and "click." The "internal turmoil" (*iżṭirābī*) that ʿIrāqī experiences here could be read as the palpable, visceral feeling of frustration that is the necessary precursor to the experience of a "click."

the *qalandars* and exclaims, "The whole world could not contain me in this joyful state," if, to paraphrase, the beloved would return his love. He is a prisoner of love, but counterintuitively the surge of positive æffects from this imprisonment makes him feel more expansive than the universe. The account seems to suggest that after this intense experience in the *qalandars*' surprise *samāʿ* session, some time passes before they leave Hamadān. The anonymous author does not tell us precisely what happened during this period. But they say that once the *qalandar* band leaves, ʿIrāqī is overcome with a "passionate desire" (*shawq*). It "conquers[s] [him]," forever transforming "his state of being" (*ḥāl*). This tidal wave of intense affects/effects has effected a new him—it has, in short, æffected him.

This final image of "passionate desire" overwhelming ʿIrāqī exemplifies love's modus operandi in medieval Sufism. The word used in the original Persian is *ghālib*, which has a range of related meanings, depending on the verb with which it is paired, that revolve around literal and metaphoric notions of conquering, overpowering, or getting the upper hand over something or someone. Love ultimately approaches the Sufi body as a battleground. It sees the traditional pious habitus of the love-naive, *ʿaql*-controlled Muslim, such as the ʿIrāqī of the beginning of this account, as an opponent, an enemy who must be destabilized, conquered, and, ultimately, vanquished from the Sufi's body, if they are to become a lover.[21] Love is like the wild *qalandar* troop, portrayed as a radical external force that first disturbs and then destroys the existing habitus. Once dispatched, it sets to work training the young lover, "mounting" them and "breaking [them] in," as ʿAyn al-Qużāt Hamadānī frames it in his richly illustrative discussion of love's pedagogical method:

> Do you know why God placed all these veils on the path? He did so in order that the lover and his eye would become more "seasoned" until it can bear encountering God without a veil. Dear one, Laylā's beauty is bait placed in a trap. Do you know what the trap is? Since the eternal hunter wanted to make a riding horse (*markab*) out of Majnūn's being (*nihād*) and Majnūn was not yet ready to fall into the trap of eternal love's beauty (where you are destroyed), God ordered that love of Laylā make a riding horse of Majnūn's form for a while until he became "seasoned" enough through that love to bear the love of God. Dear one, see what the Qurʾān says about Moses: "And we brought him close" [19:52]. Have you not seen that when there is an excellent riding horse—worthy of none except the king—first a horse trainer mounts it and breaks it in, transforming its wildness and stubbornness into tameness and reserve?[22]

Love, with the help of an earthly beloved (Laylā, the *qalandar* youth, Ḥasan), disciplines the somato-affective body of the lover, as ʿAyn al-Qużāt so colorfully suggests, teaching it how to be a lover of God, how to "bear the love of God." This

21. Although "habitus" was a term in use in medieval Europe, the medieval conception of habitus differs in important ways from its more typical Bourdieuan deployments in modern affect theory and history of emotions (Crocker, "Medieval Affects Now," 93–94).

22. Hamadānī, "Tamhīdāt," 104–5 no. 148. An earlier version of my translation of this passage appears in Miller, "Embodying the Beloved," 5.

instruction is not aimed at teaching the lover intellectual knowledge or the fine points of Sufism's philosophy of love. It is a form of knowledge that is somatic and æffective in nature. It is about teaching the body of the "riding horse" how to respond differently to its rider and what it feels like to be ridden and under the control of another. It is a process of inculcating a new series of bodily dispositions. The trainer, as ʿAyn al-Qużāt says, must work out the "wildness and stubbornness" of the novice horse/lover. It must teach it what it means to be tamed and reserved for the master rider/God. This is the most fundamental felt experience that love must æffect in the Sufi lover-to-be: They must learn to lose themselves to the point where their body and its æffective system is like a tamed horse under the control of a master horseman, going wherever the rider leads it, including, as we have seen in this account, to do all sorts of previously unimaginable things, from tossing robes of honor to the *qalandar*s and abandoning family and promising careers to, quite literally, throwing the entirety of the traditional Islamic sciences to the wind.[23]

To bring these examples together, whether it is the sense of internal turmoil, the burning of the fires of love, the loss of one's (rational) self, or the utter helplessness (in this case, perhaps a merry one) as an external force seems to seize control of one's body, these are all complex bodily experiences that ʿIrāqī feels as a result of the *qalandar*s' performance and physical presence. They are felt forms of meaning that operate in those spaces prior to, between, and after language. The words in the *qalandar*s' poetry play a role in evoking these experiences, and these experiences may be imperfectly and partially described in the language of the anonymous author's account, but their meaning is conveyed through particular orchestrations of the body's languages of sense and æffect. These somato-affective productions of meaning do not rely on intellectual concepts or logic *to mean* for their audience. They æffect their audience, persuading and instructing them about the proper habitus for lovers of God through a somatic form of inscription. ʿIrāqī, in other words, is made a lover on the Path of Love because he is taught how it *feels* to be one. God/Love (with a capital "L"), through his earthly surrogate beloved, the *qalandar* youth, has, in short, begun to entrain ʿIrāqī's somato-affective system to respond as lovers should to their beloved.

PRACTICING "LOVE PLAY" (*ʿISHQ-BĀZĪ*), LEARNING ITS "CUSTOMS": AFFLICTIONS, MISFORTUNES, AND THE NEED FOR NEEDINESS

After this dramatic conversion to the Sufi path of love, ʿIrāqī leaves Hamadān to follow his beloved *qalandar* youth, abandoning his life, family, and career there, and catches up with the *qalandar* troop a few miles down the road to Iṣfahān. They

23. It is worth noting here, as Bashir has pointed out, that it is not only God's love that can control the Sufi lover's body; the love of a Sufi master can control the body of a Sufi disciple too (*Sufi Bodies*, 107–34; see especially a particularly "gripping" account on pages 122–24).

are delighted to see him and immediately welcome him into their antinomian band with their signature initiation, shaving their new novice's hair and eyebrows.[24] ʿIrāqī, now divested of both hair and the false epistemological certainty of the traditional Islamic sciences, then travels with them as a spiritually liberated man (*mujarradvār*) throughout the Persian lands of ʿIrāq before heading with them to India.

This period of ʿIrāqī's life is focused on the practice and refinement of his amorous arts. ʿIrāqī, the biography tells us, "spent his time loving that young man" (*bā ʿishq-i pisar bi-sar hamī burd*) throughout the time they traveled together. It may have been love at first sight when ʿIrāqī saw the youth in the *samāʿ* performance in Hamadān, but ʿIrāqī's love affair with him lasted a considerable period of time as they traveled together over an enormous stretch of land from Persian ʿIrāq (*ʿIrāq-i ʿajam*) to Delhi and several places in between. ʿIrāqī's conversion to the path of love at the hands of the *qalandar* youth is just the beginning of his earthly love story. He does not instantaneously jump from falling in love with this earthly beauty to the heights of Sufi love theory and ritual that we see him espousing and practicing in the later parts of the biography. To put this in the terms of the standard philosophical framing of Sufi love theory, ʿIrāqī did not just experience a flash of embodied earthly (*majāzī*) love and then rush across the "metaphoric" bridge it provides to engage exclusively in the arts of divine love.[25] Like Zulaykhā in Rūmī's poem quoted in the Introduction, ʿIrāqī practiced embodied love with this young *qalandar* for a substantial period of time, using him and the love he evoked in ʿIrāqī to learn how to love God.

True, all love ultimately has its origin and final destination in God, as ʿIrāqī himself states in his much-later-authored *Lamaʿāt*. "Whomever you love, to whatever you turn your face, it is [God]—although you may not know it. . . . Loving other than [God] is not improper but rather impossible. Because whatever we love, we love for either its beauty or its goodness, and both of these cannot be other than [God]."[26] But too often, the ultimately divine nature of love is used subtly (even if not consciously) as a pretext to hurry modern readers across the embodied (*majāzī*) amatory bridges to divine (*ḥaqīqī*) love. This divinizing approach to Sufi love is problematic, however, because it obscures the essential role that embodied experience on these earthly bridges played in Sufi amatory spirituality, especially in its earliest "training" stages. Scholars have not paid as much attention to this type of love training for more than one reason. Chief among them has been the historical reluctance of many scholars of Sufism to see the body as central to Sufi spirituality.[27] Relatedly, the modern

24. On the practice of shaving the hair of the head and face in Islamic antinomian groups, see Ridgeon, "Shaggy or Shaved?"; Karamustafa, *God's Unruly Friends*.

25. For more on the scholarly treatment of such Sufi love play and the translation issues associated with the complex term *majāzī*, see the following two sections.

26. ʿIrāqī, *Kulliyyāt-i ʿIrāqī (Muḥtasham)*, 474–475; ʿIraqi, *Divine Flashes*, 85.

27. On this point, also see the Introduction.

(heteronormative) discomfort with the predominantly homoerotic nature of Sufis' earthly love practices has made proper appreciation of its foundational role in the Sufi Path of Love piety difficult (though this has slowly begun to change in the last couple of decades).[28] But medieval Sufis of the Path of Love are unequivocal in the importance they ascribe to this æffective mode of pedagogy.

The late thirteenth/early fourteenth-century Sufi Muḥammad Zangī Bukhārī, in his treatise *Nuzhat al-ʿāshiqīn* (*The pleasure of lovers*), presents a modestly detailed picture of this pedagogical process and the role he saw it playing in the early period of Sufi spiritual training in which ʿIrāqī found himself while traveling with the *qalandars*. He advises other Sufi shaykhs that if they have a disciple who is not making spiritual progress through traditional isolated retreats (*chillah*), they should dispatch them to the local winehouse (*kharābāt*), where they will inevitably fall in love with one of its "beautiful youth[s]." Then, in words closely following ʿIrāqī's account above, the "fire of desire (*havā*) will completely burn up the haystack of their piety."[29] This *experience* of earthly love prior to formal Sufi training—or, at least, prior to æffective advancement on the spiritual path—is of such importance that he claims that the "shaykhs of the Sufi way and the Sufi masters of Truth do not even have confidence in a Sufi disciple who has not been captivated by earthly love and they do not search for [love's] human (*mardumī*) pain inside of them."[30] This advice may seem shocking or counterintuitive to some. Send a young Sufi to what most upright Muslims would have regarded as a cesspool of sin to fall in love? The risks for going astray from the spiritual path were significant. But Zangī argues that this practice is God's own mechanism for forming his ideal spiritual subjects: lovers.

> They say that when God—glory be to him and may he be exalted—wants to grant a disciple the honor of love and put the crown of divine love (*maḥabbat-i ḥaqīqī*) on them, he afflicts them with earthly love (*ʿishq-i majāzī*) so they learn the customs of love play (*rusūm-i ʿishq-bāzī*) and experience its tribulations and tricks (*makāʾid*), and drink earthly love's wine. They cannot endure the blows of misfortunes and afflictions from divine love, which requires the shower of arrows from love and grief. He, in his infinite wisdom, afflicts the disciples on the earthly path with the misfortunes of love of a human being so that they can reach the "seasonedness" of need from the "rawness" of coquetry.[31]

Sufi amorous training, love play (*ʿishq-bāzī*), as Zangī terms it here, is the means by which aspiring Sufis are "seasoned" and made ready for the "crown of divine

28. See Najmabadi, *Women with Mustaches and Men Without Beards*; Andrews and Kalpakli, *Age of Beloveds*; Kugle, "Sultan Mahmud's Makeover"; Miller, "Embodying the Beloved"; Kugle, *Sufis and Saints' Bodies*; Bashir, *Sufi Bodies*.

29. Zangī Bukhārī, "Nuzhat al-ʿāshiqīn," 140.

30. Zangī Bukhārī, "Nuzhat al-ʿāshiqīn," 139.

31. Zangī Bukhārī, "Nuzhat al-ʿāshiqīn," 139. Of note is that immediately following this quote, Zangī goes on to cite a poem that uses the toy-sword motif that Rūmī employs in the poem I discuss in the Introduction.

love." This is the same process of amorous training and subjugation to love I discuss in different terms above, but Zangī's treatment foregrounds a different face of this process. He portrays earthly love not as subjugating the budding lover but "afflict[ing]" them. God is ultimately driving this process, deftly deploying the tool of earthly love to visit all sorts of tribulations, misfortunes, and tricks on his targeted disciple. God does this for a reason. The God of the Sufi Path of Love is not a masochist or proponent of somato-affective mortification. He is God the Beloved, a Dionysian God of merriment and wine. He lovingly afflicts his chosen lovers with purpose, because wearing the "crown of divine love" is not easy. To be capable of bearing this blessed burden, God must first build up the capacity of the lover's somato-affective system so it can play in the big leagues, so to speak, of divine love. Moments of elation and union are certainly part of the experience of love, earthly or divine, as the many stories and poems celebrating love's merry drunkenness throughout this book amply demonstrate. But the real masters of the "customs of love play" are the ones who learn how to endure in the face of the many trials and tribulations on the path of divine love. The obstacles on this path are not boulders or external enemies that the lover can dodge or fight off as they traverse its circuitous path. They, as Zangī's language suggests, need to be understood as æffective in nature. They are what in contemporary colloquial parlance we might term "emotional burdens." The terms he uses to characterize the nature of these experiences—e.g., "blows" and "showers of arrows"—underline this point: These myriad "afflictions" are keenly felt in the body as, to put it frankly, intense external assaults on the lover's somato-affective sovereignty.

What the true lover needs is practice in responding properly, or, in another sense, practice in how *not* to respond. God's ultimate goal in this process is to teach the lover to *need* better, to need more. Immature lovers still do not understand that it is their residual sense of self that marks them as untrained, "raw" lovers unready for the "crown of divine love." Spiritual maturity is marked by the lover's realization that all they need is to deeply need God. They need to learn to yearn and long for God, to feel as if they are nothing without him, to feel that utter incompleteness that one can only know through the experience of love. This feeling of abject need is not unrelated to the experience of love's subjugation discussed above. It is, in fact, its prerequisite. To æffect the "seasonedness of need" is to be ready for love's conquest. It is the æffective posture required for the realization of Sufi lover subject formation.

Like Rūmī and Abū Ḥāmid al-Ghazālī, Zangī explicitly understands the lover's process of suffering "incalculable afflictions" on earthly love's path to "neediness" in epistemological terms. He remarks that the "raw" lover's sojourn into the winehouse of love will yield "many" new "unveilings" (*gushāyish*) for them when they again try to advance on the Sufi path, under the guidance of a Sufi master.[32] It is these æffective experiences, which God visits upon the lover through the

32. Zangī Bukhārī, "Nuzhat al-ʿāshiqīn," 140–41.

experience of love with an earthly beloved, that make the later spiritual unveilings possible. The spiritual breakthroughs ʿIrāqī achieves in the Sufi lodge he subsequently joins should be understood in this context. It is his "spend[ing] . . . time loving that young man," learning the "customs of love play," and ultimately, experiencing the great affliction of losing his first earthly beloved that prepare ʿIrāqī to be the master Sufi lover he becomes in the next part of our story. Those pangs of neediness that he first feels when his beloved *qalandar* youth leaves him in Hamadān would have reached a crescendo when he loses him for good, searing into him a palpable sense of his incompleteness and need for something more. This moment is thus clarifying too for the young, half-"seasoned" ʿIrāqī, because it reveals that this need and yearning he feels are deeper than any one earthly beloved can quench.

But I am getting ahead of the story.

IT'S COMPLICATED: LOVERS, SUFIS, AND THE POLITICS OF THE PRACTICE OF ÆFFECTIVE PIETY

Zangī presents his discussion of the importance of practicing love from the perspective of a Sufi master. He offers it as an answer to what was likely a common problem: What do you do if your disciple is not making spiritual progress? His answer evinces no conflict between the practices of "love play" and the discipline of Sufi institutional orders. He sees the experience of love outside the walls of the Sufi lodge as the most powerful scaffolding for a young Sufi aspirant. His discussion implicitly assumes that these young lovers' play with their wooden-sword beloveds ultimately needs the spiritual structure of a Sufi lodge and training under a Sufi master to be worthy of the big leagues. But it understands the relationship between the extra- and intra-Sufi lodge practice of amorous piety as symbiotic. It was not always this simple, however, for a young, raw lover to join an established Sufi order. Not all Sufi masters held Zangī's view that the Path of Love and its associated practices of love play (such as *samāʿ* or *shāhid-bāzī*, ritual gazing on beautiful individuals) were productive or even licit tools for Sufi formation. Some, as we will see, vigorously opposed them as antinomian innovations and sites for generating illicit desire. Other Sufi masters seemed to tacitly accept their spiritual validity but protested their open practice or dissemination because, to put it frankly, of the public-relations problems it created for Sufis. The politics of love in medieval Sufism could make becoming a Sufi disciple complicated for a young lover.

This tension is well illustrated in ʿIrāqī's biography. After his time practicing with his "wooden sword" during his sojourn with the *qalandar*s around the Middle East and South Asia, his first recorded stop in South Asia is the city of Multān (located in present-day Pakistan), where the famous Sufi master Shaykh Bahāʾ al-dīn Zakariyyāʾ (d. 1262) headed a powerful Suhrawardiyya lodge. He and his merry band of antinomian rogues were granted an audience with the saint, which is somewhat surprising given Bahā' al-Dīn's reported general antipathy toward *qalandar*s and other antinomian dervish types.[33] During this gathering, Bahā' al-Dīn sees 'Irāqī and immediately recognizes his spiritual potential. He turns to his leading disciple 'Imād al-Dīn and says, "This youth ['Irāqī] possesses perfect spiritual preparedness (*isti'dād-i tāmm*). He should remain here." 'Irāqī intuits Bahā' al-Dīn's interest in him and, not prepared yet to depart from his beloved *qalandar* youth and become a disciple in a Sufi order, he encourages his *qalandar* troop to leave quickly before the powerful saint detains him. On 'Irāqī's recommendation, the *qalandar* band leaves and heads to Delhi. He rejects institutional Sufi life and training in favor of continuing to "lov[e] that young man"—for a little while longer, at least. Bahā' al-Dīn might think 'Irāqī is fully prepared, but 'Irāqī apparently feels that he still required more "season[ing]" to be fully ready for institutional spiritual formation. Or perhaps he does not know yet the depths of the yearning he needs to *feel* to realize that his *qalandar* youth is not ultimately what he longs for.

Alas, as suggested above, 'Irāqī's first love was not fated to be his last. After some time in Delhi, the *qalandar*s depart for Somnath. En route, they encounter a large storm, and the members of the troop are scattered. 'Irāqī is separated from his beloved and almost his entire crew. After several days of searching unsuccessfully for his troop, 'Irāqī makes the decision to return to the Sufi lodge of Bahā' al-Dīn and become his disciple. This moment marks an important step in 'Irāqī's spiritual development. 'Irāqī's "perfect spiritual preparedness" will now be formed into a more mature spirituality under the direction of Bahā' al-Dīn. But 'Irāqī has reached this state only because of his practice of love with the *qalandar* youth. He is prepared for the higher amorous arts of the Sufi path of love because he has loved, and love is now the guiding force in his life—much to the chagrin, we will see, of many in Bahā' al-Dīn's lodge.

'Irāqī's time in Bahā' al-Dīn's lodge is marked by both incredible spiritual breakthroughs and controversy. And it begins almost immediately. 'Irāqī, like all novices, is ordered by Bahā' al-Dīn to sit for a secluded retreat, which typically would have lasted forty days. But he is in seclusion only ten days when he has a powerful spiritual experience (*vajdī*), begins crying, and breaks into a poem.[34] The language that the anonymous author uses to describe this moment is almost identical with that of 'Irāqī's initial experience of falling in love. The *vajd*, they tell us, "seized him" (*bar ū mustawlī shud*), and "crying overcame him" (*giryah bar vay ghālib gasht*), emphasizing again the way Sufi audiences understood these events as full-body æffective experiences. This behavior scandalizes the other disciples in the lodge, and they run immediately to Bahā' al-Dīn to report 'Irāqī's transgression

33. Nizami, "Bahā' al-Dīn Zakariyyā."

34. I discuss the experiences of *vajd* (Persian)/*wajd* (Arabic) in more detail, including the complexities of easily translating this word into English, in chapter 3.

against the strict Suhrawardiyya rule of only permitting Qur'ānic and *ḥadīth* recitation during such retreats. This perceived violation of the order's *adab* (rules of comportment) pales in comparison to ʿIrāqī's next transgression only days later: ʿImād al-Dīn—Bahā' al-Dīn's leading disciple—hears ʿIrāqī's poem being recited with musical accompaniment in the marketplace and, even worse, the winehouse (*kharābāt*). ʿImād al-Dīn is shocked and takes this news to Bahā' al-Dīn, with the implication that ʿIrāqī has not been keeping his secluded retreat and instead is out cavorting with the musicians, poets, drunks, and, of course, beautiful youths in these off-limits social spaces.

The primary issue that Bahā' al-Dīn's disciples—represented here by ʿImād al-Dīn—take with ʿIrāqī's spiritual practices is one that resurfaces repeatedly in his biography. The most succinct presentation of it is the charge they level against ʿIrāqī nearly twenty-five years later, after Bahā' al-Dīn has died and named ʿIrāqī his spiritual successor and leader of the powerful Multān Suhrawardiyya lodge. A group of Bahā' al-Dīn's disciples go to the local sulṭān to protest his selection of ʿIrāqī as the leader of the Sufi lodge with the charge that he "does not keep the traditions of [Bahā' al-Dīn]" and, by extension, the Suhrawardiyya order. Instead, "All his time is spent immersed in poetry and he retreats with [male] youths (*amradān*)." Their opposition to ʿIrāqī, at least as the anonymous biographer records it, is rooted in their disagreement with his mode of spiritual practice, centered on the musical-poetic performances of *samāʿ* and the ritual cultivation of love through gazing at beautiful youths (*shāhid-bāzī*). In the biography, these opponents of ʿIrāqī register and represent an important social reality that the author was likely intimately familiar with: The amatory piety that ʿIrāqī embraced and became a leading proponent of was socially and spiritually suspect for many in the premodern Islamic world. There are considerable controversies surrounding its belief in the unrivaled spiritual power of poetry, music, and, especially, the (beautiful) human body to act as epistemological bridges to the divine.[35] And its critics were not only Islamic legalists or intellectuals who believed in the superiority of the traditional Islamic sciences that ʿIrāqī so cavalierly discarded in his conversion to the Sufi Path of Love. There were many Sufi orders that evinced a similar discomfort, and some outright rejected these practices. Bahā' al-Dīn, and the Suhrawardiyya order in which he was a major figure, are historically known to be in this camp. Abū Ḥafṣ ʿUmar al-Suhrawardī (d. 1234), the second leader of the Suhrawardiyya and the major force in its expansion, opposed *shāhid-bāzī* and viewed *samāʿ* ambivalently, and Bahā' al-Dīn himself did not permit *samāʿ* in his lodge—in sharp contrast to the other major Sufi order in medieval South Asia, the Chishtīyya.[36]

35. On the controversy surrounding different forms of *ʿishq-bāzī*, see Ridgeon, "Controversy"; Pourjavady, "Stories of Ahmad Al-Ghazālī"; Miller, "Embodying the Beloved"; Zargar, *Sufi Aesthetics*, 115–19. See also chapter 2 and studies cited therein for treatments of the legal issues and controversies around *samāʿ*.

36. Ohlander, *Sufism in an Age of Transition*, 239–42; Sobieroj, "Suhrawardiyya"; Nizami, "Bahā' al-Dīn Zakariyyā"; Lawrence, "The Early Chishtī Approach to Samāʿ," 74, 80–81. For an overview of

The anonymous biographer's narratological decision to foreground these controversies in ʿIrāqī's early spiritual journey makes sense in this context. As the biography's readers would have known, the opening triumph of love over ʿIrāqī is not without social consequence and would immediately raise questions, such as "What *kind* of love is this?" and "Is this love spiritually pure or licentious?" The anonymous biographer sets to work immediately defending ʿIrāqī's amorous spirituality through the stories of his early spiritual formation in Bahāʾ al-Dīn's lodge, and he continues doing so, as we will see, throughout the rest of the biography.

The account of ʿIrāqī's interactions with Bahāʾ al-Dīn functions as the opening volley in this information war. Bahāʾ al-Dīn's responses to his disciples' reports that ʿIrāqī's spiritual practice seems inescapably linked to poetry, music, and the illicit site of the winehouse (where beautiful youths hang out) registers both the social stigma associated with these practices in spiritual contexts and the biographer's view of their incomparable spiritual purity and efficacy *in the right hands.* Faced with the first report above, Bahāʾ al-Dīn coolly responds to his leading disciple, "This [ecstasy-fueled poetry recitation] is not permitted for you, but it is for him [ʿIrāqī]." In the second instance, the fact that ʿIrāqī's ecstatic poetry has escaped the confines of the lodge and is being performed to music in the marketplace and winehouse—suggesting that ʿIrāqī himself has been frequenting these places, perhaps in search of beautiful young *shāhid*s—is initially quite disturbing to Bahāʾ al-Dīn. The biography tells us that upon hearing this news, he immediately moves to confront ʿIrāqī, saying, "Are you doing your prayers in the winehouse? Get out here!" ʿIrāqī does not apologize for his behavior, but he does submit to Bahāʾ al-Dīn's spiritual authority, placing his head at his feet and crying, and recites a new poem as his defense. The poem's content moves Bahāʾ al-Dīn deeply, and he realizes that ʿIrāqī has plumbed the depths of Sufism. Instead of responding with the anticipated castigation, he honors ʿIrāqī by placing his cloak on him and marrying him to his daughter.

Bahāʾ al-Dīn's exoneration of ʿIrāqī, and indeed his endorsement of his spiritual bona fides, means all the more because of Bahāʾ al-Dīn and his Suhrawardiyya order's reputation for being sober-minded Sufis who were lukewarm at best toward ʿIrāqī's amatory mode of piety.[37] According to the biographer, despite Bahāʾ al-Dīn's better judgment and desire to uphold the strict Suhrawardiyya position on these matters, his spiritual insight allows him to see past these accusations and understand these practices as part of an amorous mode of spirituality licit only for the elect Sufi lovers: "This is not permitted for you, but it is for him [ʿIrāqī]." Much is implied in this simple rebuke from a towering Sufi figure. There is a tacit admission that these practices are indeed spiritually potent. They should

---

Bahāʾ al-Dīn spirituality, see Huda, *Striving for Divine Union*, 137–72. On other Sufi opponents of *shāhid-bāzī*, see Kugle, *Sufis and Saints' Bodies*, 210.

37. On the "sober" school of Sufism, see chapter 3 and Mojaddedi, "Getting Drunk."

not be dismissed, as many medieval Sufi and non-Sufi writers did, as just spiritual patinas for the enjoyment of illicit sensual pleasures. But there is also a palpable fear that can be sensed in Bahā᾽ al-Dīn's denial of recourse to this amorous mode of piety for ʿImād al-Dīn, who, remember, is his leading disciple, not a spiritual dilettante from the streets. Bahā᾽ al-Dīn knows that its erotically charged rituals are powerful, and in the wrong hands they can destroy one's spiritual development just as easily as, for others, they can function as unparalleled bridges to God. But for ʿIrāqī, there is no other way to truly come to know God and his divine realities than to traverse these embodied bridges to the divine *and* experience their æffective instruction, as we will see.

"THE TRUTH IS IN THE BINDS OF *MAJĀZ*": THE POWER OF THE BODIES OF EARTHLY BELOVEDS

While Bahā᾽ al-Dīn was alive, his blessing was more than sufficient to keep ʿIrāqī's critics inside the lodge in check, but with him gone, ʿIrāqī's position in Multān becomes much more tenuous. As mentioned, his critics among Bahā᾽ al-Dīn's disciples determine that they have had enough of his poetry, music, and carousing with beautiful youths and take their case to the local sulṭān. Bahā᾽ al-Dīn's command that ʿIrāqī lead the order after his death does not matter to this ruler, who harbors a grudge against the order and happily sides with ʿIrāqī's accusers. ʿIrāqī reads the writing on the wall when the sulṭān summons him, so he flees Multān with a small group of devoted followers. The stakes of who got to lead a powerful Sufi lodge in the premodern Islamic world could be high, and ʿIrāqī likely feared for his life if he stayed.

ʿIrāqī's escape takes him first to Oman, then Damascus, and finally Anatolia. Throughout his travels, he is welcomed and honored wherever he goes. His first stop in Anatolia is Konya, where he spends time with Ṣadr al-Dīn al-Qūnawī (d. 1273–74), studying the works of the towering Sufi figure Muḥyī al-Dīn ibn al-ʿArabī (d. 1240)—an intellectual experience that plays an important role in his conceptualization of his spirituality in his treatise on love theory, the *Lamaʿāt*.[38] During his time there he also reportedly gains many followers and supporters, some with considerable political and financial resources. One of these was the local governor, Amīr Parvānah, who built ʿIrāqī a Sufi lodge in Tūqāt. It is here that the next major event in ʿIrāqī's spiritual biography takes place. This is the story of the special *samāʿ* session with the legendary musician-singer Ḥasan, which I sketched in the opening lines of the Introduction.

This anecdote presents to the reader a more spiritually developed performance of Sufi "love play" (*ʿishq-bāzī*) with an earthly beloved, which, as we will

38. On this work and ʿIrāqī's melding of Ibn al-ʿArabī's metaphysical Sufism with the Sufi Path of Love tradition in it, see Chittick and Wilson, "Introduction"; Miller, "Ocean of the Persians."

see, also functions as a performative riposte to ʿIrāqī's accusers—both those in Multān and those yet to come in his biography. The inset poetry presents a versified metaphysical defense of ʿIrāqī's æffective spirituality while ʿIrāqī and Ḥasan perform it. Although I will argue in chapters 3 and 4 that we need to move beyond readings of Sufi poetry as versifications of Sufi metaphysics, this is not the same thing as saying the metaphysical content of poetry is not important. What I am arguing implicitly in the way I read ʿIrāqī's poetry here in conversation with the bodies of its performative context is that its true significance can only be seen when poetry is reembodied—that is, when the symbols and conceptual content of poetry are no longer just referring to abstract symbolic or philosophical systems but are forced into Sufi life and fuse with real-life bodies in a ritual such as *samāʿ* as well. Studying Sufi texts and, by proxy, Sufi theory, in this way enables us to see that a large part of what texts, symbols, and concepts *meant* historically to Sufis was always bound up with the performative, æffective, and material dimensions of Sufi life that they participated in and referenced. Texts are not their own symbolic worlds. Intellectual ideas have embodied and, indeed, even felt dimensions too.

When I broke away from the analysis of that epic *samāʿ* session in the Introduction, I had reached the end of the first poem, where Ḥasan sings of lovers like ʿIrāqī "entangled in [God's] tresses," occupied now only with "lassos and traps." To recap, the image here may seem to be a somewhat unclear follow-up to the preceding "tresses" image. But it is these enigmatic "lassos and traps" that tie this poem to its performance context in a powerful way. Poetically, these "lassos and traps" are extensions of the "tresses" image of the first hemistich: In medieval Persian literature, the beloved's curls are also considered to operate as "traps" or "snares" for lovers. These traps are what ʿIrāqī will later term *majāzī*, but they are not purely symbolic or metaphorical, as this term is often translated into English. They are interpreted in the Sufi hermeneutic tradition as a symbol representing the phenomenal world.[39] They represent an element of God's limitless beauty, manifested in the world, with the express purpose of luring humans into falling in love—but not with God, at least not directly. Rather, God's "tresses," the "lassos and traps" that he lays out on Earth, are the beautiful bodies of people like the *qalandar* youth and Ḥasan. As we saw in ʿIrāqī's conversion story and the theoretical discussions of Sufi love play from ʿAyn al-Qużāt and Zangī, God uses these earthly beauties to ignite the fires of love in humans, to ensnare their hearts, to afflict them with an incurable love sickness, because in loving these earthly manifestations of God's beauty, they learn to love God.

39. For tresses as a symbol of the phenomena of the manifested world in the Sufi hermeneutical tradition, see Nurbakhsh, *Sufi Symbolism (I–XVI)*, 1:76–77. Given the context of this poetic citation in ʿIrāqī's biography, it is likely that the anonymous author had this interpretation in mind. Also see ʿAyn al-Qużāt's discussion of God's use of earthly beloveds as "traps" above.

With this richer meaning of the "tresses"/"lassos and traps" now in place, the interpretative possibilities for the poem's final line open up in interesting ways and connect with the scene of Ḥasan and ʿIrāqī in the latter's lodge in Tūqāt. ʿIrāqī's line 12 ("Since our hearts became entangled in your tresses / our work has been nothing but lassos and traps") comes to have a very tangible and immediate meaning that attaches to the body of this *samāʿ* session's "lasso and trap": Ḥasan. The poem's exhortation to God in the final line, "Begin a love affair with ʿIrāqī," becomes two-pronged or, rather, operates at two levels simultaneously, the ambiguity being productive. ʿIrāqī wants ultimately to be God's lover, "entangled" in his "tresses," but fortunately those "tresses" extend into the phenomenal world, embodied in the form of earthly beauties. One of them, Ḥasan, sits before him in this imagined performance context, reciting this poem—ʿIrāqī's own poem!—back to him, making it all the more powerful. It is almost as if the author of the biography wants us to believe that ʿIrāqī's opening poem here was an invocation to God to give an amorous boost to his budding "love affair" with this earthly idol, a tryst that in an ultimate sense is really a *ménage à trois.*

The second poem in the trio composed by ʿIrāqī and performed by Ḥasan picks up exactly where the first leaves off: with ʿIrāqī "entangled" in another one of the Beloved's earthly "tresses." This poem is one of ʿIrāqī's famous *tarjīʿ-band*s or strophic poems, and it elaborates in exquisite poetic detail for a full seven stanzas (fifty-six lines in total) the poet's pursuit of an elusive beloved in the poetic world of the winehouse.[40] It develops the story of the "love affair" that ʿIrāqī seeks in the second half of the first poem, but there are no abstract or philosophical discussions of love here, as in the first and third poems. The winehouse world of the second poem revolves around a more concrete, even if still somewhat distant, beloved: one who has seduced the poet-lover (5:2) and entrapped him (6:4; 7:4) through "amorous glances," "coquetry," "fair cheeks," luscious lips, and "beautiful images and idols."[41] The beloved is portrayed as a Ganymede figure, a "cupbearer" (*sāqī*) with a "downy cheek" (4:3) that contains the "the secret of the two worlds" and whose beauty puts even Khiżr and the waters of life to shame.[42]

40. The extraordinary length of this *tarjīʿ-band* prevents a full analysis of it here. The poem itself is a masterpiece and was apparently one of ʿIrāqī's most famous in the premodern period. In addition to appearing in the anonymous introduction, it also is cited in Kāshifī's poetic treatise and ʿAbd al-Nabī Qazvīnī's famous *Tazkirah-yi may-khānah.* There is a disagreement over the length of this *tarjīʿ-band.* Qazvīnī lists it as fourteen *bands* long, and Nafīsī puts it at fifteen, but in her critical edition Muḥtasham splits these longer versions into two separate shorter *tarjīʿ-bands.* As elsewhere, I have followed Muḥtasham's edition here. See ʿIrāqī, *Kulliyyāt-i ʿIrāqī (Nafīsī),* 133–40; Kāshifī Shīrāzī, *Badāʾiʿ al-afkār,* 74; ʿIrāqī, *Kulliyyāt-i ʿIrāqī (Muḥtasham),* 91–98, 264–268; Qazvīnī, *Tazkirah-yi may-khānah,* 50–56. For a more in-depth discussion of this poem, see Miller, "'In the Winehouse with Our Fellow Rascals.'"

41. Since stanzaic poems are typically cited by stanza and line, I have used the following in-text citation format when discussing this poem: stanza:line(s).

42. The figure of the cupbearer in Persian poetry, like many of its European counterparts, has a long tradition of being understood as a beautiful, youthful male. See Yarshater, "Theme of Wine-Drinking,"

The young man for whom ʿIrāqī is "pining" in this poem is ultimately a figuration of the divine Beloved. However, as ʿIrāqī quite explicitly asserts in a number of lines, he is still striving to reach the latter. Despite his best efforts, he has not reached him yet (1:3; 3:1,7; 5:6; 6:6); his work, as he says in the first poem, remains only with his "lassos and traps." ʿIrāqī begins the poem by stating this, informing the reader of his position on the earthly/divine love spectrum:

Sit, drink wine, and be merry
with the rogues in the winehouse!
Recite the secret of the two worlds from the pleasant down of the idol's cheek,
but don't reveal it!
I have been seduced by beautiful images and idols—
for this reason I am not arriving to the master artist.[43]

Far from incidental, it is ʿIrāqī's "not arriving to the master artist [the divine Beloved]" that is the driving force of the poem and, not incidentally, the *samāʿ* session in which it is being performed. The "master artist" has "seduced" him, and he has fallen in his earthly traps, but ultimately, "[the Beloved] has not yet become [his] intimate" (3:1; 6:4). ʿIrāqī hopes to "one day" reach the divine Beloved (6:6–7), but it is clear that in this poem he remains at some remove from this "seducer of the age" whom he seeks to "catch a whiff of" in the winehouse (3:1; 5:2; 6:4; 7:4), as he says repeatedly in the poetic refrain:

I am drinking a goblet in the winehouse
in hopes that I will catch a whiff of you.[44]

The poem as a whole is a sustained meditation on the Sufi lover's predicament: They have awoken to the reality that there is a divine Beloved above and beyond all these earthly beloveds, but they are drawn to the embodied forms of beauty—that is, the Beloved's "tresses," "idols," and "bait"—on Earth that reflect Him while they await reunion with the "master artist" (1:2–3; 6:4; 7:1, 4). While true Sufis will never be completely satisfied with these embodiments of The Real (they should always be searching, like ʿIrāqī in this poem), this does not mean that they will not avail themselves of divine assistance when the divine Beloved offers one of His beautiful, embodied tresses to help draw them closer to Him. As ʿIrāqī says in an illustrative image in the seventh stanza of this poem: "His curls grabbed my hand" (7:4). Even at the end, however, ʿIrāqī is still left searching for "whiffs" of the Beloved in the winehouse—an excellent metaphor for the Sufi lover's practice of

---

48–53. For this reason, this poem has often been identified as a *sāqī-nāmah* (cupbearer ode). On this thematic genre, see Maḥjūb, "Sāqī-nāmah—Mughannī-nāmah"; Golchin-Maʿānī, *Taẕkirah-yi paymānah*; Sharma, "Hāfiz's *Sāqīnāmah*"; Riżāʾī, *Sāqī-nāmah dar shiʿr-i Fārsī*; van Ruymbeke, "Iskandar's Bibulous Business"; Losensky, "Vintages of the Sāqī-nāma"; Losensky, "Saqi-Nameh."

43. ʿIrāqī, *Kulliyyāt-i ʿIrāqī (Muḥtasham)*, 264–68.

44. ʿIrāqī, *Kulliyyāt-i ʿIrāqī (Muḥtasham)*, 264–68.

contemplating the beauty of the Beloved with a capital "B" in the form of earthly beloveds. For like the bodily sensation of catching a wafting whiff, the various Sufi practices of "love play" (*ʿishq-bāzī*) simultaneously ground the lover in a present embodied reality while pointing them to something beyond it, or rather to something that is there, but is only perceptible in residual form. The prolific fifteenth-century poet and intellectual ʿAbd al-Raḥmān Jāmī (d. 1492) in his poetic commentary *Lavāmiʿ*, which I will analyze in more depth later, explicitly draws this connection between this poetic image of "catch[ing] a whiff" of the Beloved in the winehouse and the embodied Sufi practice of utilizing earthly (*majāzī*) lovers as bridges to God:

> Embodied love (*ʿishq-i majāzī*) is like a whiff of true love's (*ʿishq-i ḥaqīqī*) winehouse, and love (*maḥabbat*) of the traces (*āṣār*) is like a sunbeam of essential love's (*maḥabbat-i ẕātī*) sun. If one had not smelled that whiff, they would not have reached true love's winehouse. If this sunbeam had not appeared, they would not have gained a share of essential love's sun. *Rubāʿī*:
>
> > Happy is the one who catches a whiff of the winehouse;
> > they went after that fragrant bouquet and ended up at the winehouse.
> > A flash appeared from the winehouse's quarter,
> > and in its beam, he saw the sacred grounds of the winehouse.[45]

The "whiffs" of ʿIrāqī's poem, in other words, like the "tresses" and "lassos and traps" of the first poem, would have meant something very concrete and bodily to this scene's audience members. These conventional poetic images would not have been understood to be just poetic "signs" (*ishārāt*) or "symbols" (*rumūz*) pointing to heavenly realms of spiritual meanings (*maʿānī*) or metaphoric "reflections of God" (*tamaththul*) in form, as poetic beloveds and *shāhid*s are often abstractly described in the heavily philosophical language of Sufi symbolist hermeneutics and theoretical treatises (though, of course, they are these too).[46] This may be what they *are*, according to Sufi theory, but this is not all they *meant* to the audience members that night. And this is a key difference. Those listening to the performance of this poem in ʿIrāqī's Tūqāt lodge would have naturally seen them as quite obvious textual gestures toward this scene's "whiff" from "true love's winehouse," this scene's *majāzī*

45. Jāmī, "Lavāmiʿ (Afṣaḥ et al.)," 371.

46. On Sufi symbolist hermeneutics, see discussions in the Introduction and chapter 4. Theoretical discussions of *shāhid-bāzī* likewise generally discuss the figure of the *shāhid* as a reflection of God's beauty in form—the "*shahid* of meaning within the *shahid* of form," as Zargar terms it (*Sufi Aesthetics*, 102). These philosophical presentations of the theory of *shāhid-bāzī* are not incorrect. But their almost exclusive focus on using the term "form" instead of "body" does have the effect of presenting this deeply embodied ritual in a distinctly disembodied way. The best summary of theoretical underpinnings of *shāhid-bāzī* is given by Zargar, *Sufi Aesthetics*, 85–119. For a critique of this disembodying tendency in the discussion of *shāhid-bāzī*, see Miller, "Embodying the Beloved." For an approach to *shāhid-bāzī* that ably reembodies this practice while maintaining a high level of philosophical sophistication in its discussion of *shāhid-bāzī*, see Ingenito, *Beholding Beauty*.

beloved and *shāhid* extraordinaire, Ḥasan.[47] In such performance contexts, poetic imagery and symbols become bound up with real bodies, creating additional vectors of meaning as the line between poetic texts and performance context blurs.[48] What these lines of poetry mean here becomes inseparable from what the body of Ḥasan means to the audience members. And it means a lot.

In this account, Ḥasan is actually foregrounded more than the poems themselves. The majority of the anecdote's written real estate is devoted to elaborating his renowned beauty and the complex process by which he is brought—over the objections of his lovers—from his hometown to Tūqāt. (He meant a lot to them, too: He had quite the pull on them.) Ḥasan is portrayed as the inspiration and intended performer of the poems as well, since ʿIrāqī composes the poems after meeting him and specifically for him to perform. The poems flow out of the encounter with him and, as texts, they function in the biography to defend the amorous mode of piety of which he is the centerpiece. All eyes—of admirers and critics alike in the "historical" and readerly audiences—are squarely fixed on Ḥasan in this anecdote. Any serious discussion of what these poems mean in this imagined performance context must take the meaning of him and his body seriously.[49]

The Ḥasan of this account is not a static entity. He is not a mere passive "reflection" (*tamaththul*) of God's limitless beauty adorning this *samāʿ* session and whom Sufis gaze upon without æffect. Ḥasan is an active force. He shapes the audience members' experience of this *samāʿ* session because he is inseparable from the powerful æffective response of love that he evokes in all who gaze upon him—a perfectly natural response to human beauty, as we learn in the poems, that was

47. Although it is not made explicit in the narrative, it is likely that the reader would have interpreted Ḥasan's role in the *samāʿ* session as both a singer-musician and a *shāhid*. The writings of ʿAyn al-Qużāt Hamadānī, Ruzbihān Baqlī, and other prominent Sufi figures indicate that singers—the *qavvāls*—also functioned as *shāhids* in some cases, and given ʿIrāqī's strong association with *shāhid-bāzī* and Ḥasan's celebrated beauty, it is likely that premodern readers would have understood him as functioning in this dual role. See Hamadānī, "Tamhīdāt," 321 (this passage is translated and discussed in detail below); Ridgeon, "Controversy," 9; Ritter, *The Ocean of the Soul*, 513–14.

48. In their analyses of Persian poetic performance contexts, Lewis ("Reading, Writing and Recitation," 102–3) and Ingenito (*Beholding Beauty*, 166ff; "Tabrizis in Shiraz," 94–96) have gestured towards this point as well from different perspectives. Abu-Lughod, writing on the use of short Arabic poems in a modern Bedouin society, also emphasizes the centrality of performance context for interpreting poetry, especially its affective import (*Veiled Sentiments*, 175–78). Relatedly, Samer Ali has shown how poems' intended meanings/referents can be radically remade in new performance contexts (*Arabic Literary Salons in the Islamic Middle Ages*; see especially 75–116).

49. For a different reading of the importance of the body in *shāhid-bāzī*, see Ingenito, *Beholding Beauty*, especially 271, 321–23. He too sees bodies and the act of gazing at them in *shāhid-bāzī* as having "epistemic" value for Sufis, though the knowledge he proposes Sufis gain in their meditation on beautiful bodies is primarily rooted in the supernal realm, not the bodies of the Sufis themselves or the somato-affective experiences evoked in the process of gazing. Ingenito does comment once on the role that physical beauty plays in exciting emotion, saying that it can "lead to a deeper understanding of the invisible balances of the universe" (474), but this is not a point he develops.

written in humanity's genetic code (to hazard an anachronism) by Love itself.[50] His very presence adds an æffective vector to the embodied experience of the ritual, which communicates a type of meaning about God, his nature, and the relationship between humanity and God. This somatically mediated form of meaning is so important for the spiritual efficacy of the ritual that some Sufis even went so far as to say that the mystical heights and unveilings of spiritual realities (*maʿānī*) promised in *samāʿ* are only achievable when in the presence of a beautiful beloved like Ḥasan, as ʿAyn al-Qużāt Hamadānī asserts:[51]

> Know that a singer must be a beautiful *shāhid* [i.e., exemplar of divine beauty] in order that when they sing these lines of poetry one iota of their spiritual meanings (*maʿānī*) may be shown:
>
> That idol, that exemplar of divine beauty, who we love with all our soul,
> Separation from him is pain; union with him, our salve and cure.
> His face, our religion and direction of prayer; his tresses, our infidelity and polytheism.
> Without a doubt, he himself is both our infidelity and our faith.[52]

This is a profound hermeneutical/epistemological statement. It uncompromisingly links the acquisition of even "one iota" of the spiritual significance of these lines (and by extension poetry generally)—its *maʿānī*—to the co-presence of embodied beauty in the form of a *shāhid*.[53] What ʿAyn al-Qużāt impresses on his audience here is that

50. In addition to the stories related here, also see the stories covered in Bashir, *Sufi Bodies*, 139–43, dealing with the role gazing and the sense of sight play in evoking love in Sufism.

51. Sufis use the term *maʿānī* (which is the plural of *maʿnā* or *maʿnī*) to refer to higher spiritual (as opposed to literal linguistic or "external appearance") "meanings" of words or phenomena. For clarity and conceptual accessibility, here I prefer the translation of "spiritual meaning or reality." Other scholars of Sufism have translated this term in a variety of ways, such as "supernal meaning" or "ideal meaning," among others (for example, see Ingenito, *Beholding Beauty*; Zargar, *Sufi Aesthetics*). For the use of this term in Perso-Arabic linguistics, see Key, *Language*. See following chapters for a more embodied, æffective understanding of *maʿānī*.

52. Hamadānī, "Tamhīdāt," 321. Translated also in Ridgeon, "Controversy," 9.

53. This requirement is not unique to ʿAyn al-Qużāt. Ritter also points out that Jāmī asserts in his entry for Rūzbihān Baqlī in *Nafaḥāt al-uns* that Rūzbihān likewise maintained that "the singer (*qawwāl*) must be beautiful, for there are three things that are necessary for the fanning/refreshment of the hearts of mystics in the *samāʿ* assembly: pleasant perfumes, a beautiful face, and a melodious voice" (my translation) (Ritter, *The Ocean of the Soul*, 513; for original Persian, see Jāmī, *Nafaḥāt al-uns (Tawḥīdīpūr)*, 256). Jāmī prefaces this comment by saying that Rūzbihān asserts this in his book "*al-Anwār fī kashf al-asrār*," which presumably is what we know today simply as *Kashf al-asrār*, though I have been unable to locate the original passage Jāmī is referring to. Minimally, this passage in *Nafaḥat al-uns* indicates that the idea that the singer must be beautiful for *samāʿ* to achieve full æffect (i.e., communicate its full meaning) was circulating in Sufi circles and was attributed to Path of Love Sufis, such as Rūzbihān. This same phrase is attributed to Rūzbihān Baqlī in later South Asian works too, such as *Naghmat-i samāʿ*. See Ernst and Lawrence, *Sufi Martyrs of Love*, 45; Ernst, *Teachings of Sufism*, 114. For the broader Islamic perspective on the potential salutary impacts of scent on the human soul and affect (including the excitation of love), see King, "Medieval Islamicate Aromatherapy," 42–47. Relatedly, as Patel argues in his overview of al-Jaḥiẓ's discussion of "singing girls," experience is often multisensorial,

the presence of the beautiful body infuses the *samāʿ* experience with *something*, a *je ne sais quoi* that makes the poem's words *mean* in a different register or dimension.[54] They are no longer just conventional poetic symbols and motifs strung together, albeit artfully. In such a performance context, with such extraordinary beauty on display, the symbols "click" into place in a new way. Suddenly the power and force of the lines hit the audience members like a ton of bricks. Why? Because they "get," to invoke a close relative of the experience of "click," the poetry in a new way, which enables them too to attain to previously inaccessible *maʿānī*. They *feel* what these lines are talking about as the beauty of this *samāʿ*'s *shāhid* naturally induces the feeling of love (and its ancillary affects, such as the pain of separation, yearning, sense of being overwhelmed, etc.) in the audience members.[55] And it is this æffect that enables them to reach new spiritual levels of understanding.

Just as in the scene of ʿIrāqī's conversion, ʿAyn al-Qużāt is suggesting here that words alone, even versified, often are not themselves sufficient to convey knowledge about God and divine realities. Texts and their philosophical concepts and symbolic references alone cannot always get it done; they are not always *æffective* enough. But bodies—both of earthly beloveds like ʿAyn al-Qużāt's *shāhid*, the *qalandar* youth, Ḥasan, etc., and of the audience members—can help. They become coproducers of the poem's meaning in the performance context. They give life to the poem's symbols and ideas. They are powerful engines of nondiscursive meaning, as much for what is experienced in and inscribed upon them as for what they evoke in others' bodies. This is why Ḥasan must be foregrounded here. For ʿIrāqī's audience in his lodge that evening, it is his beautiful body that evokes the experience of love that ʿIrāqī's poems (and the Sufi metaphysical ideas they versify) textually reference. It is only through that embodied, experiential symphony of æffects called love that the audience(s) can hope to discover even "one iota of their [the poems'] spiritual meanings" (*maʿānī*), as ʿAyn al-Qużāt puts it. Without Ḥasan's body, the poems cannot *mean* the same thing. He must be there to light the

and the "potency" of the experience is heightened when multiple senses work in concert ("'Their Fires Shall Not Be Visible,'" 7–9).

54. Relatedly, see Elias's argument that beauty in Islamic "visual piety" exists not just for "purely aesthetic contemplation," but rather to "serve a pious didactic purpose." Islamic visual piety, he argues, has a "corpothetics" (borrowing a term from Christopher Pinney)—a "sensory, corporeal aesthetics" that includes the "somatic engagement of the viewer with the object of contemplation." See *Aisha's Cushion*, 173–74.

55. The extraordinary power of beautiful bodies to evoke desire—regardless of the gazer's strongest intentions otherwise—can also be seen in the concerns that many Sufi and non-Sufi figures expressed about their potential to lead Muslims astray through lust. For a discussion of Ibn al-Jawzī's views on the irresistible nature of the desire that is evoked when gazing at a beautiful body, see Miller, "Embodying the Beloved," 14–15. Abū Ḥāmid al-Ghazalī's treatments of *samāʿ* also discuss this negative æffective potential of bodies in the context of *samāʿ* in al-Ghazālī, *Iḥyāʾ*, 2:280, 2:285. Bashir also relates a telling response by Shaykh Ahrar (d. 1490) to the question of whether gazing without any form of illicit desire is permissible. He responded indignantly, "Even I cannot have a lust-free gaze; where have you come from that you can do it?" (*Sufi Bodies*, 149).

fires of love in their hearts, to teach their bodies how it *feels* to love so that audience members can hope to achieve the spiritual heights of *ma ʿānī*. The Sufi must feel to truly come to understand poetic texts and their *ma ʿānī*.

COMING TO EXPERIENTIALLY KNOW "THE SECRET": BODY AND ÆFFECT IN THE SUFI *MAJĀZĪUM*

All the threads from the first two poems come together sharply in the third and final one, which the anonymous author lists as being composed by ʿIrāqī in his encounter with Ḥasan. It is a long ghazal reminiscent of the more theoretical treatment of Sufi love theory seen in the first poem.[56] It begins with the cosmic, pre-eternal image of Love bringing "the nine spheres" into "motion, searching" (*tak ū tāz*).

1 Who knows which instrument is the instrument of Love's merriment
whose bow sets the nine spheres in motion, searching?
2 It brought the whole universe into a dance with one stroke of the bow;
the soul of the world is itself a melody of this musician (*pardah-navāz*).
3 The world is a veiled echo of this tune (*pardah*)—who knows
what this song (*pardah*) is and what secret is in this tune/veil (*pardah*)?[57]

Punning in these lines on the word *pardah* (which can be either "veil" or "tune, song, musical mode"), ʿIrāqī returns in this poem to explicate in rich poetic imagery the Sufi metaphysics of love. Love, absolute being, does not just create the world but brings "the whole universe into a dance with one stroke of the bow" (line 2). The created world may only be a "veiled echo" of Love's original tune (*pardah*), but within it there is hidden a secret that the cognoscenti can discover (lines 3–4).[58]

4 There is a secret in this song/veil (*pardah*)—when you come upon it
(lit. experientially know it/*bi-shināsī*),
you will understand (*dānī*) why The Real is in the binds of *majāz*.
5 You will understand why Maḥmūd's mind
is always distraught in the tresses of Ayāz,
6 (and) why the beauty of the fair ones' faces—who all are the essence of coquetry—
is in need of the need of the lovers' hearts.[59]

56. Also of note is the fact that it is the only one of the three that Jāmī reproduces in his account of ʿIrāqī's biography in *Nafaḥāt al-uns*, making it apparently, in Jāmī's view, capable of encapsulating the message of all three poems. See Jāmī, *Nafaḥāt al-uns (Tawḥīdīpūr)*, 603; Jāmī, *Nafaḥāt al-uns (ed. ʿĀbidī)*, 601.

57. ʿIrāqī, *Kulliyyāt-i ʿIrāqī (Muḥtasham)*, 322.

58. For what this poem suggests about the epistemological and ontological importance of music in Sufism, see chapter 2.

59. ʿIrāqī, *Kulliyyāt-i ʿIrāqī (Muḥtasham)*, 322.

ʿIrāqī does not divulge explicitly the secret that he alludes to in lines 3–4. But the context that follows indicates that what he is referring to here is the fact that Love underpins all existence.[60] It created the world, and the world moves only to its tune. Love is in everything—ergo, all the created world, humans especially, have a reflection of God within them. Nothing truly exists except Love/God. But this is a secret that you must uncover in your heart. You must learn it through *experience* in the world, the *pardah* (lines 3–4)—a pivotal point that he underlines by using the Persian verb *shinākhtan*. Persian has two verbs for "knowing": *shinākhtan* and *dānistan*. The former connotes a type of knowing that is perceptual, embodied even, in the sense that it is not a form of conceptual knowledge. It is something that you "know" as you know persons because you have physically met them or places because you have actually gone to and experienced them. *Dānistan*, on the contrary, refers primarily to a more intellectual or rational mode of understanding, to "know" an idea or concept. ʿIrāqī is cleverly playing with these different meanings of the verbs in line 4, with his assertion that only after you experientially know (*bi-shināsī*) the secret can you (intellectually) understand (*dānī*) why "The Real" or "The Truth" (*ḥaqīqat*) is "in the binds of *majāz*" (*dar band-i majāz ast*).

ʿIrāqī's privileging of this mode of knowledge gleaned through experience rather than intellection reflects the common Sufi distinction between and valorization of *maʿrifat* over *ʿilm*.[61] *Maʿrifat* (Persian) or *maʿrifa* (Arabic) is experiential knowledge of a special type—that is, insights obtained through spiritual states and "unveilings" (e.g., *ḥāl*, *vajd*, *mukāshafāt*) that accompany the process of drawing closer to God, concluding in the profound mystical experience of *fanāʾ*, the annihilation of the individual self and actualization of the highest ideal of God's *tawḥīd* in the person of the mystic.[62] As we will see in greater detail when I return to discuss spiritual states in chapter 3 and *fanāʾ* in chapters 4 and 5, one of their chief characteristics is the prominent role that *feeling* plays in them. Sufis certainly can derive notional knowledge from these experiences too, but a substantial part of the knowledge communicated during them is grounded in the somato-affective nature of the experience, a point that ʿIrāqī echoes later in this poem.

60. See quote from ʿIrāqī's *Lamaʿāt* on this point in the Introduction (*Kulliyyāt-i ʿIrāqī [Muḥtasham]*, 473).

61. Ingenito also comments on the parallels between Arabic *ʿ-r-f* words and Persian *shinākhtan* (*Beholding Beauty*, 277).

62. On the experiential basis for *maʿrifat* in Sufi spiritual states, see Shah-Kazemi, "The Notion and Significance of Maʿrifa in Sufism," 157, 159, 170–72, 174, 174n72, n74; Knysh, "Tasting, Drinking and Quenching Thirst"; Ingenito, *Beholding Beauty*, 271–351, 384. Ingenito even goes as far as to translate *ʿārif* (the active agent form of the same Arabic verbal root as *maʿrifat*) as "spiritual beholder" to emphasize the visual grounding of the form of knowledge termed *maʿrifat* in Saʿdī's lyrics (e.g., 280). He does, however, distinguish Saʿdī's notion of *maʿrifat* from that of his more "ecstatically" inclined contemporaries, Jalāl al-Dīn Rūmī and ʿIrāqī (309–12). Regardless of the finer distinctions in these figures' conceptions of *maʿrifat*, they all remain grounded in an experiential, as opposed to intellectual, form of knowledge acquisition.

Moving to the second hemistich of line 4, ʿIrāqī claims that "The Real," "The Truth"—that is, God or Love—is "in the binds of *majāz*." But what is *majāz* and why am I resisting translating it? Few terms have proven as problematic for routine translation. Its more common adjectival form, *majāzī*, is typically translated in the Sufi context as "figurative" or "metaphoric."[63] Scholars working in the Islamicate philosophical and theological traditions—on which Sufis heavily drew for their ontological reformulation of what Wolfhart Heinrichs and Emma Gannagé call the "*ḥaqīqa-majāz* dichotomy"—have adopted other translations, such as "derivative reality," "mundane, derived reality," "defective reality," or, simply, "the world," to try to better capture the important distinction that needs to be made between *majāz* as a rhetorical and ontological term.[64] All these translations of *majāz/majāzī* are defensible in a strictly literal and metaphysical sense. However, they are not optimal for the Sufi context, as I have argued elsewhere.[65] They obscure more than they reveal, at least analytically, because these terms inevitably carry with them a whole range of connotations that devalue, obscure, restrict, or deform the Sufi idea of *majāz* in different ways. They reduce it to something that is only unreal, defective, imaginal, or even just a decorative flourish. That is, they suggest something that is not grounded in reality, or is disembodied and ultimately not essential—certainly, in other words, not something central to Sufi epistemology.[66] *Majāz*, thus, becomes scholarly shorthand in much of Sufi studies for something that is not really worth analytical attention.

What makes this translational issue particularly complicated, though, is that Sufis *do* use *majāz/majāzī* to mobilize all these pejorative meanings as well. They

63. Shahab Ahmed pushes these traditional translations the furthest in a positive direction, translating them as "Seen World of Metaphor," and "earthly = metaphorical" (*What Is Islam?*, 394–96). But these translations still carry some of the same baggage as the others discussed below. Plus, they are terribly awkward to use. Lewisohn's recent suggestion goes in an even more theoretical and disembodying direction, translating *majāz* as "the fictional," "the unreal form," and "world of Appearance" ("Sufism's Religion of Love," 167, 177).

64. For a full intellectual history of the development of these concepts, see Heinrichs, "On the Figurative (*Majāz*)"; Heinrichs, "On the Genesis"; Heinrichs, "Contacts"; Gannagé, "Al-Kindī on the *Ḥaqīqa–Majāz* Dichotomy." Heinrich and Gannagé also discuss "figurative" and "metaphoric(al)" as potential translations for *majāzī* but decide to stick with the options enumerated above.

65. Miller, "Embodying the Beloved." For another recent assessment of the best way to translate *majāz*, see Ingenito, *Beholding Beauty*, 397–401. Although Ingenito's approach to the translation of *majāz* differs from mine, he also has pointed out the seemingly "paradox[ical]" positive and negative valuation of the *majāz* and the bodies that populate it (385–86).

66. On *majāz*'s meaning in the Perso-Arabic philosophical and theological traditions, see footnote 64 of this chapter. On its meaning in Persian and Arabic linguistics, see Key, *Language*, 87, 101–6; Heinrichs, *The Hand of the Northwind*, 31. Key pithily summarizes the linguistic understanding of *majāz* and its opposite *ḥaqīqa* as follows, with a helpful example: "If you call an actual donkey 'a donkey,' then you are using the vocal form 'donkey' with lexical accuracy, according to its precedent in the original lexicon. But if you call a stupid human being 'donkey' you are going beyond the lexicon and using the vocal form 'donkey' in a new way. This is how *ḥaqīqah* and *maǧāz* are used as categories for language" (104).

apply them to their ontological view of the world. Earthly life, the manifested world and all its phenomenal forms are *majāzī* in Sufi metaphysics. They are in a certain sense "figurative," "unreal," "derivative," "fictional," "defective," etc. vis-à-vis the only thing that actually exists in the universe: God and His attributes. They are, as ʿIrāqī says in the poem, "veil[s]" and "bind[s]" for "The Real" (lines 3–4).

But, and this is the crucial point to underline, the *majāzī* realm was not just negatively valenced for Sufis, as these terms might seem to suggest at first blush; it was equally an epistemologically rich domain too. ʿIrāqī is exceedingly clear on this point. He tells us in lines 5–6—which are meant to elaborate through example the theoretical point advanced in lines 3–4—that the *majāz* is as revelatory as it is confining and concealing. Indeed, for those who have (experientially) learned the "secret," the "Truth/Real" can be found within it in/through the bodies of all Earth's beautiful beloveds. ʿIrāqī points specifically to one of the most famous examples of earthly (homoerotic) love affairs in the Persian tradition, the slave and beloved of King Maḥmūd, Ayāz, in line 5, but God ultimately can make use of anyone in which one finds beauty and goodness to communicate with Sufi lovers.[67] It is the human form's capacity to embody the lovely qualities of God that makes it the privileged site of divine self-disclosure or self-manifestation in the phenomenal world, to use the standard philosophical framing of this process. This extraordinary power of the human body gives it a central role in the Path of Love Sufi spirituality, making it a "bridge to The Real" (*al-majāz qanṭarat al-ḥaqīqa*), as the famous saying goes.

My suggestion, then, for the *majāz*/*majāzī* translation conundrum is that we adopt a translation that conveys both these positive and negative connotations and privileges clarity and analytical utility over perceived philosophical exactness. Medieval Sufis were quite explicit on what *majāz* was to them: It was the embodied world of human experience in its full somato-affective, perceptual, and linguistic variety. While the technical terminology that the Sufi theoretical literature uses to discuss *majāz* may make this more difficult to see and appreciate, Sufi poetry and biography are exceedingly clear on this point. *Majāz* meant the "embodied world" to them, which would have already carried with it the negative connotations associated with translations such as "derivative" or "derived reality." We do not need complicated literary-philosophical translations such as "metaphoric"/"figurative" or "derivative reality" to do this work, I would argue. Such metaphysicalizing just takes modern readers further from what the *majāz* meant to medieval Sufis in an everyday experiential sense.

Here I especially want to emphasize this last point: the *majāz* is not just the phenomenological world outside the self with which we interact; it encompasses the full range of embodied lived experience, including its attendant somato-affective

67. On the figure of Ayāz as the beloved of King Maḥmūd, including how their relationship has been refigured and contested in the modern (heteronormative) period, see Kugle, "Sultan Mahmud's Makeover."

dimensions. The *majāz* does contain many beautiful *majāzī* bodies, such as those of Ḥasan, Ayāz, and Yūsuf. This is where most innovative scholarship to date has focused.[68] But the *majāz* is also more than just the physical bodies of these earthly beloveds and their potential to point observers to God and the supernal realm of spiritual realities (*ma ʿānī*). It is the arena of *human experience*—a *majāzī*um, to adapt the "sensorium" term from sensory history—whose reach plunges beneath the skin, into the body's somato-affective circuits.[69] The bodies of earthly beloveds are *majāzī* and operate as bridges to The Real/God, but so too are those æffective waves that they evoke in us, pulsating our bodies, creating our felt realities, and connecting us to each other. These æffects form bridges between bodies and ultimately between human bodies and God. They are equally important implements in the somatic epistemology that the Sufi concept of *majāz* embraces.

This point emerges clearly from the second half of the poem. ʿIrāqī's theoretical treatment of love as absolute being and the way it is reflected in the *majāzī*um only occupies the first five lines. Even by the second hemistich of line 5, ʿIrāqī begins to shift the focus of his poem to the æffects of the human encounter with Love/Beloved/a beloved (this trio, as we have seen, are inseparable to a certain degree). ʿIrāqī/Ḥasan continues:

7 Love appears each moment in a different color,
in one place coquetry, in another need.
8 When it appears in the form of the lover, all is painful pining;
when it appears in the garb of the beloved, all is merriment and music.
9 From that spark that Love struck from the fair faces of the beautiful idols,
the lovers' hearts are all on fire and melting and withering away.
10 The Path of Love is very close and merry;
any way other than this is long and far.
11 A drunk that is drunk on the Path of Love,
his merry drunken dreams are the very essence of prayer.
12 Last night when they did not permit us to enter the Sufi lodge,
I went to the door of the winehouse and saw it was shut too.
13 But then a song arose from within the winehouse:
"ʿIrāqī, lose yourself, for the door of the winehouse is open!"[70]

Love, when it strikes, leaves the lover "distraught in [their beloved's] tresses" (line 5), "painful[ly] pining" and "on fire and melting and withering away" for their

68. See Ingenito, *Beholding Beauty*; Zargar, *Sufi Aesthetics*, 85–119; Bashir, *Sufi Bodies*; Kugle, *Sufis and Saints' Bodies*; Takacs, "Transposing Metaphors and Poetics from Text to World."

69. Shahab Ahmed makes a related attempt to expand the traditional understanding of *majāz* when he argues that as a mode of meaning-making it needs to be understood not only in a discursive way but also "praxial[ly]," i.e., actions and human experiences can produce *majāzī* meanings too. See *What Is Islam?*, 393–96.

70. ʿIrāqī, *Kulliyyāt-i ʿIrāqī (Muḥtasham)*, 322.

beloveds, whom they experience as a genuine bodily "need" (lines 6–9) that cannot be quenched. Intermixed with this poignant sense of longing is "merriment"—an equally potent æffective sequel a of the arrival of love (lines 8, 10–11). Finally, the whole experience of love itself is here compared (directly and indirectly) to being "drunk" (lines 11–13), a reference to a complex and multifaceted embodied experience that intends to evoke, as we will see in chapter 4, a whole series of æffective and sensorial associations in the audience. The primary result of Love's "appear[ance]," according to ʿIrāqī in this poem, is the æffective transformation of the lover. This morphing series of æffective experiences is God's pedagogical aim. This is how he instructs his disciples, articulating the somato-affective dispositions necessary for a true lover's habitus, as we have seen in ʿAyn al-Qużāt and Zangī's discussions above.

One might object that these are just stock motifs of Sufi love poetry into which we should not read Sufi "experience," or that we should interpret them with the lexicons of the Sufi hermeneutic tradition to find the "real" spiritual meanings (*maʿānī*) of these poetic symbols.[71] But ʿIrāqī makes the same point in quite literal terms in his theoretical treatise on love, the *Lamaʿāt*, where he says: "While the beloved shows his beauty to the lover in the mirror of form, pleasure and pain take shape. Sorrow and happiness appear. Fear and hope come together. (Spiritual) contraction and expansion take hold (of them)."[72] The dyadic interaction between the Sufi lover and Beloved is inextricably bound up with these somato-affective experiences. They mediate the Sufi experience of God while they remain in the *majāzī*um, the world of forms. The *majāzī*um is never fully escapable during the lifetime of the Sufis, and the *majāzī*-focused spiritual practices of followers of the Path of Love reflect this unavoidable fact. Medieval Sufis, as we have seen here and will continue to see throughout this book, were not bashful about this, though you would not always know it by the strong tendency of modern scholarship to focus on the philosophically inclined hermeneutic and theoretical works treating the divine side of the *majāzī* bridge and its metaphysical realities. The Sufi spiritual path, however, was not so unidirectional: Most Sufis did not dive into the "ocean of unicity" or pass away in "self-annihilation" (*fanāʾ*), never again to return to the world of forms.[73] They went back and forth on the *majāzī* bridge—bridges,

71. Reading Sufi poetry as transparent accounts of Sufi spiritual experience (i.e., the idea that Sufi poetry can be read as a Romantic lyric expressing a poet's specific experience) is problematic in other ways, but so too is the desire to completely sever it from the experiential domain of lived Sufism. The relationship is a bit more complex, as I will argue throughout this book. On problems with reading Persian poetry as Romantic lyrics expressing personal experiences, see Meisami, *Structure and Meaning*, 2–4, 7–8. I will take up the relationship between Sufi somato-affective experience and poetry in greater depth in chapters 4 and 5.

72. ʿIrāqī, *Kulliyyāt-i ʿIrāqī (Muḥtasham)*, 483; alternative English translation available in ʿIraqi, *Divine Flashes*, 91.

73. Even when the Sufi crosses that bridge and drowns "in the ocean of unicity" (*muḥīṭ-i aḥadiyyat*), and these æffective experiences subside, as ʿIrāqī continues, this very lack of æffect is itself a felt sense.

after all, are (usually) bidirectional—and they continued to use embodied spiritual tools, such as the Sufi rituals of love, *shāhid-bāzī* and *samā*ʿ, to refine and deepen their relationship with God and learn more of his divine realities.[74] ʿIrāqī reportedly remained a frequent traveler on this somato-affective bridge until his final days. Even after reaching the spiritual heights that allowed him to write one of the most celebrated premodern treatises on Sufi love and command the respect of illustrious Sufis such as Bahāʾ al-Dīn and al-Qūnawī, his biography portrays him still making regular use of *shāhid-bāzī* and *samā*ʿ in his spiritual practice well into the period of his spiritual prime and even in his final days in Cairo and Damascus.[75] And he was not unique in this regard.[76]

One of these accounts from ʿIrāqī's biography, the story of his engagement with a beautiful young cobbler near the end of his life, is a fitting point to end on. The story takes place in Cairo, where ʿIrāqī has fled after falling on the wrong side of changing political regimes in Anatolia. He was entrusted by his former patron and now fallen political ruler in Anatolia, Amīr Parvānah, with bringing tribute to the Mamlūk sulṭān of Cairo in hopes that this would secure the release of his imprisoned son there. Struck by ʿIrāqī's integrity in delivering a fortune's worth of tribute and yet not apparently pilfering even a dirham, the sulṭān names him the chief shaykh of Cairo, gives him a daily allowance, and even parades him on his horse in robes of honor in front of all Cairo's elite. ʿIrāqī is not in Cairo long, however, before he falls in love (again).[77]

> One day ʿIrāqī was passing through the shoe market and his gaze fell upon a young man, and he became enamored with him. He went to him and said "hello" and asked

---

The intense affliction of these different æffects gives way to the stillness of no-feeling or feeling of the loss of feeling—itself an æffective marker of a different spiritual state. Moreover, as we will see in the discussions in chapters 4 and 5, many Sufis also describe *fanāʾ* as *feeling* in a multitude of ways.

74. Algar quotes Jāmī powerfully making this point too: "Those who have realized the perfection of inner meaning but can imbibe the wine of love only from the goblet of [beauteous] form; they are constantly pulled back and forth, for no sooner are they released from [infatuation with] one form than they fall prey to another" (*Haft Awrang I*. 269) (Algar, *Jami*, 74–75). On this point, also see Ingenito, *Beholding Beauty*, 389, and O'Malley, *The Poetics of Spiritual Instruction*, 244–47, who suggests that ʿAṭṭār's works demand a "continuous conversion" from their readers.

75. Copious biographical accounts of other prominent Sufi figures similarly indicate that these amorous rituals were considered lifelong spiritual catalysts, not only early-stage pedagogical devices. See Pourjavady, "Stories of Ahmad Al-Ghazālī"; Ridgeon, "Controversy"; Shamīsā, *Shāhid-bāzī dar adabiyyāt-i Fārsī*.

76. For a discussion of some of these other anecdotes of ʿIrāqī engaging in *shāhid-bāzī*, see Miller, "Embodying the Beloved."

77. I will just note in passing that the other half of this story is focused—like the earlier stories of controversy in Bahāʾ al-Dīn's lodge in Multān—on exculpating ʿIrāqī from his opponents' accusations that he is using the amorous rituals of the Sufi Path of Love to engage in proscribed sexual actions. They take their case to the sulṭān of Cairo, but he, who is the symbolic representative of God on Earth, has the perspicacity to ask the right questions and penetrate to the heart of the matter, clearing ʿIrāqī of wrongdoing.

> the cobbler: "Whose youth is this?" The cobbler said: "He is mine." The shaykh stretched out his hand and grabbed the lips of the youth and replied: "Is it not oppression that a mouth, lips, and teeth such as these are the companion of leather?" The cobbler replied: "We are poor people and our craft is this. If his teeth do not tear leather, then they won't eat bread." The shaykh asked him: "How much does this young man earn per day?" He replied: "Four dirhams per day." The shaykh ordered: "I will give him eight dirhams per day, and he must not do work like this anymore." Every day the shaykh would go with his friends and sit in the shop and gaze at the youth without a care in the world, recite poetry, and cry.[78]

The scene described here is one of *shāhid-bāzī*, potentially including sessions of *samā'*, though music is not explicitly mentioned. The sulṭān of Cairo has named him its chief shaykh. As the next page of his biography will reveal, he is actually very near to the end of his life. Nevertheless, that morning in the Cairo market he is still on the prowl for earthly beauty. He does not rush across the embodied *majāzī* bridge in that moment when he sees the cobbler youth, proclaiming that he has already passed beyond such frivolous formal earthly spiritual crutches, immersed as he certainly was—at times, at least—in the formless and affectless "ocean of unicity."

No, he stops at that cobbler's stall, and does not just admire the beautiful young man but even reaches out and "grab[s]" him by the lips.[79] This action is partly a dramatic gesture, perhaps a rhetorical flourish on the part of the biography's author, to emphasize the "oppression," as 'Irāqī says, of letting a beauty such as this cobbler youth fritter away his time making shoes, using his exquisite "mouth, lips, and teeth" to do the menial task of "tear[ing] leather." 'Irāqī may also be partially performing a cultural script, reflected in the conventional poetic imagery of this period, that identifies the "mouths, lips, and teeth" of the figure of the beloved as particularly evocative of desire.[80] But the physical nature of the encounter is too tangible to explain away. Interestingly, it is almost the inverse of the line from 'Irāqī's *tarjī'-band* discussed above, where he says that "his [God/Beloved's] curls grabbed my hand" (7:4). Here, 'Irāqī takes the initiative and grabs for one of God's earthly tresses: the beautiful lips of the cobbler youth. It is a symbolic action that nevertheless reinforces the continued importance of the body to 'Irāqī's spirituality. Not only is he not disengaged from these "formal" pursuits in his final days, he is still actively grabbing for them and going to extraordinary financial lengths to secure them for his spiritual practice.

78. Anonymous, "Muqaddimah-yi dīvān," 63.

79. Though not my focus here, it is also important to point out that the "grabbing" of another person certainly highlights the unequal power relation at work in *shāhid-bāzī* and indeed in most relationships in the premodern world. On age, class, and power differentials in premodern same-sex relationships, see Afary, *Sexual Politics*, 79–107.

80. On poems as cultural scripts, see Andrews and Kalpakli, *Age of Beloveds*, 37–38. For a poem of 'Irāqī using this exact image, see Miller, "Ocean of the Persians," 265–67.

Here is where our story of ʿIrāqī ends. The biographer tells us that after paying the father of the cobbler youth for the use of his beautiful son in this ritual, "Every day the shaykh would go with his friends and sit in the shop and gaze at the youth without a care in the world, recite poetry, *and cry*" (emphasis added). It is not just the gazing that is important here; the crying is arguably more so, because these rituals of the Sufi Path of Love aim above all to evoke *æffects* in their Sufi participants. Æffect, if we believe the Sufis of the Path of Love, is the highest language of God, who is, after all, Love. It is æffect that gets inside the lovers and forms them as loving subjects. It is through the symphony of somato-affective experiences produced by love that spiritual seekers can "come upon" (i.e., experientially come to know, *bi-shināsī*) new spiritual knowledge, new divine "secret[s]," in the *majāzī*um, as ʿIrāqī suggests in his last poem. It is the convulsions of tears (or conquering fires of love, pangs of longing, etc.) that form the Sufi lover, teaching them what it feels like to be a lover.

CODA: FEELING MEANING

Meaning in the Sufi Path of Love must be *felt* to be fully understood. The privileging of this æffectively mediated experiential mode of spiritual formation does not mean that words are not important in medieval Sufism. Quite the contrary. But what words mean to audiences cannot be reduced to their intellectual content or a symbolist-inspired hermeneutic reading of their symbols alone. As ʿAyn al-Qużāt says, we cannot hope to understand even "one iota" of the spiritual meaning of poetry in the absence of the beautiful bodies and the æffects they induce in the audience. This means words *also* mean by engaging with bodies and marshaling their æffective forces to convey a form of knowledge rooted in the felt sense of the body—a type of power/feeling-knowledge akin to Foucault's famous power/knowledge.

This more deeply embodied understanding of meaning means purely logo- or ratiocentric approaches to Sufi epistemology are not sufficient. This, of course, is not to say that they have no role. It is just that such disembodied approaches cannot fully appreciate ʿIrāqī's continual assertion throughout all three of the poems examined here that one can only come to know God's "secret[s]" by falling in love, or Rūmī's claim that one can only learn to wield a real sword in war by "playing" with it, potentially for years, until the body at a visceral level—below the level of normal ratiocentric consciousness—learns its secrets and no longer needs to *think*, much less read, about it. (As anyone who has become an expert in a physical activity that relies on muscle memory knows, "thinking" about your next move is a surefire way to mess up.) The central assertion of this chapter is that Sufism's amorous mode of piety is built to a large degree on an analogous somato-affective form of play-based epistemology. Stated differently, to become a true Sufi lover in the *majāzī*um, God/Love must entrain your somato-affective body to the rhythms of love as much, or more, than convey any intellectual knowledge to your mind.

2

"An Internal Turmoil Overtook the Shaykh"

The Æffects of Music and Place in Samāʿ

ʿIrāqī's dramatic conversion to the Sufi Path of Love in the last chapter began when "an internal turmoil overtook the shaykh" (*iżṭirābī dar darūn-i shaykh mustawlī gasht*). This passing moment of uncertainty and internal upheaval is, as noted there, a common first felt experience on the Sufi Path of Love. It prepares him for the "click" moment when he spots the beautiful *qalandar* youth in the troop and the forces of love take over his body, somato-affectively inducting him as a novice Sufi lover in the amatory order.[1] The way the anecdote's narrative is structured does not allow us to assign responsibility for ʿIrāqī's palpable disquietude in this transitional moment to the love the beautiful youth unleashed.[2] It is, rather, something in the *qalandars*' *samāʿ* performance in the seconds prior that irrevocably destroys the psycho-intellectual foundations of the self-assured scholastic ʿIrāqī of the mosque, leaving in its wake a "ruined" ʿIrāqī, ripe for plundering by love, ready to head to love's Mecca, the "dilapidated wine house" or "*kharābāt*" (a word literally meaning "ruins"). The scene again:

> Suddenly a group of antinomian rogues (*qalandar*) arrived and entered the assembly with all their merry commotion. They started doing a poetic concert (*samāʿ*) and sang this *ghazal* with a sweet song and perfect rhythm:
>
> We moved our belongings from the mosque to the dilapidated wine house (*kharābāt*),
> We crossed out the pages of asceticism (*zuhd*) and miracles.
> We sat in the ranks of lovers in the Magian (Zoroastrian) quarter,

1. On the felt experience of "click," see discussion and citations of Schaefer in chapter 1.

2. My reading here differs slightly from my interpretation of this account in Miller, "Embodying the Beloved," where I lump the feeling of "internal turmoil" and ʿIrāqī's subsequent experience of love together.

> We took goblets from the hands of the dilapidated winehouse's libertines.
> It is fitting if the heart beats the drum of honor henceforth
> For we raised the flag of fortune to the heavens.
> We have passed beyond all asceticism and spiritual stations (*maqāmāt*)—
> From asceticism and stations we only drew many goblets of toil and fatigue.

> When the *qalandars* had finished their melodious performance of this *ghazal*, an internal turmoil overtook the shaykh.

Most of the real estate in this *samāʿ* anecdote is dedicated to the poem that the *qalandar* troop performs, visually anointing it as the central player in ʿIrāqī's destabilization. The poem's sizable, four-line text block performs the dual labor of creating a stylistic break in the prose narrative and a break in the life trajectory and internal sense of self for young ʿIrāqī. The catalyst that ignited his "internal turmoil" must lie in the meaning of the words of this poem, right? Yes . . . and *no*, this chapter will argue.

Sufis and modern scholars alike have long regarded *samāʿ* as an unparalleled—though not uncontroversial—catalyst for spiritual transformation (rivaled only, according to some, by the related spiritual ritual of *shāhid-bāzī*, discussed in the previous chapter).[3] Abū Ḥāmid al-Ghazālī famously argues that *samāʿ* is spiritually even more powerful than Qurʾānic recitation.[4] The flip side of this potent spiritual power is its equally unparalleled potential for spiritual peril. *Samāʿ* brings together poetry, music, and, often, beautiful beloveds in the form of the sessions' musicians or *shāhids*—all individually viewed as worldly enticements that could lead unprepared Sufi novices to spiritual ruin, and how much more when combined in one context! This Janus-faced nature of *samāʿ* led many of its medieval Sufi proponents to take great pains to defend this ritual from its critics and elaborate its correct practice in substantial detail. The resulting proliferation of discourse around *samāʿ* makes it one of the most well-documented windows into how medieval Sufis understood the process of meaning creation in performance contexts.

Building on the previous chapter's discussion of the æffective meaning of bodies in the *majāzī*um, this chapter and the following will disaggregate and flesh out *samāʿ*'s multiple vectors of meaning by reading the accounts of *samāʿ* in ʿIrāqī's biography alongside the writings of one of this ritual's leading theorists, Abū

3. For the legal and social controversies surrounding *samāʿ*, see Robson, "Introduction"; Lawrence, "The Early Chishtī Approach to Samāʿ"; Nelson, *The Art of Reciting the Qur'an*, 32–51; Gribetz, "The Samā' Controversy"; Lewisohn, "The Sacred Music of Islam," 1–4, 25–26; Ernst and Lawrence, *Sufi Martyrs of Love*, 34–45; Michon, "Sacred Music and Dance in Islam," 469–72; Klein, "Music, Rapture and Pragmatics"; Klein, "Musical Instruments in Samāʿ Literature." M. S. Rizvi looks at the legal debates surrounding *samāʿ* and argues that divergent understandings of the emotions engendered by *samāʿ* play a key role in the different approaches to its legality ("Music, Emotions and Reform in South Asian Islam"). For an in-depth study of some of the earliest Sufi sources discussing *samāʿ*, see Pourjavady, "Dow asar-i kuhan dar samāʿ."

4. al-Ghazālī, *Iḥyāʾ*, 2:295–98; al-Ghazālī, *Kīmiyā*, 370–72. See discussion also in chapters 3 and 4 and the Conclusion.

Ḥāmid al-Ghazālī.[5] As we will see, these medieval sources understand meaning in *samāʿ* to be much more than the sum of the intellectual content and abstract spiritual realities (*maʿānī*) alluded to by the symbols in its poetic text. The ritual's music and performance context play independent roles in fashioning the nondiscursive elements of æffective meaning in these scenes. And even the full import of the poem's words, spiritual *maʿānī*, and the resulting "states" (s. *ḥāl*, pl. *aḥwāl*)) and "ecstasy" (*wajd*) are only realized when we analyze how they are imbricated with æffect and the somato-affective bodies of the participants (chapter 3).[6]

WHAT DOES *SAMĀʿ* MEAN? TWO EPISTEMOLOGICAL ROUTES, AND THE (ÆFFECTIVE) ONE NOT TAKEN

Most existing scholarship on *samāʿ* would read this opening scene of the *qalandars* performing *samāʿ* differently—not incorrectly, but partially, as I will argue across this and the following chapter.[7] It would suggest to us that we first direct our attention to the text of the recited poem as the primary site of meaning creation. The nonverbal components of a *samāʿ* performance, when they are mentioned at all, are portrayed as supporting actors for the main event where the *real* meaning is created: the recitation of the poem. Discussions of the performance context are largely reduced to the permissible locations to hold *samāʿ* performances. Treatments of dance or other bodily posturing done in *samāʿ*—when discussed at all—typically revolve around the diversity of Sufi views on whether and when such actions are appropriate or regard them simply as products of spiritual states (*aḥwāl*) or "ecstasy" (*wajd*) achieved as the result of a spiritual insight inspired by the poem. Music, similarly, only helps "sharpen . . . [the participant's] attention" or "arouses," "stimulates," "incites," "evokes," or "intensifies" the emotional atmosphere of the *samāʿ* performance or what is already in the heart of the listener.[8]

5. al-Ghazālī's influence in the Islamicate world is, as Elias has remarked, "truly pervasive" and extends well beyond elite intellectual registers: "For several centuries, he has been one of the most popular religious thinkers across the entire Muslim world, with the majority of his works widely translated and extensively read by a broad cross section of Muslims" (*Aisha's Cushion*, 162). And his importance is not limited to the premodern period. As Weinrich has observed in her research in contemporary Syria and Lebanon, his treatise on *samāʿ* is still frequently cited in modern Islamic communities ("Sensing Sound," 1).

6. Although I disaggregate these different meaning vectors of *samāʿ* in my treatment in this and following chapter for illustrative purposes, they obviously all work together to produce the rich experience of *samāʿ*. Human experience, as Lange shows in his study of al-Jāḥiẓ's sensory theory, is always an "integrated" product of multiple sense perceptions working in "collaboration" ("Al-Jāḥiẓ on the Senses," 28). Also, see my discussion of *wajd* in chapter 3 for why I think its common English translation as "ecstasy" is problematic.

7. Though I will discuss *samāʿ* as one tradition in order to drill down on the question of the ways in which it produces meaning for the audience, Jean During rightly points out its diversity too ("What Is Sufi Music?," 278–81).

8. For examples of these perspectives, see Meier, "Dervish Dance"; Qureshi, "Listening to Words Through Music"; Michon , "Sacred Music and Dance in Islam"; Lewisohn, "The Sacred Music of Islam";

But, as Qureshi says, articulating frankly what is implicit in other studies, "words still reign supreme" in *samā*ʿ; "musical features" are there to "serv[e] textual enhancement."[9] In many scholars' view, then, the nontextual components do not convey meaning themselves, or if they do, their importance is so marginal relative to the text that it quickly fades from view. Meaning, and thus Sufi knowledge and subject formation, becomes primarily a textual matter in this approach to *samā*ʿ—and "textual" understood in a limited way at that.[10]

This points to the second difference in the existing scholarship's approach to this opening scene: how it understands the poetic text's words to *mean* to the participants in the *samā*ʿ session. In Sufi studies, the dominant approach to poetic interpretation in *samā*ʿ has been different flavors of what I will call the cogno-spiritual hermeneutic.[11] It sees Sufi poetry's meaning—and, by extension here, *samā*ʿ's meaning—as produced through a spiritualizing hermeneutic in which the audience members rationally meditate on the potential associations between the poetic symbols and their "archetypal" or "supernal" spiritual meanings (*maʿānī*). In this system, words, and especially the imagery of Sufi poetry, are understood to represent or embody *maʿānī* in a limited linguistic form or to act as pointers (*ishārāt*) to them. A few studies even extend this hermeneutic method to the musical component of *samā*ʿ performances, arguing that its music is "in essence . . . a manifestation of the Divine Word," where each individual instrument has a specific "symbolic value" or a "sacred connotation and archetypal meaning

During, "What Is Sufi Music?" Lewisohn, in his seminal study on *samā*ʿ, advances the most sophisticated version of this argument, laudably foregrounding music's importance in *samā*ʿ, but then also still reducing it (and the æffects it produces) to just a tool to facilitate the apprehension of what he understands to be the real meanings—the abstract, archetypal spiritual meanings (*maʿānī*)—in the ritual's poem: "Poetry and words, as vehicles capable of communicating the Transcendental, are themselves highly inadequate. Music alone is capable of bridging the gap between the literal and anagogic levels of meaning, for the intense emotionality of any Sufi poem cannot be properly expressed except within the sacred ambience of the *Samā*ʿ ceremony. Music constitutes the poem's emotional body of water; the poem-fish is born and swims in the ocean of *Samā*ʿ—for without music, the vertical dimension of *Samā*ʿ, the poem expires on the dry land of literal and horizontal meanings" ("The Sacred Music of Islam," 15). See below for more on this cogno-spiritual approach.

9. Qureshi, "Listening to Words Through Music," 220–21, 236. Despite my concern with her framing of meaning as emanating primarily from the poetic text in *samā*ʿ, Qureshi's study is an interesting ethno-musicological analysis of contemporary *samā*ʿ performance in India, which tries to contextualize it with premodern sources.

10. Klein critiques this exact point in his study of al-Ghazālī ("Music, Rapture and Pragmatics"), pushing the field to include "non-verbal" forms of meaning. For a more detailed discussion of Klein's views on this point and where we depart from one another, see footnotes 40 and 50 in this chapter.

11. Literary scholars of Persian and Arabic poetry have pushed back in different ways against this interpretative approach to Sufi poetry, though not in the context of *samā*ʿ specifically (with the exception of Ingenito's work, discussed subsequently). See citations to Sells, Homerin, Stetkyvch, Meisami, and Keshavarz in chapters 4 and 5 and the works of Lewis, Brookshaw, and Ingenito on aspects of the performance context and bodies within it cited in chapter 1.

(*maʿnā*)," which its role in the ritual is to "incarnate" and "express."[12] Lewisohn summarizes this approach:

> It is important that the mystic audit 'the hidden mysteries' within the poetry. Audition to such poetry/music during *Samāʿ* is not merely an aesthetic experience requiring attention to the words and music alone: it is rather a concentration on the *symbolic correspondences and mystical references* of Sufi poetry with the ear of the heart; an audition to the 'hidden' melody within sound, to the secrets within the silent intervals as well as the notes of the music.[13]

Ingenito's recent masterful study of Saʿdī represents a much more nuanced, flexible, and theoretically sophisticated presentation of this spiritual hermeneutic, which he terms the "rational-inferential" approach to "spiritual cognition" (*maʿrifa*).[14] Laudably, he rescues it from the disembodying tendencies of its earlier proponents, convincingly showing that its medieval Sufi theorists, especially Abū Ḥāmid al-Ghazālī, regard the body of the beloved in *samāʿ* as a similarly potent pointer to the ritual's potential "supernal meanings" (*maʿānī*).[15] But I would like to suggest that we need to expand the bounds of what constitutes meaning production in *samāʿ* even beyond what this richer embodied cogno-spiritual approach allows. Why? Because the way that all these cogno-spiritual approaches frame meaning creation in *samāʿ* as a fundamentally "rational," "mental," "cognitive," or "intellectual" exercise of establishing correspondences between these (textual or embodied) earthly "pointers" and the *maʿānī* of the celestial realm risks obscuring the diverse ways in which participants produce meaning in *samāʿ* as much in and through the feelings of their somato-affective body as the intellectual or symbolic domains of their "mind" (understood in the traditional ratiocentric sense of this term).[16]

12. Michon, "Sacred Music and Dance in Islam," 477–79; Lewisohn, "The Sacred Music of Islam," 13–15. Ingenito similarly sees music's role in *samāʿ* as a potential catalyst for reaching "supernal" (*Beholding Beauty*, 443–518).

13. Lewisohn, "The Sacred Music of Islam," 15–16, emphasis original. For more examples of cogno-spiritual approaches to meaning in *samāʿ*, see Qureshi, "Listening to Words Through Music"; Michon, "Sacred Music and Dance in Islam"; Meier, "Dervish Dance."

14. Ingenito, *Beholding Beauty*, 443–518.

15. al-Ghazālī did not invent this hermeneutic approach; it has its roots in Ibn Sīnā's metaphysics, which is built on the work of earlier Islamic philosophers as well. For comprehensive studies of the Ibn Sīnian foundations of al-Ghazālī's "theory of mystical cognition," as Alexander Treiger terms it, or the "rational-inferential" approach, as Ingenito calls it, see Treiger, *Inspired Knowledge in Islamic Thought*; Ingenito, *Beholding Beauty*, 205–518. See also my discussion of Ingenito's perspective on the importance of bodies and gazing in chapter 1.

16. Lewisohn is the most emphatic on this point, stating that *wajd*, the primary epistemic experience of *samāʿ*, has an "intellectual basis" and "intellectual character." It is, as he says, a "cognitive experience" that the "mystical subject" arrives at as the "objective fruits of a heightened consciousness rather than the subjective vagaries of a hyper-emotional imagination" ("The Sacred Music of Islam," 15–16, 23–24). Ingenito, likewise, maintains throughout his work that *samāʿ* and the process of deriving

We see the results of such a logo- and ratiocentric framing of *samā ʿ*'s spiritual hermeneutic in how these studies do—or, sometimes, do not—treat æffect or emotion (the latter term is more typically used in studies of *samā ʿ*). It is usually not completely absent in their discussion, but it is generally relegated to the background, to an undefined part of the ritual's ambience (often associated with its musical backdrop or "body of water," as noted above), or portrayed as a byproduct of the ceremony without a clear function, almost as a type of spiritual offgassing. *Samā ʿ* has "emotive aspects," an "affective quality," or a powerful emotional atmosphere. Other times *samā ʿ* is said to operate as a "spiritually emotive stimulant," inducing and fanning the flames of love, and resulting in ecstatic states (s. *wajd, ḥāl*).[17] Interestingly, many of these studies quote—sometimes at length—passages from Sufi sources that discuss the role of æffects in *samā ʿ*. We will look at several of these passages in both this and the following chapter. This is not a case, then, of a lack of attention to the right primary sources or sections within them. It is a matter of where scholars have directed the field's attention. Æffect/emotion seem unworthy of analytical focus. Or, more charitably, the analytical lens with which they have approached *samā ʿ* have not enabled them to appreciate æffect's constitutive role in Sufi epistemology and subject formation.[18] They have not been able to see it, in other words, as a coproducer of Sufi knowledge of God in *samā ʿ*.

meaning from it should be understood as "rational," "cognitive," or "intellectual," at least in the case of al-Ghazālī and Saʿdī. For Ingenito's "rational-inferential" approach or "rationalizing approach to spiritual cognition (*ma ʿrifat*)," see *Beholding Beauty*, 205–518 and especially 443–518. For some specific representative examples of Ingenito's argument about meaning creation in *samā ʿ* in al-Ghazālī and Saʿdī as having a "rational," "cognitive," "intellectual," etc. basis, see 230, 266, 272, 281, 290, 292, 298, 300, 302, 384, 388. That said, it is important to note that he makes a distinction between this more "rational" approach in al-Ghazālī and Saʿdī's works and the perspective of other more "mysticism-inclined," ecstatic-type Sufis, whose approach differs. (For his perspective on this split see Introduction and *Beholding Beauty* 309–12, 335, 353, 380–83, 394–95). Meier does not discuss this point at length, but does remark that *samā ʿ* comes to primarily be a "more mental activity" ("Dervish Dance," 35).

17. Papan-Matin, *Beyond Death* 191–2; Meier, "Dervish Dance," 31, 36–37; Lewisohn, "The Sacred Music of Islam," 15–17; Papas, "Creating a Sufi Soundscape." Avery points to the "'emotive'" dimensions of *samā ʿ*, especially when discussing *wajd* and *ḥāl*, which he sees as affective overflows, going as far as translating them as "emotive response" at times (*A Psychology of Early Sufi Samāʿ*, 65–74, and variously throughout his overview of ecstatic experiences in chapters 4–5). Robson refers elliptically to *samā ʿ*'s "powerful influence," which "stir[s]" humanity ("Introduction," 4–5). Gribetz says *samā ʿ* "bring[s] about religious emotion and ecstasy" and "longing" ("The Samāʿ Controversy," 43, 52–54).

18. Avery is a partial exception to this general rule. He seems to see affect as potentially epistemological, remarking in a discussion of the uses of the word *qalb* (heart), "This suggests that the heart does lay claim to knowledge, gained by observation and understanding, and that this knowledge involves an emotional and ecstatic element rather than a purely intellectual content" (*A Psychology of Early Sufi Samāʿ*, 80; relatedly, see his passing comment about the "evocation power" of the "non-semantic aspect of poetry" on 142). This is a keen observation that he unfortunately does not elaborate, even though he extensively catalogs the different somato-affective sequalae of *samā ʿ* throughout his book. He also provides useful brief summaries of several key treatises on *samā ʿ*, though his "altered states of consciousness" and the comparative psychological framing of much of his study is problematic.

To properly see affect's role in *samā*ʿ's meaning production, we need to apply an æffective lens of analysis to all aspects of this ritual, from the elements of its performance context to the different experiences participants undergo. This is the task of the next two chapters. This chapter will foreground æffects' machinations in *samā*ʿ's performance context and music, analyzing how these components of the ritual æffect those in attendance in meaningful ways. The following chapter will turn to examine the Sufi poetic hermeneutic in *samā*ʿ alongside the peak spiritual experiences of "states" (*aḥwāl*) and "ecstasy" (*wajd*) that flow out of it and show how what these all mean to Sufis is inescapably imbricated with æffect.

"MINDING THE TIME, PLACE, AND COMPANY": ÆFFECTIVE ATTUNEMENT AND SETTING THE STAGE FOR *SAMĀ*ʿ

To return to our opening anecdote, when the *qalandar*s arrive to the mosque in which ʿIrāqī is teaching, they do so with dramatic intent. I use "dramatic" not in the histrionic or melodramatic sense of that term, as it is often used colloquially, but rather in its meaning of something that is intensely æffecting—one of those moments when you can feel the gravity and intensity of a scene or situation in your body, viscerally giving you goosebumps, making your heart race, etc. ʿIrāqī, surrounded by his students—perhaps in the mosque courtyard, perhaps in the mosque building proper—would have been holding forth on one of the traditional Islamic sciences. His students, the account leads us to believe, would have been transfixed by ʿIrāqī's brilliance. But their enrapturement would have been a sober one, an astonishment of their intellect at ʿIrāqī's remarkable erudition at such a young age. The atmosphere likely felt rarefied, but decidedly solemn, perhaps even a bit staid and stuffy at times for any of those in the audience who were less soberly inclined.

Into this environment, the *qalandar*s enter, *hāy u hūy zanān*—literally, "making a ruckus." They are outsiders to the normative space of the mosque.[19] They have not come to solemnly say their prayers or sit reverentially at the feet of the young intellectual phenom and quietly learn a day's lesson drawn from the traditional Islamic sciences. They are raiding the mosque, proselytizing for their antinomian mode of piety: what the poets Sanāʾī and ʿAṭṭār refer to in the eponymous genre celebrating the *qalandar*s, the *qalandariyyāt*, alternatively as their "way," "path," even "religion" (*rāh, maẕhab, dīn, ṭarīq*).[20] Their riotous entrance, made all the

19. *Qalandar*s and many other antinomian groups of the medieval Islamic world made their name on social and religious transgression and disruption of normative spaces and piety. On *qalandar*s and similar antinomian types in the premodern Islamic world, see Karamustafa, *God's Unruly Friends*; Algar, "Impostors"; Watenpaugh, "Deviant Dervishes."

20. See, for example, Sanāʾī, *Dīvān-i Sanāʾī*, 393–394, 506, 653–54; ʿAṭṭār, *Dīvān-i ʿAṭṭār*, 361, 491–92. On the *qalandariyyāt* as a poetic genre, see de Bruijn, "The *Qalandariyyāt* in Persian Mystical Poetry"; Miller, "The Qalandar King"; Miller, "The Poetics of the Sufi Carnival."

more shocking by their antinomian attire, is not an empty performative spectacle or narrative flourish, as some may be tempted to read it. It is central to their missionary goal. Conversion to their "path"—which is synonymous in the Sufi imaginary with the "Path of Love"—requires not just rejecting normative Islam but also its æffective entailments and assemblages of feeling. *Qalandar*s are the people of wine and merriment (*khwushī, ṭarab*). They are done, as they say in the final line of the poem they perform in the subsequent *samāʿ* session, draining the "many goblets of toil and fatigue" offered by the ascetic mode of piety (*zuhd*). The *qalandars*' "commotion" (*hāy u hūy zanān*) should be understood through this lens. It is intended to be deeply disruptive to the mosque atmosphere and ʿIrāqī's class but in a distinctly festive way. *Hāy u hūy*-ing is not a scary or threatening type of social upheaval, at least to those with the proper aptitude for seeing beauty and spiritual insight in the *qalandars*' antinomian praxis. It is carnivalesque.[21]

In this context, the *qalandars*' "merry commotion" has a specific goal: It sets the stage for the deployment of their most potent proselytizing tool, *samāʿ*. Premodern Sufi commentators going all the way back to Junayd (d. 910) maintain that *samāʿ* is only effective when the "time (*al-zamān*), place (*al-makān*), and company (*al-ikhwān*)" of its performance are properly arrayed.[22] At first glance, this phrasing may seem to suggest that Sufis were principally concerned with delineating the precise times during the day, specific physical locations, and categories of licit and illicit attendees for the performance of *samāʿ*: for example, hallowed Sufi lodges or mosques with an audience restricted to pious (male) spiritual adepts, not potentially corrupting social sites such as the market or winehouse, where the composition of the audiences would be completely unregulated. Such legalistic concerns are addressed to a degree in these accounts.[23] But Sufi discussions of "proper time, place, and company" are equally (or more) concerned about how aspects of these three elements work together to construct a particular *ambience* for *samāʿ*'s performance. al-Ghazālī is the clearest on this point:[24]

21. See Miller, "The Poetics of the Sufi Carnival."

22. This tripartite requirement is, as Lewisohn observes, "mentioned by nearly every Sufi who subsequently wrote [after Junayd] on *Samāʿ*." Lewisohn provides a comprehensive overview of the traditional reading of these "preconditions" in "The Sacred Music of Islam," 6–12.

23. See, for example, al-Ghazālī's lengthy discussions of the legality of *samāʿ*, its protocols of comportment, and what can block its spiritual efficacy: *Kīmiyā*, 358–367, 374; *Iḥyāʾ*, 2:266–284, 298–302. Or, for another example, see Muḥammad al-Ṭūsī's recommendation that *samāʿ* only be performed in Sufi lodges or mosques, discussed in Lewisohn, "The Sacred Music of Islam," 9.

24. The following account is excerpted from al-Ghazālī's magnum opus, *Iḥyāʾ*, which he composed in Arabic. He later wrote a highly abridged version of this work in his native language of Persian, titled *Kīmiyā-yi saʿādat*. The relevant passages from both works discussed here closely follow one another. The differences in his accounts, however, are at times instructive and emphasize different aspects of his thought on particular issues. The full translation of the Persian version is as follows: "Know that one must mind three things in *samāʿ*: [proper] time, place, and company. *Samāʿ* is useless any time that the heart is occupied, or it is the time of prayer or eating, or it is a time when hearts are more distressed and preoccupied. Regarding place, when it is [near] a roadway, or an unpleasant and dark place, or in a

> al-Junayd said: "[True] *samāʿ* requires three things, and if they are not there, do not practice *samāʿ*: [proper] time, place, and company." The meaning of this is that it is useless to engage in it [*samāʿ*] at a time of the presence of food, argumentation, prayer, or anything that diverts one with turmoil of the heart. This is the meaning of observing [proper] time (*al-zamān*). Thus, one may maintain a state of emptiness of the heart for it. Regarding place (*al-makān*), if it is [near] a busy street or some ugly place or a place where there is something that may trouble the heart, one should avoid it. And the reason for company (*al-ikhwān*) is that if there is present someone of a different type (*al-jins*), who disapproves of *samāʿ*, makes a show of his ascetic piety, and is poor of the subtleties of the heart, he is [felt] to be unbearable in the assembly, and the heart will be preoccupied by him. Likewise, if there is present an arrogant, worldly individual to whom attention and regard must be paid, or one of the Sufis who make a show and fake ecstasy and are ostentatious in ecstasy, dance, and rending their garments [in *samāʿ*]—all these are disturbances.[25]

His overriding concern in this passage is to caution his readers against engaging in *samāʿ* in any context that has the potential to distract or disturb the participant's heart. (He does not even mention the typical recommended locations, e.g., Sufi lodges and mosques, that are seen in some other Sufi accounts of the "[proper] time, place, and company.") Some of the distractions he lists are mundane. He recommends, for example, not trying to engage in *samāʿ* when food is present or near busy streets. He also notes that the coperformance of the required daily Islamic prayers could impinge on the heart's focus in *samāʿ*.[26] But the majority of his account above addresses types of distractions that share a common uniting feature: their ability to shape the æffective ambience of the ritual, and to do so in a decidedly negative fashion.[27] Mundane, value-neutral, or, in the case of prayer, religiously laudable distractions can be a problem for the *samāʿ* participants'

house of oppression, it will be disturbed all the time. Regarding company, it is necessary that all who are present are true practitioners of *samāʿ*. *Samāʿ* is of no use when an arrogant worldly person is present, or a person who knows only the outward aspects of religion, or an ostentatious person is present who always exaggerates in their ecstasy and dance, or a group of ignorant people are present who do *samāʿ* with useless thoughts or are occupied with useless stories and look all around and are not reverent, or a group of women are looking and among the group is young men, and if they are not empty of thoughts of one another. The meaning of this is what Junayd has said: 'The necessary conditions for *samāʿ* are [proper] time, place, and company'" (*Kīmiyā*, 373–34).

25. al-Ghazālī, *Iḥyāʾ*, 2:298. Duncan MacDonald has translated al-Ghazālī's treatise on *samāʿ* from the *Iḥyāʾ* in a three-part article: al-Ghazzālī, "Emotional Religion" (1901a; 1901b; 1902). The translation is passable, but its English is dated and sometimes misses nuances and obscures some technical aspects in the original Arabic. Thus, I have decided to translate all passages from the *Iḥyāʾ* myself.

26. He reiterates these items in his Persian work as well: al-Ghazālī, *Kīmiyā*, 373.

27. Papan-Matin gestures towards a similar idea as "affective ambience" when she says that "*Samāʿ* sessions were to be held in specific physical and *emotional environments*" (*Beyond Death*, 196, emphasis mine). But she does not elaborate further.

concentration, but it is the contextual forces that ruin the mood, so to speak, that are the real enemies of *samāʿ*'s spiritual efficacy.

The words that he most frequently uses in both his Arabic and Persian accounts to talk about these distractions are derivations of the Arabic root *shīn-ghayn-lām*. *Shīn-ghayn-lām* words can have positive or value-neutral meanings. They can be used, for example, to talk about working or, as al-Ghazālī says in the second sentence above, in the generic sense of "to engage in [something]" such as *samāʿ* (*al-ishtighāl bihi*). But in his discussions of *samāʿ* most *shīn-ghayn-lām* words need to be understood as carrying the negative connotation that this root can have for "troubling," "disturbing," "disquieting," etc.—"occupying," that is, in the distracting or anxiety-laden sense of "preoccupying." The predominant focus in his accounts on elements of the context that can, as he says, cause "turmoil of the heart" (*iḍṭirāb al-qalb*) underlines the vexatious valence he associates with these *shīn-ghayn-lām* words.[28] He warns his readers to avoid "ugly place[s]" (*mawḍiʿan karīh al-ṣūra*) or ones in which there is "argumentation" (*khiṣām*). His Persian version of this passage is more emphatic on these points, urging his readers not to attempt *samāʿ* at times when "hearts are more distressed (*parākandah*) and preoccupied (*mashghūl*)" or in "unhappy and dark places" (*jāʾī-yi nā-khwush va tārīk*) and "houses of oppression" (*khānah-yi ẓālimī*). In such locations, one will be "disturbed (*shūrīdah*) all the time." They, to return to the Arabic version, "trouble the heart" (*yashghal al-qalb*).

The pejorative ways that he characterizes what he later terms "all these . . . disturbances" (*mushawwashāt*) deeply embeds them in æffective nets of meaning. Having one's heart "preoccupied" (*ishtaghala*) with these types of distractions is not an intellectual matter. These cannot all be reduced to annoying, though disembodied, passing thoughts or bodily temptations (e.g., to eat) that pop up to break the concentration of the *samāʿ* participant. The environmental conditions he admonishes his audience to avoid are felt as forces that impinge upon them. They create certain assemblages of feeling in the ambience that are somatically realized in the participants.

al-Ghazālī provides a clear example of this in his discussion of the third requirement, "[proper] company," where he presents myriad examples of bad company, from deceptive Sufis and superficially focused religious antagonists who do not understand *samāʿ* to high-maintenance "arrogant, worldly individuals." He ends his first sentence in this section with a revealing observation: "And the reason for company (*al-ikhwān*) is that if there is present someone of a different type (*al-jins*), who disapproves of *samāʿ*, makes a show of his ascetic piety, and is poor of the subtleties of the heart, *he is [felt] to be unbearable in the assembly*" (*kāna mustathqalan*

28. Words derived from the *ḍād-rāʾ-bāʾ* root, like the *shīn-ghayn-lām* root, can be used in positive—as we have seen previously and will see again repeatedly throughout this book—or negative senses, as in this example.

fī al-majlis) (emphasis mine). In this concluding observation, al-Ghazālī makes explicit something that is implicit in the rest of his discussion: Environmental conditions and other actors impact the way the ritual's atmosphere *feels* to the participants. In this example, it is people with discordant natures and motivations "preoccupy[ing]" the true practitioners of *samā'*, making their session's invisible æffective atmosphere heavy with a palpable sense of insufferable weight, burden, or, annoyance.[29] These negative free radicals in the assembly mess up the session's vibe, which makes it impossible to focus one's heart and feel the way one must for this deeply æffective form of meditation.[30]

al-Ghazālī's final point here, however, needs to be extended backward to the other environmental elements he previously mentioned. Dark, oppressive, disgusting, contentious, and unhappy places would likewise modulate the assembly's ambience, impacting its æffective charge and shaping how the participants somatically experience it. These may not all be felt exactly as the negative pressure of the "unbearable[ness]" that al-Ghazālī explicitly mentions in his final example, but they would each change its assemblage of feeling, inducing different flavors of "turmoil of the heart" that are not just metaphoric or rhetorical but somatically realized.

At a broader level, what I want to argue is that al-Ghazālī is presenting the case here, though in the negative, for the necessity of æffective attunement between all aspects of the performance ambience and the hearts of the *samā'* participants. How participants feel changes their ability to engage in spiritual practice. Indeed, as we will see in the following chapter, it even modulates how they interpret poetry. To achieve the "sacred ambience" required for *samā'*, the Sufi participants must begin by carefully constructing a performance context that somato-affectively primes their body for the realization of the sacred.[31] Because al-Ghazālī presents his case in this what-to-avoid structure, the inverse—i.e., what should be in the *samā'* ambience—gets a bit obscured, at least in this section in his works. But other Sufi authors are unequivocal on this point, as is al-Ghazālī elsewhere.[32]

29. The æffect of those around one can work in the positive direction too. al-Ghazālī maintains in his section on *tawājud* that one way to help cultivate "states" (*aḥwāl*) is to be in the company of those who embody those states (*Iḥyā'*, 2:293).

30. I am grateful to Jonathan Allen for the suggestion of "vibe" here.

31. Lewisohn also emphasizes the importance of the ambience of the *samā'* performance, though the ambience he is concerned with is what he terms the "sacred ambience"—that is, the "ontological priority of the Sacred in the *Samā'* ceremony," the way "the Sacred preludes, preconditions, encompasses and, ultimately, defines the ambience of the Sufi's audition" ("The Sacred Music of Islam," 12).

32. al-Ghazālī is not only focused on the important role of æffect/emotion in *samā'*; he takes up their importance in multiple places in his works. For other discussions of al-Ghazālī's treatment of æffect/emotion, see Vignone, "Fear and Learning in Medieval Islam," 41–43, for the importance al-Ghazālī assigns to fear in scholarly piety; Gade's overview of his discussion of the role of affect in Qur'ānic recitation (*Perfection Makes Practice*, 138–41); Katz's study on how Islamic jurists and intellectuals use the "gendered emotional trait" or "affective disposition" of "jealousy" to "articulate the

This is where we return to the *qalandar*s. They know these basic preconditions for *samāʿ*, if not through reading Sufi treatises and manuals of comportment like al-Ghazālī's, then through spiritual intuition and practice. They may realize these three requirements for *samāʿ* in somewhat different ways than their more sober, mainstream Sufi brethren, such as al-Ghazālī. But they share with them the recognition that an individual *samāʿ* session's success in æffecting spiritual insight is tied as much to the ambience in which it is performed as to its recited lines of poetry. Bursting in *hāy u hūy zanān*-ing, they reset the mood of the mosque's classroom and bring it into attunement with the æffective posture their disciples must adopt for spiritual advancement in the Path of Love. This act of æffective modulation is not external to the *samāʿ* ritual. It is coextensive with and integral to it. It is its prerequisite, as we have seen, because *samāʿ*—especially in its *qalandarī*, Path of Love varieties—will not work in a stuffy, solemn environment like a mosque classroom. Its ambience must resemble that of an uproarious carnival for the full force and range of its intended meaning(s) to be conveyed. It must be made drunken and "merry" (*khwush*), as ʿIrāqī says below, for the Sufi participant to feel the sense of ruination they need to advance spiritually:

> In the banquet of the rascal Qalandars—
> sit, drink wine, and be merry (*khwush*)![33]

"STRANGE AND WONDROUS" IMPRESSIONS (*ĀTHĀR*): MUSIC, ÆFFECT, AND MEANING IN *SAMĀʿ*

The *qalandar*s' entrance into ʿIrāqī's assembly that day was not silent. Their "merry commotion" would have had a powerful aural component to it as well. This may have been chanting or the general commotion of a sizable group of "God's unruly friends" entering a venue—the account does not make it explicit. Their entrance could equally likely have been accompanied by some form of instrumental performance—a premodern "walkout" song of sorts.[34] At the minimum, the account makes clear that the *qalandar*s moved swiftly in this melodic direction. No sooner did they enter the mosque than "they started performing *samāʿ*, reciting this *ghazal* with a sweet (*khwush*) song and perfect rhythm." The poem, whose meaning we will return to in the following chapter, occupies the next four lines of the page. When the text is done, the narrator returns to tell us, "When the *qalandar*s had finished their melodious performance of this *ghazal*, an internal turmoil

boundaries of proper interactions between the sexes" ("Beyond Ḥalāl and Ḥarām"); and Gruber's elaboration of what she calls Islam's "affective ethics" ("In Defense and Devotion," 99–100).

33. ʿIrāqī, *Kulliyyāt-i ʿIrāqī (Muḥtasham)*, 80–81. A variation on this line is found in arguably one of ʿIrāqī's most well-known poems. For further discussion of that poem, see chapter 1.

34. Antinomian groups, such as *qalandar*s, were strongly associated with music. See Karamustafa, *God's Unruly Friends*, 20, whose term I borrow.

overtook the shaykh." The watershed moment of "internal turmoil" is clearly tied to the poetic performance. But we must not allow the more substantial physical space the poem occupies on the page to obscure that the poem, as a text, does not stand alone here. It is not just a poem being declaimed out loud, much less read silently, as we still too often implicitly imagine medieval reading practice. It is a musical performance of a poem, with a specific æffective quality to it.

The word that the anonymous author of ʿIrāqī's biography uses here to describe the *samāʿ* music, *khwush*, is the same one we saw above in two forms: first, in the negative, in al-Ghazālī's account, where he warns his audience not to engage in *samāʿ* in an "unhappy" or "unpleasant" location, and, second, in ʿIrāqī's poem, exhorting his audience to be "merry" at the "banquet of the *qalandars*." The importance of *khwush* reverberates throughout Sufi Path of Love literature, especially poetry and discussions of *samāʿ*. Sufi lovers and beloveds are routinely described as or implored to be "*khwush*," as ʿIrāqī says. The (in)famous wine of the Sufi tavern, as we will see in chapters 3, 4, and 5, reduces all who imbibe it to that familiar state of drunken *khwush*-ness. Its shades of meaning, depending on context, can range from "merry," "pleasant," "happy," or "delightful" to "charming," "elegant," and "well/good" (in the sense of well-constructed, skilled, or pleasing in presentation). The way in which *khwush*, and related æffective states and qualities such as *ṭarab* or *ladhīdh*, pop up throughout Persian and Arabic discussions of Sufi poetry, music, and spiritual experience is not coincidental. It is rooted in the foundational role that æffect plays in Sufi subject formation and epistemology.

In his opening discussion of *samāʿ* in *Kīmiyā*, al-Ghazālī gives us a window into the interlinked world of music, æffect, and Sufi spiritual experience.[35]

> Know that there is a secret of God in the human heart. It is concealed inside it like fire in iron, and just like with a strike of flint the secret of fire is made manifest and disclosed, so too *samāʿ* with a sweet (*khwush*) and rhythmic song excites that inner human essence and makes something appear in them without them having any control over it. The cause of this is the relation that the essence of the human heart has with the celestial world, which is called the world of spirits. The celestial world is the world of excellence and beauty (*ḥusn va jamāl*) and the foundation of beauty is proportionality. Whatever is proportionate is an illustration of the beauty of that world, and all beauty and proportionality in this sensory world is the fruit of the beauty of that world. Thus, sweet, rhythmic, well-proportioned song resembles the wonders of that world. For this reason, an awareness is discovered in the heart; movement and longing (*shawq*) appear that the person themselves does not know what it is. This is in a heart that is simple and empty of the love and longing that is involved in

35. For a concise overview of al-Ghazālī's book on music and poetry and the larger context of music theory of the Late Antique world out of which it comes, see Weinrich, "Sensing Sound." Like many studies of music in the premodern Islamic world, Weinrich highlights the way music seeks to "arouse" emotions in al-Ghazālī's *Iḥyāʾ*. She does not, however, connect this to questions of Sufi epistemology or subject formation; instead, like Klein, she discusses it only as part of the "experience" of the music.

> this path. But when a heart is not empty and is engaged with something, that [thing it is occupied with] starts to move, and like a fire that is blown upon, it increases in intensity. For the ones whose hearts have been conquered (*ghālib*) by the love of God the most high, *samāʿ* is important because that fire [of love] will burn hotter. But for those who have trivial (*bāṭil*) love in their hearts, *samāʿ* is a deadly poison for them and is forbidden.[36]

In this passage, al-Ghazālī uses a complex metaphor to explain why *samāʿ*, despite its serious spiritual dangers, is a critically important tool for Sufi seekers. He begins by revealing that there is a "secret of God in the human heart." The secret here is multilayered. It is built first upon the foundational reality that the human heart has the ability to connect to the "celestial world" or "world of spirits." But this connection is "concealed inside [the heart] like fire in iron." It is, in other words, a potentiality that can only be realized if elicited by the right combination of earthly stimuli, just as "fire" can only be produced by striking flint on iron.

The second layer of this secret is the "How-To" portion. The real and metaphoric hidden "fire" that is effected in both of these scenarios does not happen accidentally or haphazardly. It is predicated on the specific qualities of the two interacting objects. Striking flint on iron produces fire because of the chemical properties of these two substances. The precise "relation" of these properties to one another makes the fiery product of this chemical reaction possible. The same action would fail to ignite anything if done with flint and a piece of wood. So too in the case of the spiritual "fire" to which al-Ghazālī is comparing it. What catalyzes the spiritual flame depends on the nature and qualities of the two interacting substances. In al-Ghazālī's metaphoric setup, the actors in this interaction are the human heart, specifically its aperture to the "celestial world," and *samāʿ*. What is important to underline, however, is that when he discusses *samāʿ* in this passage his focus is decidedly not on any linguistic meaning conveyed in its sung poetry. "*Samāʿ* . . . excites that inner human essence" because of its particular qualities, because it is "sweet (*khwush*) and rhythmic."[37] Music that is *khwush* and rhythmic—like the "sweet (*khwush*) song and perfect rhythm" of the *qalandars*' *samāʿ* performance before young ʿIrāqī—speaks directly to the heart of human beings because, as he continues, it "resembles the wonders of [the celestial] world." But how?

It is here that he makes a series of key linkages. The celestial world, the "world of spirits," is also "the world of beauty (*ḥusn va jamāl*)," and beauty ultimately is based on

36. al-Ghazālī, *Kīmiyā*, 357–58.

37. In discussions of music, *khwush* could be used in both the sense of "merry" and "well-constructed" or "pleasing in presentation." al-Ghazālī likely intends both meanings of *khwush* here to some degree, but his use of Arabic words derived from the *lām-dhāl-dhāl* root (associated with a web of meanings clustered around being "sweet," "pleasing," "delightful," etc.) in his account in the corresponding passages in *Iḥyāʾ* suggests that he does intend *khwush* here in its meaning of "sweet," "merry," or "pleasing" as much or more than "well-constructed" (*Iḥyāʾ*, 2:266).

"proportionality" in his framework.[38] Rhythmic sound echoes this proportionality, and "sweet" (*khwush*) tunes, he implies, function as a musical embodiment of beauty. The rich web of connections he draws between all these concepts and qualities in this handful of sentences makes explicit what the insightful reader of chapter 1 may have begun to suspect by association. Music, in its *khwush* forms at least, operates in ways strikingly similar to earthly physical beauty. "Sweet, rhythmic, well-proportioned song," as he says later, is music to the ears, so to speak, of the human heart's window unto the celestial world because it is an "illustration (*namūdgārī*) of the beauty of that world." Indeed, as he continues, ultimately, "all beauty and proportionality in this sensory world is the fruit of the beauty of that [celestial] world." Beautiful earthly beloveds and merry music both recall and renew the vision of this world for earthly audiences. Or, in the case of neophytes, who al-Ghazālī refers to as those with "a heart that is simple and empty of . . . love and longing," these earthly embodiments of beauty and proportionality introduce them to the celestial world by shaking loose the dust covering this aperture to the celestial world, awakening in them the realization that there is something more to long for.[39]

This inchoate impetus to search and to long for something not yet understood is arguably what ʿIrāqī experiences at the end of the *samāʿ* performance. He has been conquered by a palpable sense of discomfort, but he does not yet completely understand the source of it. His heart has not yet been conquered by love (of either God or an earthly beloved—the latter happens moments later when he sees the beautiful *qalandar* youth), but he feels something strong moving in him that he does not yet have the words or concepts for. It is just an "internal turmoil." al-Ghazālī, in a rich passage in *Iḥyāʾ* discussing the æffects of "the strings and the rest of the musical melodies (*naghamāt*)" compares this stage on the spiritual path to the situation of a hypothetical youth who grew up without having ever seen a woman or learning of sex.[40] This youth, when he reaches puberty and sexual

38. For the link between beauty and proportionality in Islamic aesthetic theory, see Elias, *Aisha's Cushion*, 156–61.

39. As Kukkonen observes in a different context, al-Ghazālī sees all "pleasant" things as essentially evocative of love: "Love is an expression for a given nature's inclination towards something that is pleasurable (*al-ḥubb ʿibāra ʿan mayl aṭ-ṭab ʿ ilā sh-shay ʾ al-muladhdh*). . . . Put another way, every pleasant thing is loved (*kull ladhīdh maḥbūb*)" ("Al-Ghazālī on the Emotions," 143).

40. al-Ghazālī, *Iḥyāʾ*, 2:292. Klein discusses this fascinating passage too in his excellent overview of al-Ghazālī's treatment of music and *samāʿ*. He comments on the way al-Ghazālī sees music as having "a great influence on the soul" and "heart," and how he compares this "difficult to explain in words" influence (which, I assume, is another translation of "*āthār*"—he also uses "trace" and "impressions") to "longing." Elsewhere in his study he refers to music's "various emotive effects." In the introduction and conclusion, he lays out the broader implications of al-Ghazālī's project in his treatise on *samāʿ* and suggests that one important takeaway is that we need to move beyond language as the conveyor of meaning and knowledge in Sufism. He sees music and "sound" as central to this "nonverbal language," this "nonverbal channel of meaning," but he does not frame this non-linguistic mode of meaning/knowledge creation (which he calls "musical cognition") as necessarily affective or felt in nature. It is

desire (*shahwa*) "conquers him," will "feel the fire of sexual desire," but he will not understand what he is longing for. This, al-Ghazālī argues, is the state of the yet-to-be converted Sufi lover who has not yet had love and longing sparked in their heart. They, like all humanity, have an unlearned connection to the celestial world and its beauty, which is now obscured by engagement with the world. But there is a way to (re)discover it: firing up, so to speak, that secret aperture in the heart with the right types of earthly "flint." Earthly beauty can play this role, as we saw in chapter 1, but al-Ghazālī's focus on this passage is on the musical dimension of *samā*ʿ.

> But regarding the state (*al-ḥāl*), how many people grasp (*yudriku*) a contraction (*qabḍan*) or expansion (*basṭan*) in their heart in the moment [*al-waqt*] in which they wake up and do not know its cause. A person may (*qad*) contemplate (*yatafakkar*) something and then this imprints (*yuʾaththir*) an impression (*atharan*) in his soul (*nafs*). Then, he forgets that cause, but the impression (*al-athar*) remains in his soul (*nafs*) and he feels it (*yuḥiss bihi*). Sometimes the state (*al-ḥāla*) that he feels may be delight that is buried in his soul because he was contemplating (*bi-tafakkur*) something that induces (*mūjib*) delight, or [likewise, the same way with] sadness. Then, he forgets what he had been thinking about, but he still feels the impression (*al-athar*) subsequently. Other times, this state (*al-ḥāla*) [he feels] is a strange (*gharība*) state that neither the words delight nor sadness express clearly and he does not find for it a fitting and clear expression for the intended [i.e., the feeling]. Having a sense for properly metrical poetry and for the difference between it and not properly metrical poetry, is something some have in distinction to others. It is a state in which the poetry aficionado [lit. the one who possess this "*dhawq* of poetry"] knows—without any doubt—the difference between metrical (poetry) and the non-metrical (*al-munzaḥif*). It is not possible for him, however, to express it [this state] with anything that would make intelligible what he means by it to someone who is not an aficionado. In the soul (*al-nafs*), there are strange states (*aḥwāl gharība*) like this. Not (*bal*) the well-known meanings (*maʿānī*) of fear, sadness, and delight that rather (*innamā*) arise only in listening to (*al-samā*ʿ) an intellectually comprehensible song (i.e., one with words) (*ghināʾ mafhūm*). But regarding the tunes and the rest of the musical melodies (*naghamāt*) produced by strings, which are not intellectually comprehensible (*laysat mafhūma*), they imprint (*tuʾaththir*) in a strange and wondrous way (*taʾthīran ʿajīban*) in the soul (*nafs*). While it is not possible to give clear expression to the strange wonders (*ʿajāʾib*) of these impressions, sometimes (*qad*) they are called "desire" (*shawq*), but this "desire" is a desire where the possessor [of the desire] does not know for what they desire. It is, thus, strange and wondrous (*ʿajīb*). He whose heart is disturbed (*iḍṭaraba*) by listening to strings or the flute (*shāhīn*) and the like does not know for what he desires and he discovers in his soul a state that is as if it is demanding something that he does not know what it is.[41]

---

just "delicate, ineffable meanings" or an "ineffable" "experien[tial]" form of "understanding." See "Music, Rapture and Pragmatics," 216, 220, 229–30, 233, 239–40.

41. al-Ghazālī, *Iḥyāʾ*, 2:292.

Occuring in the course of his treatment of *wajd*, al-Ghazālī here illustrates the powerful role music plays in the excitation to desire in his Sufi framework. And, like beauty, it does not require words to communicate with its audience members, nor intellectual comprehension. He is quite direct on this point. He is not talking about the "intellectually comprehensible song[s] (i.e., with words) (*ghinā ʾ mafhūm*)."[42] He is focused here on how music, as "melodies" and instruments, expresses meaning to listeners engaged in *samā ʿ* (in both the general and technical Sufi sense of this term) in a way that is not discursive or "intellectually understood (*laysat mafhūma*)."[43] Music, rather, produces meaning for humans by "imprint[ing] (*tu ʾaththir*) in a strange and wondrous way (*ta ʾthīran ʿajīban*) in the soul (*nafs*)."[44] It is because of this "impressive" mode of nondiscursive meaning conveyance that, for example, instruments alone, "even though they have no meaning (*ma ʿnī*)," and Arabic verses in non-Arabic speaking audiences, can both still be very æffective bases for *samā ʿ*. Even babies and camels, who certainly cannot claim the powers of linguistic or intellectual comprehension, are deeply æffected by music.[45]

al-Ghazālī, uncharacteristically, seems a bit uncertain about how to conceptualize and describe these powerful "impression[s]" (s. *athar*, pl. *āthār*) and the internal "state[s]" (*al-ḥāla*) they produce.[46] (The interlinked way he discusses these two makes it difficult to completely disaggregate them.) He describes them multiple times as "strange" and "wondrous" in varying verbiage. He asserts that it is not possible "to give clear expression" to the "strange wonders" (*ʿajā ʾib*) that are realized in the person from them. They are not, he avers a bit more confidently, the "well-known"—i.e., socially recognized and constructed—emotional "meanings

42. See also chapter 3 on al-Ghazālī's different levels of "hearing" (*samā ʿ*). His first stage is hearing without "(intellectual) understanding" (*fahm*). Also see chapter 3 for discussion of why *fahm* cannot be understood only as "intellectual understanding," at least in the Sufi context.

43. Although al-Ghazālī's concern here is primarily instrumental music, he does see this same non-discursive aspect of meaning creation (described subsequently) involved in the contemplation (*tafakkur*) of other "thing[s]" as well, as he points to at the beginning of this passage. I will return to this point and its implications for Perso-Arabic theories of meaning and mind in the following chapters.

44. al-Ghazālī also uses very similar phrasing in other passages touching on music's "strange and wondrous" impressions that "move the heart" and induce more specific æffective responses, such as joy, sadness, etc., and physical movements of the limbs in its listeners, without "understanding the meanings (*ma ʿānī*) of the poetry" (*Iḥyā ʾ*, 2:273, 277). See his broader discussion of the imbrication of music, poetry, and affect/emotions in *Iḥyā ʾ*, 273–79 and in *Kīmiyā*, 360–62. Ibn Sīnā uses this same phrasing—"imprint[ing] (*tu ʾaththir*) in a strange and wondrous way (*ta ʾthīran ʿajīban*) in the soul (*nafs*)"—when discussing "image-evoking utterances" (*al-mukhayyilāt*) and links them to æffective responses (*al-Ishārāt*, 362). For more on this, see chapter 4.

45. al-Ghazālī, *Kīmiyā*, 365; al-Ghazālī, *Iḥyā ʾ*, 2:273.

46. While I do *not* want to collapse the full sense and meaning with which Sara Ahmed uses the term "impressions" in her works into the Perso-Islamic concept of *āthār*, it is worth pointing out that she talks about emotions as acting through exerting "impressions" on people and society in her influential works *The Cultural Politics of Emotion* and *Queer Phenomenology*.

(*ma ʿānī*)" of fear, sadness, and joy that one obtains from the intellectually understood component of songs.[47] And they are not volitional or part of a deliberate rational interpretative process (at least in the case of music).[48] They are "something" that just "appear[s] in [humans] without them having any control over it," to return to the passage from the *Kīmiyā* above.[49] Sometimes they can only be described as "strange states (*aḥwāl gharība*)," as al-Ghazālī says in the middle of this passage.

But al-Ghazālī is certain of one thing: These "impression[s]" (*āthār*) and "state[s]" (*al-ḥālāt*) are *felt*.[50] He repeats this several times in this passage. Underlining their enduring nature and æffective power, he says that even if the "cause" of the "impression" is forgotten, "the impression (*al-athar*) remains in his soul (*nafs*) and he *feels it* (*yuḥiss bihi*). . . . [H]e still *feels* the impression subsequently" (emphasis mine).[51] The feeling may be akin to "delight" or "sadness," but often it just "a strange (*gharība*) state that neither the words delight nor sadness express clearly," and for which one "does not find for it a fitting and clear expression." These impressions and their states sometimes just *feel* weird and wondrous in a way that no words seem capable of conveying exactly. They are an unnamable æffect impinging on the body's somato-affective sensorium.

al-Ghazālī vacillates several times throughout this passage on whether specific socially legible categories of feeling such as delight, sadness, fear—i.e., emotions—can capture the way these states and impressions feel.[52] At first, he seems to believe

47. See chapter 4 for discussion of the somato-affective dimension of *ma ʿānī*.

48. See subsequent discussion in this chapter, and also chapters 3–4 and the Conclusion, for how "impression[s]" (*āthār*) are imbricated with rational processes of understanding and meditation.

49. This understanding of music can ultimately be traced back to the Islamic and Greek philosophical traditions (e.g., al-Kindī, *Ikhwān al-safāʾ*). See Weinrich, "Sensing Sound."

50. Compare this discussion of *āthār* to their conceptualization and treatment in Islamic philosophy: Key, *Language*, 163–68; Black, "Intentionality." Klein comments in passing on the connection between these "trace[s]" and their ability to induce emotional states such as "happiness" and "sadness" in his brief discussion of this passage ("Music, Rapture and Pragmatics," 232). Implicit in his introduction and conclusion is that these emotional states contribute in some way to the general "nonverbal" "experient[ial]" form of knowledge he argues al-Ghazālī champions (in addition to the verbally "mediated" forms), but this is not an argument he develops explicitly.

51. He also mentions that "impressions" are "felt" (*maḥsūs*) even by animals; see *Iḥyāʾ*, 2:273.

52. The view that music and Qurʾānic recitation convey affect/emotions or evoke them in listeners is widespread in scholarship in these fields. See, for example: Nelson, *The Art of Reciting the Qur'an*; Gade, *Perfection Makes Practice*; Wolf, *The Voice in the Drum*; Schofield, "Emotions in Indian Music History"; Schofield, "Learning to Taste the Emotions"; Lunn and Schofield, "Delight"; Schofield, "Music, Art and Power"; Gill, *Melancholic Modalities*; Osborne, "The Experience of the Recited Qurʾan"; Osborne, "Aural Epistemology"; Elias, *Alef Is for Allah*, 52–53. In addition to role of music in evoking emotions, Elias also points to philosophical literature that gives colors this power too. Several scholars have even pointed specifically to the link between *āthār* (and derivations thereof) and emotions in the context of music. See Weinrich, "Sensing Sound," 50–58; Schofield, "Emotions in Indian Music History," 186–88; Schofield, "Learning to Taste the Emotions," 414, 417; Shahid, "Saif Al-Mulūk," 236, 294. While all these studies are consonant with my reading here, I want to lean in more on the way in which these *āthār* can be a much

they are nameable. Then he backtracks and suggests other times they are not. But, in the final section of this passage, he proffers what he seems to think is the best approximation of what the feelings of these strange impressions and states can be labeled as: "Sometimes (*qad*) they are called 'desire' (*shawq*)."[53] It is a desire, though, of a special type, and here we return to the examples of ʿIrāqī and the sexually frustrated young man. This sense of full-body yearning is akin to the visceral yet poorly understood feeling experienced by the budding Sufi lover and sexually naive youth: The powerful inner sense of desire for something that is paradoxically not known, yet still exerting an indelible force on one's inner sensorium. It escapes easy conceptualization and articulation, but it conquers people entirely, consuming them like a fire—an image al-Ghazālī and the anonymous biographer of ʿIrāqī both use. On one hand this feeling is "strange and wondrous (*ʿajīb*)." But it can also be disturbing at the same time, as both note too, because, as al-Ghazālī says, when the "heart demands something [but] it does not know what, it becomes perplexed, bewildered, and disturbed. It is like one who is being strangled and does not know how to free himself."[54] This striking final image is worth pausing to consider. What does it say about the nature of music's meaning, realized through its elusive "impressions" and "states," to compare it to such an experience?

The Arabic words he uses to discuss these "impressions" in the *Iḥyāʾ* are permutations of the *ʾ(hamza)-thāʾ-rāʾ* root and circle around meanings having to do with affecting, influencing, producing an effect on/in, or even making a physical impression upon something. It is, as he characterizes it in Persian in the *Kīmiyā*, something that moves inside us—a *ḥarakat*.[55] This semantic web suggests that he sees music's meaning experienced as a type of internal energy or force.[56] It does not present itself to our mind for intellectual comprehension; it moves in and operates on our body and soul.[57] It imprints or impresses its meaning on us by pushing or exerting itself upon us. It leaves marks.

---

wider range of less-easy-to-pin-down feelings rather than the more limited number of socially and intellectually constructed and categorizable emotions, as I will show in the coming chapters.

53. al-Ghazālī's tentative willingness to give a label to this feeling here is echoed in the other passages discussed in this chapter and chapter 3, where he specifies that music induces certain æffective responses, which he does name there. But his equivocating qualification here still evinces a lingering uncertainty or discomfort with affixing any particular label to these diffuse yet powerful internal assemblages of feeling.

54. al-Ghazālī, *Iḥyāʾ*, 2:292.

55. See also quote in final paragraph of chapter 4 where al-Ghazālī discusses "poetic verses and music" as "mov[ing] [the heart] in a way not found in any other."

56. Relatedly, see chapter 3 for al-Ghazālī's discussion of *wajd* as a force and chapters 4 and 5 for his discussion of *fanāʾ* in similar terms.

57. Weinrich's observation that al-Ghazālī's discussion of music is "mainly concerned with sensations and processes that are triggered through listening" comes close to this idea, but she ultimately sees these "sensations and processes" as "channeled" as vague "religious experiences," rather than as a component of an alternative felt epistemic vector ("Sensing Sound," 2).

We need to be careful, though, at this juncture for two reasons. First, talking abstractly about some woolly notion of music's meaning as ill-defined "impressions" or a New Age-y "force" or "energy" runs the risk of de-legitimizing and rendering academically suspect this important epistemic vector.[58] Second, as we saw in the discussion of the problems with reducing love to an abstract concept in the previous chapters, we need to be careful not to intellectualize this felt form of meaning creation or gloss over it in a rush to get to the "real" source of meaning in *samāʿ*, that is, the poem. This is where affect theory's formulation of affect-as-force can lend analytical aid and precision to our study of Sufism. I would offer that we should understand these ill-defined "impressions" in al-Ghazālī's account as æffects. (We could even potentially translate *āthār* using this book's "æffect" neologism in many contexts, though I will not push this point here.) We need to be okay with the strange way they feel and their ability to elude capture in language and its socially legible categories of feeling (i.e., emotions) because these "impressions" exercised tremendous power in Sufi spiritual formation, in music, and, as al-Ghazālī gestures to in the last quoted passage, even seemingly in forms of "contemplation" (*tafakkur*) as well. They were not subtle or marginal actors. They were so deeply felt that al-Ghazālī deems it appropriate to compare the experience of them to the explosive cacophony of somato-affective responses felt when being strangled. While luckily few of us will have experienced being strangled, anyone who has seriously choked on food or almost drowned will testify to the fact that the combined response of one's physical and emotional resources in that moment is astounding. As a tsunami of adrenaline surges through every limb, the body mobilizes all physical capabilities to free itself. Utter terror overcomes the mind as the very real possibility of imminent death suddenly and unexpectedly presents itself. The complex array of bodily *feelings* in that moment cannot be put into words. But they will *leave a mark* on you for the rest of your life, and they are often so meaningful that they lead those who escape death to change their life in profound ways.

al-Ghazālī's image does offer some hope on this front to his audience. He says that this musically induced longing feels like being strangled *for the person who does not know how to free themselves*. What this suggests is that the metaphor of strangulation should only be taken so far, or rather the unstated conclusion of it

58. Jean During suggests something along these lines when he says that the *samāʿ* musicians invest music with their "psychic energy," which they pass to their listeners through their music, relying on the audience members to "decipher the message and 'decode the spiritual lesson' (*ʿibrat*) hidden in the music." Or, he offers, this energy could be framed through "'energetics,' a science which is part of Western 'New Age' psychology." I think During is correct when he concludes this section by saying, "For the Sufi singer or musician, the essential thing in the art of interpretation is the circulation of this energy" ("What Is Sufi Music?," 286). But I think we need to be a bit more specific in how we conceptualize this "energy" because dehistoricized and analytically imprecise framings of this very real dimension of musical meaning will contribute to its continued occlusion and marginalization.

needs to be played out in the reader's head. This untargeted, and thus unrelievable, desire does produce a powerfully disturbing somato-affective response that overwhelms the body and makes it feel on the verge of death. *But* if one figures out how to direct this longing, that release is as sweet as that moment when the object standing between you and the rest of your life is finally removed and that first gasp of air enters your hungry lungs. The experience of desire is wondrous, but it is disturbing too, particularly if the destruction it wreaks in its conquest of the person is not followed by a channeling of it. This is ʿIrāqī's experience after that *samāʿ* session. He is disturbed, but he does not understand, nor can he conceptualize and express, the felt sense of "turmoil" that has conquered him.

What al-Ghazālī's accounts of music's role in *samāʿ* make clear is that we do not *necessarily* need to seek the source of ʿIrāqī's internal disequilibrium in the lyrics of the song. They would likely have played an important role too, as we will see in the following chapter. But it is just as likely that the *qalandar* band's music is responsible for awakening that aperture of ʿIrāqī's heart—its sweet tune and perfect rhythm exciting the first taste of desire in ʿIrāqī by providing an earthly "illustration" (*namūdgārī*) of the beauty of the celestial world. As in the case of the bodily "illustrations" of beauty in the preceding chapter, the key point here is not to reduce the meaning of music to this—that is, to serving merely as a reflection of divine beauty. This may be what it *is*, but it is not what or how it *means*. These are two different things. Music means through those strange and wondrous "impressions" that al-Ghazālī sees fit only to call "longing" (*shawq*). Music, in short, speaks the ancient language of æffect. It educates as it æffects the participants' somato-affective bodies. Before the lyrics ever begin, it provides the unconverted the first lesson in the Sufi Path of Love by making them desire, by forcing their body to become its subject and experience its totalizing somato-affective logic—to get strangled by it.[59]

"THERE IS A SECRET IN THIS SONG/VEIL (*PARDAH*)": MUSIC AS AN EPISTEMIC AND ONTOLOGICAL FORCE

ʿIrāqī experienced the *qalandars*' *samāʿ* as a person whose heart was yet "simple and empty of . . . love and longing," as al-Ghazālī phrases it above. This pre-Path-of-Love-conversion ʿIrāqī needed something different from the *samāʿ* session that day than the spiritual leader ʿIrāqī of the later *samāʿ* session portrayed in his biography. The beauty of the music still needed to move within this

59. Although I will not focus on this point here, we also should resist the temptation to collapse the meaning of a song into only the linguistic meaning of the words that are sung; how a singer modulates their voice in singing the words of a song transforms their meaning. Rūmī, a prolific historical practitioner of *samāʿ*, argues that the *samāʿ* singer sets the æffective tone for the ritual through the way they sing; see *Fīhi mā fīhi*, 127. Schofield also makes this point in a later Islamicate musical context ("Learning to Taste the Emotions," 414.)

spiritually immature ʿIrāqī and act upon his heart, destabilizing the foundation of his old self and exerting upon him the "strange and wondrous" "impression" that al-Ghazālī eventually concludes is an æffective force most akin to "desire" (*shawq*). He still needed to be converted to the Path of Love. But how would the spiritually mature ʿIrāqī of the grand *samāʿ* assembly of Tūqāt, whom al-Ghazālī would characterize as one "whose heart ha[s] been conquered (*ghālib*) by the love of God," experience music, and how would it mean to him?

The most common response given to this question in the existing scholarship on *samāʿ* is a variation of the "emotional intensifier" answer.[60] That is, music acts to inflame or intensify the love that is already in the hearts of those "conquered" by it. al-Ghazālī himself lends credence to this position, arguing near the end of the quote from the *Kīmiyā* above that *samāʿ* remains central for mature Sufi lovers because their "fire [of love] will burn hotter"—a point he reiterates in different ways at various points throughout both his works treating *samāʿ*.[61] The "burn hotter" phrasing is taken as proof of music's supplementary role. It is a catalytic substance or tool that helps amp up the general æffective atmosphere of the ritual, but in essence it is separate from the real meaningful action of *samāʿ*. To put it in terms of the metaphoric image used here, music stands like an attendant on the side of the action, fanning the flames of love that engulf the ceremony and burn up its participants' hearts. At most, the spiritually attuned participant may be able to discern a symbolic meaning (*maʿnā*) or two in its tune.

But this reading of *samāʿ*'s role in the spiritual life of mature Sufi lovers misunderstands, or at least understands incompletely, how medieval Sufis saw music operating in this sacred ceremony. Music, as we saw above, is constitutive of meaning in *samāʿ*, and æffectively so. It is not outside of it nor reducible to its linguistically mediated dimensions of meaning or the spiritual inferences (*maʿānī*) its participants arrive at. This comes through when we recontextualize al-Ghazālī's famous "burn hotter" remark in his larger discussion. He prefaces this remark by saying: "But when a heart is not empty and is engaged with something, that [thing it is occupied with] *starts to move*, and like a fire that is blown upon, it increases in intensity" (emphasis added). As we see in more detail in the following chapter, what the participant's heart "is engaged with" does guide their hermeneutic approach, and there is usually continuity between this prior æffective state of the heart and the transformed state (*ḥāl*) *samāʿ* produces in it. But what the music actually means in this context is how it transforms the listener's state. Its meaning is the state "transformation" it effects, as al-Ghazālī will term it in passages I discuss in the next chapter.

Here, al-Ghazālī frames this transformation as movement—*ḥarakat*—the same term he uses to talk about those difficult-to-define, though powerful, internal

60. See the review of scholarship on *samāʿ* in the second section of this chapter.

61. See, for example, al-Ghazālī, *Kīmiyā*, 358, 361; al-Ghazālī, *Iḥyāʾ*, 2:273, 277.

assemblages of feeling that music creates and through which it makes its wordless meaning known to us. These internal movements are what he is comparing to the fire, which "increases in intensity" or "burns hotter" when "blown upon" by *samāʿ*. It is another way of metaphorically imagining the ways these "impression[s]" push on us and move things in us: They can also feel more intense. But these movements, of whatever type, are not separate from the meaning of the music for an audience member. If music increases the "intensity" of one of these movements, it is not because it is an external catalytic agent that throws its gasoline on a fire created separately by a poem or beloved. It is because that is what it means, which is to say, that is what it feels like (at least for that listener).[62] Intensity *means* something. Music, remember, is flint in al-Ghazālī's formulation; it can create its own (æffecto-epistemic) fires when it strikes the human heart; it does not just fan the flames of others' creation.[63]

This understanding of music as its own powerful epistemic force diverges from those of the existing literature on *samāʿ*, but it is very much in tune with medieval presentations of music's role in Sufi life. In fact, in some Sufi accounts, music functions not only as an epistemic force, but also at times even as an ontological one.[64] We see an example par excellence of this much more dynamic perspective on music—appropriately—in the final poem written by ʿIrāqī and performed by Ḥasan in the *samāʿ* ceremony in Tūqāt. It is a new poetic tale of creation. I discussed one dimension of this poem's striking series of epistemological claims in the preceding chapter. But the poem presents an even richer—more musically inspired—picture than I gave it credit for there.

1 Who knows which instrument is the instrument of Love's merriment
whose bow sets the nine spheres in motion, searching?
2 It brought the whole universe into a dance with one stroke of the bow;
the soul of the world is itself a melody of this musician (*pardah-navāz*).
3 The world is a veiled echo of this tune (*pardah*)—who knows
what this song (*pardah*) is and what secret is in this tune/veil (*pardah*)?
4 There is a secret in this song/veil (*pardah*)—when you come upon it
(lit. experientially know it/*bi-shināsī*),
you will understand (*dānī*) why The Real is in the binds of *majāz*.
5 You will understand why Maḥmūd's mind
is always distraught in the tresses of Ayāz,

62. On the highly subjective assignment of meaning to phenomena in Sufism, see chapter 3.

63. al-Ghazālī gestures to music's ability to engender æffects in this metaphor, but he also mentions that songs can help create desire (*shawq*) in someone if it is not already their heart in a passage about devotional poetry for *hajj* (*Iḥyāʾ*, 2:273). See also passage in chapter 3 in which al-Ghazālī indicates that *samāʿ* both "excites and strengthens" æffective states. Relatedly, see discussion in chapter 3 about *tawājud*, or the practice of "æffecting *wajd*," as another illustration of how *samāʿ* does not just intensify feelings; it seeks to cultivate them—that is, both create *and* foster affect.

64. Lawrence also gestures to this point in his passing observation that "music was both the ontological and epistemological sine qua non of Islamic mysticism" ("The Early Chishtī Approach to Samāʿ," 71).

6 (and) why the beauty of the fair ones' faces—who all are the essence of coquetry—
is in need of the need of the lovers' hearts.
7 Love appears each moment in a different color,
in one place coquetry, in another need.
8 When it appears in the form of the lover, all is painful pining;
when it appears in the garb of the beloved, all is merriment and music.
9 From that spark that Love struck from the fair faces of the beautiful idols,
the lovers' hearts are all on fire and melting and withering away.
10 The Path of Love is very close and merry;
any way other than this is long and far.
11 A drunk that is drunk on the Path of Love,
his merry drunken dreams are the very essence of prayer.
12 Last night when they did not permit us to enter the Sufi lodge,
I went to the door of the winehouse and saw it was shut too.
13 But then a song arose from within the winehouse:
"ʿIrāqī, lose yourself, for the door of the winehouse is open!"[65]

Linking from primordial time (instrumental) music and the twin æffective forces of love and merriment, ʿIrāqī portrays God as a musician (*pardah-navāz*) who uses his "instrument of Love's merriment" (*sāz-i ṭarab-i ʿishq*) to engender the universe, bringing its "nine spheres in motion, searching" and "the whole universe into a dance with one stroke of the bow" (lines 1–2).[66] The world's soul is a "melody" of God, and the material world "a veiled echo of this tune" (lines 2–3). Music and æffect are running the show, playing the role of *the* combined ontological force animating the world and its celestial and earthly bodies (lines 2–3). The way ʿIrāqī links Love (God), music, and "merriment" (*ṭarab*)—an Arabic-derived noun that captures the same assemblage of feelings as our familiar merry adjectival friend *khwush*—echoes al-Ghazālī's discussions above. Music speaks through æffect, and, according to ʿIrāqī's portrayal here, it is a creative force that brings the world to life—"into a dance"—too.[67]

Words are conspicuously absent from this creation story—an absence that the *samāʿ* audience would have felt poignantly because of its contrast with the traditional Qurʾānic account. The Qurʾān presents God as bringing the world into existence through the spoken command "Be!" (*kun*): "He says to it 'Be, and it is'" (*yaqūlu lahu kun fayakūnu*).[68] It privileges *logos* as God's tool of creation. It is a verbal imperative that animates the universe. Ontology proceeds from language, and language, with the aid of the human intellect (*ʿaql*), thus naturally forms the primary bridge by which humanity can come to know God and about existence

65. ʿIrāqī, *Kulliyyāt-i ʿIrāqī (Muḥtasham)*, 322.

66. On the role of musical performance in eliciting *ṭarab*, see Moukheiber, "Gendering Emotions."

67. al-Ghazālī also links God and his way of communicating with his followers to the æffects of *ṭarab*, arguing that His goal in sending the holy scriptures was to fill humanity with joy and desire (*Iḥyāʾ*, 2:279).

68. This phrase appears eight times in the Qurʾān (2:117, 3:47, 3:59, 6:73, 16:40, 19:35, 36:82, and 40:68). See Nasr, et al., *The Study Quran*. Translations of the Qurʾān here are mine. Arabic text referenced from A. Ali, *Al-Qurʾān*.

itself (e.g., through the Qur'ān, or through the prophetic example preserved in the *ḥadīth*).[69] Though superficially these two creation accounts seem to posit mutually exclusive origin stories, they are better read as symbolically representing competing epistemological impulses within the Islamic world.[70] Their disparity indexes and metaphorically distills the wide spectrum of intellectual and spiritual approaches to the question of "How do we come to know God and the nature of his creation?" Despite their sometimes theatrical and seemingly categorical rejection of the rational (*ma'qūl*) and "(linguistically) transmitted" (*manqūl*) fields of the traditional Islamic sciences (e.g., *tafsīr*, *ḥadīth*, *kalām*, philosophy), Sufis do not deny the power of linguistic and intellectually mediated forms of knowledge to guide human behavior and reveal (certain limited) aspects of the nature of God and the universe.[71] But Sufis believe that there are other, more efficacious modes of drawing closer to God and learning the true nature of divine realities. God does more than speak to believers' rational minds.

'Irāqī brings these other epistemic modalities together in the figure of the "secret" in this poem. The secret is in the merry "tune" (*pardah*) that Love plays on its instrument, but that tune is also the earthly world of embodiment (line 2). Music and the bodies of the *majāzī*um are fused here as *the* primary sites for revealing knowledge about God. In my reading of this poem in the previous chapter, I discussed the embodiment half of this dual-natured "secret"—that is, the realization that God is the basis of the entire universe and thus is within everything to a limited degree. Since God is Love and Beauty, as the Sufis of the Path of Love insist, He is especially apparent in the beautiful, love-evoking bodies on Earth—the Ayāzs and Ḥasans of the world (lines 4–6). *But* God makes Himself known to humanity in more than just beautiful earthly forms too. He has other tools for forming lovers.

Before the secret becomes embodied, it is wrapped in a merry musical tune. At first glance, these two modalities of conveying divine secrets, musical notes and bodies, seem very different. But, as al-Ghazālī tells us, these both, at their root, are "illustrations" of celestial beauty and proportionality that disclose their secrets to our soul through their sweetness and the desire they evoke—through, that is, the way they make us *feel*. Nothing captures this experiential epistemological reality

69. See Rahman and Chittick, "'Aql," on *'aql* in Qur'ān as means of knowing God through scripture. See Boer and Rahman, "'Aḳl," on linking together *'aql* and logos.

70. As shown by the example from 'Irāqī's *Lama'āt* discussed in the opening of chapter 3, where he imagines the Qur'ānic creative command "Be!" as a song, language and music are not necessarily opposing forces in Sufism. They often work together to convey æffective and intellectual forms of meaning. I have separated my discussion of them in this book to help illustrate the different ways they can operate as independent, though, usually mutually re-enforcing, vectors of meaning. See chapters 3, 4, and 5, where I bring language, in the form of poetry, back into the discussion.

71. For an example of a dramatic Sufi account purportedly wholesale rejecting transmitted and intellectual forms of knowledge, see the story of 'Irāqī's conversion in chapter 1.

more succinctly than the scene in Tūqāt. As Ḥasan performs ʿIrāqī's poem, he functions in this dual epistemic role. His musical and physical presences are both earthly forms of flint that will produce the "spark[s]" (line 9) and "strange and wondrous" impressions that æffect Sufi bodies, conquering them and teaching them what it feels like to be a Sufi lover.

CODA: FELT MEANING

The Introduction opened with a scene from the epic *samāʿ* session of a spiritually mature ʿIrāqī with the legendarily beautiful and talented *shāhid*-cum-musician Ḥasan. Chapters 1 and 2 discussed ʿIrāqī's first (recorded) *samāʿ* session with the *qalandar*s who converted him to the Path of Love. The centrality of *samāʿ* to ʿIrāqī's spiritual life is not surprising. As a ritual, its importance is nearly unparalleled in Sufism, especially among those Sufis who cleave to the Path of Love. It also provides a perfect window onto medieval Sufism for this study because it brings together—indeed, performs—the arguments that I am making throughout the first three chapters of this book.

Samāʿ is a multifaceted performance in which language in the form of poetry shares the stage, so to speak, with multiple other vectors of nondiscursive meaning produced by the presence of beautiful musicians, their music, and the carefully curated ambience of the ritual. Most scholarship in Sufi studies has focused primarily to date on linguistically mediated meaning production in *samāʿ*. These logo- or ratiocentric approaches to medieval Sufism study the central ritual of the embodied amatory spirituality of the Path of Love as if its meaning can be located primarily in the participants' act of decrypting the recited poem's symbolic references to archetypal spiritual "meanings" and Sufi metaphysical treatises.

But in the scenes of *samāʿ* I have analyzed in this and the previous chapter, large parts of Sufi meaning are æffectively, rather than linguistically or intellectually, realized—in how the performance context (and its bodies) makes the participants feel, or not feel, properly, and in the ways the accompanying music moves them. To see these nonlinguistic dimensions of meaning, we need to decenter the text and broaden our scope of what we consider to be spiritually *meaningful* in this ritual performance. Meaning in medieval Sufism is about much more than the words recited in its rituals or recorded on the pages of its textual products, a point that has understandably been obscured at times by our inescapable reliance on texts for the study of medieval Islamic culture. Sufi meaning cannot be determined through a intellectualizing spiritual hermeneutic or symbolist reading of the words of the poem *alone*. It must be *felt*, too.

3

Getting into the Habit(us) of Being a Lover

Æffective Hermeneutics and the Formation of Sufi Feeling Subjects in Samāʿ

In chapter 18 of his theoretical treatise on love, the *Lamaʿāt*, ʿIrāqī tells another version of the Islamic story of creation.[1] It is similar in many respects to the versified account he provides in the final poem of his grand *samāʿ* session in Tūqāt with Ḥasan, discussed in the previous two chapters. The scene: the lover is lying in repose in the pre-eternity before existence. He has not yet even seen the face of the Beloved because it does not yet exist. There is only Love. Suddenly the "tune of '*Be!*'" (*naghmah-yi kun*), the divine Qurʾānic command of creation, "stirs him from the sleep of nonexistence."[2] Love places its familiar "fiery agitation" (*shūrī*) in his being (*nihād*) and "overtakes [him]" (*mustawlī shud*) because, as ʿIrāqī says in an inset Arabic hemistich, "Sometimes the ear falls in love before the eye." A poetic song (*tarānah*) forever ends his inner and outer tranquility, bringing it into a "motion and dance" (*ḥarakat va raqṣ*) that will never stop as long as he exists. Creation, again, is portrayed as the initiation of a cosmic love affair, even as an inaugural *samāʿ* of sorts. And, like his earlier discussed poem, the music or "tune" in this version is presented as both the primordial ontological and epistemic agent: "Tasting that tune" (*ẕawq-i ān naghmah*), as ʿIrāqī says, initiates an æffective transformation that entrains his somato-affective body to be a lover—that is, to move and dance and feel and, quite literally, *be* in the world in particular ways.

But this account also foregrounds two other components of the Sufi ritual of *samāʿ* that this chapter will focus on. The music that initiates creation is no longer doing a solo, as in ʿIrāqī's poem of the last chapter. It is now accompanied by words, such as "Be!" and the verses of the poetic ditty (*tarānah*), and it results in

1. ʿIrāqī, *Kulliyyāt-i ʿIrāqī (Muḥtasham)*, 505.
2. See the discussion of the traditional Qurʾānic accounts of creation in chapter 2.

specific spiritual experiences, the "motion and dance" and "ecstasy" (*vajd*) that ʿIrāqī reports "hearing" (*samāʿ*) these songs effect. Picking up where the last chapter left off in its consideration of the ritual experience of *samāʿ*, this chapter will center these linguistic and experiential components while also recontextualizing them as part of what al-Ghazālī argues is the full three-"station" (*maqāmāt*) or "stage" (*daraja*) unfolding of the ritual experience of *samāʿ*: "Know that the first stage of *samāʿ* is the understanding (*fahm*) of what is heard and dispatching (*tanzīl*) it to a meaning that comes to the listener. Then, understanding (*fahm*) bears the fruit of *wajd*, and then, ecstasy bears the fruit of movement (*ḥaraka*) of the body's limbs."[3] In al-Ghazālī's treatment of *samāʿ*, all three of these stages *mean* something important to the ritual participant. Each stage "bears the fruit" of the next, which we need to be careful not to interpret as establishing a hard and fast separation between them. I suggest instead that we see al-Ghazālī's fruit-bearing metaphor here as indicating a transformative cycle: A seed "bears the [metaphoric] fruit" of a sapling, which in turn becomes a more elaborated mature plant. The original seed nurtures the mature plant and remains a part of it. The sapling is not a "response to" the seed; it is the next stage of its development. You cannot separate one from another. They require each other to develop into the full form of a mature tree.

al-Ghazālī, I will argue in this chapter, also sees the hermeneutic process of meaning and knowledge production in *samāʿ* in this way. The upcycled forms—*wajd* and its æffective states (*aḥwāl*) and "movements" (*ḥarakāt*)—should not be understood as separate experiences "actualize[d]" by or "responses"/"reactions" to the original seed of meaning and knowledge creation in the first *fahm-tanzīl* stage (i.e., where most considerations of Sufi hermeneutics stop).[4] They are elaborations, ramifications, rhizomatic shoots, or even transubstantiations of the meaning the participant establishes in the first phase. They are the final fruition of the spiritual meanings (*maʿānī*) participants find in *samāʿ*, realized in the participants' somato-affective and physical bodies, as we will see. The participant's experience of these is very much part of what a poem's words and imagery *mean* to them in this ritual context. To understand what and how *samāʿ* means to its Sufi participants, we need to see the ways in which Sufi participants may also have derived forms of meaning from these rituals that are not reducible to what has often been presented as the "rational" or "intellectual" process of establishing correspondences

3. al-Ghazālī, *Iḥyāʾ*, 2:285; see also parallel Persian passage: al-Ghazālī, *Kīmiyā*, 368. Lewisohn and Ingenito likewise discuss al-Ghazālī's presentation of *samāʿ* as a three-stage process, but, as we will see subsequently, they focus on the rational/intellectual dimension of this process. See Ingenito, *Beholding Beauty*, 475–80; Lewisohn, "The Sacred Music of Islam," 23.

4. For examples of this framing of the æffects and æffective states evoked by poetry as responses or reactions to, rather than constituent of, meaning or knowledge production, see Lewisohn, "The Sacred Music of Islam," 22–28; Ingenito, *Beholding Beauty*, 30, 472 n42, 476–80, 482–83.

between poetic symbols/imagery and *ma ʿānī*.[5] We need to follow the long tail of Sufi meaning/knowledge production into the somato-affective Sufi body to see how æffects are imbricated with and even at times directing this complex process of meaning generation.

ḤĀL YOU FEEL, IS HOW YOU UNDERSTAND (*FAHM*) (STAGE 1): THE DRIVING FORCE OF ÆFFECT IN THE SUFI HERMENEUTIC MECHANISM (*TANZĪL*) AND THE ILLUSION OF RATIONAL CONTROL

Past treatments of *samāʿ* often point to a number of "locus classicus" passages from al-Ghazālī's *Iḥyāʾ* and *Kīmiyā* as anchors for their understanding of meaning production in *samāʿ*.[6] In these frequently cited selections, al-Ghazālī outlines how humans of all spiritual dispositions (or lack thereof) interpret amatory poetry and defends its use in the Sufi context—an issue that clearly remained controversial in his time. His discussion considers the legal and authoritative traditions on the topic, but he ultimately builds his central line of defense on a hermeneutic maneuver.

> And about love poetry (*al-nasīb*)—i.e., amatory poetry[7] on the cheeks, lovelocks, beauty of the physique and figure, and all other descriptions of women—there has been debate. The correct view is that it is not prohibited to compose and recite it, with or without a tune, [but] it is incumbent on the listener that he does not dispatch [the poetic images] to a specific woman, [or] if he does, that he dispatch [the poetic images] to one among his wives or slaves. And if he dispatches [the poetic images] to

5. Lewisohn is especially insistent on the "highly intellectual," as opposed to emotional or æffective, nature of Sufi meaning making in *samāʿ*, from the act of interpreting poetry to the ecstasy it can produce, arguing that "the mystical subject consciously recognizes the origin and end of his ecstasy; his transports may thus be better described as the objective fruits of a heightened consciousness rather than the subjective vagaries of a hyper-emotional imagination" ("The Sacred Music of Islam," 23–24; see also subsequent citations of Lewisohn in this chapter). Ingenito, to take another seminal case, presents a much more nuanced and expanded overview of al-Ghazālī's open hermeneutic (including a critique of the more static symbolist approach advanced by Lewisohn, 247–48, 255), but he does present the Sufi hermeneutic process as fundamentally "rational," "intellectual," "cognitive," etc., at least in the case of Saʿdī. For some representative examples see *Beholding Beauty*, 230, 254, 266, 272, 281, 290, 292, 298, 300, 302, 384, 388; see also discussion of Ingenito's work in chapter 2. Compare my treatment here to Ingenito's at 246–47, commenting on the corresponding passage from *Kīmiyā*, or 475–80, where he discusses al-Ghazālī's "psycho-physiology of the lyrical ritual" and calls it "predominantly rational" (475n51). Ingenito does touch on æffect/emotion's involvement in *samāʿ* and poetic meaning in a few places, but he does not seem to see the felt, æffective dimension as an epistemic element, or at least this is not a line of argument he develops (e.g., 343, 468–79, 520–22).

6. Lewisohn, MacDonald, and Klein (citing MacDonald) use this term "locus classicus" to refer to the two major passages from al-Ghazālī's *Iḥyāʾ* that I analyze in this chapter. Ingenito does not use this term, though he points to and discusses corresponding passages from *Kīmiyā* (*Beholding Beauty*, 165–72, 246–55, 475–80).

7. Reading *tashbīb* for *tashbīh* here, as in al-Ghazālī, *Iḥyāʾ*, 259.

> a foreign woman, then he is a sinner in thus dispatching [the poetic images this way] and letting his thoughts wander. For one of this description, they should avoid *samāʿ* categorically. Because one whom passionate love (*ʿishq*) has conquered (*ghalaba*) dispatches all [poetic images] they hear to it [their *ʿishq*], regardless of whether the words fit it or not, because there is not a word (*lafẓ*) that cannot be dispatched to meanings (*maʿānī*) through metaphor (*istiʿāra*). Hence, [when] the one whose heart has been conquered (*yaghlibu*) by the love of God [hears] the [image of] "the blackness of the lovelock," they think, for example, of the darkness of infidelity (*kufr*); [when they hear the image of] "youthful radiance of the [beloved's] cheek," [they think of] the light of faith; with the mention of [the image of] "union," [they think of] reunion with God; with the mention of [the image of] "separation," [they think of] the veiling of God for those turned away; and with the mention of [the image of] "the guardian [of the beloved] who disturbs the joy of union," [they think of] the hindrances of the world and its calamities that disturb the continuance of their intimacy with God. And intuitive discovery (*istinbāṭ*), meditation (*tafakkur*), and time for reflection (*muhla*) are not necessary when dispatching [these images] to [those meanings], for the dominant meanings in the [listener's] heart are what first comes to their understanding (*fahm*) when they hear a word (*lafẓ*).[8]

Positing a radically open and subjective hermeneutic approach, al-Ghazālī predicates the permissibility and spiritual efficacy of love poetry on how the individual listener interprets the poem's specific imagery.[9] This interpretative process is what he later characterizes as the "first stage" of *samāʿ*: the "understanding" (*fahm*) of poetry.[10]

al-Ghazālī opens his discussion of the *fahm* stage by differentiating between the numerous types of "hearing" (*samāʿ*). There is the preunderstanding form of hearing of animals—which is not true *fahm*—that they engage in when they hear music, for example.[11] Then there are three levels of hearing "with understanding (*bi-fahm*)": that of the young and "lords of lust," that of the disciples (*al-murīdīn*),

8. al-Ghazālī, *Iḥyāʾ*, 2:280. This is the "locus classicus" section of al-Ghazālī's *Iḥyāʾ* on the Sufi approach to poetic imagery that Lewisohn cites and discusses in "The Sacred Music of Islam," 17–18. al-Ghazālī reiterates this same spiritualizing interpretative method a few pages later when discussing how Sufi disciples interpret poetry (*Iḥyāʾ*, 2:285), which is the section that MacDonald describes as the "locus classicus" for Sufi hermeneutics (al-Ghazzali, "Emotional Religion" (1901a), 707n1). There are similar passages (though with much less detail) in al-Ghazālī, *Kīmiyā*, 364, 368–69. To provide the most complete picture possible, I will discuss all these passages together in this chapter.

9. al-Ghazālī's discussion of his hermeneutic approach to poetry is spread across his works, but the most important passages are *Iḥyāʾ*, 2:280–88; *Kīmiyā*, 364–65. For another discussion of al-Ghazālī's "open interpretative" framework, see Ingenito, *Beholding Beauty*, 246–49. Cf. Leaman, "Poetry and the Emotions in Islamic Philosophy," 149–50.

10. It is clear in the quote discussed earlier in the chapter that he sees this first stage as named "*fahm*," even though he also mentions "*tanzīl*" as well. In the following sentence he corroborates this reading by characterizing it as "The first station: On understanding (*fī fahm*)."

11. See the previous chapter on how music communicates meaning to animals *and* humans without requiring *fahm*.

and that of those whose self has been annihilated in *fanāʾ*.[12] Members of all these groups hear and understand (*fahm*) the "surface meanings" of the words and images (*ẓawāhir*) uttered in a poem—their literal "meaning" in everyday parlance—in the same way. This yields an initial literal understanding, what I will call a "*fahm*1." What ultimately differentiates these three groups of listeners from one another is what they then do with this *fahm*1 of the poet's imagery. He terms this second part of the *fahm*ing stage "*tanzīl*," the "dispatching" of the poetic imagery to a referent outside of the poem. He presents *tanzīl* as an active and dynamic process. Its interpretative energies can be trained on poetry of any type to make seemingly any meanings out of its imagery, even if they seem patently opposed to the author's original intent.[13] As he says above, "there is not a word (*lafẓ*) that cannot be dispatched to meanings (*maʿānī*) through metaphor (*istiʿāra*)," even, he emphasizes, "whether the words fit it or not."[14]

Each of these groups of listeners who hear "with understanding" approach the *tanzīl*ing of *fahm*1 differently. They each build meaning from the poem by attaching its imagery to different external referents, but their hermeneutic efforts achieve dramatically different results based on "the capaciousness of the listener's knowledge and purity of their heart." For the young and "lords of lust" of the second group, the bodily charms of their earthly beloveds will come to their mind when they hear the images of the poetic beloved's "lovelock" and "cheek" and their sweet moments of illicit rendezvous when the obligatory "union" of poetic lovers is mentioned. This is where these metaphoric images are dispatched for them. This type of *tanzīl*ing is "forbidden" (*ḥarām*) unless the earthly beloved that the poetic imagery is dispatched to is licit, such as a wife or slave.[15] It is this second step in their "understanding"—a *fahm*2—that establishes what the poem's imagery represents to them. The poem ultimately becomes about their earthly beloved. This is what it means to them.

But these images do not necessarily need to be interpreted in this mundane erotic manner. The spiritually attuned, those true "disciples" of the third group, can also read these same images as pointers (*ishārāt*) or cryptic allusions (*rumūz*) to divine realities or metaphysical concepts. It is on the interpretative process of this group that al-Ghazālī focuses.[16] After listening to and understanding (*fahm*)

12. The entire treatment of these different types of hearing stretches from al-Ghazālī, *Iḥyāʾ* (1873), 285–89.

13. In *Kīmiyā* al-Ghazālī uses the verb *bar zanī* in one place to correspond to *tanzīl* in the Arabic discussion, and in another he uses the phrase "[mundane image] *fahm konand* (understand) as [spiritual meaning]." In a later passage, he uses the word *tanzīl* with *kardan* to make a compound Persian verb. See *Kīmiyā*, 364, 368.

14. He uses a similar phrase in al-Ghazālī, *Iḥyāʾ*, 2: 285 and 288.

15. al-Ghazālī also discusses this form of interpreting love poetry in reference to illicit earthly lovers in *Iḥyāʾ*, 2:280, 285; *Kīmiyā*, 364.

16. There is some ambiguity in al-Ghazālī's accounts regarding what role he sees the *fahm* stage, with its hermeneutic mechanism of *tanzīl*, playing for those who have experienced self-annihilation

the literal meaning of the words (*fahm1*), their hermeneutic tool directs them away from potential mundane erotic referents and toward celestial referents among the spiritual *maʿānī* of the supernal. In contrast to the "lords of lust," when Sufi disciples "[hear] the [image of] 'the blackness of the lovelock,' they think, for example, of the darkness of infidelity (*kufr*); [when they hear the image of] 'youthful radiance of the [beloved's] cheek,' [they think of] the light of faith; with the mention of [the image of] 'union,' [they think of] reunion with God," as al-Ghazālī says in the passage above. Their *tanzīl* makes these "spiritual inference[s]," establishing "spiritualized correspondences" between these mundane poetic images and higher spiritual meanings (*maʿānī*) of the supernal, to use Ingenito's terminology.[17] While they may agree with the more carnally inclined lovers on the *fahm1* of poetry, their *fahm2*s could not be more different. The same words, the same poem, do not mean the same thing to them.

At this point, the reader is likely wondering why I have insisted on awkwardly using the passive voice in the previous two paragraphs discussing *tanzīl*. The reason is tactical: I want to focus attention here on what drives this central interpretative mechanism of the Sufi hermeneutic. Because it is not the individual listener, at least not in the traditional sense of the rational director "I" who controls normal quotidian mental and bodily functions. al-Ghazālī, in terming this first stage of *samāʿ fahm*—a term for "understanding" that typical denotes an "intellectual," "conceptual," or "rational" form of comprehension—has been read as indicating that the listener's rational faculty is driving this first stage of *samāʿ*'s hermeneutics.[18] But when we dive deeper into al-Ghazālī's treatment of this stage, its primarily rational basis becomes hard to sustain.

(*fanāʾ*). His discussion focuses more on the details of the hermeneutic process for the Sufi disciples than this final elite group of the *fanāʾ*-ed. When discussing the self-annihilated in this section, he says seemingly conflicting things. On one hand, he refers to them as occupying the "level of the upright ones in understanding (*fahm*) and ecstasy"—an appellation that he gives to the *fanāʾ*-ed at the end of the story of Abū Ḥasan al-Nūrī (d. 907), discussed in chapter 5 (where I delve into the Sufi experience of *fanāʾ* in detail). But then he also says that the *samāʿ* of the self-annihilated is "not by means of the *fahm*-ing of *maʿnī*" (*nah bar sabīl-i fahm-i maʿnī bāshad*") and that they "do . . . not understand (*fahm*) anything other than God anymore" because they directly "hear . . . for God and through God and in God and from God." See *Kīmiyā*, 369; *Iḥyāʾ*, 2:288. Compare to Klein ("Music, Rapture and Pragmatics," 228), who sees al-Ghazālī as including *fahm* as part of the self-annihilated's engagement with poetry in *Iḥyāʾ*.

17. Ingenito, *Beholding Beauty*, 247, 251.

18. Lewisohn cites this passage and uses it to argue that since al-Ghazālī employs the word "understanding" (*fahm*), this indicates that *samāʿ* has an entirely "*intellectual* basis"—that is, not æffective ("The Sacred Music of Islam," 23, emphasis original). Ingenito's perspective is more nuanced. He does at one point in his discussion of the parallel passage in *Kīmiyā* translate *fahm* as "[rational] understanding" (brackets original). But he does see æffect involved in this stage to some degree, characterizing it as a "semi-rational and aesthetic response" and as having a "twofold irrational/rational aspect" (with "irrational" here meaning "emotional") and "stand[ing] out for its mix of spiritual and mundane forms of sensorial emotionality." As discussed previously, however, affect/emotion is there in the background;

If we look again at the "locus classicus" passage from al-Ghazālī quoted above, we see that he opens it by defining amatory poetry and briefly discussing practical examples of its licit and illicit use. He then proceeds *not* directly to elaborate the mechanism of *tanzīl* and the *ma ʿānī* to which it dispatches the listeners' initial "understandings" (*fahm*1s), but rather to prefatory framing that explains what drives *tanzīl*. It is not a tool that each individual can freely manipulate with their rational mind—even if "they" are the ones doing it. al-Ghazālī is very clear on this point: It is a hermeneutic implement that must be aimed, and it is what "rules" or has "conquered" (a derivation of the same *ghayn-lām-bā* ʾ root we have seen repeatedly) the individual's heart that directs the interpretative energies of *tanzīl*. Those who have been "conquered (*ghalaba*)" by love (*ʿishq*) for an earthly woman will, for example, "dispatch . . . all [poetic images] they hear" to her, as al-Ghazālī says above. But if the individual's heart has been "conquered (*yaghlibu*) by the love of God," then these same poetic images (and the bodies of any earthly beloveds present, as Ingenito argues) are seen as signs pointing to higher spiritual "meanings" or "realities" (*ma ʿānī*) of the supernal.[19]

In the passage above, al-Ghazālī refers at the most general level to the different types of love that have "conquered" the hearts of these two groups as being what directs *tanzīl*. But *tanzīl*'s hermeneutic powers are actually far more fine-grained than this. Any change, even slight, in the listener's internal state will impact the final *fahm*2 meaning it makes for the listener. In the second "locus classicus" passage discussing Sufi hermeneutics, al-Ghazālī provides an extensive list of different poetic motifs that he suggests correspond to different "states" (*ḥālāt*) that will "meet" the Sufi listener in his "interactions" (*mu ʿāmalāt*) in his spiritual "search."

> When he [the listener] hears the mention of rebuke, censure, assent, rejection, union, separation [from the beloved], proximity [to the beloved], distance [from the beloved], lamentation for what has passed, thirsting for what is awaited, desire for what is arriving, craving, hopelessness, desolation, companionship, faithfulness to a promise, breaking of a covenant, fear of separation, or joy upon union [with the beloved], or mention of observing the beloved, fending off the [beloved's] guardian, bathing in tears, incessant sighing, lengthening of separation, promise of union [with the beloved], and so forth that poems include in their descriptions, then inevitably some of these [poetic motifs] will fit with the state (*ḥāl*) of the disciple in their search and then that will engender a spark that will inflame the kindling (*zinād*) of his heart. Then, through that, [the heart's] fire will flare up and the emission (*inbi ʿāth*) of desire

it is not a driving force of the hermeneutic process in his framework. He also prefaces this section on the *fahm* stage of *samā* ʿ by saying (in a footnote) that "as often emphasized, what is unique to al-Ghazālī's treatment of the techniques and habits leading to the spiritual quest for the unseen is his non-institutionalized and yet *predominately rational approach* to these topics" (*Beholding Beauty*, 475–80, emphasis added).

19. On this point of æffective states of the listener directing the interpretative process of *tanzīl*, see also the parallel Persian passage: al-Ghazālī, *Kīmiyā*, 368. On Ingenito's argument on the importance of bodies, see citations to his study in chapters 1 and 2.

> (*shawq*) and agitation will strengthen through it and attack him [the listener], [and] because of it, unfamiliar states (*aḥwāl mukhālifa li-ʿādatihi*) [too], and he has a free hand [lit. wide scope] in dispatching the words (*alfāẓ*) to his states (*aḥwāl*).[20]

The implied states span the spectrum from distinctly negative æffective experiences—rebuke, rejection, and hopelessness—to manifestly positive ones—union, proximity, and "desire for what is arriving"—and a full set of polyvalent states combining the positive aspects of longing with the negative of frustrated or postponed fulfillment (e.g., craving, distance from the beloved, and even the "fear of separation," the last of which, of course, implies current union). al-Ghazālī also references the somatic response of crying ("bathing in tears") and the palpable bodily feeling of longing that he terms "thirsting for what is awaited." The range of "states" he expects Sufis to experience are not limited to these either. They could be any others "that poems include in their descriptions," too. But how could these much more specific æffective states direct *tanzīl*'s arrow of meaning? al-Ghazālī anticipates this question and immediately follows this more theoretical opening with concrete "examples" of this process of "dispatchings and understandings" (*al-tanzīlāt wa al-fuhūm*) so that the "ignorant" do not think that Sufis latch onto only the "literal" or "surface [meanings]" (*ẓawāhir*) of erotic poetry when they listen to it.[21]

One of the most intriguing examples he gives revolves around two lovers of God who both hear the same verse declaimed but have diametrically opposed responses. The story illustrates the deep reach of the listener's æffective state into the Sufi hermeneutic process, revealing that it even shapes the listener's interpretative evaluation of the relevance and metaphoric truth value of poetic imagery to the listener. It opens with the recitation of this verse: "How great is God, the omnipotent of Heaven! / Verily, the lover is in agony."[22] After the reciter of the verse concludes, the first lover announces, "You speak the truth!" But a second instantly retorts, "You lie!" The story's context presumes both lovers already have the love of God firmly ruling their hearts, yet curiously their interpretations of the verse are diametrically opposed. An anonymous "possessor of insight" in the crowd steps forward to resolve the confusing deadlock, declaring, "They both have squarely hit the bullseye."

While the perspicacious observer's adjudication perhaps defuses the budding lovers' poetic spat, it only further confounds the average reader. How can they both be correct? And would not the love of God ruling their hearts have led them to similar assessments of the veracity of this verse's meaning? It is at this point that

20. al-Ghazālī, *Iḥyāʾ*, 2:285. A similar but shorter list appears in al-Ghazālī, *Kīmiyā*, 368.

21. The "examples" (*amthila*) of *tanzīl-fahm* that al-Ghazālī propounds begin immediately following the passage immediately above and stretch for a few pages. For all examples, see al-Ghazālī, *Iḥyāʾ*, 2:285–88.

22. This example can be found in al-Ghazālī, *Iḥyāʾ*, 2:287. Compare to Klein's reading of this story in Klein, "Music, Rapture and Pragmatics," 227–228.

al-Ghazālī steps back into the narrative to explain why the "possessor of insight" is right in his enigmatic response. The first lover, he explains, is correct in his interpretation of the verse being true because he, like the lover of the verse, is himself currently in agony as a result of being denied and separated from his beloved. His interpretation of it as true is correct because the verse accords with his present internal "state," captured in the imagery of the lover pining away in pain in the second hemistich of the verse. It "fit[s] with the state (*ḥāl*) of [this] disciple," as al-Ghazālī says above. It *feels* right.

The second lover, on the other hand, is also correct in his interpretation that the verse is false, according to al-Ghazālī, because he, unlike the lover of the verse, is currently in the thralls of love and *enjoying* it. The image of the distressed, pining lover does not jibe with his internal "state," al-Ghazālī continues, because of "the seizure of his heart by hope and favorable assessment [of love]" (*ḥusn al-ẓann*). The feelings in his heart tell him this verse is not true. They guide his interpretative compass to read the imagery of the second hemistich as a poor representation of the reality of being a lover. His strong, accusatory exclamation of "You lie!" indexes a powerful internal felt sense of indignation that this line of poetry misrepresents the reality of love.

Love in a broad sense is guiding the interpretative process of both these lovers, but the broad æffective assemblage of Sufi feelings termed "love" (*ishq* or *ḥubb*) is not monolithic. The Sufi Path of Love is a long, winding, and highly variegated emotional rollercoaster, as the widely disparate æffective positions of the two lovers in this story and al-Ghazālī's theoretical preface both illustrate well. The Sufi lover can be pining away in a type of merry agony upon separation from the beloved, elated beyond bounds in union with the Beloved, excitedly on the hunt for the Beloved, or a seemingly incongruent combination of these and many others.[23] Being in love does not mean uniformity in æffect—*or* hermeneutics. The different *aḥwāl* the lovers feel in these various moments of love's journey co-constructs the meaning they derive from this poem because, as al-Ghazālī avers, all "understanding (*fahm*) differs [in accordance] with the states (*aḥwāl*) of the listener," because each listener "*tanzīl*s based on their *aḥwāl*."[24] Or, as he says in a parallel passage in the *Kīmiyā*, listeners interpret poetry in ways "agreeable with their state" (*dar khwar-i ḥāl-i īshān*).[25] Listeners' æffective states can even lead to a sort of failed or negative *tanzīl* where they reject the æffective correspondence of the poetic image and the state of their current "interactions" with God, as we saw in the preceding example.

23. Compare the complexity of the diversity of *aḥwāl* and intricacies of its felt dimension in al-Ghazālī's account here to the standard list of "qualities" of Sufi "states" presented in most general accounts of this experiential dimension of Sufi spirituality, such as in Khalil, "Ḥāl in Ṣūfism."

24. al-Ghazālī, *Iḥyāʾ*, 2:287; al-Ghazālī, *Kīmiyā*, 368.

25. al-Ghazālī, *Kīmiyā*, 364.

Aḥwāl, in sum, are not just passive abstract "psychological states," "meanings preexisting in [the] heart," or "state[s] of mind" that have some emotional content or vague æffective "qualities" to them.[26] They need to be understood as diverse somato-affective assemblages of feeling that *do* things in the bodies and minds of the Sufis. Indeed, they control *samāʿ*'s hermeneutic show. Whatever is "dominant" in the listener's heart, whatever "fits" between their heart and the æffectively charged motifs of the poem, fundamentally structures how they make meaning out of language.[27] It supplants any literal semantic "understanding[s]" of the verses (*ẓawāhir*) with an æffectively drenched *fahm2* that corresponds to what the heart wants to see in the poetic imagery, "regardless," remember, "of whether the words fit it or not." With æffect steering the hermeneutic horse, dispatching (*tanzīl*) the imagery to meanings that "fit" its desires, the heart gets what the heart wants in Sufism's æffective hermeneutics.[28]

This is a hugely consequential statement for Sufi poetics and epistemology more broadly. It means that æffect is inescapably constitutive of Sufi interpretation and knowledge. It is the dominant player in fashioning Sufi—in this case, poetic—understanding (*fahm*). The rational appraisal of the literal semantic meaning of poetic imagery (*fahm1*) yields to a *fahm2* that is inextricably imbricated with æffect. The rational-intellectual mind, in fact, as al-Ghazālī presents it, has little to no influence on the central hermeneutic/epistemological mechanism of *tanzīl*, as al-Ghazālī says in the final sentence of the first block quote above. Recourse to (presumably) rationally based modes of interpretation, such as "intuitive discovery (*istinbāṭ*), meditation (*tafakkur*), and time for reflection (*muhla*)[,]" he argues, "are not necessary" in the meaning/knowledge production process in *samāʿ* because, he concludes, "*the dominant meanings in the [listener's] heart* are

26. This is how *aḥwāl* are generally portrayed in the scholarship. Even when their æffective "qualities" are noted, this central dimension of their experience is not presented as itself a form of meaning and they are certainly not understood to be acting as an agent in the process of knowledge/self production. The quotations, and other similar framing, are from Klein, "Music, Rapture and Pragmatics," 224–28, 236, 240; Khalil, "Ḥāl in Ṣūfism." Gade, in her introduction to affect and emotion in Islam, begins to take the field in the right direction with her observation that states (*aḥwāl*)—as well as unveilings/discovery (*mukāshafāt*) and stations (*maqāmāt*)—can be thought of as "sentiments" and "qualities of experience," that "represent named 'emotions' or emotional orientations" ("Islam," 42–43).

27. See also Shahid's intriguing ethnography of modern YouTube viewers' responses to a "*samāʿ*" of *Sayf al-mulūk* for a consonant treatment equally concerned with emphasizing the æffective import of the Sufi hermeneutic ("Saif Al-Mulūk," 235–97).

28. Compare to Klein's conclusions on the nature of the Sufi hermeneutic that al-Ghazālī presents. It is not just the "*relation* between words and the listener's state of mind" (emphasis original) or "correspond[ence]" between the text and "the meanings residing in him or her" or even "in [the] heart" that drive the hermeneutic process. "The mystic" does not just "listen . . . to the poem looking for anchors to connect with images in his imagination," as Klein says in another place. The Sufi hermeneutic is not just one of "allegorical subjective interpretation" ("Music, Rapture and Pragmatics," 224, 227, 236, 240). It is driven by æffect. It is an æffective hermeneutic that forms the basis of an æffective epistemology.

what first comes to their understanding (*fahm*) when they hear a word (*lafẓ*)" (emphasis added).[29] *Fahm*ing poetry, in al-Ghazālī's account, is ultimately, predominately, an æffective process.

FINDING MEANING (*WAJD*) AND MOVING (*ḤARAKA*) TO IT IN *SAMĀ*ʿ: *WAJD, AḤWĀL, ḤARAKA*, AND MEANING'S EXPANDING WAKE (STAGES 2–3)

The traditional cogno-spiritual approach sees the conclusion of this *fahm* stage, with its pinpointing of spiritual inferences or correspondences, as *the* moment of Sufi meaning construction.[30] Meaning production proper, in this framework, begins with the literal linguistic understanding of the words and images in a verse (*fahm*1) and ends when the listener "dispatches" these poetic images and symbols to an appropriate celestial *maʿānī* of the supernal realm (*fahm*2). When the *samāʿ* participant uses this method to, for example, interpret the earthly poetic lovers' union as referring to their mystical union with God, or they understand the various marks of the beloved's beauty (radiant cheeks, tresses) to refer to aspects of faith or God's beauty, *this* is when they discover the true, spiritual meaning of the poetry (for them, at least). Poems and their words *mean* to *samāʿ* participants through the ways they *represent* different *maʿānī*. Meaning is rooted in representation. To identify a poem's "symbolic correspondences and mystical references" (i.e., the *maʿānī*), as Lewisohn refers to them, is to find its meaning in this paradigm.[31]

To be sure, establishing the *maʿānī* that correspond to the allusive poetic images is a key step in the Sufi hermeneutic process. But, as I have argued in different ways in this and previous chapters, this conception of what *samāʿ*, and even poetry itself, means is too limited.[32] The completion of *fahm*2 is not where Sufi meaning/knowledge production ends in *samāʿ*, and what a poem means in a particular performance context of *samāʿ* cannot be separated from the rest of this hermeneutic arc. There are still two more stages in al-Ghazālī's formulation of the complete ritual experience of *samāʿ*, and they flow out of the participant's

29. *Istinbāṭ* has a wide semantic range in Sufi and non-Sufi sources, as Sara Sviri has documented (*Perspectives on Early Islamic Mysticism*, 298–324). Its juxtaposition here with *tafakkur* and *muhla* seems to suggest that al-Ghazālī intends it in the general non-Sufi sense of "understanding by means of wise extrapolation and discernment" (302), *not* as proceeding from a particular mystical source of knowledge, such as *aḥwāl*, as it was sometimes used in early Sufi sources.

30. See chapter 2 for a more detailed treatment of the cogno-spiritual approach to *samāʿ*.

31. Lewisohn, "The Sacred Music of Islam," 16. As discussed in chapters 1 and 2, Ingenito enriches our understanding of this hermeneutic considerably by including earthly bodies in it, connecting poetic symbols of the beloved with earthly beauties in a collaborative effort to point Sufis towards God and the supernal *maʿānī*.

32. The way *maʿānī* are consistently portrayed as or implied to be *just* abstract, celestial, or archetypal ideas or concepts in the supernal is also problematic, as I will discuss in chapter 4. They can be all of these things too, but that is only one of their aspects.

interpretative engagement with its poetic component. We see this in the second block quote from al-Ghazālī above. How/*ḥāl* the participant feels guides their *tanzīl*ing to *ma ʿānī* that "fit with the state (*ḥāl*) of the disciple in their search" (*fahm2*). This "fit"—that is, that moment of finding a celestial *ma ʿānī* that corresponds to the poetic imagery—is, in many ways, where meaning/knowledge production is just getting started: "[The fit] will engender a spark that will inflame the kindling (*zinād*) of his heart. Then, through that, its [the heart's] fire will flare up and the emission (*inbi ʿāth*) of desire (*shawq*) and agitation will strengthen through it and attack him [the listener], [and] because of it, unfamiliar states (*aḥwāl mukhālifa li- ʿādatihi*) [too]."

Achieving this "fit" ignites a somato-affective conflagration of the heart, producing an amalgamation of "spark[s]," "fire," "desire," and "agitation" that crescendos in intensity until it "attack[s]" the listener. It is an "attack" that transforms the state of the interpreter, creating within them "unfamiliar states" (*aḥwāl mukhālifa li- ʿādatihi*). al-Ghazālī does not elaborate further here on these "unfamiliar states." Instead, he wraps up his more theoretical presentation of stage one by reemphasizing how truly wide a scope listeners have in "dispatching the words (*alfāẓ*)" to their states (*aḥwāl*). But this mention of "unfamiliar states" marks his first gesture toward the second stage of the *samā ʿ* ritual experience: *wajd*.[33]

Wajd, typically (though problematically) translated as "ecstasy," is often portrayed as an "experience" separate from the act of poetic interpretation in *samā ʿ*.[34] It is an experiential "reaction to" the poem. It is something that follows it, something that the poem triggers. The "states" (*aḥwāl*) evoked may convey other spiritual (read: intellectual) knowledge. Its "movements" (*ḥarakāt*) may be discussed as curious anecdotes or to adumbrate the Sufi protocols (*ādāb*) on these bodily responses. But in these readings of *samā ʿ*, these second and third stages are not themselves portrayed as integral parts of the poem's unfolding meaning/knowledge production process.[35] As I discuss in the Introduction and the previous chapter, this subtle scholarly elision of these predominately somato-affective stages from the main show of the poetic meaning/knowledge production process of *samā ʿ* is to a great degree an innocent byproduct of the modern academy's tendency to look at texts primarily for their intellectual, historical, or discursive content (the "linguistic fallacy").[36] But, as I will show in the remainder of this chapter

33. Immediately following this passage is where he begins providing examples of these "dispatchings and understandings" (*al-tanzīlāt wa al-fuhūm*). Most of the examples include explicit mention of *wajd* (al-Ghazālī, *Iḥyā ʾ*, 2:285–88), which, as he says in the quoted passage below, includes the experience of "find[ing] states within himself that he was not encountering before *samā ʿ*"—a clear parallel to the "unfamiliar states (*aḥwāl mukhālifa li- ʿādatihi*)" mentioned here.

34. As the subsequent discussion will show, the semantic range of *wajd* is much broader and refers to epistemological experiences of a much more diverse variety than can be captured by the English "ecstasy."

35. See studies cited in chapter 2's larger review of the existing secondary literature on *samā ʿ*.

36. On the modern academy's "linguistic fallacy," see the *Introduction*.

through a rereading of al-Ghazālī's account, this misunderstands how he views poetry and ultimately *samā'* as creating meaning/knowledge for listeners. *Samā'* aims as much to cultivate somato-affective as intellectual realizations. It is, in fact, poetry and music's ability to create this form of paralinguistic meaning that make them the stars of *samā'*'s first stage and the *sine qua non* of stages two and three. The somato-affective forms of meaning/knowledge produced in stages two and three, in other words, are also what the poem of stage one means to the participants in specific *samā'* performance contexts.[37]

WHAT IS *WAJD* AND WHAT ARE ALL THESE "STATES" (*AḤWĀL*) DOING IN IT?

Let's return for a moment to the conversion story of 'Irāqī from chapter 1. In the previous chapter, I steered us away from the poetic centerpiece of this surprise antinomian *qalandar samā'* session, focusing instead on the unique ways that performance ambience and music each would have æffectively created meaning for *samā'* participants like 'Irāqī that fateful day. But, of course, what he heard the *qalandar*s melodiously recite for him in those four verses would have also played a central role in æffecting the dramatic state transformation that 'Irāqī experiences in this anecdote. The anonymous author does not give us direct insight into the æffective state 'Irāqī was in at the beginning of this *samā'* session or elaborate the details of his hermeneutic process as the recitation unfolded. But, as a Sufi narrative, we can assume that readers would expect 'Irāqī's interpretative engagement with these verses to broadly follow the contours al-Ghazālī provides in the passages discussed above. His æffective state, transformed by the performance ambience and music, would have guided his interpretation of the poetic images in those beautifully chaotic moments.

What seems clear from the subsequent events is that together the ambience, music, and poetry of the *qalandar*s' performance awaken something in 'Irāqī—likely the sense of inchoate longing discussed in the previous chapter—which prepares him for the baptism by the fires of love that was to come next. Now, all that was required to bring the glowing embers of an undirected desire into a fiery conflagration was a blow from one of God's earthly bellows. Then it happens: The anonymous biographer reports that at the moment the *qalandar*s concluded their *samā'* session, 'Irāqī sees a beautiful youth in their midst, and "the bird of his heart fell in the trap of love and the fire of loving desire burnt up the haystack (*khirman*) of his rationality." Sighting the striking young man among the *qalandar*s was the final straw in 'Irāqī's conversion; it gave the smoldering ruins-cum-kindling of

37. Abuali also touches on how the "bodily sensations of pleasure and pain" that are "triggered" by *wajd* or "cultivate[d]" in *wajd* play a role in Sufi spiritual practice in his recent study looking at how Sufi food practices "reconfigur[e] the experience of the body within the framework of piety" and "mobilize all the potentials of the body in 'sensing' and 'feeling' the divine" ("'I Tasted Sweetness,'" 55–57, 66).

ʿIrāqī's former self the requisite final blow of oxygen needed to produce the raging fire that would engulf him entirely.

This powerful moment when love seizes control of ʿIrāqī and fundamentally reorients his life is the culmination of a large team effort of the different components of *samāʿ* discussed so far.[38] Performance ambience, music, poetry, and the beautiful body of an earthly beloved all have been working in concert on his somato-affective body in different ways throughout the performance, and *together* they produce in him this profound spiritual experience where an æffective state—here, love (*ʿishq*)—transforms his life, religious practice, and "state of being" (*ḥāl*). This is ʿIrāqī's first experience of *wajd* and its "unfamiliar states," as al-Ghazālī terms them above. It is a powerful, though difficult to translate or describe, spiritual experience. As we saw in ʿIrāqī's account, its æffects on the individual seem to be both deeply felt and epistemologically profound. It is this experience, after all, that leads ʿIrāqī in short order to throw away his entire collection of Islamic intellectual-tradition classics and transforms his "language of speech . . . into the 'tongue of spiritual experience'"—literally, the "tongue of *ḥāl*."

But what is *wajd* and how does it operate in the broader context of the Sufi hermeneutic arc of the ritual experience of *samāʿ*? These are questions, as al-Ghazālī forthrightly says, that have elicited no shortage of responses from Sufis and other "wise ones" (*ḥukamāʾ*).[39] But, in a certain sense, what *wajd* is is actually quite simple in al-Ghazālī's estimation. *Wajd* is what is "found"—that is, experienced—as a result of *samāʿ*: "All which is found subsequent to *samāʿ*, due to hearing (*al-samāʿ*), in the soul, is *wajd*."[40] This deceptively simple characterization of arguably the most important and enigmatic aspect of Sufi spiritual experience points us to two foundational features of *wajd*: its fundamentally subjective experiential nature and its place within the unfolding ritual process of *samāʿ*. As he elaborates in more detail in another passage, *wajd* should be understood as the experiential realization of *samāʿ*'s first stage:

> The seventh [type of listening (*samāʿ*)] is the *samāʿ* of those who love God, passionately love Him, and desire to meet Him. He does not look at anything without seeing Him—Glory be to God—in it. No decibel reaches his ear except that he hears it from Him [God] and in Him. *Samāʿ* [for him] is a stimulant of his passionate desire (*shawq*) and accentuator of his love (*ʿishq wa ḥubb*) and striker of the flint of his heart and it elicits from it [the heart] states (*aḥwāl*), which fall under [the categories of] unveilings (*mukāshafāt*) and caresses (*mulāṭafāt*) that description cannot fully grasp and that those who have tasted (*dhāqahā*) them know while they are denied by those who are too dull to taste them. These states are called in the language of the Sufis "*wajd*," which is from "finding" (*al-wujūd*) and "encountering" (*al-muṣādafa*),

38. On the importance of the diverse ways æffects "orient" subjects, see chapter 4.

39. al-Ghazālī cites, seemingly approvingly, many of these views in his account and comments on their extraordinary proliferation in *Iḥyāʾ*, 2:289–90.

40. al-Ghazālī, *Iḥyāʾ*, 2:293.

> that is, he finds states within himself that he was not encountering before *samāʿ*. Then, these states become the causes of shoots that spring up (*rawādif*) and of effects of them, which burn the heart with their fires and cleanse it from impurities just as fire cleanses substances immersed in it from impurities.[41]

This passage is drawn from al-Ghazālī's lengthy discussion of the legality of listening to music and poetry.[42] What guides his approach to this topic is the same concern as his later discussion of amatory poetry, discussed previously. Its legality is premised on the intention with which the listener is engaging with it. Music and poetry have as many laudable social, and even religious, functions as illicit ones. The principal praiseworthy one is the focus of his account in this treatise: the use of music and poetry in Sufi *samāʿ*. As we saw in his more detailed discussion of poetic interpretation, what both makes this form of "listening" (*samāʿ*) licit and directs its hermeneutic rudder is the Sufi's (presumed) æffective disposition: the fact that they approach listening as *lovers of God*. He does not elaborate the *fahm-tanzīl* process here, but this is the æffective hermeneutic mechanism operating in the background to guide "anything" he sees and any "decibel" he hears to a divine association.

al-Ghazālī begins his treatment in this passage with a more cursory overview of where he left off in the previous passage: the inflection point between stages one and two of *samāʿ*, where the *fahm*ing of poetry is experientially realized in *wajd*—or as he calls it elsewhere in his account, "phase two" of *samāʿ*. There, as we saw previously, the listener *tanzīl*s the poetic images of the poem that "fit with the[ir] state" to relevant spiritual meanings (*maʿānī*). This click moment ignites their heart, producing a fiery desirous conflagration that grows in intensity and agitation until it "attack[s]" the listener.[43] It is "because of" this "attack" that the *samāʿ* participant then experiences "unfamiliar states."

In this passage, al-Ghazālī presents this transition point in similar, though less detailed, terms, portraying *samāʿ* as a "stimulant" and "accentuator" of desire and love and a "striker of the flint of his heart." As before, he characterizes this moment primarily as a fiery amalgamation of love and desire that forcefully acts on the participant and thereby "elicits" the "states" that come from "unveilings (*mukāshafāt*) and caresses (*mulāṭafāt*) that description cannot fully grasp." These states, he continues, "are called in the language of Sufis '*wajd*,'" and, echoing the framing of these states above as "unfamiliar," he defines them solely here as internal experiences that they have "not encounter[ed] before *samāʿ*." *Wajd*'s defining feature is the experience—i.e., the "finding" (*al-wujūd*), "encountering" (*al-muṣādafa*), "tast[ing]" (*dhāqahā*) (a verb from the same root as *dhawq*)—of something new

41. al-Ghazālī, 277; see similar discussion in al-Ghazālī, *Kīmiyā*, 361–62.
42. al-Ghazālī, *Iḥyāʾ*, 2:266–84.
43. See discussion of "click" moments in chapter 1.

and typically difficult to explain in words.[44] These states are not just passively experienced or afterthoughts to the main event of meaning production in *ma ʿānī* identification; they reveal new things to the *samā ʿ* participant. They are epistemological events that the *fahm*ing of poetry in phase one makes possible.

In another passage, al-Ghazālī explicitly frames *aḥwāl* as sites of knowledge/meaning production as he disaggregates *wajd* into two possible types of epistemological experience:

> There are many reported statements about *samā ʿ* and *wajd*, and it is meaningless to mention the surfeit of them, so let us occupy ourselves with elucidating the meaning which *wajd* expresses. We say that it is equivalent to the state (*ḥāla*) that *samā ʿ* bears as its fruit and it [*wajd*] is something new and true that arrives subsequent to *samā ʿ* that the listener finds in their soul. This state (*ḥāla*) necessarily is of two types: either it goes back to unveilings (*mukāshafāt*) and witnessings (*mushāhadāt*), which are of the intellectual (*min qabīl al- ʿulūm*) or exhortative (*al-tanbīhāt*) type, or it goes back to transformations and states (*taghayyurāt wa aḥwāl*), which are not of the intellectual sciences (*min al- ʿulūm*), but rather are such as desire, fear, sadness, uneasiness, joy, regret, remorse, expansion, or contraction. *Samā ʿ* excites these states and strengthens them.[45]

The distinction that al-Ghazālī makes here between these two types of experiences in *wajd* is the one that I have been suggesting throughout this book. There is, al-Ghazālī maintains, an "intellectual (*min qabīl al- ʿulūm*) or exhortative type" of knowledge involved in *wajd*'s "unveilings (*mukāshafāt*) and witnessings (*mushāhadāt*)."[46] But this is *not* the only epistemological path offered to the Sufi in *wajd*. Equally important is the participant's experience of profound "transformations and states" (*taghayyurāt wa aḥwāl*).[47] What these are is a more complicated matter. al-Ghazālī is confident that they "are not of the intellectual sciences (*min al- ʿulūm*)"—a crucial starting point. But when we try to drill down on his understanding of their exact nature and texture as epistemological events, we see that

44. For more on *dhawq*, see Introduction.

45. al-Ghazālī, *Iḥyā ʾ*, 2:290; on the role of unveilings (*mukāshafāt*) and witnessings (*mushāhadāt*) in *samā ʿ*, see al-Ghazālī, *Iḥyā ʾ*, 2:277. He makes a series of similar points about *wajd* in his discussion in *Kīmiyā*, covering points from the previous quote and this one, including the distinction (though not as detailed), between *ahwāl* and *mukāshafāt* (369–70).

46. For a broader look at al-Ghazālī's varied uses of *mukāshafa* and the Sufi background of the term—from which it draws and expands upon—see Treiger, *Inspired Knowledge in Islamic Thought*, 35–47.

47. Throughout most of his discussion, al-Ghazālī does not seem to regard these two hierarchically. But at one point in *Iḥyā ʾ* he does appear to suggest that unveilings (*mukāshafāt*) and witnessings (*mushāhadāt*) represent a higher level than the *aḥwāl* (277). This assertion, however, is belied—or at least complicated—by the fact that much more of his discussion in his treatise focuses on *aḥwāl*. And it should be noted too that feeling/æffect remains central in *fanā ʾ*, which is beyond all these types of experience (see chapter 5).

he offers several answers and, as we have seen already, he admits repeatedly in the process that they are difficult to capture precisely in words.

There are three ways in which he discusses the content of *aḥwāl* throughout his treatises on *samāʿ*. First, as exemplified in the preceding quote, at times he characterizes them explicitly as well-defined emotions (i.e., socially legible æffective states), such as "desire, fear, sadness, uneasiness, joy, regret, remorse," which "conquer (*ghālib*)" the participant and make them feel like it is "intoxicating" them, as he characterizes it in the corresponding Persian passage in *Kīmiyā*.[48] He makes this association at numerous other points too, sometimes in the context of discussing examples (see one such below) and other times in passages where he simultaneously suggests that *aḥwāl* are both like and also not quite like emotions.[49] A prime example of this, the reader may recall, can be seen in a quoted passage from the previous chapter.[50] There he vacillates between characterizing the experiences of *ḥāl* as an emotional state of "delight," "desire," or "sadness" and then also denying the ability of these emotional categories to exactly capture the full range of what *aḥwāl* can feel like.

Such ambivalent statements typically occur when he is treating *aḥwāl* in the context of music.[51] Music, as discussed in more detail in the previous chapter, can produce "strange states" (*aḥwāl ghariba*) in listeners through the mechanism of "impressions" (*āthār*). These "impressions"—which is the second major way al-Ghazālī discusses the content of *aḥwāl*—are definitely felt, but what they feel like is harder to articulate. They are "strange and wondrous." They can "disturb" the listener and feel sort of like "desire" (*shawq*), but only a mysterious, undirected form of it. In one place he seems certain that they are "[n]ot (*bal*) the well-known meanings (*maʿānī*) of fear, sadness, and delight," which, remember, he says "arise only in listening to (*al-samāʿ*) an intellectually comprehensible song" (that is, one with words) (*ghināʾ mafhūm*).[52] But then, in a passage that follows the first block quote of this section above, he repeats a very similar list of emotions in his attempt to explicate what these enigmatic impressions that music effects feel like:

> The cause of these states (*aḥwāl*) occurring to the heart through *samāʿ* is God's secret in making rhythmic musical melodies and souls harmonize (*munāsaba*) and making souls subservient to and impressed (*taʾaththur*) by them [the melodies] in desiring (*shawqan*), merry (*faraḥan*), sad (*ḥuznan*), expanding (*inbisāṭan*), and contracting (*inqibāḍan*) ways. The (experiential) knowledge (*maʿrifa*) of the cause of the

48. al-Ghazālī, *Kīmiyā*, 370.

49. al-Ghazālī identifies experiences in *wajd* with these and other æffective states at numerous points throughout his works. For other examples, see al-Ghazālī, *Iḥyāʾ*, 2:291–95; al-Ghazālī, *Kīmiyā*, 370.

50. See discussion of al-Ghazālī, *Iḥyāʾ*, 2:292, in chapter 2.

51. Both the passages discussed subsequently occur in the context of al-Ghazālī discussing *wajd* and what constitutes it.

52. See detailed discussion of the full passage (al-Ghazālī, *Iḥyāʾ*, 2:292), from which these quotes are drawn, in chapter 2.

> impressing of souls by tunes (*aṣwāt*) is among the rarefied points of the knowledge of unveilings (*mukāshafāt*). The dull-witted, hard-hearted, stern one, excluded from the pleasure of *samāʿ*, is astonished at the delighting of the listener and his *wajd* and at the agitating (*iḍṭirāb*) of his state (*ḥāl*) and transforming of his complexion (*lawn*). . . .[53]

As the melodies make the souls of the listeners "subservient to" them, the souls are "impressed" in "desiring (*shawqan*), merry (*faraḥan*), sad (*ḥuznan*), expanding (*inbisāṭan*), and contracting (*inqibāḍan*) ways." The structure of his sentence leaves a bit of a gap between the actual feeling of these impressions in the listener's somato-affective feelingscape and these more well-defined emotional categories of experience. The impressions are felt "in [these] ways"—that is, they feel like the "well-known" emotions these words typically denote, hence the frequent resort to them in the discussions of these enigmatic impressions. But they also are not quite them either, hence the equivocation whenever they are mentioned in this context. They remain elusive æffects, perhaps best left described as delightful "agitat[ions]" of the listener's "state" (*ḥāl*), "transform[ations] of his complexion" (*lawn*), or "strange states" (*aḥwāl gharība*), as al-Ghazālī calls them in one of the moments when he concedes their inexplicability.

al-Ghazālī also advances a third category of *aḥwāl* experiential content: somatic sequelae. These diverse physical realizations cannot be fully disaggregated from the other somato-affective experiences previously discussed or even from the more well-defined emotions. It is, after all, the internal power and valence of æffective/emotional states that effect the types and intensities of their bodily realizations. These somatic sequelae begin to encroach on the domain of the third stage, "movement" (*ḥaraka*), as well in certain cases (e.g., falling unconscious, weeping). But, despite this lack of clarity on their precise classification, these manifestations of æffect deserve to be highlighted separately because they constitute a new mutation or stage in the development of their somato-affective realization. al-Ghazālī elaborates several cogent examples of these and how they interlink with the broader unfolding of the Sufi ritual experience of *samāʿ* in another passage in which he returns to the question of how to define *wajd:*

> True *wajd* is what develops from excessively loving God Almighty and truly wishing for Him and passionately desiring to reunion with Him. This [*wajd*] is excited by hearing the Qurʾān too. What is not excited by hearing the Qurʾān, on the contrary, is love of creation and created things. Those words of God Almighty point to this: "Are not hearts at peace in the remembrance of God?" [13:28]. And the Almighty's saying: "[A Book] paired, whereat quivers the skin of those who fear their Lord. Then their skin and their hearts soften unto the remembrance of God" [39:23]. All that which is found subsequent to *samāʿ*, due to *samāʿ*, in the soul, is *wajd*. Thus, the tranquility, trembling, fear, and tenderness of the heart—these all are *wajd*. God Almighty has said: "Only they are believers whose hearts quake with fear when God is

53. al-Ghazālī, *Iḥyāʾ*, 2:277.

> mentioned" [8:2]. And the Almighty said: "Had We made this Qur'ān descend upon a mountain, thou wouldst have seen it humbled, rent asunder by the fear of God" [59:21]. Thus, fear and humility are *wajd* of the *aḥwāl* kind, even if not of the unveilings (*mukāshafāt*) kind. But it may become the cause of unveilings (*mukāshafāt*) and exhortations (*al-tanbīhāt*). . . . And there are a lot of narrations showing that *wajd* has overcome the lords of hearts upon hearing the Qur'ān. His [the Prophet's] saying, "The Sura Hūd and its counterparts made my hair white," is a narration of *wajd* because having white hair is produced by sadness and fear, and this is *wajd*. It is related that Ibn Mas'ūd recited to the Prophet the Sura al-Nisā' and when he got to the words of the Almighty "How will it be when We bring forth a witness from every community, and We bring thee as a witness against these?" [4:41], he [the Prophet] said: "Enough!" And tears poured from his eyes. There is also a narration in which he [the Prophet] recites this verse, or it is recited to him, "Truly with Us are fetters and Hellfire, food that chokes and a painful punishment" [73:12–13], and then he was made unconscious. And there is another narration in which he [the Prophet] recited, "If Thou punishest them, they are indeed Thy servants" [73:12–13], then he cried. And when he passed a verse of compassion, he prayed and rejoiced—and rejoicing is *wajd*. God Almighty extolled the people of *wajd* in the Qur'ān, saying, "And when they hear that which was sent down unto the Messenger, thou seest their eyes overflow with tears because of the truth they recognize" [5:83]. And it is narrated that the Prophet prayed with his chest bubbling like the bubbling of a cauldron.[54]

This passage, interestingly, inaugurates a section in which al-Ghazālī provides examples of what he argues is *wajd* from the Qur'ān and *ḥadīth*. He wants to root *wajd* in the Qur'ānic and prophetic universe. It is not something new that Sufis developed. It is a form of spiritual experience as old as Islam. The Qur'ān can produce it, and the Prophet Muḥammad regularly experienced it.[55] Indeed, as al-Ghazālī implicitly suggests elsewhere, producing *wajd* was the main aim of all God's past revelations to humanity too.[56] Establishing *wajd*'s impeccable pedigree in traditional sources is important for al-Ghazālī because he proceeds after this section to advance one of his most controversial arguments: that is, why *samā'* with poetry and music is typically more effective in effecting *wajd* than God's own words in the Qur'ān.

This discussion of *wajd* in the Qur'ānic and *ḥadīth* traditions provides one of the most extensive windows into the range of somato-affective feelings

54. al-Ghazālī, *Iḥyā'*, 2:293–94. Translations of the Qur'ānic verses are drawn from Nasr, et al., *The Study Quran.*

55. See al-Ghazālī, *Iḥyā'*, 2:293–95. Many of the æffective/emotional states and somatic sequelae mentioned in the preceding block quote are then elaborated in further examples in the following pages.

56. "The [Holy] Scriptures were not sent down except that they produce joy with the mention of God Almighty. Someone said: 'I saw written in the Gospels,' we sang to you, but you did not move with joy, we played a windpipe for you, but you did not dance.' Meaning: We filled you with desire with the mention of God Almighty but you did not desire" (al-Ghazālī, *Iḥyā'*, 2:279). This summative comment comes in response to a story in which a young man is so overjoyed at his mother's responses to his questions about God's creation of the world that he flies into *wajd* and throws himself off a mountain.

that al-Ghazālī believes constitute *aḥwāl*. We see mention of the now familiar emotion states, such as fear or rejoicing.[57] We also see slightly less-well-defined æffective states, such "hearts at peace"/"tranquility"/"tenderness of the heart" or "humility," which all entail complex assemblages of feeling, from varying degrees of the senses of openness, safety, warmth, and wholeness in the first case to a diverse series of relational somato-affective feelings and psychological dispositions (e.g., restraint, meekness, powerlessness, openness vis-á-vis God) in the second. But then there is a third group of experiences that do not quite fit into these categories: The "trembling" and "quiver[ing of] the skin of those who fear their Lord," the "soften[ing]" of the "skin and . . . hearts" of believers when they remember God, the "bubbling" of the Prophet's chest "like the bubbling of a cauldron" when he prayed, and the Prophet's hair turning white upon reception of the Qur'ānic Sura Hūd. Even this final story is a "narration of *wajd*," al-Ghazālī asserts, because white hair is brought about by "sadness and fear, and this is *wajd*." It is "*wajd* of the *aḥwāl* kind," as he says in the middle of the passage.

al-Ghazālī's discussion here underlines the fact that he certainly sees the experience of æffect as central to *aḥwāl*. But this passage does more than this, too, in its focus on the diverse internal and external somatic elaborations of æffect in *aḥwāl*. It adds considerable depth, texture, and richness to our understanding of the experiential content of æffect in *aḥwāl*. *Aḥwāl* can make Sufis tremble in fear or rage or their skin quiver, goosebump, or flush with heat and color. They can æffect a sense of internal emptiness or fullness or closed-offness or retraction out of fear or from the weight of grief on the heart. Or the opposite: they can electrify the Sufi, making them feel as if they are flying or their chests are "bubbling" like a roaring cauldron, as al-Ghazālī tells us the Prophet Muḥammad was said to feel when he prayed. They can even etch themselves into aspects of their physical appearance over the long term, turning their hair grey/white, wasting their bodies, etc., as a (stress) response to negative æffective states.

These all—from the "well-known," socially legible emotional states and difficult-to-describe æffects to their diverse somatic realizations—are what *aḥwāl* is. All these can be "f[ound]," "encounter[ed]," "discover[ed]," "unveil[ed]," "witness[ed]," or "grasp[ed]" in *aḥwāl* and the "transformation[s]" they æffect.[58]

57. Knysh, in his recent short study "Tasting, Drinking and Quenching Thirst," analyzing *dhawq* and related terms such as *aḥwāl* and *wajd*, also asserts that in early Sufism these phenomena can be understood as "psychological (primarily ecstatic) states experienced by Sufis in their quest for intimacy with God, God's presence and God's pleasure." He sees the "psychological and emotive aspects" of these "states" waning as more "metaphysical and cognitive connotations . . . come to the fore in later Sufism," though never disappearing entirely (38–40). I am uncomfortable with this last characterization, and I also would push back on the distinction Knysh appears to draw in his conclusion between later Sufism's interest in the "gnoseological (epistemological) ramifications" of "states and stations" and earlier Sufism's emphasis on their "psychological and emotive aspects" because this seems to imply that somato-affective information is not epistemological in nature (40). But Knysh is a bit unclear on this point.

58. For all of the terms quoted here, see the preceding quoted passages and al-Ghazālī, *Iḥyā*ʾ, 2:290.

And, importantly, together they constitute a form of knowledge, according to al-Ghazālī. They are "a type of knowledge" (*ʿilm*), he concludes, "that helps illustrate matters not known about before [their, i.e., the *aḥwāl*'s] arrival" (*lam takūn maʿlūma qabl al-wurūd*).[59] This bears repeating: Æffects and their diverse, even if ill-defined, amalgamations of feeling are a "*type of knowledge*" that teaches and reveals to Sufis something new about divine realities and God. This somato-affective form of knowledge is the sine qua non of becoming a lover, because you can only be a lover if you know how *to love*. You do not primarily need to know about love as a theoretical construct; your somato-affective body must be entrained to its somato-affective rhythms. This is the work of *wajd* and specifically its *aḥwāl*. In advancing æffective states as sites of knowledge, al-Ghazālī does not abandon rationality or cognition as part of the Sufi epistemological repertoire, as some seem to fear.[60] But what his treatment suggests is that our modern scholarly abandonment of the epistemological value of æffect has impoverished our understanding of how Sufis produced meaning and knowledge.[61]

It is important to underline again too that æffect does not just show up at this final part of stage two, dropping felt knowledge on the participants. To a large degree, it subtends and directs the whole process leading up to it as well, as we have seen. The *samāʿ* participant enters the ritual with a certain æffective disposition —ideally, one informed by love of God. The *samāʿ* session's contextual ambience and the music that precedes the recitation of the poem can both impact the nature of this æffective state in negative or positive ways. The precise æffective state that the participant has at the moment of poetic recitation then leads them to focus

59. He also mentions the other potential epistemological route in this passage: "instruction" (*al-tanbīh*). Relatedly, Elias's passing observation that al-Ghazālī sees "pleasure (*ladhdha*) . . . itself [as] a form of perception (*idrāk*), such that to enjoy (or 'taste,' *dhāqa*) something is to know it" supports this reading too (*Aisha's Cushion*, 164).

60. Regarding reading al-Ghazālī's use of the word "heart" in place of rational soul or intellect, Treiger cautions against reading "emotion" into al-Ghazālī's epistemology: "In calling it heart rather than rational soul or intellect, al-Ghazālī did not intend any radical departure from philosophical noetics in the direction of a more 'emotional' noetics of the heart. He merely intended to defuse the concept's philosophical connotations so as to make it more palatable to the broader circles of religious scholars (*ʿulamāʾ*), while leaving its content essentially the same" (*Inspired Knowledge in Islamic Thought*, 18). For a more positive appraisal of role of emotions in al-Ghazālī's works, see Kukkonen, "Al-Ghazālī on the Emotions." Kukkonen suggestively notes in a number of places how the intellect/rationality and emotions are more intertwined than many accounts give them credit for. See especially examples on page 150 where he notes that the emotion of "shame" requires reasoning and that the emotion of "anger" is believed to be able to exert power over intellect.

61. Æffect can perhaps be reintegrated into the more disembodied, "immaterial" conception of al-Ghazālī's thought advanced by those such as Treiger (see preceding footnote) through the "connection" that the "heart" (i.e. the rational soul, soul, intellect) has with the "physical heart." But I am not concerned here with effecting a reconciliation of these perspectives. See Treiger, *Inspired Knowledge in Islamic Thought*, 17–18. See also Bauer, who similarly argues that traditional Islamic view is that the heart is the site of understanding of both rational and æffective types ("Emotion in the Qur'an," 14–16).

on specific mundane imagery in the poem and interpret it in highly specific ways. What guides this interpretative process is the æffective resonance between the listener's state and the æffect gestured toward in the poetic imagery. The poetic imagery must "agree with," "fit," or, perhaps better, "speak to" the æffective state of the *samāʿ* participant. Æffective affinity acts as a rudder, steering the spiritual hermeneutic process of *tanzīl*ing toward a higher spiritual meaning (*maʿānī*), a *fahm*2. While some form of rationally directed association of the poem's symbols/imagery with archetypal *maʿānī* may happen in this process, this is not al-Ghazālī's primary concern in his treatises on *samāʿ*. His main focus is the æffective import the *tanzīl*ing process produces for the participant. Put a different way, a cluster of poetic imagery may be inferred to be a symbol or poetic representation of one or another set of *maʿānī*. But this does not encapsulate the full extent of what the imagery actually *means* to the participant.

Sufi meaning is about much more than this. What poetic imagery means, as al-Ghazālī makes clear, is the highly subjective result that begins, *not* ends, with the æffectively guided *tanzīl*ing process of the listener. Identifying spiritual *maʿānī* that "fit" may represent a "click" moment, but it is the way this "click" subsequently æffects their *ḥāl* that determines what it really means to the listener in a deeper sense. This is the entire gist of his concluding argument in the second chapter of his *samāʿ* treatises on why *samāʿ* is typically more likely to produce *wajd* than Qurʾānic recitation. After walking the reader through several examples of the truly elaborate maneuvers that Olympic-level hermeneuts engaged in to achieve *wajd* from legalistic Qurʾānic verses, he concludes:

> And examples like this may excite *wajd*, but only for him who has two characteristics: one of them is that he [is experiencing] a dominant (*ghāliba*), utterly absorbing, overpowering state, and the other is profound understanding (*tafaṭṭun balīgh*) and perfect and keen alertness (*tayaqquẓ bāligh kāmil*) capable of pointing him to distant [i.e., abstract] *maʿānī* through those things that are close at hand [i.e., concrete]. But that is rare. So because of that, refuge is taken in singing, which has words so affinitive to the states (*alfāẓ munāsiba li-l-aḥwāl*) that their [the states'] excitement is hastened.[62]

In all the examples he gives that precede this summation, the "overpower[ed]" hermeneut does exhibit their "profound understanding and perfect and keen alertness capable of pointing him to distant [i.e., abstract] *maʿānī* through those things that are close at hand [i.e., concrete]." But, as we know, this associative hermeneutic process is driven by their "dominant (*ghāliba*), utterly absorbing, overpowering state." And, most importantly, in all the cases he provides, the end point of this hermeneutic process is an æffective state-cum-*wajd*. The first ends with "fear and apprehension conquer[ing]" the hermeneut, the second in "hope," "rejoicing," and "merriness." What these texts mean, in other words, is not just what their

62. al-Ghazālī, *Iḥyāʾ*, 2:295; al-Ghazālī, *Kīmiyā*, 371.

hermeneuts associate the words and images with in a philosophical or even spiritual sense. What is most important to al-Ghazālī is how this association makes them feel, which is realized in the *aḥwāl* transformations of *wajd*. This is why singing/poetry (they are interchangeable in this section) is ultimately the most æffective base for *samāʿ* because they are fundamentally concerned with conveying æffects. "[Poetic] verses," al-Ghazālī argues, "are only set down by poets to give expression through them to states of the heart so it is not required to force their [i.e., the state's] affectation (*takalluf*) when understanding the state from them."[63] The poet's primary aim is to capture and convey somato-affective, not intellectual, information.[64] This is why it is so *æffective* in producing *wajd*. One way, then, of understanding *wajd*, "of the *aḥwāl* type" at least, is as the subjective realization in the somato-affective body of the meaning produced in the first stage of *samāʿ*'s three-part hermeneutic process.[65] It is this stage's somato-affective epistemic "fruit," to return to al-Ghazālī's original framing of the relation between the stages of *samāʿ*. It makes the bodies of *samāʿ* participants *feel*—that is, understand—the highly subjective and context-dependent somato-affective meaning(s) of a particular recitation of a poem.

LETTING THE "MEANINGS" OF *WAJD* MOVE YOU (OR NOT): THE FORCE OF *WAJD* AND ITS "MOVEMENTS" (*ḤARAKA*)

In one of the passages above, the Prophet Muḥammad is said to have experienced *wajd* at the recitation of numerous Qurʾānic verses. The evidence of this, al-Ghazālī suggests, is the bodily reactions he is reported to have performed. One verse causes "tears [to] pour . . . from his eyes." Another likewise elicits crying. A third renders him "unconscious." And, al-Ghazālī argues, even the Qurʾānic reference to early Muslims crying when they hear new revelations speaks of *wajd*: "God Almighty extolled the people of *wajd* in the Qurʾān, saying 'And when they hear that which was sent down unto the Messenger, thou seest their eyes overflow

63. al-Ghazālī, *Iḥyāʾ*, 2:295.

64. This, in fact, is his main line of argument throughout this entire final section on why poetry and music are better able to æffect the soul than the Qurʾān. It is, in short, their superior ability to convey/generate æffect for the audience that is key to their spiritual efficacy, for all the reasons discussed in this and the previous chapter. See the Conclusion for more on al-Ghazālī's discussion of these points, and also al-Ghazālī, *Iḥyāʾ*, 2:295–98; al-Ghazālī, *Kīmiyā*, 370–72. For a good English summary of this section in the *Iḥyāʾ*, see Klein, "Music, Rapture and Pragmatics," 234–37. For an in-depth look at al-Ghazālī's discussion of the role of musical modes (also covered in this section in his treatise) and their relation to "emotional states," see Weinrich, "Sensing Sound," 59–65.

65. Compare to Klein's discussion of *wajd* passages in "Music, Rapture and Pragmatics," 228–34. Although Klein does mention that *wajd* can "include . . . pure emotions," he ultimately characterizes *wajd* as a "moment of deep understanding, a realization of profound reality" or "unique state of mind that allows for meaningful communication [of "delicate, ineffable meanings that cannot be expressed by words"] between the heart and the listener" (230).

with tears because of the truth they recognize' [5:83]."[66] These external manifestations of *wajd* in bodily actions—"the æffect (*athar*) of *wajd*, that is, that which leaks out from it externally," as al-Ghazālī phrases it—are the third and final stage of the ritual experience of *samā*ʿ. But these dramatic acts of "losing consciousness, crying, movement (*ḥaraka*), tearing garments, and the like" are much more than the colorful, even if legally suspect (in the eyes of some), hagiographic flourishes that they often are presented as (when discussed seriously at all).[67] The diverse ways that *ḥarakāt* are realized in and through the body, manipulating both the external physical bodies of Sufis and their internal feelingscapes, is another key implement in the toolbox of Sufism's æffective pedagogy. "Going through the motions," as the phrase goes, turns out to be quite meaningful.

The section of al-Ghazālī's treatise explicitly dedicated to "movement" (*ḥaraka*)—the third stage—is the shortest of his treatment of the stages of the ritual experience of *samā*ʿ.[68] But the seemingly short shrift given to *samā*ʿ's culminating stage is more apparent than real because al-Ghazālī discusses *ḥaraka* throughout the other sections as well. In fact, one of his most pithy discussions of it occurs immediately following one of the quoted definitions of *wajd* above in that stage's section:

> If it [the state experienced in the soul] is weak so that it does not affect the external movement [of the person experiencing it] or render him calm or transform his state (*ḥāl*) so that he moves contrary to his custom or starts or stops seeing and speaking and moving contrary to his custom, then it is not called *wajd*. If it manifests externally, it is called *wajd*, be it weak or strong, depending on whether it manifests externally and on whether it ends up transforming someone's external conduct. It causes movements [of the body] in accordance with the power of its arrival, and [the ability to] preserve the exterior from transformation is in accordance with the power of the person experiencing *wajd* and his power to restrain his extremities. So, the *wajd* may be powerful on the inside but the outside is not transformed due to the strength of the person experiencing it. But it [*wajd*] may also not manifest externally due to the weakness of the arriving [*wajd*] and its inability to move [the person] and loosen the binding of his composure.[69]

Prior to this section, the reader will remember from above, al-Ghazālī defines *wajd* as consisting either of "unveilings (*mukāshafāt*) and witnessings (*mushāhadāt*), which are of the intellectual (*min qabīl al-*ʿ*ulūm*) or exhortative (*al-tanbīhāt*) type," or of "transformations and states (*taghayyurāt wa aḥwāl*), which are not

66. al-Ghazālī, *Iḥyā*ʾ, 2:293–94. He follows these remarks with numerous other reports of the Prophet's companions and followers and Sufi luminaries likewise crying, losing consciousness, and even dying from *wajd* induced by Qurʾānic recitation (294–95).

67. al-Ghazālī, *Iḥyā*ʾ, 2:298. Most scholars either ignore the different forms of *ḥaraka* or discuss their legality. Lewisohn, for example, primarily treats the legality and "genuine[ness]" of "dance"—passing over other "movements" or any broader discussion of their function in *samā*ʿ—and Ingenito does not take up the issue in his otherwise quite comprehensive account in any significant way (Lewisohn, "The Sacred Music of Islam," 25–28; Ingenito, *Beholding Beauty*, 476, 483).

68. al-Ghazālī, *Iḥyā*ʾ, 2:298–302; al-Ghazālī, *Kīmiyā*, 372–73.

69. al-Ghazālī, *Iḥyā*ʾ, 2:290.

of the intellectual sciences (*min al-ʿulūm*) but rather are such as desire, fear, sadness, uneasiness, joy, regret, remorse, expansion, or contraction."[70] Both of these, he suggests, are types of *wajd*. Although this study has focused primarily on the latter, it is crucial to underline before proceeding that he then goes on to assert that *wajd of both types* come to be realized somato-affectively in stage three. Even "intellectual" or "exhortative" *wajd* feels like something in the end. It is expressed in the body as either a "strong" or "weak" force that tries to "move [the person experiencing it] contrary to his custom." It is agonistic: Its goal is to "loosen the binding of his composure" and manifest itself externally in the form of valence-appropriate actions, such as crying, wailing, falling unconscious, and a bevy of "movement[s]" of the "extremities" (flailing arms, dancing, or tearing cloaks), that the director "I" of the participant was not previously doing or wanting to do.[71] This point is key for al-Ghazālī. The participant should aim to "preserve the exterior from transformation." He should strive to be "motionless in external appearances." He should only move "*if wajd* conquers him and moves him without his will" (emphasis added). And, "whenever his will returns to him, then he should return to his stillness and motionlessness."[72] al-Ghazālī makes this exhortation to remain still and not move if one can help it as a part of his cautioning *samāʿ* participants not to engage in ostentatious or inauthentic performances of external movements. But it also highlights another important point: Stage three of *samāʿ* is experienced as a struggle of wills, with *wajd* squaring off against its experiencer's director "I" self in a battle (sometimes to the death, as we will see shortly) over who will control the *wajd*-ified body.[73]

al-Ghazālī's discussion of the experience of *wajd* attempting to take control of the participant's body and their subsequent efforts to stay composed evinces a certain degree of ambivalence. We might even say that his account seems a bit conflicted on this point. On the one hand, he seems to suggest that it is not truly *wajd* unless the body of the person is forced to move "contrary to his custom": "If it [the state experienced in the soul] is weak so that it does not affect the external movement [of the person experiencing it] . . . then it is not called *wajd*. If it manifests externally, it is called *wajd*, be it weak or strong." But then, on the other hand, al-Ghazālī also suggests that the spiritual elite can control even *wajd*'s most powerful volitional onslaughts. Through the countervailing force of their "intellect and composure" (*al-ʿaql wa al-tamāsuk*), these masters can "restrain [their] external

70. For this passage, see the previous section.

71. See the fascinating quote from the biography of the Sufi saint Aḥmad Bashīrī, cited by Bashir, for a lively imaginal portrayal of this process. In this account, it is the "flames of love" (the æffect) "reach[ing]" the different parts of the body (eye, mouth, hand, legs) that make them externally manifest the æffective state of love. See *Sufi Bodies*, 139–40.

72. al-Ghazālī, *Iḥyāʾ*, 2:299.

73. The portrayal of *wajd* as an agonistic force is also paralleled in the presentation of the force of God acting in the Sufi's body who has experienced self-annihilation (*fanāʾ*). See chapter 5.

appearance," even when experiencing extremely powerful bouts of *wajd*: "Despite the strength of the *wajd* on the interior," he says, no movement is "manifested externally due to the perfection of the power of restraining the extremities." And "this," he argues, "is perfection."[74]

al-Ghazālī cites the great early Sufi Junayd (d. 910) as the paradigmatic example of this more self-composed approach to *wajd*. Junayd is widely portrayed as the founder of the so-called "sober" path of Sufism.[75] Unlike the Sufis of the "intoxicated" or "drunk" path of Sufism (which would include most, if not all, of the Sufis following the Path of Love), "sober" Sufis generally remained more restrained in their ritual practices, avoiding charged external expressions of *wajd*, wild "ecstatic sayings," or the more controversial aspects of Sufi amatory rituals.[76] al-Ghazālī's praising of the Junaydian example of restraining oneself from externally perceptive movement in *wajd* as "perfection" gestures toward his sympathies with this more "sober" approach to physical realizations of *wajd*.

One would not necessarily know that this is al-Ghazālī's favored position, however, by reading most of his account. He elaborates a surfeit of examples of the most accomplished Sufis and even the Prophet Muḥammad himself, as we saw, engaging in various forms of "movements" (*ḥarakāt*) as a result of their *wajd*. Indeed, it is precisely these "external manifestation[s]" that he pointed to earlier as proof that the Qur'ān and stories of the Prophet contain examples of *wajd*. To suggest that al-Ghazālī interprets these stories as representing examples of deficient spiritual practice or a lack of perfection in the spiritual preparedness among these elite Sufis and the Prophet and his closest companions is difficult to imagine.

Further complicating this picture, al-Ghazālī also relates striking stories about the seeming irresistibility of *wajd*'s force. In one shocking story involving Junayd, the sober master orders a young follower who keeps crying out when he hears anything in Sufi chanting (*al-dhikr*) not to do this any longer, otherwise he will be disallowed from associating with him. Not wanting to lose his venerable spiritual master, the young man does his utmost to restrain himself, keeping the force of *wajd* from being realized in any discernible external way. But this is a fool's game—and a *very dangerous* one at that. Eventually, the internal force is too much. As he keeps trying to keep himself under control, little drops of sweat start pouring out of his every pore, and then "one day he is strangled by the force on him from restraining it." The power of the internal force of *wajd* was just too much to bear. It cleaved his heart clean in half before dispatching his soul.[77] This is because, as al-Ghazālī says in another place, the "conquering (*ghalaba*) of the intoxication of *wajd*" is a "compelling"—in the "coercive" sense of this word—force that does not

74. al-Ghazālī, *Iḥyā'*, 2:299.

75. For an overview and critical interrogation of the "sober" vs. "intoxicated" approaches to Sufism and the development of this distinction, see Mojaddedi, "Getting Drunk."

76. On "ecstatic sayings," see Ernst, *Words of Ecstasy in Sufism*.

77. al-Ghazālī, *Iḥyā'*, 2:299.

take no for an answer.[78] It makes people do things no matter how much they will otherwise. Comparing gasps of breath to movements and the indomitable force of *wajd* to the body's unstoppable ability to force one to breathe against their will, he says: "A human being cannot stop doing all acts that they realize through their will. Breathing is an act one realizes through self-will, but if a human being intends to restrain their breathing for a while, they would be forced to will [themselves] to breathe from within themselves." This is what, he concludes here, truly powerful *wajd* is like. Like breathing, you cannot just decide to stop it and control it with your will. If you try, the best-case scenario is that it will force you to do its bidding by making you will to do what it wills to do. Or worse: if you doggedly fight it, as Junayd's young follower discovered, the extraordinary pressure of this battle of wills might kill you.[79] These portrayals do not reconcile easily with al-Ghazālī's passing mention that the ideal is to use "intellect and composure" to suppress *wajd's* external manipulations of the Sufi body, nor with the prolific history in Sufism more broadly of elite Sufis regularly engaging in dramatic displays of *wajd*-induced *ḥarakāt* (some of which al-Ghazālī himself mentions in his account).

But let's return to al-Ghazālī's discussion of Junayd, because one of the stories he relates about him provides an important clue about how to possibly—at least partially—reconcile these two divergent positions. The section in which al-Ghazālī praises those whose "intellect and composure" can restrain them from manifesting their *wajd* externally does not end where he calls this "perfection." It continues into an illustrative anecdote about Junayd that suggests that perhaps the question of whether the Sufi moves externally is actually not, in the end, as significant as it would first seem: "Junayd used to move [in *wajd*] in *samāʿ* in the beginning, but then he started not to move. So something was said to him about this. He responded: 'And thou seest the mountains that thou dost suppose are solid pass away like clouds—the Work of God, Who perfects all things' [Qurʾān 27:88]. This is an indication that the heart is agitated (*muḍṭarib*), roaming about the 'Unseen Realm' (*malakūt*) while the extremities are properly self-controlled in external appearance, motionless."[80]

When Junayd was a bit less spiritually developed, *wajd did move* him. His power to control its external manifestations was something he developed as he spiritually matured. So far, this tracks with al-Ghazālī's comments above about those who have reached perfection being able to restrain *wajd*'s powerful æffects on their external members. Young Sufis, the implication is, must develop this purportedly ratiocentric power, so that *wajd* will stop moving them so powerfully—to tears, to dance, to cry out and wail, to express externally the powerful force impinging on them. Intellect and self-control, the implication is, can keep these immature

78. He uses several words here derived from the *iḍṭirār* root, whose meanings circle around ideas of "compulsion," "coercion," "forcing to do something," etc.

79. al-Ghazālī, *Iḥyāʾ*, 2:301.

80. al-Ghazālī, *Iḥyāʾ*, 2:299–300. Qurʾānic quotations are from Nasr, et al., *The Study Quran*.

outbursts from happening. The intellect and self-will—itself a projection of the rational director "I"—of the Sufi adept can control æffect's external realization.

This interpretation is tempting, not least because it is consonant with the tendency in the existing scholarship to see the experience of *samāʿ* in its true or proper Sufi form as guided fundamentally by a rational or intellectual process. But we need to pay close attention to how Junayd's story ends: with his heart "agitated (*muḍṭarib*), roaming about the 'Unseen Realm' (*malakūt*)." His limbs may have been at rest, "properly self-controlled in external appearance, motionless," through the force of his intellect and the self-control that emanates from it. His heart and internal somato-affective feelingscape, however, are another story. They are in motion, moving and being moved. The "strength" of *wajd* and the intensity of its *aḥwāl* and "transformation[s]" have rocketed Junayd into orbit in the Unseen Realm. Their æffects are still profoundly felt deep inside even the soberest and most externally equanimous of Sufis. As al-Ghazālī says above: "The *wajd* may be powerful on the inside but the outside is not transformed due to the strength of the person experiencing it." The felt experience of the staggering power of *wajd* does not disappear, even if the Sufi has reached the levels of "perfection" that enable them to control their external movement. It just stays bottled up inside, exerting itself on the heart and the somato-affective body of the Sufi. It still engenders movement, and its movement still very much makes the Sufi feel something, powerfully.

When taken in the aggregate, al-Ghazālī's discussion of *ḥaraka* suggests that these different forms of "movement" are best understood as one of *wajd*'s mechanisms for conveying meaning, a somato-affective one akin in some ways to the wordless "impressions" left by music and *aḥwāl* in the Sufi's soul.[81] Their manipulations of the external physical and somato-affective bodies' equilibrium offer felt glimpses of the æffective life of God and his Sufi lover saints. Through their internal and external machinations, they entrain the somato-affective systems of aspiring Sufis to become lovers by teaching them how they must feel and enact æffect to be lovers. To be a lover is to know how to, and how it feels to, cry from grief and longing; to yell out or fall unconscious when overwhelmed by awe, joy, or majesty; to be forced to rip one's garment against one's better judgment . . . or to be launched soaring into the Unseen Realm with *wajd* riling one's heart, even while performing the herculean task of keeping this almost irresistible force from leaking outside of the bounds of the physical body. These are complex assemblages of feeling that the body must experience to learn to do. This is why *samāʿ* is not complete unless it moves the participant. And how it moves them is also what it

81. al-Ghazālī implicitly makes this association in a few places (see preceding discussion of *aḥwāl* in this chapter and chapter 2). Also see Klein's similar observation that the "movement of the body to music, rather than a side-effect of audition, is a delicate and meaningful nonverbal language. Rather than being irrational, bodily movements in the state of *wajd* are a 'rational' language in themselves, a delicate one, not bound by the constraints of speech" ("Music, Rapture and Pragmatics," 229). He does not, however, present "movement" in general as playing a pedagogical or epistemic role per se.

means—to them, and those around them.[82] The meaning-production process of *samā'* does not end with the participant "dispatching" imagery to *ma'ānī* in stage one. To, for example, cut off the feelings of longing or joy (*aḥwāl* of stage two) and their realizations in tears or dancing (*ḥarakāt* of stage three) is to reduce meaning and knowledge production to a mechanical philosophical game of abstract conceptual representation. Fully understanding *samā'* as an epistemological event—that is, as a ritual process that "illustrate[s] matters not known about before," as al-Ghazālī says regarding *aḥwāl*—requires us to follow the long tail of meaning production into the somato-affective body of its Sufi participants.

CODA: GETTING IN THE HABIT(US) OF BEING A LOVER AND THE FORMATION OF SUFI FEELING SUBJECTS

In a small section, almost an aside, in his discussion of *wajd*, al-Ghazālī mentions that there are actually two types of *wajd*: the *wajd* that "assaults" (*hājim*) you and the *wajd* that you "æffect" or "force" (*mutakallaf*).[83] The former is the *wajd* discussed throughout this chapter. The latter is what he terms *tawājud*. At the most basic level, *tawājud* is the act of æffecting or *acting like* one is experiencing *wajd* by engaging in some external movement—a *ḥaraka*—that is typically characteristic of real *wajd*. It is quite literally faking it until you make it, or as proponents of the practice theory approach to emotion and affect would prefer, "practice[ing] until [it] become[s] automatic," to adapt Scheer.[84] A Sufi, to be explicit, cannot always wait for *wajd* and its æffects to happen *to them* (to, that is, be "triggered" in them, as the common framing has it); sometimes they have to initiate and practice it.[85]

It may come as a surprise to readers that, far from universally condemning all *tawājud* as dissimulation or fraudulent, al-Ghazālī actually praises the proper performance of *tawājud*. When well-intentioned, he portrays it is a supremely effective means for "summoning" the *aḥwāl* of real *wajd*—for, that is, literally effecting *aḥwāl*'s "illustrious" æffective states. *Tawājud*, in his formulation, is the *samā'* equivalent of the pedagogical play with the toy wooden swords-cum-earthly lovers of Rūmī's poem or ritualized gazing upon the beautiful *shāhid*s. It is an

82. As Bashir notes (*Sufi Bodies*, 76–77), the expression of "corporeal agitation" in the "intense states" of *samā'* impacts the other participants in the session as well—a point which is rooted in the need for "æffective attunement" in *samā'* (discussed in chapter 2).

83. al-Ghazālī, *Iḥyā'*, 2:292–93. The parallel Persian section, although just a few sentences, is al-Ghazālī, *Kīmiyā*, 370. Klein provides a brief summary of this entire section in the *Iḥyā'* ("Music, Rapture and Pragmatics," 238). He correctly calls *tawājud* "a device (*ḥīla*) allowing to acquire a noble state by practice" (sic). But he leaves the point there. al-Ghazālī also reiterates a few related points on *tawājud* in passing in *Iḥyā'*, 2:300.

84. See Introduction.

85. On this point, see Scheer, "Are Emotions a Kind of Practice," 206–7.

"expedient," "maneuver," or even "artifice" (*ḥīla*) that functions as a pedagogical tool for scaffolding Sufis up to real *wajd*.

As humans, we all have to engage in diverse forms of pedagogical "play" or "training" to learn how to do anything. Learning how to properly embody, feel, and perform æffects—such as how to truly love another person or God, or cry and feel sadness when reciting the Qur'ān, as al-Ghazālī offers as examples here—is no exception. These often first require that we æffect these states, he asserts.[86] In fact, this practice has prophetic precedence: The Prophet ordered his followers to cry when reciting the Qur'ān even if they did not actually feel like it deep down because "these states may be æffected in the beginning but then in the end become real." This process of learning æffective modes of being, he continues, is just like learning to memorize the Qur'ān or write. It requires "forcing" (*takalluf*) it—in the sense of unartfully or unnaturally practicing it with great difficulty and concentration—at first until one has done it so much that it becomes part of their mental or physical muscle memory of sorts, so they do not have to even think about it anymore. All types of learning function this way: skills and behaviors "become one's nature through habit" (*yusīr bi-l-ʿāda ṭabʿan*), through practice. This, al-Ghazālī concludes, is the main reason for engaging in *samāʿ*: It is among the best ways of "summoning" *aḥwāl*. Its primary aim, or at least one of them, is to provide a practice ground for *aḥwāl*'s rigorous mode of æffective training to make being a lover of God the Sufi participant's fundamental nature. *Samāʿ*, in this sense, can be understood as what Scheer terms an "emotional practice": all its components and stages, from its performance ambience and music to its poetry and movements, are to a significant degree instruments aimed at effecting the æffective states that together, over time, form the ideal Sufi lover (feeling) subject.[87]

86. For a resonant and theoretically rich discussion of how embodied performance of æffective "dispositions" can cultivate and actualize them in the production of an "ideal virtuous self," see Mahmood's seminal study of women's performance of "Islamic virtues" (e.g., modesty) in the women's mosque movement in Cairo in the 1990s (*Politics of Piety*, especially chapter 5).

87. For a discussion of "emotional practices" see Scheer, "Are Emotions a Kind of Practice," 209–20.

4

"Expressing Meanings (*Ma ʿānī*) in the Clothing of Forms"

Sufism's Æffective Poetics

ʿIrāqī, the Sufi lover whose life has punctuated the discussion across the preceding chapters, is remembered as the quintessential rogue poet. As the reader will recall, he falls head over heels in love with a young man in the *qalandar* band, gives his garments and turban (symbols of his social status) to them, tosses away all his prized books by the leading Islamic philosophers and theologians, and leaves his family and high social position behind in Hamadān to join this wandering crew of spiritual reprobates. He becomes a "madman"—at least in the eyes of normative Islamic society. His place of worship, as the inset poem sung by the *qalandar*s in his conversion narrative suggests, is now the "dilapidated winehouse" (*kharābāt*) of the Magian (Zoroastrian) quarter. This is the hub of the Sufi lover's imaginal world. As the etymology of *kharābāt* suggests, it is where one goes to get drunk, wasted, literally destroyed (*kharāb*) on wine and to learn the normatively destructive, "wine"-fueled piety of the *qalandar*s—what the more sober Sufi master Abū Ḥafṣ ʿUmar al-Suhrawardī famously denounced as their seemingly single-minded drive to "destroy [normative socio-religious] customs" (*kharabū al-ʿādāt*).[1]

A reader with only a passing knowledge of Islam and Sufism could be forgiven for asking how and why wine and associated anacreontic imagery became one of the most generative symbolic complexes in Sufi poetry. Imbibing wine, after all, is directly proscribed in the *Qurʾān* and is against *sharīʿa* law.[2] Although this

1. al-Suhrawardi, *ʿAwārif al-Maʿārif*, 89. All three of these words are derived from the same Arabic trilateral root *khāʾ-rāʾ-bāʾ*, which is associated with destruction, ruins, and intoxication (i.e., metaphorically being "wasted"). On Arabic's trilateral root system, see footnote 17 in the Introduction.

2. Although all forms of alcohol eventually came to be proscribed in most schools of Islamic law, there is some complexity on the prohibition of alcohol in both the Qurʾān and the Islamic legal traditions. For example, the Qurʾān initially did not completely proscribe alcohol consumption (only

proscription did not stop many medieval Muslims and even some antinomian Sufi or Sufi-aligned groups from partaking of wine, drugs, and other intoxicants, the more mainstream Sufi lovers discussed in this book would not have been advocates of such a literal interpretation of quaffing the "wine of love" of which they sing in thousands of poems.[3] So why, then, is the imagery of the wine ode (*khamriyya*) their primary poetic means of expressing their amatory spirituality? The simple answer to this question is, of course, that the wine imagery is metaphoric. These Sufis do not literally mean they were imbibing goblets of wine in the local *kharābāt* from the hands of beautiful cupbearer beloveds.

But what does it mean when we say they use wine imagery to metaphorically represent the Sufi Path of Love? What does "metaphor" mean here, and what does metaphoric imagery do for the Sufi author and audience members? This is a more complicated set of questions. Interpreters of Sufi poetry from the medieval to modern periods have proffered different answers, sometimes explicitly and other times implicitly. How each understands the operation of metaphoric imagery in Sufi wine poems differs in important ways along multiple axes. Some regard metaphoric imagery, as I have discussed in preceding chapters, as only symbols pointing to higher spiritual meanings (*ma ʿānī*) or concepts and figures in Sufi metaphysics or scripture. Others read this imagery biographically, as gesturing toward some aspects of the author's life. Modern literary critics tend to caution against these approaches and encourage readings that foreground the poetic function of imagery in each poem. Some combine different components of more than one of these interpretative tendencies in their analyses. All these ways of reading poetry have merit and, to varying extents, are represented in the reception history of Sufi poetry down to the present day. But what has often been missed in all these approaches is the *æffective* function of Sufi metaphoric imagery—the basis of what I will call here Sufism's æffective poetics.

Analyzing Jāmī's commentary on the famous wine ode (*khamriyya*) of ʿUmar ibn al-Fāriḍ (d. 1235), this chapter will show that one of the most important roles of Sufi imagery is to operate as a device for bridging the gap between somato-affective aspects of embodied spiritual experience and language as an intellectual system. Imagery, from this perspective, embodies poetry—indeed, language more broadly—not as a straightforward biographical reflection of Sufi life, but rather by

drunkenness) but eventually came to prohibit wine (*khamr*) consumption. Or, to take another example, the Ḥanafī legal school, especially in its early years, focused their prohibition on drinking to intoxication and wine (because the latter was explicitly prohibited in the Qurʾān). For an overview of these complexities, see Matthee, *Angels Tapping*, 62–71.

3. On Sufi antinomian groups and the long history of the consumption of intoxicating substances in the Islamic world, see Karamustafa, *God's Unruly Friends*; Algar, "Impostors"; Matthee, *The Pursuit of Pleasure*; Matthee, *Angels Tapping*. See also Shahab Ahmed's argument for why wine, in a certain sense, is very "Islamic"; *What Is Islam?*, 3–4, 57–71, and 420–24 for one intriguing example of how he interprets "wine" as "Islamic."

acting as a mechanism for conveying somato-affective meaning and knowledge about its referent. Imagery—the "clothing" of *ma ʿānī*, to use Jāmī's terminology—does not just represent or point audience members to abstract spiritual meanings in the celestial realm or concepts and references in Sufi metaphysics and Islamic scripture; it conveys or "express," as Jāmī says, somato-affective meanings, too.

THE MODALITIES OF SUFI IMAGERY: WINE AS SYMBOLIC POINTER AND WINE AS SOMATO-AFFECTIVE EMBODIMENT

1 In memory of the beloved we drank wine;
we were drunk with it before creation of the vine.
2 The full moon its glass, the wine a sun circled by a crescent;
when mixed, how many stars appear!
3 If not for its bouquet, I would not have found its tavern;
if not for its flashing gleam, how could imagination picture it?
4 Time preserved nothing of it save one last breath,
concealed like a secret in the breasts of wise men.
5 But if it is recalled among the tribe, the worthy ones
are drunk by morn without shame or sin.[4]

These lines are drawn from Ibn al-Fāriḍ's *The Wine Ode*, among the most famous and influential poems in medieval Sufism. It was widely read in both the Persian and Arabic-speaking worlds. As its opening suggests, the poem imagines the relationship between the Sufi seeker and the divine beloved in anacreontic terms, with the intoxicating substance of wine functioning as a metaphor for the equally stupefying and overflowing love of God. Most of the poem (lines 7–20) is a kaleidoscopic poetic exploration of wine as a force of inconceivable proportions, concluding with a descriptive section (*waṣf*) on its "attributes" (lines 21–27) and an exhortation (lines 28–33) to its listeners to head to the "tavern" posthaste and "try to uncover [the wine] there amid melodious tunes" (line 29),

32 For there is no life in this world for one who lives here sober;
who does not die drunk on it [i.e., the wine], prudence has passed him by.
33 So let him weep for himself, one who wasted his life
never having won a share or measure of this wine.[5]

Wine here is obviously intended metaphorically. But *how* did this anacreontic metaphoric imagery mean to different Sufis across the ages and vast geographic spread of this poem?

4. Ibn al-Fāriḍ, "Wine Ode," 47. The translation of Ibn al-Fāriḍ's *khamriyya* is Homerin's. Both his translation of this poem and al-Qayṣarī's commentary on it are excellent, so I have elected to use these.

5. al-Qayṣarī, "Commentary," 14.

Ibn al-Fāriḍ's wine ode is one of the most widely commented upon poems in the medieval Sufi tradition. This commentary tradition offers us numerous windows into how medieval Sufis interpreted this poem for their spiritual practice. It is a voluminous and complex interpretative tradition that I cannot treat exhaustively here. Instead, in this chapter, I focus on two of its most important commentaries as a window into the diversity of ways in which wine was understood to function as a metaphor for the love of God in medieval Sufism. These two examples illustrate contrasting—though potentially symbiotically—interpretative tendencies within the broader history of the reception of Sufi poetry: what I will call the metaphor-as-symbolic-pointer and metaphor-as-imaginal-embodiment approaches. This latter type should be further subdivided into branches that treat metaphoric imagery as embodiments of physical entities (i.e., the fusion of the imaginary of the beloved with real-life beloveds that I discuss in chapter 1) and those that interpret metaphoric imagery as somato-affective embodiments of Sufi experience. It is this second category that is the principal concern of this chapter. But it is important that we do not reify these different approaches to imagery into opposing camps or imagine them as mutually exclusive. They are better understood as interpretative modalities that different readers of these texts—including, importantly, modern scholars—have made use of in varying degrees throughout the centuries, each illuminating different dimensions of Sufi poetry.

Among the earliest and most influential in the long commentary tradition on Ibn al-Fāriḍ's wine ode is Dāwūd al-Qayṣarī's (d. 1350) *Sharḥ khamriyyat Ibn al-Fāriḍ*.[6] al-Qayṣarī was a prominent Anatolian Sufi who is credited—alongside his teacher ʿAbd al-Razzāq al-Kāshānī (d. 1329–35), Muʿayyid al-Dīn Jandī (d. ca. 1300), and Ṣadr al-Dīn al-Qunawī (d. 1274)—with laying the foundations of the so-called "'school' of ibn ʿArabī" through their voluminous commentary on his works. Often termed "Akbarian" Sufism, this highly metaphysical formulation of Sufi thought would become one of the leading intellectual currents within Sufism in the coming centuries.[7] al-Qayṣarī's commentary on Ibn al-Fāriḍ's wine ode is an attempt to understand the poem as a versification of Ibn al-ʿArabī's metaphysical Sufism (despite the fact that Ibn al-Fāriḍ likely had no knowledge of Ibn al-ʿArabī), and it should be understood as part of his broader project of reinterpreting Sufi texts and reformulating Sufi metaphysics along Akbarian lines.

Much of his commentary on Ibn al-Fāriḍ's poem exemplifies the application to poetry of what I call in earlier chapters the cogno-spiritual hermeneutic. al-Qayṣarī's overriding concern throughout his commentary is, as he forthrightly says in his

6. Homerin, *The Wine of Love and Life*, xiii.

7. On al-Qayṣarī, see Hussain, "Dāwūd Al-Qayṣarī." On the Akbarian commentary tradition, see Morris, "Ibn ʿArabi and His Interpreters Part II"; Morris, "Ibn ʿArabi and His Interpreters Part II (Conclusion)"; van Lit, "Ibn ʿArabī's School of Thought." ʿIrāqī too played a central role in the spread of Akbarian thought in the Persian world through his *Lamaʿāt*, which gives an Akbarian metaphysical foundation to the Sufi Path of Love.

prefatory remarks, that the reader obtains a correct understanding of the "symbols" in the poem.[8] The term he uses here for "symbols," "*rumūz*" (s. *ramz*), tells us something important about his interpretative method and theory of poetry and language more broadly. In this paradigm, language and, in particular, poetry contain symbols (*rumūz*) or "allusions" (*ishārāt*) that point to or stand as allegorical representations of Sufi concepts and spiritual meanings (*maʿānī*).[9] At the literal or surface level (*ẓāhir*) of language, these symbols and symbolic actions may be exceedingly mundane and even sacrilegious (e.g., wine and its consumption, infidelity, love affairs), but ensconced within them are higher, "inner" (*bāṭin*) meanings, as we saw in chapter 3 as well. These spiritual meanings will not be apparent to most members of society. Only learned Sufi adepts have the requisite knowledge of inner mystical realities to responsibly decipher and explicate the welter of esoteric "mysteries" hiding in plain sight in everyday earthly symbols. al-Qayṣarī's exhaustive interlinear interpretations of Ibn al-Fāriḍ's wine ode aim to provide this service. His hermeneutic charge, as he sees it, is to illuminate the true, "inner" meaning of Ibn al-Fāriḍ's *khamrīyya* by revealing for the reader the elaborate, sub- or supra-literal network of allusions to myriad Qurʾānic passages, *ḥadīth*, Sufi metaphysical concepts, and supernal *maʿānī* that are contained in the symbols of each verse.[10]

Most of his commentary follows a predictable pattern, with some variation. Sometimes, for example, he initiates his interpretation on a line with brief definitions of words or discussions of grammatical points in it. Other times he moves straight to the identification of the "symbols" or symbolic actions (e.g., drinking) in the line and the provision of their true meaning with the phrases, "The aim of / What is intended by [x, y, or z symbol. e.g., beloved, wine]" (*al-murād*) or "that is" (*ay*). There is also some variation in terms of each section's interpretative focus: Some expend more ink providing scriptural linkages to the Qurʾān and *ḥadīth* for the poetic images; others are more concerned with explicating the imagery in terms of the panoply of concepts in Akbarian metaphysics. In his commentary on the second verse of the poem (provided above), for example, he begins with a few grammatical notes and clarifications before proceeding to discuss what Sufis would call the "inner meaning" of the line—that is, how its images represent Akbarian metaphysics in verse.

> "*Its*" refers to the wine, with the subject being "*the full moon*" and "*cup*" as the predicate, i.e., "*The full moon is a cup for it.*" The "*crescent*" is what goes around [the sun], while "*how many*" refers to the stars, i.e., "*Many are the stars that appear.*" What is meant by "*the full moon*" is the face (*wajh*) of the divine beloved with respect to manifest existence; this is the Muhammadan Essence (*al-dhāt al-muhammadīyah*), which exists in true being. It is illuminated by the light of the sun of the essence of

8. al-Qayṣarī, "Commentary," 1–13.

9. On *ramz*, see Heinrichs and Knysh, "Ramz."

10. For more on this Sufi symbolist approach, see earlier discussion of it in the Introduction and chapters 2 and 3.

> exclusive oneness (*al-dhāt al-aḥadīyah*), via reflection due to opposition between the two essences, by virtue of the two comprehensive levels of existence, namely that of unity and that of differentiation. However, this is not with respect to essential exclusive oneness (*al-aḥadīyah al-dhātīyah*), since that has neither differentiation nor separation within it. Therefore, [the poet] made the full moon a cup, a drinking bowl full of drink, and thus something limited, which can only be in the world.[11]

The image of the "full moon" is taken not as a concrete referent to an earthly beloved but as pointing to the divine beloved in a particular state of manifestation, which is linked to the concept or reality (depending on how you view it) of the "Muhammadan Essence" (*al-dhāt al-muḥammadiyyah*)." The implied light from the image of the "sun" is then grafted onto the central image of the poem—i.e., wine—which he tells us here is also the "essence of exclusive oneness (*al-dhāt al-aḥadiyyah*)." This sets up the following image complex: Wine (*al-dhāt al-aḥadīyyah*), like the sun of this line, pours out (as light) into "cups," the delimited vessels of phenomena in the manifested world, represented here by the moon reflecting the sun's light in its own limited form.

Wine and its consumption, as he says in his interpretation of the opening verse, similarly are defined primarily in terms of scriptural references and, to a lesser extent here, Akbarian metaphysics.[12]

> What is meant by "*wine*" is the drink of Zanjabīl, and the spring of Salsabīl, which delights its drinker and intoxicates him, driving out his reason, and baffling his mind. This is indicated in the Lord's Word, that immortal text in which He, most high, has said: "They will be given there [in Paradise] a cup to drink whose blend is Zanjabīl from a spring there named Salsabīl" [76:17–18]. Indeed, by means of it, the drinker loses his sense of self, as all the properties of his human nature disappear along with his natural traits regarding the designations of actions, characteristics, and essence. For the ruling property of duality disappears from him as he becomes one then with the divine essence that was from the beginning when there was nothing with it. Just as [the Prophet], God bless him and give him peace, has said: "God was, and there was nothing with Him!" with the passing away of what is not, and the abiding of Him who never disappears. . . . The source of this drink is also mentioned in His, most high, saying: "Lo, the righteous will drink from a cup whose blend is from Kāfūr, a spring from which God's servants drink as they cause it to flow abundantly" [76:5–6]. First, [the drink] is blended with Kāfūr, then with Zanjabīl, as indicated by the sequence in the Glorious Word. There, He mentions the Kāfūr mixture, to which He endowed the cool refreshingness of certainty only for the drinkers among the righteous, while its soothing revelation is for the spirits of lovers who shun multiplicity. He speaks of this again regarding the third [and

11. al-Qayṣarī, "Commentary," 16–17 (English text), 21 (Arabic text).

12. al-Qayṣarī rarely relates Ibn al-Fāriḍ's poetic imagery to concrete referents (e.g., as the commentaries that Zargar and Takacs point to below) or to the somato-affective "similitude" of the experience of the earthly imagery and its spiritual referents, as Jāmī terms it in his commentary on this poem discussed below. But there are limited exceptions such as the one discussed in footnote 31 of this chapter.

> higher] level belonging to "those brought near" as having the choice, sealed wine, in His, most high, saying: "They are served a choice wine sealed with musk. So let those who strive, strive for this! Its blend is from Tasnīm, a spring from which drink those brought near" [83:25–28]. Only those brought near him will receive it. He said: "Of a choice wine sealed with musk," which arises and perfumes the breaths of existence, and whose taste quenches the burning thirst of those parched for the beatific vision. He mentions Tasnīm [lit. "ascension"] as an indication of [the drink's] high place and exalted (131a) rank. What is intended by *drinking* is the reception of the everlasting divine effusion which descends in levels over the entities and their capacities, [and which] is the cause for the manifestation of the perfections hidden in the unseen of the servant's entity. [These perfections] are the divine states concealed in the treasury of the unseen, firmly rooted in the servant's reality.[13]

Ibn al-Fāriḍ's poetic image of wine, according to al-Qayṣarī's interpretation, is a mixed drink drawn from the Qur'ānic waters of the spring of Kāfūr and the Zanjabīli spring of Salsabīl. Even the order of the blending of these springs is defined by the implied sequence of their appearance in the Qur'ān. Further close reading of passages mentioning wine leads al-Qayṣarī to develop a typology of Qur'ānic wine, with the most select drinkers—"those brought near"—being offered a "choice wine sealed with musk." This wine is associated, he argues, with the third spring the Qur'ān mentions, Tasnīm, whose literal meaning, "ascension," confirms this wine's superior status. When al-Qayṣarī discusses Ibn al-Fāriḍ's copious imagery of imbibing wine, he shifts his interpretative approach from one primarily grounded in a Qur'ānic-*ḥadīth* hermeneutics to one rooted in metaphysics. The intoxicating nature of wine is defined as the passing away of aspects of humanity and the "ruling property of duality" as the Sufi becomes united with the "divine essence," while drinking represents the final stage of the Neoplatonic emanation—that is, earthly entities receiving their share of the "everlasting divine effusion," which brings forth the "divine states" that are from the "treasury of the unseen" but available to worthy "servant[s]."

Sufi commentaries can continue in these interpretive veins sometimes for hundreds of pages, explicating each important poetic image and imaginal action in a poem as a representation of different metaphysical concepts and linking them to sources of authority within the Islamic tradition, such as the Qur'ān, *ḥadīth*, and the writings of other important Sufi and religious scholars. This process of linking Sufi poetic symbols to the tradition's sources of textual authority and metaphysics was an important part of legitimating this sometimes controversial mode of expressing mystical insights in the eyes of less "intoxicated" Muslims.[14] It also often functioned as an important site for intellectual creativity and poetic

13. al-Qayṣarī, "Commentary," 14–15 (English text), 18–20 (Arabic text).

14. Take, for example, the famous case of Ibn al-'Arabī's *Tarjumān al-Ashwāq*: After accusations were made against him regarding the scandalous nature of this love poetry, he wrote a poetic commentary elucidating the poem's meaning in terms of Sufi metaphysics. See Zargar, *Sufi Aesthetics*, 121.

transmission.[15] And it represents an undeniably important interpretative community within Sufism that informed the writers and audiences of Sufi poetry (especially after the thirteenth century) in varying degrees.[16]

But, as numerous scholars have argued, this mode of interpretation—if used in isolation—is quite limiting too because it approaches poetry primarily as a versification of Sufi thought. Poetic imagery becomes exclusively representational. It is always just an "allusion" to some other text, philosophical concept, or spiritual reality (*ma ʿnī*).[17] The diverse and dynamic Sufi poetic tradition becomes an encoded data repository that can only be decrypted and analyzed with the aid of Sufi commentaries and lexicons (*iṣṭilāḥāt*)—a "mechanical" interpretative approach that, if applied too rigidly, does not always even work. Sometimes the purportedly "real" esoteric meanings posited for each poetic image do not always even make sense when "plugged into" specific poetic contexts.[18] What imagery comes to mean in this interpretative framework is only accidentally connected to the imagery itself. Strictly speaking, there is no real reason why a particular image (e.g., wine) or imaginal action (e.g., drinking) is the symbolic representation of a metaphysical concept or spiritual experience. Poetic imagery does not do any other work for the poem's audience except to be a static, stylized, and conventional "pointer" to their *real* meanings that are located elsewhere.[19] It is all just "symbolic references encoded in poetic language," as Leonard Lewisohn argues in his discussion of Ḥāfiẓ's carnivalesque (*rindī*) poetics.[20]

15. The large interpretative tradition that grew up around Ibn al-Fāriḍ's poetry is an example *par excellence* of this dynamic. Commentaries on his poem became one of the primary vehicles for spreading Akbarian Sufism in both Persian and Arabic-speaking domains, even though the poem itself was written prior to the rise of Ibn al-ʿArabī's metaphysical Sufism. On this poem's commentary tradition, see Morris, "Ibn ʿArabi and His Interpreters Part II"; Morris, "Ibn ʿArabi and His Interpreters Part II (Conclusion)"; van Lit, "Ibn ʿArabī's School of Thought."

16. Ingenito argues that this symbolist hermeneutic approach expands significantly beginning in fourteenth and fifteenth centuries (*Beholding Beauty*, 247–48).

17. Meisami, "Allegorical Techniques"; Meisami, *Medieval Persian Court Poetry*, 239–42; Meisami, *Structure and Meaning*, 48–50, 387–403; Meisami, "Nāsir-i Khusraw"; Keshavarz, *Reading Mystical Lyric*, 18–20, 72–74; de Bruijn, *Persian Sufi Poetry*, 122; Yarshater, "Ǧazal II"; Hunsberger, "'On the Steed of Speech'"; J. Stetkevych, *The Zephyrs of Najd*, 92ff; Ingenito, *Beholding Beauty*, 247–48.

18. Meisami, *Medieval Persian Court Poetry*, 240–42; Keshavarz, *Reading Mystical Lyric*, 73–74; Meisami, *Structure and Meaning*, 48–50, 387–403; Meisami, "A Life in Poetry"; Homerin, *Wine of Love*, xxii.

19. Chittick, in his translation and discussion of part of the same chapters from Jāmī's commentary on Ibn al-Fāriḍ's wine ode that I examine in detail in this chapter, exemplifies this view. In his concern to make sure that no reader thinks Sufis were literally talking about real wine in their wine/love poetry, he disembodies the symbol of wine completely, arguing that Sufi imagery should only be seen as having metaphysical referents: "No doubt when Ḥāfiẓ speaks of wine, he means wine. The question is, 'What is wine?' All Sufi thought goes back to a cosmology and metaphysics. In order to understand the nature of wine, we must refer to the philosophical and metaphysical beliefs of the Sufi poets who employ the image" ("Jāmī on Divine Love," 193).

20. Lewisohn, "Prolegomenon to the Study of Hafiz," 55. This view of Sufi poetry has contributed to the current state of Sufi literary studies, where it is not uncommon, for example, to find studies on Sufi

With this critique of the symbolist interpretative method lodged, we also need to be careful to not reduce the entire Sufi commentary tradition to the most extreme versions of this one interpretative mode. Sufi commentaries do not all treat Sufi poetry as a ciphertext composed of archetypal symbols, abstracted out of contact with the world. There is more diversity in this interpretative genre than its modern critics have sometimes given it credit for. This is just one modality of Sufi hermeneutics. Zargar and Takacs have convincingly shown this in their studies looking at how some Sufi commentaries analyze poetic imagery as simultaneously pointing to embodied *and* supernal realities, both of which are capable in different and mutually reinforcing ways of revealing divine knowledge (for those with spiritual insight, at least).[21]

In what follows, I want to extend this reassessment of the Sufi commentary tradition further by focusing on two chapters from Jāmī's commentary on Ibn al-Fāriḍ's *khamriyya* that present his case for why Sufis employ the poetic symbol of wine (*khamr*) and the imaginal actions/experiences associated with it (e.g., drinking, intoxication) in poetry treating the spiritual love of God.[22] Sufi poets, in his assessment, did not just borrow or inherit the imagery of love and wine poetry and decide randomly to use it as the metaphoric representation of Sufism's amatory metaphysics, as some premodern and modern readers seem to implicitly suggest. Their engagement with and adaptation of it was motivated by, as Jāmī says, the "complete similitude" (*mushābahatī-yi tamām*) of wine and love—a deceptively simple characterization that conceals a complex implicit theory of the embodied nature of metaphoric imagery. As we will see below, what becomes clear in Jāmī's analysis is that what he ultimately means by "similitude" boils down to similarity in experiential somato-affective content. It is the structural parallels in the way something would present itself to one's body—as an event, as a set of possible affordances for engagement, as a felt experience, etc.—that makes it an apt

poets that read largely as intellectual biographies or histories of Sufi thought. These works, of course, are important in their own right, but they analyze Sufi poetry as everything except what it is—that is, poetry. They primarily employ what Jonathan D. Culler terms the "hermeneutics" approach to analyzing texts, which he characterizes as a "practice of interpretation, whose goal is to discover or determine the meaning of a text." While I certainly make use of "hermeneutic"-type approaches to Sufi poetry in this book too, my contention is that the full potential set of a text's meanings can only be surfaced if we place equal focus in our analyses on what Culler terms "poetics": the "devices, conventions and strategies of literature, of the means by which literary works create their effects"—"how," in other words, "works produce the effects they have for readers" (Culler, *Structuralist Poetics*, vii–viii; for a similar argument in the Persian literary studies, see also Meisami, "Nāsir-i Khusraw").

21. Zargar, *Sufi Aesthetics*, 120–150; Takacs, "Transposing Metaphors and Poetics from Text to World." Their arguments resonate in important ways with my arguments in chapter 1 and Ingenito's throughout *Beholding Beauty*.

22. My study here is focused on Jāmī's treatment of the symbol of wine in his commentary; it does not aim to be comprehensive. For an exhaustive look at wine symbolism and its connection to love in Persian Sufi literature, see Pourjavady, *Bādah-yi ʿishq*. For an equally exhaustive study of the theory and development of Persian poetic imagery, see Shafīʿī-Kadkanī, *Suvar-i khiyāl dar shiʿr-i Fārsī*.

image to metaphorically represent something else.[23] This is an embodied theory of metaphoric imagery, though, not embodied in the sense of poetic imagery being linked to external corporal referents in the poetic performance context.[24] It is an embodied theory of poetry rooted primarily in the somato-affective body and its feelingscape.

In presenting Jāmī's embodied theory of imagery, I do not mean to suggest that it is somehow *the* only right way to read Sufi poetry. Multiple approaches to poetic interpretation existed side by side in the Islamic world, from the tightly grammar- and philology-focused investigations of individual lines and rhetorical devices to more expansive Sufi symbolist interpretations of poems and philosophical reflections on the nature of poetry and imagery. In the case of Jāmī's commentary, we see more than one approach represented even in the same work.[25] My focus here on this one part of Jāmī's interpretative approach in his commentary aims to enrich our understanding of Sufi poetics, stressing especially the way it harnesses the body and its somato-affective system to convey nondiscursive meaning, and to act as a corrective to tendencies in the history of Sufi poetic analysis (premodern and modern) that read it as just another source for the study of Sufi ideas, "worldview," or even history, on the one hand, or as too conventional, allegorical, and rhetorical in nature to be connected to any sort of lived experience of the author, on the other.[26] Jāmī's account insists that there is a connection between the language of poetry and the lived reality of the author; it is just not a direct biographical or historical one. It is a somato-affective one mediated through an embodied conception of metaphor. If language, as Schaefer suggests, is a "highly sophisticated bodily tool that can circulate and distribute affects with amazing precision," it is

23. Zargar, in a couple of places, seems to start to move in this direction with comments such as: "A successful poem is one that is able to recreate best the experience known and shared by all gnostic lovers, indeed all lovers, since the experience of love is in fact one. . . . This representational form (the poem), if effective, will then induce a parallel experience in its audience" (*Sufi Aesthetics*, 121, 136, 148–49). Shahab Ahmed also, in his discussion of love and wine poetry, encourages readers to realize that there is a "*meaningful* relationship between 'metaphorical = earthly wine' and 'Real-True' wine" (*What Is Islam?*, 396, 422–23, emphasis original). Keshavarz too, criticizing the "'suitcase' theory" or "poetry as a container for a pre-existing meaning" approach, has strongly argued for the "inseparability of the poetic and mystical self" and, using a combination of Rūmī's reflections on poetry and Heidegger, that Sufi poetry is "ground[ed] . . . in mystical experience" (*Reading Mystical Lyric*, 18–30). See also citations to Sells's arguments on the relationship between "mystical" texts and experience in chapter 5.

24. This is the approach that I take in chapter 1, and also taken by Zargar, *Sufi Aesthetic*, 120–150; Takacs, "Transposing Metaphors and Poetics from Text to World"; Ingenito, *Beholding Beauty*.

25. This is a testament, as Meisami has pointed out, to the dynamism and diversity of perspectives on poetry (*Structure and Meaning*, xi). On the Arabic poetic commentary tradition, also see Larkin, "Abū l-ʿAlāʾ Al-Maʿarrī's Muʿjiz Aḥmad."

26. For examples and discussion of these different perspectives, see J. Stetkevych, "Arabic Poetry and Assorted Poetics"; Sells, "Guises of the Ghūl"; Meisami, *Structure and Meaning*, x, 2–4, 7–8, 346, 349–52, 379, 394, 471n37; de Bruijn, "The Ghazal in Medieval Persian Poetry," 342.

metaphoric imagery, Jāmī would emphasize (and al-Ghazālī would concur), that plays the central role in their dissemination through Sufi poetry.[27]

THE FORCE OF IMAGERY: THE "COMPLETE SIMILITUDE" OF EARTHLY WINE AND THE EMBODIED EXPERIENCE OF LOVE

Jāmī occupies a dual place in the cultural memory of the Persianate world. He is remembered as both a prolific Sufi intellectual and a first-class poet. His voluminous writings in a number of different genres, covering a wide range of disparate topics, show he was keenly aware of the breadth and depth of the Islamic sciences. At the same time, later litterateurs regarded his poetry so highly that they also cast him as the last great poet of the "classical" Persian poetic tradition—the "seal of the poets" (*khatam al-shuʿarā*) (a bold play on Prophet Muḥammad's designation in Islam as the "seal of the prophets"). While this framing of his poetry and place in Persian literary history is a bit problematic, it does capture at the broadest level a key point: Jāmī brings together a powerful command over the Islamic intellectual tradition with a master poet's sensitivity to language and meaning creation.[28] His works project both an intense impulse to intellectually theorize Sufism and explore it poetically.

This dually attuned approach is evidenced in his work that I consider in this chapter: his commentary on Ibn al-Fāriḍ's wine ode, entitled *Lavāmiʿ* (Flashes). It presents the reader with two distinct ways of analyzing the poem's central image of wine. Most of this work reads as a traditional Sufi symbolist commentary. His interlinear interpretations largely follow the patterns set down in al-Qayṣarī's work, with the exception that he spends significantly more space providing Persian definitions and glosses for the Arabic originals. He echoes al-Qayṣarī in framing his work as a "commentary on the words, phrases, unveiling[s], symbols, and allusions (*sharḥ-i alfāẓ va ʿibārāt va kashf va rumūz va ishārāt*) in the *Mīmiyyah khamriyyah* of Ibn al-Fāriḍ."[29] This goal, he continues, following al-Qayṣarī's example, is only possible if he first elaborates the "definition and division[s] of love (*maḥabbat*)" and explains "its root and branch[es]."[30] After this theoretical exploration of love, al-Qayṣarī moves on to his interlinear commentary on Ibn al-Fāriḍ's wine ode. Jāmī, however, adds two additional chapters, or "flashes" (s. *lāmiʿah*), as he terms them, at this point in his commentary. The first explains why Sufis use the image of wine when poetically treating the topic of love. The second expands on this discussion, abstracting it out to a broader exploration of the "several reasons" for

27. Schaefer, *Wild Experiment*, 19. al-Ghazālī similarly sees poetic imagery as central to the conveyance of æffect in verse, as we saw in chapter 3 and will see further in this chapter and the Conclusion.

28. Algar, *Jami*, 85–86. See this full work for a thorough recent overview of Jāmī's life, works, and thought; see also the excellent studies in Hubert and Papas, *Jāmī in Regional Contexts*.

29. Jāmī, "Lavāmiʿ (Afṣaḥ et al.)," 344.

30. Jāmī, "Lavāmiʿ (Afṣaḥ et al.), 344; al-Qayṣarī, "Commentary," 3.

"expressing meanings (*ma ʿānī*) in the clothing of forms" (EMICF)—the terminology he uses to characterize this process of employing earthly imagery to poetically convey meaning about divine realities (i.e., the *ma ʿānī*).[31]

Jāmī, as we will see in more detail below, anchors EMICF in the same æffective poetics as al-Ghazālī in the last chapter. Jāmī's discussion of poetry and æffect, however, takes an important step that al-Ghazālī's does not. He elaborates, in considerable detail, at least one way of precisely *how* Sufi metaphorical imagery can convey somato-affective meaning by drawing on embodied experience. al-Ghazālī, as we saw in the previous chapter, is certainly keenly aware of the importance of æffect in producing poetic meaning for the audience. But his treatment does not delve into the mechanics of how poetic imagery may convey somato-affective meaning to audience members in the way Jāmī's does. (The closest he comes to treating the *how* of this process is when he discusses the various ways in which audience members of varying levels of spiritual preparation "dispatch" (*tanzīl*) poetic images to different meanings, some wholesome and spiritual, others decidedly not, but all conveying somato-affective import).[32] This is where Jāmī's detailed consideration of why Sufis use the image of wine and intoxication for the poetic treatment of love adds an important new dimension to our understanding of the Sufi Path of Love's æffective poetics.[33]

31. Discussions of Sufi imagery that link the meaning of poetic images with the embodied experience of the earthly object or action are not isolated to Jāmī's commentary. Less developed comments push in this direction in other commentaries as well. al-Qaysarī, for example, in his discussion of line 2, also remarks,

> Just as he uses the word '*full moon*' metaphorically for the cup, he uses '*the sun*' as a metaphor for the spiritual drink due to the existence of the supra-sensory heat causing ecstasy, intoxication, and the illumination that enlightens hearts and spirits, indeed, the whole world. In fact, the light of the visible sun is its form and manifestation in the sensory world. (The poet) uses the noun '*crescent*' as a metaphor for the cup-bearer, drawing on the association they both have to turning in a circle. While the crescent moon circles in terms of its form, the cup-bearer actually turns in a circle to pass the cup around among the companions. What is meant by (the crescent) is the commander of the Faithful, (the forth (sic) caliph, Prophet Muḥammad's cousin and son-in-law) ʿAlī ibn Abī Ṭālib (d. 40/660), may God honor him!" ("Commentary," 17 [English], 21–22 [Arabic]).

In between dense passages focused on elaborating this line's poetic symbols as references to Islamic texts, figures, and Sufi concepts, al-Qayṣarī allows too that the sun is chosen as the figurative representative of the "spiritual drink" in this poem because it is experienced as a form of "supra-sensory heat" that causes "ecstasy, intoxication, and illumination." Similarly, when discussing the "crescent" image, he notes that the poet uses this image because the moon "turn[s] in a circle" like the cupbearer. Like Jāmī, he anchors the reason for the selection of this imagery in the structural similarity between the embodied experience of them and the spiritual experience he sees as treated in this poem. But unlike Jāmī's foregoing discussion of wine and love, he does not elaborate this point at length and his sporadic observations in this vein easily get lost among his much more extensively grammatical and metaphysical commentary.

32. For an examination of this aspect of al-Ghazālī's approach to poetry, see chapter 3.

33. al-Ghazālī's (and other Sufi authors') lack of an analogous detailed analysis of the nitty-gritty mechanics of imagery does not necessarily mean that they did not have similar ideas about how Sufi

Jāmī opens this discussion in the thirteenth chapter by asserting, "Passionate desire and love (*ʿishq va maḥabbat*) has complete similitude (*mushābahatī-yi tamām*) with earthly (*ṣūrī*) wine. Thus, the words and phrases that correspond to this topic [i.e., earthly wine] in Arabic and Persian are employed as metaphors for it (*az barā-yi ān ʾistiʿārah mī-kunand*) and they explain love with the various names for wine, such as *rāḥ*, *mudām*, and *may*. There are various facets and numerous aspects of this similitude."[34] Jāmī takes the reader in the opposite direction of the symbolist approach of most Sufi commentaries in the opening lines of this chapter. He does not rush to the esoteric levels of meaning by explaining the metaphysical realities and philosophical concepts these poetic images may represent or by indicating the verses of sacred texts to which they may allude. Instead, he presents a case for why earthly wine is used to metaphorically convey meaning about love (*ʿishq*, *maḥabbat*) in Sufi verse. He grounds his argument in the claim that the embodied experiences of these two substances possess a "complete" and multifaceted "similitude" (*mushābahat*). He never explicitly defines what he means by "similitude."[35] But the way he elaborates the "various facets and numerous aspects of th[e] similitude" of wine/love in the remainder of the chapter reads as an exceptionally detailed case study of how different realizations of wine imagery could function as what Perso-Arabic philosophers and literary theorists have termed "image-evoking utterances" (*al-aqāwīl al-mukhayyila*)—metaphoric imagery, that is, which conveys somato-affective meaning about its referent by calling to mind structurally similar embodied experiences.

Philosophers as early as al-Fārābī (d. 950) contend that poetry uses these "image-evoking utterances" to "imitate one's subject matter" and "evo[ke]" the mental construction of images and scenes (*takhyīl*) that the listener then makes meaning from by drawing on their associated past intellectual and embodied knowledge of similar objects or experiences. The primary aim of these "poetic utterances," according to al-Fārābī, is to be "evocative" and to "prompt" certain

---

imagery worked to convey somato-affective meaning. Most poetic commentaries and treatises on poetry do not discuss at length image complexes and how they create meaning at the level of the poem either (see Heinrichs, "Literary Theory"; Meisami, "Esteʿāra"; Larkin, "Limits of Poetic Commentary"). This does not mean, as Larkin and Meisami have noted, that these critics and their contemporaries did not appreciate "complex structures," such as the function of imagery in this more holistic way. They just were not the primary concern of the poetic commentary genre as they understood it (Larkin, "Limits of Poetic Commentary," 492–93; Meisami, *Structure and Meaning*, 9–15). Medieval Persian and Arabic literary critics did sometimes comment more holistically on these "complex structures" in ways that suggest they just assumed they existed without needing to theorize them (Larkin, "Limits of Poetic Commentary," 487, 491–92; Meisami, *Structure and Meaning*, 323–41). On the general lack of explicit theorization of a "recipient-oriented poetics of didacticism" in premodern Persian literary theory, see also O'Malley, *The Poetics of Spiritual Instruction*, 92, 119.

34. Jāmī, "Lavāmiʿ (Afṣaḥ et al.)," 358.

35. On al-Ghazālī's similar discussion of "similitudes (*mesal*)" and how they "function as 'ladders' through which one can ascend upwards towards the spiritual realm," see O'Malley, *The Poetics of Spiritual Instruction*, 196, 206. See also Zargar, *Sufi Aesthetics*, 26–30, 127–28.

somato-affective experiences in their listeners and thereby to move them to do certain actions, "positive or negative."[36] Ibn Sīnā (d. 1034), ʿAbd al-Qāhir al-Jurjānī (d. 1078–81), Abū al-Barakāt al-Baghdādī (d. ca. 1164), Naṣīr al-Dīn Ṭūsī (d. 1274), and Ḥāzim al-Qarṭājannī (d. 1285) all echo this view in different ways.[37] But, perhaps not surprisingly, it is the literary theorist al-Qarṭājannī who develops this perspective the furthest, arguing that poetry "is based on the evocation through images of the things that are conveyed by its utterances and by the implantation of their images in the mind through the beauty of imitation."[38] This "image-evocation," he continues, is how

> the poet, through his words, his motifs, or his combination of motifs and syntactic arrangements represents something to the listener, rousing in the latter's imagination a form or forms whose imagining or envisioning subliminally cause him a measure of relaxation or tension, either directly or because he envisions something else in them.[39]

This classical Perso-Arabic philosophical understanding of figurative language is a deeply embodied one, which centers both bodily experience and æffect in its meaning production process.[40] Imagery does not just represent, refer, or point to

36. al-Fārābī, "Jawāmiʿ al-Shiʿr," 173–75; English translation from al-Fārābī, "Treatise on Poetry," 17–18. Relatedly, in an interesting study of the role of affect in al-Fārābī's "political theory," Ali Altaf Mian observes that "Language, Farabi seems to be suggesting, emerges in and through our affective, bodily existence. . . . In a nutshell, Farabi seems to be saying that we come to name (we step into linguistic existence) through our sense-perceptive (affective and cognitive) interaction with the world" ("Muslim Political Philosophy," 54).

37. Ibn Sīnā, *al-Ishārāt*, 362–63; Ibn Sīnā, *Kitāb al-majmūʿ*; al-Baghdādī, *al-Kitāb al-Muʿtabar*, 1:276–78; al-Qarṭājannī, *Minhāj al-bulaghāʾ*, 62–129. English translations of most relevant sections can be found in Ibn Sīnā, "Remarks and Admonitions," 25; Ibn Sīnā, "Compendium," 26; al-Baghdādī, "Lessons in Wisdom," 71; al-Qarṭājannī, "Path of the Eloquent," 85–113. al-Jurjānī's account is especially interesting for how it often walks the reader through highly focused examples of the complex ways in which poetic imagery "makes [the listener] imagine (*khayyala*)" certain scenes, conveying information that draws on embodied experience in the world and induces æffective responses in some cases. See his various readings of lines of poetry in al-Jurjānī, *Asrār al-balāgha*, 241–96, and for English translation, see al-Jurjānī, "The Secrets of Eloquence," 30–69. On Naṣīr al-Dīn Ṭūsī's views, see Landau, "Nasīr al-Dīn Ṭūsī."

38. al-Qarṭājannī, *Minhāj al-bulaghāʾ*, 62; English translation from al-Qarṭājannī, "Path of the Eloquent," 85.

39. al-Qarṭājannī, *Minhāj al-bulaghāʾ*, 89; English translation from al-Qarṭājannī, "Path of the Eloquent," 93. As pointed out in chapter 2, Ibn Sīnā actually links the æffects of the *al-mukhayyilāt* in the audience members to the same process of "imprint[ing] (*tuʾaththir*) in a strange and wondrous way (*taʾthīran ʿajīban*) in the soul (*nafs*)" that al-Ghazālī discusses in the context of music. See Ibn Sīnā, *al-Ishārāt*, 362.

40. A number of scholars have discussed Perso-Arabic philosophical poetics and pointed to this (even if they did not use these terms): Landau, *De rythme et de raison*, 213–60; Landau, "Nasīr al-Dīn Ṭūsī" (which Ingenito also approvingly cites; see *Beholding Beauty*, 520–22); Kemal, *Philosophical Poetics*, especially 41–52, 78–135, 159–69, 277–85; Abu Deeb, *Al-Jurjānī's Theory of Poetic Imagery*,

conceptual or supernal meanings (*maʿānī*) in this paradigm; it "imitates" something in its referent as it stages an imaginary performance in the minds of its audience. It is not primarily attempting to convey intellectual information or present the reader with a complex array of symbolic allusions; its ultimate goal, in fact, is to make the audience *feel* in certain ways—to "move" or "excit[e] the soul," as Harb says, in different æffectively coded ways with the aim, according to Landau, of "prompting the listener to action by stirring passions in his soul."[41]

Jāmī's analysis of the specific image of wine and its referent, love, is built upon this theoretical foundation drawn from Perso-Arabic philosophical poetics. While the general contours of this theory of poetic imagery as the somato-affective engine of language are known, what has been less explored—especially in the Sufi context—is the question of *how* imagery actually does this. How does this process work at the image level? al-Jurjānī gives more details than most on this score, but Jāmī's treatment is much more thorough.[42] His account provides a rare glimpse into how this approach to metaphor was vernacularized into medieval Sufism and, perhaps more importantly, how this philosophical theory of metaphor could be operationalized as a mode of poetic analysis.[43]

83–93, 264–66, 257–302; Key, *Language*, 196–240. The degree to which individual poets were aware of these philosophical discussions of poetics likely varied. Some may have drawn directly from them, even if they did not cite or reference them in any way. Others may have indirectly made use of these ideas through their "ambient availability," as Mikkelson has argued ("Flights of Imagination," 41–43; see also Meisami, *Structure and Meaning*, 343). At a minimum, poets and litterateurs clearly saw Persian and Arabic poetry as having the power to æffect listeners, imagining it variously as a form of "licit magic" (Bürgel, *The Feather of Simurgh*; Meisami, *Structure and Meaning*, 64; Seyed-Gohrab, "Magic in Classical Persian Amatory Literature"), a medicine or drug (*taryāk* and *mufarriḥ*) (O'Malley, *The Poetics of Spiritual Instruction*, 90–125), and a catalyst for pleasure and wonder (Kemal, *Philosophical Poetics*, 88–124; Elias, *Aisha's Cushion*, 154–55, 160–62, 168–69; Harb, *Arabic Poetics*). For the complex social and political import of "sentiments" expressed through everyday recitation of short poems in a modern Arab Bedouin context, see Abu-Lughod's classic *Veiled Sentiments*, where she argues her subjects view poetry as "linked to the feelings of the self" (182) and "poetry's purpose [as] . . . transforming attitudes" and "moving people emotionally" (242, see also 177–85). Bray also emphasizes the centrality of emotional expression to poetry's social role in her studies: "Yaʿqūb b. al-Rabīʿ Read by al-Mutanabbī and al-Mubarrad" and "Codes of Emotion" (especially see comments on 185).

41. Landau, "Nasīr al-Dīn Ṭūsī," 15–16. As Harb points out, theorists of Arabic poetics, especially in and after the eleventh century, were quite interested in the "effect of poetic speech on the listener's emotions" and poetry's ability to "produce an emotional impact on the listener that is characterized by wonder," which she discusses as an "emotional experience," "emotional reaction," or "effect" (*Arabic Poetics*, throughout her work, but see 4–8, 73, 125 for quotes). Shafīʿī-Kadkanī points to this too in his voluminous study of the development of Persian poetic imagery (*Suvar-i khiyāl dar shiʿr-i Fārsī*, 23–27).

42. See Key, *Language*, 196–240, for an overview of al-Jurjānī's efforts to explain how "Poets put words together in patterns that impact the minds of the audience" (197).

43. Although, as noted previously, poetic commentaries and manuals do not often perform the complex and detailed analysis of particular images as Jāmī does in chapter 13 of *Lavāmiʿ*, they do sometimes note the æffective impact of poetry on audience members. See, for example, the overwhelming

Jāmī begins his elaboration of the similitude of wine/love by drawing parallels between their typical physical features and basic operating procedures in the world. They both, for example, share an origin inside of another entity (i.e., a wine vat and the heart) and they proceed out of these initial places of "fermentation" to fill other containers in the world in accordance with the capacity of those vessels.

> Just as wine intrinsically has no determined shape or special form, but rather its shapes and forms are in accordance with its containers and vessels—for example, in the vat, it is in the vat's circular form; in the pitcher, it is in the pitcher's concave form; and in the goblet, it is in the internal form of the goblet—so too the meaning of true love (*'ishq-i ḥaqīqī*) is unlimited (*muṭlaq*) and its manifestations in the lords of love are in accordance with the capabilities of their containers and preparedness of their vessels [i.e., in accordance with the extent of their spiritual preparation].[44]

As amorphous substances, wine/love have no "determined shape or special form"; they are limited to the "capabilities of [the] containers and preparedness of [the] vessels" in which they are fermented or poured. These containers are restricting but also shape the specific realization of these substances in crucial ways: The pitcher's walls make wine/love "concave," and the wine goblet likewise makes them appear in a tulip shape.[45] It would be a mistake, however, to read wine/love as inert substances. For while it is true that people and objects can mold, direct, and contain wine/love to some degree, they are decidedly not passive substances. They cannot be bottled up and ignored. They are powerful, and they powerfully transform the "containers" they inhabit and, through them, the world around them. They act and are experienced as a dominant force. This point is key, and it is the primary way in which wine and love evince a "complete similitude," according to Jāmī, at least judging by the amount of space he subsequently dedicates to elaborating the similar ways in which they *forcefully* act upon individuals:

> Just as wine's original station and first abode is the belly of the wine vat and the bottom of the wine barrel, [and] by means of the strength of its boiling and bubbling [produced during fermentation] it tends toward manifestation without any external stimulus, so too does the secret of love—which is concealed in the tight cavity of the

æffect of Rūdakī's *Bū-yi jū-yi Mūliyān* poem on the ruler in Niẓāmī 'Arūżī Samarqandī, *Chahār maqālah* (123, 132–34, 150) (see Introduction and Landau's treatment of this account in Nasīr al-Dīn Ṭūsī and *De rythme et de raison*); and the incredible power of *rubā'īs* as portrayed in Qays al-Rāzī, *Al-Mu'jam*. Larkin also mentions that "we would note that the literature surrounding al-Mutanabbi repeatedly refers, albeit in general terms, to the great emotional effect of his poetry" ("Abū l-'Alā' Al-Ma'arrī's Mu'jiz Aḥmad," 480–82).

44. Jāmī, "Lavāmi' (Afṣaḥ et al.)," 358.

45. As we will see in more detail in chapter 5, far from incidental, these basic shared characteristics shape the range and operation of love/wine's myriad individual poetic realizations because they provide the primary metaphors (e.g., CAUSES ARE PHYSICAL FORCES, PRESSURIZED CONTAINER) and metaphoric schemas (e.g., COMPULSION FORCE image schema) upon which poets build their imagery.

> hearts of lovers and innermost chamber of the heart of each desirous one—require discovery and manifestation without an external cause due to [its] dominance and predominance.[46]

Wine/love may both begin ensconced in their fixed vessels of origin, but they have an inherent internal energy that grows stronger when properly cultivated and eventually propels them—"without any external stimulus" or "cause"—toward self-manifestation of their inner reality. Jāmī uses the image of wine's fermentation process to make this idea more concrete, alluding to the fact that when smashed grapes are left in a vat, they will begin "boiling and bubbling" as they ferment. Although, as we know now, this reaction is the product of microscopic yeast particles converting sugars in the grape mash into alcohol and carbon dioxide, the process appears to be autogenic. The inert grape mash comes alive with movement and its "boiling and bubbling" grows in "strength" until it has been metamorphosed into an entirely new substance with the power to intoxicate and radically transform all who come into contact with it. This internal force that "require[s] discovery and manifestation" is what he terms love/wine's intrinsic *ghalabah va istīlā ʾ* ("dominance and predominance")—terms, you will recall, that we also saw earlier in various Persian and Arabic permutations (e.g., *ghālib, ghalaba, yaghlibu, mustawlī*) in several selections from ʿIrāqī's biography and al-Ghazālī's treatment of *samā ʿ*. As in these texts, Jāmī understands the feeling of *ghalabah va istīlā ʾ* as central to the experience of wine/love. It is at the root of their "complete similitude" because, as his subsequent analysis makes clear, the primary reason that wine is used as a metaphor for love is the somato-affective parallels in how these two substances make us feel and act.

Jāmī begins expanding on the point of wine/love's *ghalabah va istīlā ʾ* by identifying it as *ʿumūm-i sarayān:*

> Among the [aspects of wine and love's similitude] is its all-embracing penetration and spread (*ʿumūm-i sarayān*). Just as the æffect (*asar*) of earthly wine flows in each limb and member of the wine drinker, so too does the command (*ḥukm*) of the wine of love flow in all the senses (*quvā*) and faculties (*mashā ʾir*) of one who it possesses. Not a single hair on their body is freed from the being afflicted by love, nor is there a single vein in their body that does not throb with the demand of love. Like blood, it [love] has worked its way into their muscles and skin. Like the soul, it has set up its lodging on their inside and outside.[47]

The portrayal of wine/love as *ʿumūm-i sarayān*, translated here as "all-embracing penetration and spread," adds complexity and body to Jāmī's earlier characterization of this potent pair as containable in fixed vessels. The "strength" and "dominance and predominance" that are fostered through the fermentation of wine in the

46. Jāmī, "Lavāmiʿ (Afṣaḥ et al.)," 358. I am reading this line as "*istīlā[ʾ] bī-bā ʿis*" instead of "*istīlā ʾī bā ʿisī*," as in the text of the critical edition. Same reading can be found in these editions too: Jāmī, *Lavāmi ʿ-i Jāmī (ʿAbd al-Aḥad)*, 16; Jāmī, *Lavāmi ʿ-i Jāmī (Āl-i Āqā)*, 19.

47. Jāmī, "Lavāmiʿ (Afṣaḥ et al.)," 359.

vat and love in the heart eventually leads them to "flow" out into "in each limb and member" and "all the senses (*quvā*) and faculties (*mashā ʾir*)" of one who partakes of these intoxicating substances. They do not slowly leak out of containers. Once activated, they gush out like an overwhelming (i.e., "all-encompassing") torrent that forces their host into submission, penetrating every inch and fiber of their body down to the level of the subject's thousands of individual strands of hair.

Jāmī characterizes the nature of love/wine's intoxication colonization of the body as a *ḥukm*.[48] Just as the drunkenness of earthly wine produces a powerful æffect (*aṡar*) in one who imbibes it, wine too, he says, æffects those who partake of it, as it "flow[s]" out into them, establishing its "command (*ḥukm*)" over them. The term "*ḥukm*" can express a range of meanings depending on the context, but they all revolve around the central notion of "control," whether that control is expressed in the form of a "command/order," "authority/mandate," or "judgment/sentencing." An invading army, for example, would impose their *ḥukm* after conquering (e.g., *ghālib*) an enemy's lands. In this figuration, wine/love become the all-powerful commander of the bodies they subjugate—not even "a single hair" or "vein" remains unafflicted as they work their way "into their [subject's] muscles and skin" and establish themselves, as Jāmī says in the last line of this paragraph, in the commanding position formally held by the individual's soul.

What is most noteworthy about Jāmī's account of *ḥukm* is its predominant focus on the somato-affective entailments of love/wine.[49] It is a sustained meditation on how wine/love's *ḥukm* feels to the conquered body and, equally important, how it then makes the somato-affective body feel and act differently. After subjugating the body, love "afflict[s]" each hair.[50] Its "demand" makes every single vein "throb." "Like blood," it is felt rushing beneath the skin and in the muscles. It is a felt presence both on the subject's "inside and outside" that is "like the soul" in its intimate connection with the self but also experienced as something other than the subject's own soul. This sense that love is both something foreign and simultaneously something more true, real, and inseparably part of their body than the subject's own self is the mystery of love. Feeling this complex assemblage of somato-affective sensations is the first step on love/wine's journey because it makes the subject grasp the incompleteness of the self by making them pine for what they only now realize is missing. It makes them feel "need," as Jāmī forthrightly says

48. Recall, too, in the previous chapter, al-Ghazālī's characterization of the *samāʿ* participant's experience of æffects in *aḥwāl* as akin to being "conquer[ed]" and "intoxicat[ed]."

49. Compare these bodily transformations to those wrought upon the body by earthly love, according to Islamic poets, philosophers, physicians, and other intellectuals. See especially Alharthi, *The Body in Arabic Love Poetry*, 189–217, and scattered discussions of the æffects of love on the body in Giffen, *Theory of Profane Love*; Bell, *Love Theory*.

50. For more discussion of how the felt sense of "subjugation" itself should be understood epistemologically, see my discussion of ʿIrāqī being conquered by love in chapter 1.

later.[51] It provides a somato-affective object lesson in the illusion of the separate and self-sufficient "I" as it dislodges the self from control and drives them to seek something outside of themselves.

This road of longing and yearning spurs the lover/drunkard to seek more, despite, as we will see below, the dire personal and social consequences of this path. "However much more they drink," Jāmī observes, "they [still] search for more. However much their drinking increases, they increase the amount of hardship (*ranj*) they expend in search for it."[52] This is what we would characterize today as addiction. This search is a compulsion. It is felt as a physical craving: The body propels the victim to do this. It is not intellectual in nature, and no amount of rational explanation, as any addict would tell you, could ever explain its visceral depths nor persuade the love/wine addicted to abandon their increasingly frantic and self-destructive efforts to quench this painful thirst.

The *ranj*—a word whose semantic range includes "pain," "toil," or even "affliction"—they endure in this search is a psychological and physical consequence of the drunk's drive for increasing amounts of their drug. In one sense, it is part of the afflictive pedagogy of love I discussed earlier: It builds the drunks' capacity to endure the increasing amounts of physical and psychological tribulation that they must be ready for as their need for more love/wine grows.[53] In another sense, it also whets their desire for what they are endeavoring to acquire because it acts as a powerful reminder that they are missing something their body needs. This missing piece is why they are *ranj*-ing. Obtaining it, they know, will grant them the bliss that they once knew. It will make them feel right and whole again. In this way, this *ranj* furthers the ultimate program of self-dissolution that wine/love set in motion as it drives them onward on their endless search for more.

The æffects of wine/love on its subject's body, however, are not only a personal matter. Wine/love also "makes," "forms," or "fashions" (*sāzand*) new æffective states for their subjects that are rooted in social webs of meaning and have deeply social consequences: "Wine makes (*sāzand*) its drinker, and love, its possessor, even if greedy and miserly in nature, generous and liberal. . . . One who is drunk [on earthly wine] freely gives away dinars, and one who is drunk on the wine of love gives away the currency of both worlds at once."[54] Here, Jāmī begins drawing out the diverse ways in which wine/love reorient their subject's æffective relation with the world in similar ways.[55] In the preceding example, wine/love make even the most "greedy and

51. Jāmī, "Lavāmiʿ (Afṣaḥ et al.)," 359. Relatedly, see discussion of the Sufi lover's need for need in chapter 1.

52. Jāmī, "Lavāmiʿ (Afṣaḥ et al.)," 360.

53. See Introduction and chapter 1.

54. Jāmī, "Lavāmiʿ (Afṣaḥ et al.)," 359.

55. Although this not a point I develop at length in this study, the way in which æffects "orient" subjects toward or away from certain objects, identities, persons, political projects/ideologies, etc. in the socio-political realm is one of the primary ways it powerfully shapes cultural politics, as Sara

miserly" suddenly "generous and liberal," ready, as he says, "to give away the currency of both worlds at once" without a care or a second thought.

In the following paragraphs, he builds on this basic point through examples illustrating wine/love's abilities to force other dramatic æffective transformations, such as making drunkards "fearless and reckless, free of the characteristics of timidity or fear"; throwing down the self-important "delicate ones from their high stations of honor and eminence to the threshold of humility and neediness"; driving the formerly honorable and God-fearing to "remov[e] the veil of shame and modesty"; and disclosing the sacrosanct divine secrets that God shares only with his closest Sufi lovers.[56] These refashionings of the drunkards' æffective selves are not subtle. The wine/love-drunk does not just become a little bolder in their daily interactions; they, according to Jāmī, "[act as if they] have had their fill of life" in truly "dangerous places" and "perilous situations."[57]

True intoxication does not just produce reputation-staining peccadilloes; it induces the drunk to actively court social calumny and "tosses the esteemed ones of the world from their pinnacles of honor and power to the depths of abjectness and contempt." They scatter the explosive and dangerous (to spiritually unsophisticated ears, at least) secrets of their beloved, the sovereign of the universe, not some furtive trifles they purloined from snatching a classmate's note in transit at school.[58] The emphasis in all these examples is on the profound gulf between the preintoxicated (socio-)æffective state of the subject and that of their later intoxicated self. The distance traveled on these spectra (e.g., from timidity to fearlessness, respectability to rascality) indexes the power and degree of control that wine/love have over their subjects.[59] It is absolute: They do not compromise with anyone or anything.

These examples bring to the fore a key point implicit in Jāmī's account. Wine/love do not flow in the bodies of those who imbibe them and remain contained there. Sufi æffect may be subjectively experienced, but it is social too. It is socially productive. It is a powerful social agent that forges not only identities but cultures and politics too.[60] After wine/love ravage and seize control of their drunkards' internal sensoria and somato-affective systems, they spill out into the world, if not

Ahmed has shown at length in *Cultural Politics* and *Queer Phenomenology*. Emotions/æffects are part of "affective economies" and, as she says in an article by that title, they "do things, and they align individuals with communities—or bodily space with social space—through the very intensity of their attachments. Rather than seeing emotions as psychological dispositions, we need to consider how they work, in concrete and particular ways, to mediate the relationship between the psychic and the social, and between the individual and the collective" (119).

56. Jāmī, "Lavāmiʿ (Afṣaḥ et al.)," 359–60.

57. Jāmī, "Lavāmiʿ (Afṣaḥ et al.)," 359.

58. Jāmī, "Lavāmiʿ (Afṣaḥ et al.)," 359.

59. Relatedly, see chapter 5 for more examples of how the extreme nature of these transformations plays out in poetic imagery.

60. This point is a mainstay of much work in affect theory and history of emotions. See studies of Sara Ahmed cited in this chapter and those studies cited in the Introduction.

literally, then at least indirectly in the form of the actions they force their subjects to perform. Jāmī illustrates this point here with his focus on this series of æffective refashionings of the wine/love-drunk's personality: greedy→generous, fearful/timid→brave/reckless, arrogant→humble/needy, honorable/God-fearing→shameless/immodest/blame-seeking, and trustworthy→unreliable. These spectra of personality dispositions are both personal and social. They are personal in the sense that, first, they each are associated with a range of internal felt senses (e.g., to be greedy is experienced as a physical sense of retraction from giving away items and agitation when forced to; fear is characterized by psychological and physical retraction and the somatic symptoms associated with fight or flight), and second, they are the realization of social codes in the individual. But what constitutes these different social mores is not the individual's prerogative. They are socially constructed, and the meaning of an individual's performance of them is socially determined.

Sufis of the Path of Love are most (in)famous for their performances of a constellation of behaviors that draw on the fearful/timid→brave/reckless and honorable/God-fearing→shameless/immodest spectra. We saw powerful examples of such bold and disreputable antinomian social performances in ʿIrāqī's biography (chapters 1 and 2) and we will see further poetic figurations of it in the next chapter in an example of ʿAṭṭār's "rogue poetry" (*qalandariyyāt*). No longer held back by the tethers of fear, shame, or modesty and their somato-affective senses of retraction and control, Sufi lovers are frequently portrayed as rushing forth to engage in "blame-seeking" (*malāmatī*) behaviors.[61] These social performances are doubly æffective. They externally manifest the profound æffective transformation of the Sufi, and they aim to æffectively transform others through their spectacle of shocking impropriety. They want to performatively spill a bit of wine/love for their audience so they too might catch a drop and join the search for more. Those in the audience who are not ready to seize this opportunity play a different, though not less æffective, role. They read this roguish behavior as blameworthy—a response that plays right into the hands of the Sufi lovers. Sufi lovers welcome this blame as a tool for (æffectively) disciplining what remains of their self. Social opprobrium joins forces with wine/love to dispatch any remnants of the lover's self, ensuring no pride or arrogance in their (now former) high socio-religious position remains inside them to prop up the beleaguered self. Æffect, in its subjective somato-affective and social dimensions, is the catalyst, language, and spiritual tool of these performances. It is how they mean socially and personally to both their audiences and performers.

Jāmī brings this chapter to a conclusion with the image of the lover reunited with the source of their love, engulfed in "happiness" (*inbisāṭ*): "When love's

61. On *malāmatī* in Sufism, see Karamustafa, *God's Unruly Friends*, 34–36; Sviri, *Perspectives on Early Islamic Mysticism*, 77–101; Salamah-Qudsi, "Yūsuf ibn al-Ḥusayn al-Rāzī."

intoxication becomes dominant (*istīlā ʾ yābad*), the lover turns their face away from everything else and sits on the carpet of happiness (*inbisāṭ*) and rids themselves of anything opposed to it."[62] The drunk's feeling of "happiness" here is complex. It needs to be seen as the resolution and culmination of the æffectively variegated path of the wine/love drunkard. It is part satiation from acquiring what their body was craving. It is part relief at reaching the end of their long, *ranj*-filled search. It is part elation at reunion with their beloved. It is part, as the Persian and Arabic *inbisāṭ* suggests, that sense of openness, expansion of horizon, and unlimited possibilities we feel when something exhilarates us.[63] It is part release or freedom, in a triple sense: from the physical tension and agitation that builds from being put off from what one craves, from the other enticements and social mores that would prevent their exclusive devotion to the object of their love ("the lover turns their face away from everything else . . . and rids themselves of anything opposed to it"), and, most importantly, from the reins of the self.[64] Indeed, this is ultimately the greatest joy for the love-drunk: to achieve self-annihilation (*fanā ʾ*), to be rendered "unconscious" and "free from the shackles of existence and self-worship," to pass away in the beloved's arms.[65]

This experience of self-annihilation should not, however, be understood as free of feeling. As Jāmī reminds his readers, returning to his key opening point, it is only when "love's intoxication becomes dominant (*istīlā ʾ yābad*)" over them that they can even hope to approach this "carpet of happiness (*inbisāṭ*)." They must feel, as I will discuss in more detail in chapter 5, *dominated* if they are truly self-annihilated. It is the forceful nature of love/wine that makes all the other transformations discussed here possible. And it is the experience of this force that ultimately communicates the greatest of God's divine secrets: the illusion of the self and its corollary, the absolute unity of God and existence. The drunken Sufi Path of Love leads, as Jāmī says in this same account, to "the perfection of perception (*shu ʿūr*) and awareness of the Beloved (God)," "secrets of divine unity and the realities (*ḥaqā ʾiq*) of spiritual tastings and ecstasies (*az̲vāq va mavājīd*)," and "the heights of the degrees of proximity and union."[66] But the path there is not through Sufi metaphysics. The Sufi lover must *feel* their way to God and his divine secrets. Drunks do not imbibe wine/love to learn about it intellectually; they do it

62. Jāmī, "Lavāmiʿ (Afṣaḥ et al.)," 361.

63. On this feeling, see also ʿIrāqī's inset poem in the anecdote on his conversion to the Sufi Path of Love at the hands of the *qalandar* youth, where he says "The whole world could not contain me in this joyful state / if for but one moment you would be my bosom buddy" (chapter 1).

64. On the tension and agitation that comes from not being able to achieve what is longed for, see discussion in chapter 2 of al-Ghazālī's example of the youth who does not know for what he longs and therefore cannot release his sexual drive.

65. Jāmī, "Lavāmiʿ (Afṣaḥ et al.)," 360.

66. Jāmī, "Lavāmiʿ (Afṣaḥ et al.)," 360.

to taste something, to *feel* something—to get taken over and dominated by it, to lose oneself.

By the time the reader reaches the end of Jāmī's account of wine/love's "complete similitude" in chapter 13 of *Lavāmiʿ*, they could be forgiven for forgetting that it starts with the goal of explaining why the primary imagery Sufis use in poetry to metaphorically treat their love for God is that of earthly wine and its consumption and intoxication. The account is so focused on exploring the somato-affective experiential affinity of wine/love that the initial stated aim of discussing their poetic operation as metaphoric imagery seems to fade into the background. But this is precisely why Jāmī's account here is instructive. It shows us a different face of poetic meaning in Sufi poetry. As most scholarly treatments of Sufi poetry emphasize, for Jāmī, wine and its associated paraphernalia and experiences do function as symbols (*rumūz*) representing divine realities and spiritual meanings and as allusions (*ishārāt*) to complex metaphysical concepts and scriptural passages, all of which he deftly explores at length in later chapters of *Lavāmiʿ*. But this is not *why* wine was chosen as the preeminent imaginal embodiment of love. What drives its selection, Jāmī argues here, is that it is best able to communicate what love *feels* like—which is *also* what it means—to the Sufi body.[67] Jāmī's theory of imagery is a motivated one, and it roots the meaning of Sufi imagery as much in the body and its somato-affective feelingscape as in Sufi metaphysics or the supernal realm.[68]

FROM "FEELING AN INCLINATION" TO "FALLING INTO AGITATION": EMICF AND THE DISTRIBUTION OF ÆFFECT

In chapter 14 of *Lavāmiʿ*, Jāmī zooms out from his detailed analysis of the "various facets and numerous aspects of [wine/love's] similitude" in the previous chapter to explore at a more theoretical level why Sufis adopt this approach to poetically treating love. He aims to defend this technique, which he terms here the "expression

67. There are some interesting parallels between Jāmī's analysis here of how an individual poetic image conveys æffective meaning and what Osborne identifies as Sayyid Qutb's "affective mode of reading" the Qurʾān, in which he focuses on the "nondiscursive" dimension of its meaning and how he "experiences" "the words of the Qur'an" and how they "feel to him," as "Qur'anic imagery produces images in his mind, evoking feelings." Judging from Jāmī's account here, I believe he would concur completely with Osborne's reading of Qutb's Qurʾānic hermeneutics: "The Qur'an . . . communicates those lessons through meanings that are felt in addition to being comprehended through intellectual means. The words of the lesson do not appear on the page, rather they can be gleaned only through imagining or feeling the images that they describe and evoke" ("Feeling the Words," 5, 8).

68. Jāmī's view of language has interesting overlaps with contemporary theories of meaning and language coming out of the broad interdisciplinary tent of disciplines, termed embodied cognition and cognitive linguistics, in particular. On this perspective on language and meaning, see Introduction and Conclusion.

of meanings (*ma ʿānī*) in the clothing of forms (*suvar*)" (EMICF), by situating it on a firm Islamic philosophical and Sufi theoretical foundation.[69] He claims that there are a "few reasons" for the Sufi use of the technique of EMICF, all of which revolve around the paradoxical capacity of "forms"—both physical bodily and imaginal bodily ones—to both veil and unveil higher spiritual realities.

Jāmī begins by rooting the EMICF approach in the common philosophical understanding of the progression of knowledge from what can be sensed in the world (*maḥsūsāt*) to what can be cognized (*maʿqūlāt*).[70]

> One [reason] is that a human in the beginning state arrives to the intellected (*maʿqūlāt*) from the sensed (*maḥsūsāt*) by means of the application of the tools of sense (*ḥiss*) and imagination (*khiyāl*) and knows the universals from the particulars. Thus, comprehending meanings is not familiar to their soul and habitual for their nature except in the cover of forms. If it is done in a different way, it is possible that the strength of his understanding (*fahm*) will not reach it [i.e., the meaning] and the power of his comprehension will not grasp it.[71]

The movement from sensed/particular to intellected/universal is one of ascension up an epistemological ladder. Those "in the beginning state" start off immersed in the embodied world—the world of forms—unable to use anything but their bodily senses to understand their material environment and place in the universe. They cannot directly understand higher spiritual or intellectual meanings and ideas (*maʿānī, maʿqūlāt*) because it is not "familiar to their soul and habitual for their nature." The power of their "understanding" (*fahm*) and "comprehension" (*idrāk*) is not sufficient to do this act alone. But there is hope yet for this group of fledgling, world-enmeshed novices, and it comes in the garb of our familiar friend "forms."

Applying the "tools of sense (*ḥiss*) and imagination (*khiyāl*)" to the material and imaginal forms of the world, they can begin to progress on the epistemological

69. The EMICF phrase is not Jāmī's invention. It, and close variations on it, also show up earlier in the Sufi tradition in a lexicon (*iṣṭilāḥāt*) (mis-)attributed to ʿIrāqī and a passage from ʿAṭṭār's *Mukhtār-nāmah*, for example, which indicates that this understanding of metaphoric imagery was much more widespread and not just an idiosyncrasy of Jāmī. See Zargar, *Sufi Aesthetics*, 132–33; O'Malley, *The Poetics of Spiritual Instruction*, 78–79.

70. The broader philosophical-literary framework for this progression has been extensively discussed elsewhere. For the philosophical and Sufi background of using what can be sensed (the particular) as pedagogical ladder to what can be intellected (the universal) (especially its roots in Ibn Sīnā's philosophy), see Kemal, *Philosophical Poetics*, 125, 269; Zargar, *Sufi Aesthetics*; Ingenito, *Beholding Beauty*, 168–70, 295–96, 322–23; Landau, "Nasīr al-Dīn Ṭūsī," 54; Elias, *Aisha's Cushion*, 218–35; Harb, *Arabic Poetics*, 138–70, especially relevant statements on 141, 157–58; O'Malley, *The Poetics of Spiritual Instruction*, 196, 206. For the literary background of this concept see Meisami, *Structure and Meaning*, 203–4, 389–92, 439n4, 464–65n8, 470n33; Heinrichs, "On the Figurative (*Majāz*)"; al-Jurjānī, "The Secrets of Eloquence," 57.

71. Jāmī, "Lavāmiʿ (Afṣaḥ et al.)," 361.

path to grasping *ma ʿānī* and *ma ʿqūlāt* more directly. Forms, in their linguistic and bodily manifestations, mediate this process, functioning in a dual role. On the one hand, Jāmī regards them as a protective "veil" that conceals the "secrets" and "states" of those "intimates of the secrets of Truth (*ḥaqīqat*)" and "states (*aḥvāl*) of the [Sufi] path" when they are disclosed in language or, in the case of *shāhid-bāzī*, in bodies, as we saw in chapter 1. This act of occlusion keeps these powerful secrets "far from the eyes of the strangers" (who could be hostile to Sufism) and those not yet spiritually prepared enough to handle their explosive implications.

But, on the other hand, Jāmī also sees forms as the central means by which God reveals these "secrets." It is only in the "clothing of form" that their "benefit" can be "universal" and their "utility . . . complete." The reason for this is that "form-worshipper[s]" (*ṣūrat-parast*)—that is, those people in the world who are not (yet) spiritual adepts but have a natural aptitude for perceiving higher spiritual meanings—are "frequently" able to catch glimpses of the "beam[s] of light" that meaning "cast[s] . . . from behind the veil of form." Even though their still-underdeveloped power of understanding is not yet sharp enough to grasp the "beauty of meaning" in its raw mode of presentation, they can use their embodied tools of "sense and imagination" and the (imaginally) embodied scaffold of meaning in poetic imagery to begin the process of spiritual refinement, to start "sharp[ening]" their "understanding" and making "their secret (*sirr*) fine."[72] Forms are, thus, Janus-faced: They unveil as much as they veil.

If this reasoning feels familiar to the reader, it is because what we see encapsulated here is another iteration of the philosophical justification for the ritual practice of *shāhid-bāzī* discussed in chapter 1. Forms, in their material or imaginal bodily mode of manifestation, contain within them a bit of the Real, whether that Real is the beauty of God in the former case or the higher divine spiritual secrets that are termed *ma ʿānī* in the latter. The key point of similarity I want to draw out for the purposes of this chapter is that they also operate through a similar process of æffective excitation to knowledge. In the ritual of *shāhid-bāzī*, the shard of God's beauty embodied in the earthly beloved ignites the fires of love in the onlooker and entrains their somato-affective system to become a lover-subject. In the context of poetry, it is the "beauty of meaning" (*jamāl-i ma ʿnī*), as Jāmī terms it, that excites an "inclination" in the attuned audience member and begins an analogous process of æffective formation.

The term he uses for "inclination," "*mayl*," should be understood as an internal bodily urge, a feeling of being pushed or pulled, that moves an individual toward—that is, inclines them—or attracts them to something. It could also be translated as a "desire" or "wish."[73] It is this push or attraction, this realization of

72. Jāmī, "Lavāmiʿ (Afṣaḥ et al.)," 361–62.

73. I prefer "inclination" because it cleaves more to the root meaning of the word and better conveys the felt sense of this term as an ill-defined, though still potent, bodily push/draw towards

need and desire for something more, that propels the form-worshipper to "escape from form and enmesh themselves in meaning." As in the cases of the wine/love drunks of Jāmī's preceding chapter and the young Sufi lover practitioners of *shāhid-bāzī* in chapter 1, it is this somato-affective experience that provides the first rungs of the EMICF epistemological ladder, teaching them that they are not self-sufficient or in control. They must feel this first if they have any hope of coming to *know*—in the experiential sense of *shinākhtan* and *maʿrifat*—"the secrets and (experiential) knowledge (*maʿārif*) of the (experientially) knowledgeable ones (*aṣḥāb-i maʿrifat*)."[74]

But EMICF is not just for those in "the beginning state" or even Sufi novices. At first glance, Jāmī may seem to imply this. The way he discusses the more advanced spiritual seekers, those "people of meaning" who can "benefit from the expression of meaning without forms," suggests that they have no need for forms at all. They should, he appears to imply, be able to go straight to the *maʿānī* and *maʿqūlāt*. Their "understanding" is sufficient to dispense with EMICF and the lower, embodied rungs of the epistemological ladder to God and his divine secrets. They have a direct line already established. They are, after all, the "intimates of the secrets of Truth (*ḥaqīqat*)" from whom God does not need to veil his *maʿānī*.

This reading of Jāmī's account is tempting. But it misses a key point. While Sufi masters may well have been able to dispense with forms, in practice even many of the most accomplished Sufis continued to make avid use of imaginal and bodily "forms" in their spiritual practice. We saw this vacillation in the discussion of *shāhid-bāzī* in chapter 1 too: Sufis keep using the embodied forms of beautiful young *shāhid*s, even after they are assumed to have achieved union with the real beloved—God—and be able to grasp "meaning" directly.[75] Even past the point of spiritual mastery, Sufis continue to go back and forth on the *majāz*→*ḥaqīqa* bridge on offer in the ritual of *shāhid-bāzī*. It is no different in the case of poetry and the imaginal forms it offers to its audience members, from beginners to adepts. Most Sufis, especially those of the Path of Love (only a small number of whom are discussed in this book), were deeply engaged with poetry, often both reading/listening to and writing it. Just as in the case with their *shāhid-bāzī*-practicing brethren, they continued ascending and descending EMICF's sensed/particular→intellected/universal ladder. Neither bridges nor ladders are typically used for one-way traffic.[76]

---

something. *Mayl* is also what we feel when we love something, and it is commonplace in Sufi discussions of love. See, for example, the quote from al-Ghazālī on this point in chapter 2 (drawn from Kukkonen, "Al-Ghazālī on the Emotions," 143). It is central to love's somato-affective repertoire of feelings that it evokes in its subjects.

74. Jāmī, "Lavāmiʿ (Afṣaḥ et al.)," 361–62. See Introduction on *shinākhtan* and *maʿrifat*.

75. See also chapter 1, which contains a quote from Jāmī on this exact point too.

76. The world and its earthly forms act together to push even accomplished Sufis closer to God, as Ingenito says, summarizing Saʿdī's views on this topic: "The sensible and the suprasensible blend

This more expansive understanding of the use of forms in Sufi practice is also reflected in Jāmī's account of the "reasons for the expression of meanings (*maʿānī*) in the clothing of forms" in chapter 14 of *Lavāmiʿ*. It is, however, easy to miss because Jāmī focuses so strongly in the first three-fourths of his account on (1) the pedagogical role that EMICF plays in scaffolding "human[s] in the beginning state" to *maʿānī*, and (2) how imaginal forms block the access of those yet too immature for or hostile to the real spiritual *maʿānī*. This reading is also reinforced by the narrative weight of past scholarship, which has tended to rush readers across the embodied bridges to God and the divine realms of *maʿānī*, as I noted in chapter 1. But Jāmī indicates that there is a third (and final) reason for EMICF too, and it is as operative for more advanced Sufis as the novices.

> Another reason is that when the tastings and ecstasies (*az̤vāq va mavājīd*) of the lords of love and the secrets and (experiential) knowledge (*maʿārif*) of the (experientially) knowledgeable ones (*aṣḥāb-i maʿrifat*) are mentioned in the tongue of allusion (*ishārat*), the æffect (*taʾs̱īr*) of it in the souls of the listeners is greater than when done in explicit language. Therefore, the state (*ḥālī*) of many of this group is not transformed from listening to the verses or words of the Qurʾān, but their state (*ḥāl*) does transform and they fall into agitation (*shūr oftad*) from one or more lines of Persian or Arabic poetry containing description of the tresses or the beauty marks of the beautiful ones and coquetry and amorous glances of the beloveds or mentioning wine, the winehouse, goblets, or chalices [of wine].[77]

This final paragraph of Jāmī's fourteenth chapter is as rich as it is short. Unlike the preceding paragraphs, Jāmī does not specify which levels of individuals it applies to. There is no talk of this "reason" for EMICF being relevant for those "in the beginning state," *maʿānī*-curious "form-worshippers," "people of (earthly) forms (*ahl-e ṣūrat*)," or "people of meaning" (*ahl-e maʿnī*), as we saw before. There are two groups mentioned: Sufi masters (i.e., the "lords of love" and the "(experientially) knowledgeable ones") and generic "listeners." The following sentence then refers back to "this group (*īn ṭāʾifah*)" as not being transformed by the Qurʾān but profoundly so by a few lines of Persian or Arabic anacreontic poetry. It is somewhat ambiguous who Jāmī intends to include in "this group" whose "state" (*ḥāl*) EMICF somehow aids in transforming. But there are several indications that he intends this "reason" to apply more broadly to the whole spectrum of listeners, from spiritual novices to masters.

The way he opens this paragraph—referring to the "tastings and ecstasies (*az̤vāq va mavājīd*) of the lords of love and the secrets and (experiential) knowledge (*maʿārif*) of the (experientially) knowledgeable ones (*aṣḥāb-i maʿrifat*)," which the poetic imagery alludes to—suggests that the "listeners" he has in mind

into each other in such a way that the more the lyric subject plunges into the beautiful mud of earthly experiences, the more its heart resounds with supernal meanings" (*Beholding Beauty*, 281).

77. Jāmī, "Lavāmiʿ (Afṣaḥ et al.)," 362.

here are at the very least capable of perceiving *ma ʿānī* with the aid of forms. They must *at least* be one of those former "form-worshippers" who caught a glimpse of meaning "behind the veil of form" and had their understanding refined to the point where they could perceive such *ma ʿānī* in the "tongue of allusion (*ishārāt*)" (i.e., imaginal forms). Those in "this group," in other words, must already have had some spiritual formation, even if they are still budding Sufi novices.

We should not, however, imagine the composition of "this group" to be restricted to spiritual beginners. Sufi masters too made plentiful use of poetry for the exact purpose Jāmī lays out here. al-Ghazālī, for example, in his account of why poetry is more æffective than the Qurʾān (which Jāmī clearly echoes in abbreviated form here), gives the example of the bona fide Sufi master Yūsuf ibn al-Ḥusayn al-Rāzī (d. 916–17), who, he reports, was reading the Qurʾān all day in a mosque to no great spiritual avail.[78] But, when a traveler who had come to visit him recited a couple of lines of poetry, he broke down crying and declared: "Since the morning prayer, I have been reading the Qurʾān and not a single tear has dropped from my eyes, but the resurrection [happened for me] (*qāmat al-qiyāma*) upon [hearing] those two lines of poetry!" al-Ghazālī, reflecting on this story, then concludes, "So when hearts are ablaze in the love of God Almighty an unfamiliar line of poetry will excite in them that which the recitation of the Qurʾān cannot." The "greater" æffect of the EMICF-powered "tongue of allusion" in poetry, in other words, is not just for novices still reliant on the crutch of forms. It also æffectively drives the spiritual life of Sufi masters, those already "ablaze in the love of God Almighty."[79]

Jāmī's account parallels al-Ghazālī's treatment in another way too. He links together the "tastings and ecstasies (*azvāq va mavājīd*) of the lords of love and the secrets and (experiential) knowledge (*ma ʿārif*) of the (experientially) knowledgeable ones (*aṣḥāb-i ma ʿrifat*)" with æffect as well. When mentioned in "the tongue of allusion" in poetry, he claims, their "æffect (*taʾsīr*) in the souls of the listeners is greater" than when presented in "explicit language (*bi-ṣarīḥ ibārat*)." What EMICF communicates to the listener is not just a form of intellectual meaning. As we saw in al-Ghazālī's discussions of *taʾthīr* and æffective hermeneutics in the previous chapters as well, it *means* to the audience by acting upon them, leaving a mark, æffecting and transforming them.

---

78. See Salamah-Qudsi, "Yūsuf ibn al-Ḥusayn al-Rāzī."
79. al-Ghazālī, *Iḥyāʾ*, 2:297–98. al-Ghazālī does concede in the parallel discussion in *Kīmiyā* that ultimately *samāʿ* is more æffective than the Qurʾan in inducing *wajd* because of the "weakness of the listener." Truly extraordinary lovers can make "*samāʿ* out of anything" and, through particularly elaborate hermeneutic maneuvers, attain *wajd* from anything they hear (see the examples of the figures experiencing *wajd* even upon hearing legalistic verses of the Qurʾān, discussed in chapter 3). But this, he cautions, is very "rare," and it does not negate that many who are "ablaze in the love of God Almighty" and already Sufi masters made ready use of *samāʿ* for its unparalleled ability to induce *wajd* and transform "states." See al-Ghazālī, *Kīmiyā*, 371–72; al-Ghazālī, *Iḥyāʾ*, 2:295.

The example that Jāmī proceeds to give to illustrate this assertion is a generic version of al-Ghazālī's story of al-Rāzī mentioned above: "Many in this group" remain unmoved by Qur'ānic recitation, but then suddenly "one or more lines of Persian or Arabic poetry containing description of the tresses or the beauty marks of the beautiful ones and coquetry and amorous glances of the beloveds or mentioning wine, the winehouse, goblets, or chalices [of wine]" radically transform their "state" (*ḥāl*), inducing an "agitation" (*shūr oftad*) in them. This is where Jāmī ends his discussion of the "reasons" for EMICF. Tying his theoretical discussion of chapter 14 back to his close reading of poetic imagery in chapter 13, he concludes with a few examples of specific anacreontic imagery æffectively transforming the state of a Qur'ān-resistant Sufi. The central point: It is this *imagery*, through the mechanism of EMICF, that does this work. Because of how imagery harnesses embodied somato-affective experience to "explain" or "express" other experiential realities, it can create æffective forms of meaning—by evoking æffect—in audience members in a way that even the Qur'ān cannot (at least, not as easily, as al-Ghazālī argues; see chapter 3 and Conclusion). It can, as Jāmī says here, transform their somato-affective state and agitate them—one of the most common somato-affective realizations of love, whether evoked by a physical bodily form of an earthly beauty or, as Jāmī shows, an imaginal (embodied) form.

But the "agitation" the listener feels in this concluding example is really but one of the potential "state" transformations that they could have experienced while listening to poetry with its "meanings" "express[ed] . . . in the clothing of forms." A different listener's state could have been transformed into any number of other feeling states. In al-Ghazālī's example of al-Rāzī above, his state is similarly upended with a feeling of turmoil, but his state heads in the direction of the forlorn or sorrowful end of the æffective valence spectrum. al-Ghazālī's other three examples of the completely engrossed super Sufi hermeneuts from the last chapter, who are thrown into *wajd* upon hearing the recitation of very legalistic verses of the Qur'ān, are likewise "conquered" or "overwhelmed" (*yaghlib*) by the powerful æffective state transformations of "fear and apprehension," "hope," "rejoicing," and "merriness" as the final stage of their—quite circuitous, though seriously impressive—hermeneutic journeys. And the list could go on.

But the central point remains consistent: For Jāmī and al-Ghazālī, the final stage of the Sufi hermeneutic is not an intellectual form of comprehension of spiritual *ma'ānī*; it is somato-affective state transformation. To understand the full range of meaning a Sufi poem aims to "express," we must strive to understand how it would have made its listeners *feel*. We need to add on to the classical formulation of the sensed (*maḥsūsāt*)→intellected (*ma'qūlāt*) epistemological progression that Jāmī mentions above. As we have seen in both Jāmī and al-Ghazālī's accounts across this and the previous chapters, this progression does not end in pure intellection of abstract or archetypal spiritual *ma'ānī*. It ends in æffect. And, the reader will remember from chapter 2, this can even be true when the listener sets out to deliberately "contemplate" the poem. As al-Ghazālī says there, the process of "contemplating" (*yatafakkar, tafakkur*) something "imprints (*yu'aththir*) an impression (*atharan*) in [their] soul (*nafs*)" that they "feel" (*yuḥiss bihi*) and recognize as æffective or emotional in nature.[80] For Sufis of the Path of Love, the way to God is paved with æffect. One must *feel* to truly know God.

CODA: WHAT *MA'ĀNĪ* FEEL LIKE

Discussions of *ma'ānī* in Sufi and Islamic philosophy typically portray them as abstract or archetypal ideas or concepts, celestial spiritual truths or realities, or "mental contents."[81] But is this all that *ma'ānī* mean in Jāmī's "expressing meaning in the clothing of form" paradigm? Asked differently, does Jāmī see the poetic process of "cloth[ing]" meanings in the forms of mundane imagery as just a more effective or pedagogically productive way to convey intellectual information about Sufi metaphysics or to hint at scriptural references and the spiritual realities of the supernal? The answer to these questions is, emphatically, "no." Jāmī's two chapters together make clear that he, like al-Ghazālī, sees the *ma'ānī* of poetry intimately bound up with æffect and the somato-affective form of knowledge it conveys as well.

At the minimum, *ma'ānī*, even if understood as essentially mental in nature, evoke æffect production in the audience.[82] They can feel like something. Dressing *ma'ānī* in the forms of poetic imagery, in this view, can be said to give them an additional æffective add-on power. Jāmī's comment in his concluding paragraph that "the æffect (*ta'sīr*)" of *ma'ānī*, when "mentioned in the tongue of allusion (*ishārat*)," is "greater than when done in explicit language" could be read along these lines.

But I want to push beyond this argument because I believe that the entire thrust of Jāmī's (and al-Ghazālī's) account advances a more radical proposition. *Ma'ānī* in Sufism are not just abstract ideas or mental content that evoke æffect production;

80. For the full passage, see chapter 2. See also O'Malley's consonant reading of these terms in al-Ghazālī in his recent monograph, where he cautions readers that al-Ghazālī understands *tafakkur* and its synonyms *ta'ammul* and *tadabbur* to produce not just an "abstract, intellectual conclusion" but rather "a form of internalised and embodied knowledge." In this context, he mentions "affective stances" as one of the products of al-Ghazālī's approach to meditation as well (*The Poetics of Spiritual Instruction*, 76–77).

81. See studies cited in review of *samā'* scholarship in chapter 2. For the presentation of *ma'ānī* as "mental contents" in the intellectual domains of Perso-Arabic linguistics and philosophy, see Key, *Language*.

82. Key holds this view, keenly observing in his discussion of al-Jurjānī that "the poets al-Ǧurǧānī was interested in wanted to manipulate *ma'ānī*—mental contents—in order to create affect and make audiences feel and understand beauty" (*Language*, 196). Landau also sees the philosophical tradition indicating that *ma'ānī* and affects cannot be completely separated because the aim of poetry is the excitation of affect ("Nasīr al-Dīn Ṭūsī," 55–57).

they themselves can be amalgamations of feelings.[83] They can be somato-affective in composition.[84] His entire account in these two chapters is premised on the notion that what the "clothing" of the "forms" of wine imagery primarily provides to the audience is somato-affective information (that is, knowledge) about the experience of love. Their "complete similitude" is rooted in the structural affinity of the experience of wine and love in the human physical and somato-affective body. This is not to deny that *ma ʿānī* have an intellectual, rational, or ideational dimension too. This intellectual or mental content aspect of *ma ʿānī* is obviously important, no doubt, and Jāmī treats it at length in the rest of his commentary. But he includes these two chapters on EMICF precisely because this does not exhaust all that *ma ʿānī* are and mean to their spiritually attuned listeners.

Regardless, however, of which position we adopt on the nature of *ma ʿānī*, the argument that I want to conclude with is that we cannot separate what poetry means to Sufi audiences at a broader level from the ways it *æffects* them. Meaning is not just propositional or intellectual. We can never fully disentangle the "æffect (*ta ʾthīr*) [of poetry] . . . in the souls of the listeners" and its transformations of their "states" (*aḥvāl*) from what it means, because Sufis learn about God as much or more through their somato-affective body as through intellectually rooted forms of knowledge, as we have seen throughout this book. To ignore the æffects of poetry and their central role in this genre's ability to convey meaning/knowledge about God and his divine "secrets" is to destroy a large part of how poetry *means* to Sufis. We have to follow the long tail of meaning—and Sufi epistemology—into the (somato-affective) body to see how poetry means (as affect) to and forms (effects) Sufi lovers: how it *æffects* them.

83. Corroborating this view, Knysh also suggests that *ma ʿānī* can be understood in "psychological" terms too ("Tasting, Drinking and Quenching Thirst," 39).

84. It is also worth recalling here that al-Ghazālī refers in a passage discussed in chapters 2 and 3 to the "well-known meanings (*ma ʿānī*) of fear, sadness, and delight," linking *ma ʿānī* to emotional categories too. The context of this comment, specifically the way he juxtaposes these to the "strange and wondrous" impressions (*āthār*) and "state[s]" (*al-ḥāla*), militates against reading these phrases along the lines of the "abstract themes (*ma ʿānī*) of . . . ." It seems, rather, he sees *ma ʿānī* as capable of having felt, emotional content too. The suggestion that *ma ʿānī* and *āthār* are connected also supports this reading. See Key, *Language*, 166; Black, "Intentionality," 68–69.

5

"When the Wine of Love Started Taking Its Æffect"

Self-Annihilation (Fanāʾ) *and the Force Dynamics of Sufi Poetry*

In the previous chapter, we saw that when Jāmī interprets the poetic imagery of Ibn al-Fāriḍ's legendary poem *The Wine Ode* in his commentary *Lavāmiʿ* (*Flashes*), he sees its poetic imagery conveying at least two types of meaning at the same time: intellectual/symbolic and somato-affective. On the one hand, he participates in the robust Sufi tradition of symbolist commentaries that read the poem's individual poetic images and image complexes as symbols (*rumūz*) or allusions (*ishārāt*) pointing to a wide range of Sufi metaphysical concepts, scripture, and spiritual realities (*maʿānī*). This symbolist hermeneutic forms the basis for the majority of his interpretation of this poem in the *Lavāmiʿ*.

He also departs from this traditional interpretative tradition, however. In a series of two chapters in the *Lavāmiʿ*, he takes up the more foundational question of *why* Sufi poets use the imagery of "earthly wine" to poetically "explain" love. Terming this the "expressing meaning in the clothing of form" (EMICF) mode, he argues that wine imagery—the "forms" in the EMICF formulation—is used as a metaphor for love because the embodied *experiences* of love and wine evince "complete similitude." His account focuses on drawing out in considerable depth the similar ways in which these substances make the body feel, operate as actors in the world, and compel the intoxicated person to engage their social context in novel ways. At a broader level, what Jāmī's cataloging of their "complete [experiential] similitude" shows is that he sees poetic imagery as uniquely capable of providing a small taste of the myriad ways that love *feels* to Sufi lovers. It is the experiential affinity and parallelism between imagery and its metaphoric referent that enables poetry—as opposed to what he calls "explicit language"—to better convey this somato-affective form of meaning—to, as Jāmī says, have a more powerful "æffect (*ta ʾṯīr*) . . . in the souls of listeners" and evoke in them states and ecstasies that even the Qurʾān can not.

In his account, Jāmī does not extend the EMICF mode of poetic analysis to the level of the whole poem or even image complexes within it. He tightly focuses on the generic poetic image of wine and how it relates to its typical referent, love. But what I will argue in this chapter is that we, as modern literary critics, can build on the EMICF approach to poetic analysis, both in extending its analytical frame to the whole poem and in connecting it with modern theories of language that share a similar perspective on language and meaning as embodied, and deeply æffective, phenomena. This expanded EMICF mode of analysis—a form of æffective hermeneutics—can help us illuminate the diverse ways that Sufi imagery constructs poetic meaning beyond its symbolist import or intellectual content.

Using a hybrid analytical framework built on Jāmī's EMICF approach to imagery and the modern cognitive linguistic theory of force dynamics, I will illustrate in this chapter how the somato-affective contours of the ultimate Sufi spiritual experience of *fanāʾ*—self-annihilation—flows into and structures the metaphoric imagery treating it in a *qalandariyyāt* (rogue) poem of Farīd al-Dīn ʿAṭṭār (d. 1221). In this EMICF-inspired reading, the imagery and its imaginal action do not mean just by referring to static concepts, symbols, or scriptural references; they mean by imaginally performing "complete similitude" with the experience of *fanāʾ*. Sufi poetry, in this interpretative paradigm, is not just a "suitcase" or "vehicle" that "describe[s] or refer[s]" to symbolic meanings, as sensitive literary critics have long cautioned us. It is a "whirling dance," as Keshavarz says, or "meaning event," to adopt Sells's term. It effects a "semantic analogue to the experience of mystical union . . . that re-creates or imitates the mystical union" and "attempt[s] to evoke in the reader an event that is . . . structurally analogous to the event of mystical union," as Sells characterizes it.[1] As we will see, the "meaning" in these meaning events is as somato-affective as it is discursive, symbolic, or intellectual in nature.

"SO DISTURBED THAT HIS SELF IS ANNIHILATED FROM IT": ÆFFECT AND THE FORCE OF SELF-ANNIHILATION (*FANĀʾ*) IN SUFI LITERATURE

In a book focused on the Sufi Path of Love, it is fitting that this final chapter take up the pinnacle Sufi experience of *fanāʾ*, or "self-annihilation," and its elaborations in Sufi poetry. For, as ʿAṭṭār—the author of the Sufi poem we will analyze in this

1. Keshavarz, *Reading Mystical Lyric*, 12, 18–20, 36–39, 72–74, 77; Meisami, "Imagery as Argument"; Meisami, "Allegorical Techniques"; Meisami, *Medieval Persian Court Poetry*, 239–42; Meisami, "Nāsir-i Khusraw"; Meisami, *Structure and Meaning*, 48–50, 387–403; Sells, *Mystical Languages of Unsaying*, 9–10. Hunsberger and de Bruijn have also criticized this approach as well: de Bruijn, *Persian Sufi Poetry*, 122; Hunsberger, "'On the Steed of Speech.'"

chapter—says, it is only "those who are annihilated in essence [that] remain on the Path of Lovers."[2] To be a consummate lover requires, in the final analysis, the annihilation of the Lover's self. This experience of becoming "unconscious . . . and free from the shackles of existence and self-worship" is, as Jāmī terms it in a passing reference in his account covered in the previous chapter, the highest goal of loverhood, because it is only when the self of the lover has been destroyed that they can fully unite with their Beloved, God, and realize His—and, indeed, all of existence's—oneness (*tawḥīd*).[3] This ontological realization of the nothingness of the lover marks the summit of the Sufi spiritual path. And this realization, as we will see below, is primarily realized in and through the Sufi body and its somato-affective affordances.

Fanāʾ has been a cornerstone of Sufism since at least the time of Junayd (d. 910), who propounds this concept as a way to reconcile the Islamic conception of God/Existence's absolute unity (*tawḥīd*) with the multiplicity of the phenomenal world. Junayd argues that in the pre-eternity before creation, humans existed only in a form of "selfless existence in God," as Karamustafa terms it, and the ideal Sufi must aim to return to that state by "dy[ing] before [they] die," to adapt the famous *ḥadīth* that Sufis later frequently employed in discussions of *fanāʾ*. According to Junayd, this "death" or "passing away" of the psychosocial, "director" self (ego)—our normal sense of "I" that operates our bodies—is the only way for the Sufi aspirant to achieve true spiritual union with God, or, as the later Sufi lovers would frame it, for the Sufi lover to unite with the Beloved.[4] But this death is not a death of the physical body. As Karamustafa reminds us, *fanāʾ* "is not total annihilation of the individual since even after *fanāʾ*, the self survives in a transformed fashion."[5] It is this *fanāʾ*-ed self, which Sufis often refer to as the state of *baqāʾ* ("surviving" or "subsisting"), that Sufis aim to achieve.[6]

Beginning with Junayd, Sufis have rooted the experience of *fanāʾ* in the famous *ḥadīth qudsī* (a narration of God's words) in which God said to the Prophet Muḥammad: "My servant draws near to Me by means of nothing dearer to Me than that which I have established as a duty for him. And My servant continues drawing nearer to Me through supererogatory acts until I love him; and when I love him, I become his ear with which he hears, his eye with which he sees, his hand with which he grasps, and his foot with which he walks."[7] Although the words "*fanāʾ*," "self," and/or any of their near semantic kin are not used in this *ḥadīth qudsī*, Sufis have seen in this narration a pithy articulation of the Sufi path of spiritual

2. ʿAṭṭār, *Dīvān-i ʿAṭṭār*, 33–34.

3. Jāmī, "Lavāmiʿ (Afṣaḥ et al.)," 360.

4. Karamustafa, *Sufism*, 16–17.

5. Karamustafa, *Sufism*, 17.

6. For an extensive overview of *fanāʾ* and *baqāʾ*, see Wilcox, "Dual Mystical Concepts."

7. Translation from and Arabic text available in Graham, *Divine Word*, 173–74, which also discusses its sources. Karamustafa discusses it in reference to *fanāʾ* in *Sufism*, 16.

development, ending with a jargonless description of *fanāʾ*. The road leading to the experience Sufis report and term *fanāʾ* maps tightly onto the sequence of events described in this divine narration. The Sufi disciple (the servant) endeavors to draw nearer to God through absolute obedience to God's will and performances of extraordinary levels of devotion—actions that are done, according to Sufis of the Path of Love, out of their ardent love for God, the Beloved. When they have drawn close enough to God, God takes control of the situation and "love[s]" them back. God's love is portrayed here, as we have seen before, as a powerful force. It is not passive or theoretical; it is deeply felt. When God loves someone, according to this divine narration, he commandeers their faculties and bodies, becoming "his ear with which he hears, his eye with which he sees, his hand with which he grasps, and his foot with which he walks."

When we read later Sufi accounts of the experience of *fanāʾ*, it becomes clearer why they came to understand this *ḥadīth qudsī* to be a divine account of *fanāʾ*.[8] The key is the final moment in the narration, with its implied displacement of the director "self" of the "servant" whom God "love[s]" and its replacement by God. Later Sufis saw this as an allusion to the powerful felt experience of *fanāʾ*, which they presented at the most general level, beginning with Junayd and continuing in the treatments of al-Ghazālī, ʿAṭṭār, and Rūmī discussed below, as a total loss of volitional control over their body and the inflowing of an awe-inspiring force, interpreted as God, that begins to control and animate them. These accounts are diverse in the ways they portray the experience, but they share this fundamental somato-affective event structure.[9]

Let's begin with al-Ghazālī's discussion of those who have experienced *fanāʾ* in his treatment of *samāʿ*. This is "the level of the righteous ones in knowledge and *wajd*"—the "highest level" of spiritual attainment in Sufism.

> The fourth situation is the hearing (*samāʿ*) of him who has gone beyond states (*aḥwāl*) and stages because he does not understand (*fahm*) anything other than God anymore. He is even far from his own self (*nafs*) and its states and social engagement [with the world]. He is like one who is astonished, immersed in the sea of the essence of witnessing, whose state is akin to state of the women who sliced their hands while looking upon the beauty of Yūsuf as they became perplexed and had their senses (*iḥsās*) fail. The Sufis say of those in a similar state that they have passed away (*faniya*) from their self (*nafs*). However much they pass away from their self,

8. Whether this *ḥadīth qudsī* has to be read as referencing *fanāʾ* is not important here. For the Sufis we are concerned with, the answer was unequivocally "yes."

9. Although I will not discuss Junayd's account here, he strongly emphasizes the dominating and overwhelming aspect of the felt dimension of *fanāʾ*, describing it as "the chief, most overwhelming (*aghlab*), more deserving to be called conquering (*al-ghalaba*), vanquishing (*al-qahr*), and truly possessing (*ṣiḥḥat al-istīlāʾ*)" experience, and continues to say it completely destroys the *fanāʾ*-ed person's normal worldly human existence. See Junayd ibn Muḥammad, *Life*, 32–33 (Arabic original, and 153–54 for an alternative English translation, from which I diverge in a few places). I am indebted to Green, *Sufism*, 37 for pointing me to this account.

> they pass away ever more so from what is not Him. It is like they pass away from everything except the Witnessed One. . . . [*Fanā ʾ*] in most cases is like a sudden gripping (*khāṭif*) flash of lightning that does not endure or continue and, if it did continue, human strength could not endure it. Sometimes one becomes so massively agitated (*iḍṭaraba . . . iḍṭirāban*) under its load (*a ʿbā ʾ*) that their self is destroyed from it, as is related about Abū Ḥusayn al-Nūrī, who was in attendance at a gathering in which he heard this couplet: "Out of love for you, I over and over again stop at an abode / stopping at which the hearts in confusion throws." He stood up, æffected ecstasy (*tawājada*), and frantically wandered (*hāma ʿalā wajhihi*), and stumbled upon a reedbed that had been cut. Their stalks remained and they were like swords. He began running through it and stammering the verse until morning and blood ran down his legs and eventually even his feet and legs swelled up. He lived only a few days after that and then died, may God have mercy on him. This is the level of the righteous ones in knowledge and *wajd* and this is the highest level because listening (*al-samā ʿ*) in the states (*aḥwāl*) is a step down from the level of perfection as they [the states] are a mixture with human attributes, and that is a shortcoming. Perfection, however, is when one passes away completely from one's self and one's states—that is, they forget them and have no regard for them, like the women who had no regard for their hands and the knives. He hears for God and through God and in God and from God. This is the rank of him who has dived into the depths of the sea of spiritual truths (*ḥaqā ʾiq*) and has passed beyond the shores of states and works and has become one with the purity of unicity (*tawḥīd*) and has come to truly worship God with nothing but pure sincerity. Nothing at all remains in him from him. His humanness (*bashariyyat*) has been completely extinguished and his regard for the attributes of humanness has passed away.[10]

al-Ghazālī opens his treatment of *fanā ʾ* with the framing that is typical of such discussions by this point in the Sufi tradition. He describes the term *fanā ʾ* as used for the Sufi experience of "pass[ing] away (*faniya*) from [the] self (*nafs*)" and "its states and social engagement [with the world]." At this "level," the Sufi has "pass[ed] away from everything except the Witnessed One [i.e., God]." They have even gone "beyond [the] states and stages" of the Sufi path. They no longer show any "regard for [their] attributes of humanness," and their "senses (*iḥsās*) fail" them. Their normal self is forgotten as they plumb the "depths of the sea of spiritual truths (*ḥaqā ʾiq*)" and become "one with the purity of unicity (*tawḥīd*)." They—i.e., their director "I" self—no longer exists. There is nothing left in their body that is of this self: "[Their] humanness (*bashariyyat*) has been completely extinguished."

The focus in the beginning and end of al-Ghazālī's treatment on the disregard of the self-annihilated Sufi for their senses and human attributes could give the reader the impression that the experience of *fanā ʾ* has no felt dimension. If there is no self or sensorial self-awareness left, how could they feel anything? The examples he gives of the women gazing in astonishment at Yūsuf and the great mystic Abū

10. al-Ghazālī, *Iḥyā ʾ*, 2:288.

Ḥusayn al-Nūrī, who all engage in serious bodily harm without any care or visible bodily response, seem to confirm this reading. If they felt anything at all, certainly they would have been compelled to respond. It would be instinctual.

But, as other parts of al-Ghazālī's account make clear, *fanāʾ* is definitely a deeply felt experience. It is not that the Sufi stops feeling altogether while annihilated. God commandeers their internal and external senses, but they remain available to the Sufi in this transfigured form.[11] Citing the example of "hearing"—his primary concern in the larger context of this account—he presents the self-annihilated Sufi as continuing to hear, though now he only "hears for God and through God and in God and from God"—an oblique reference to the *ḥadīth qudsī* above. Their organs of perception, like the larger body of which they are a part, are no longer theirs to animate or direct, but they continue to exist and feed somato-affective information to the Sufi.

al-Ghazālī turns to directly address the felt experience of *fanāʾ* in the middle of this passage. Typically, he asserts, it feels "like a sudden gripping (*khāṭif*) flash of lightning." The adjective *khāṭif* here carries connotations of "quick," "fleeting," even "lightninglike" (hence, "sudden"), but also "seizing," "rapacious," and "ravenous" (hence, "gripping").[12] The experience of *fanāʾ* may last only a short time, but it is intense. It is not a subtle internal stirring or movement of the soul. In an unexpected instant, it grabs full control of one's body and attention, electrifying them in a markedly aggressive way.

al-Ghazālī also suggests that the Sufi who is experiencing such a flash of *fanāʾ* feels like they are collapsing. It is experienced as a "load" that bears down on them. There is something heavy about the experience, but not in the pejorative sense in which al-Ghazālī talks of the "unbearable[ness]" felt in a *samāʿ* session that is attended by unwelcome spiritual charlatans who ruin the mood, so to speak (see chapter 2). This heaviness is a felt realization of the awesome power of God pressing on them, so intense that if it lasts for more than a moment, "human strength could not endure it." The Arabic verb used for "endure" here is a derivation of the *ṭāʾ-wāw-qāf* root, which we saw in a Persianized instantiation in chapter 1, where ʿIrāqī's melodious Qurʾānic recitation *bī-ṭāqat*s the members of his audience, engulfing and overwhelming them with æffect(s) that they cannot control. Here, al-Ghazālī aims to convey a similar somato-affective experience of being

11. Hofer and Abuali have also recently made this point—namely, Sufi senses are not jettisoned in their spiritual experiences; they are "reconfigured," which "open[s] up an entirely new sensorium." As Hofer observes, "rather than shutting off the senses, this reconfigured self was able to experience vivid sensory inputs—sounds, smells, lights, things, persons, animals." For Sufis, such as "Kubrā, Ibn al-ʿArabī, and the others," they "do not mean the elimination of the sensing body in favor of pure cogito, but a rearrangement of the self in such a way that it can ignore one kind of sensory data in order to accommodate another" ("On the Material," 2, 19–23). See also Abuali, "Visualizing the Soul," 168. Compare to Seyed-Gohrab, "Beyond Senses."

12. Lane and Lane-Poole, *An Arabic-English Lexicon*, 2:766; Wehr and Cowan, *A Dictionary of Modern Written Arabic*, 248.

overwhelmed, though the valence of the feeling differs. The "load" of *fanāʾ* that must be "endure[d]" is "agitat[ing]" to the Sufi.

The terms al-Ghazālī uses in this passage for "agitat[ion]," variations of *iḍṭirāb*, are similarly related to ones we have seen in previous chapters for the felt experience of lovers. This is an ill-defined internal somato-affective constellation of feelings. The Sufi feels their normal sense of the world uprooted, unsettled, in disorder. It is uncomfortable. It tells them something is not right; they need to do/be something different. This feeling demands expression, sometimes verbally, but as in the examples he gives in this account, just as often physically, in the form of extreme bodily actions that shock onlookers in their intensity, as we will see shortly. This points to a key dimension of the experience of "agitat[ion]": It is felt as a foreign force operating on and within the Sufi subject's somato-affective body. al-Ghazālī himself suggests this linkage: "Sometimes one becomes so massively agitated (*iḍṭaraba . . . iḍṭirāban*) under its load (*aʿbāʾ*) that their self is destroyed from it." The somato-affective feeling of *iḍṭirāb* is, in this formulation, portrayed as an agent or tool of *fanāʾ*. The unbearable force of *fanāʾ* (i.e., its "load") agitates, disturbs, unsettles, uproots the Sufi subject so profoundly that it obliterates their self. In a sense, æffect here is the self-slayer of God. It is not knowledge that effects the apotheosis of the Sufi spiritual path; it is ultimately the felt force of God that realizes this experiential form of knowledge in the somato-affective body of Sufi subjects.

As an example par excellence of this *fanāʾ*-induced annihilation of the self through agitation, al-Ghazālī points to the story of the famous Sufi Abū Ḥusayn al-Nūrī. The way al-Ghazālī leads into the story of al-Nūrī (i.e., "as is related about . . .") makes clear that he sees this agitation-driven self-annihilation process as the operative force in the famous case of al-Nūrī's *fanāʾ*-induced death. The story begins with al-Nūrī hearing a couplet while he is attending a gathering (*majlis*) one day. The lines of poetry deeply move him, and he arises and begins to "æffect ecstasy (*tawājada*)."[13] Although al-Ghazālī does not directly state this, the implication is that at some point in his performance of *tawājud* he reaches genuine ecstasy (*wajd*) and, ultimately, self-annihilation, because he eventually departs the gathering and proceeds to "frantically wander (*hāma ʿalā wajhihi*)." The connotations of aimless roaming and lack of bodily awareness hint at what is to be poignantly confirmed in the shocking climax of this story. Stumbling into a cut reedbed with razor-sharp stalks, al-Nūrī not only does not retract in pain as these vegetative "swords" lacerate his feet and legs; he continues running through it. Like the women who famously cut their hands open at the sight of Yūsuf's striking beauty, he is "astonished," "perplexed," and shows no regard for the pain his physical senses would have been screaming to his director self.

These wounds lead to his death a few days later, but this is an afterthought. The point of this stunning story is that he had already "died before he died"—his self had

13. On "æffecting ecstasy" (*tawājud*) and its relationship with "ecstasy" (*wajd*), see the Coda of chapter 3.

already been annihilated by the divine "load" of *fanāʾ* and its agitation. al-Nūrī's director self no longer controlled his body. God was now animating his body, as we saw in the *ḥadīth qudsī* that al-Ghazālī gestures to subsequently. al-Nūrī's shocking actions index the incredible force God exerts on the self-annihilated mystic. They aim to demonstrate the awe-inspiring intensity of God's power and control. Sufi somato-affective spiritual experience can vary substantially in degree, from internal movements and inclinations to the obliterating intensity of *fanāʾ*'s agitations and control.

Another common way that the experience of bodily control in *fanāʾ* has been portrayed is as the experience of being drowned. The beautifully simple account of Rūmī's teaching on *fanāʾ* in his *Fīhī mā fīhī* takes this metaphoric route, comparing a Sufi who has been self-annihilated to a drowned person whose only movement is that produced by the movements of the ocean itself.

> It is like a fly: when it flies, its wings move, its head moves, all its members move. When it is drowned in honey, all its members become the same and do not move at all. "Being drowned" is such that he [who has drowned] is not involved, he no longer makes any exertion on himself, he no longer acts, nor moves. He has been drowned. Whatever action comes from him, does not arise from him—it is not his action, [but rather] the action of the water. If he is still thrashing about in the water, then we would not call him "drowned." Or if he is screaming, "Help! I am drowning!" then we would not call that "drowned." Now, people think saying "I am the Truth [i.e., God]" (*anā al-ḥaqq*) is a claim of greatness . . . [but actually] it is great humility because saying "I am God's servant" affirms two existences: one of his own, and another for God. However, the one who says "I am the Truth" has made himself nonexistent; he has thrown his "self" to the wind. He who says "I am the Truth" means "I do not exist—everything is He. There is no existence except God; I am completely pure nonexistence—I am nothing." There is more humility in this, [but] people do not understand this. When a man serves God, his servanthood is involved, although it is for God. He sees himself, his own actions, and God. He is not "drowned" in the water. The one who is drowned is one who does not move or act at all, but whose movements are only those of the water.[14]

The opening image is of a fly buzzing about, frenetically moving all parts of its body, as, Rūmī implies, it excitedly circles a pot of honey. Unable to resist the honey pot's sweetness, it descends to get a taste, as flies are wont to do, but drowns in the sticky goodness in the process. The act of drowning, of submersion in the honey, stills "all [the fly's] members" and they "become the same and do not move at all." Abruptly switching the protagonist of the metaphor to a human and the honey pot to the ocean, Rūmī begins speaking of the significance of this loss of movement. The key point is that the stillness of the body after "being drowned" shows the director self to have passed away, to no longer be capable of being "involved" or "mak[ing] any

14. Rūmī, *Fīhī mā fīhī*, 40–41. For an alternative English translation, see Rūmī, *Signs of the Unseen*, 45–46.

exertion on [ourselves]," "no longer act[ing], nor mov[ing]." The image of drowning is especially striking because, as the audience would know, it is not possible to fake the stillness of one's body while drowning. The deeply rooted human self-preservation instinct to breathe will not allow it: It sends the drowning body into frantic motion, "thrashing about" or "screaming, 'Help! I am drowning!'" When a drowning body ceases making these desperate final attempts to rescue itself, we know for sure the body's respective self has passed away and ceded control of its physical body, Rūmī suggests.

The drowned body will eventually begin to move again. But the origin and director of the movement changes after the waters have claimed its life. The body now moves only with the water it floats in; its "movements are only those of the water," as Rūmī concludes. The drowned person becomes a mere puppet for the boundlessly enormous and powerful ocean waters that bear down on them from all sides as they slowly disappear into its seemingly infinite depths. Their body is not theirs any longer. The body that they used to control and animate through the exertion of their will—speaking, moving, acting in the world, even "serv[ing] God"—now is supplanted by another external force: the ocean waters, which, of course, are a metaphor for God and, specifically, the felt experience of God in *fanāʾ*.

In Rūmī's teaching, what the image of God as a killer ocean seeks to convey above all else is that the God of *fanāʾ* is a powerful one, and the experience of him in *fanāʾ* follows suit. At this apotheosis of the Sufi spiritual journey—the moment when God "drowns," "t[akes] possession of," or, as God puts it in the *ḥadīth qudsī*, "loves" the mystic—he bears down so hard on the Sufi that he has no problem overpowering the greatest earthly force of them all: the illusory "self." Dispatching it with ease, seizing control of the Sufi's body, God only knows what they will do in this transformed state because He is now the force that animates them. They may even be moved to utter that paradoxically blasphemous and exceedingly "humble" phrase of the paradigmatic self-annihilated mystic Manṣūr al-Ḥallāj (d. 922), "I am the Truth" (*anā al-ḥaqq*) (that is, God). Proclaiming this phrase is, as Rūmī reminds us, evidence that the Sufi has achieved the highest spiritual realization in Sufism: "I do not exist—everything is He [God]. There is no existence except God; I am completely pure nonexistence—I am nothing." Sufis may articulate this spiritual realization of *tawḥīd* as Rūmī does, but what all these accounts of *fanāʾ* indicate is that this experiential knowledge of the ultimate nature of the universe was not, in the main at least, conceptually revealed to them. They were made to *feel* the unity of all existence (*tawḥīd*) in themselves. They had to feel their ontological nothingness and God's limitless power to fully grasp what the concept of *tawḥīd* meant at the most fundamental level. God, through the experience of the force of *fanāʾ*, had to instruct their somato-affective body for them to understand the true nature of all Reality.[15]

15. While God is the only force in *fanāʾ*, Sufis have also used the image of "total voluntary submission" in the context of the Sufi disciple-and-master relationship. On this, see Bashir, *Sufi Bodies*, 187ff.

These three examples do not fully exhaust the diverse ways in which *fanāʾ* has been metaphorically imagined in Sufism. But they do exemplify its dominant presentation in Sufi literature as a profound somato-affective experience in which God, portrayed as an overwhelming force, jettisons their director "I" self and takes absolute control of their entire body and all its faculties. Following Jāmī's EMICF approach, what I want to show in the remainder of this chapter is how this basic embodied experience of *fanāʾ* structures metaphoric realizations of self-annihilation in Sufi poetry. Sufi imagery is not accidentally chosen or arbitrarily related to its referent—it is not amodal, as linguists would say. It does not just function as an elaborate symbolist screen that cryptically encodes references to Sufi metaphysics and "spiritual realities" (*maʿānī*). As Jāmī illustrates in his analysis of the "complete similitude" of the experiences of "earthly" wine and love, the selection of Sufi imagery is motivated by its somato-affective structural affinity with its intended referent.[16] Imagery gives us a window into how it felt to be a Sufi lover, to "pass away" in the Beloved's arms, to have one's self "annihilated" in union. To interpret this form of meaning in Sufi texts we need to adopt an æffective hermeneutics that sees Sufi poetry as pointing as much to Sufi embodied experience as to its metaphysics and the spiritual realities of the supernal realm.

"THE STORY OF THE ḤALLĀJIAN MASTER OF OUR DAY": THE ROLE OF POETRY ACCORDING TO ʿAṬṬĀR'S *QALANDARIYYĀT* POEM ON *FANĀʾ*

In Rūmī's account in the preceding section, he transitions from his opening metaphoric treatment of *fanāʾ* as drowning to a more theoretical explanation of this experience by invoking the example of the (in)famous Baghdadian mystic al-Ḥallāj. al-Ḥallāj is popularly remembered throughout the Sufi tradition for being executed on charges of blasphemy for uttering the phrase "I am the Truth" (*anā al-ḥaqq*) or, in other words, "I am God."[17] Rūmī, like most Sufis, defends al-Ḥallāj from these accusations, arguing that proclaiming *anā al-ḥaqq* needs to be interpreted differently in the case of self-annihilated Sufis. al-Ḥallāj's jaw-dropping statement, he explains, is not a claim of divinity for a truly annihilated Sufi; it actually represents "great humility because," as Rūmī continues, "saying 'I am God's servant' affirms two existences: one of his own, and another for God. However, the one who says 'I am the Truth' has made himself nonexistent; he has thrown his 'self' to the wind." Rūmī draws here on the long tradition of mobilizing al-Ḥallāj's famous utterance and story to draw out the truly explosive potential of *fanāʾ*: It means realizing *tawḥīd* not just in the abstract intellectual sense but rather

16. On the "modal" or "motivated" nature of Jāmī's theory of imagery, see the Introduction.

17. On al-Ḥallāj and the more complicated history of his utterance of this phrase and reasons for his execution, see Ernst, "Introduction," 3–7; Mojaddedi, "Ḥallāj, Abu'l-Moḡit Ḥosayn"; Massignon, *The Passion of al-Hallāj*. See also Ernst's new translation (Ḥallāj, *Hallaj*).

performatively, allowing God to work in and through the body of the annihilated Sufi. Their actions, no matter how shocking, are not their own. They are the result of God puppeteering their now completely pliant body. And, as we saw in the example of al-Nūrī, the more shocking the bodily actions are that God performs through them, the more powerfully this essential point of *fanā'* is made (somato-affectively) legible to the audience.

In the remainder of this chapter, we will look at a poem treating *fanā'* by the renowned Sufi poet ʿAṭṭār. The poem, which he characterizes in the closing lines as a poetic rendition of "the story of the Ḥallājian master of our day," is an example of a Sufi *qalandariyyāt*—a thematic genre in classical Persian poetry that versifies on the various roguish figures associated, sometimes uneasily, with Sufism, and their wild carnivalesque exploits.[18] Because the raison d'être of the *qalandariyyāt* is to powerfully shock the audience, these poems lend themselves to poetic figurations of *fanā'* more than any other in premodern Persian poetry.[19] Their poetics of shock is capable of expressing, to adopt Jāmī's framing in his discussion of EMICF, a closer degree of "similitude" with the equally world-inverting experience of *fanā'* than any other types of poetry seem capable of.

1 At the crack of dawn, our master awoke
and went from the mosque to the vintner.
2 He went from the circles of the men of religion
to being within the loops of the (non-Islamic) cincture.
3 He drained a jug of dregs instantly.
He cried out and he became a dregs-drinker!
4 When the wine of love started taking its æffect on him,
he became disinterested in the good and bad of the world.
5 Stumbling like those drunk from a morning draught,
he went with a goblet of wine in hand toward the bazaar.
6 An uproar arose among the people of Islam.
How strange! This spiritual master became one of the infidels!
7 Everyone was asking: "How did this loss happen?
How did such a master become so treacherous?"
8 Whoever gave him advice made his chains tighter—
in his heart the advice of people were thorns.

18. On *qalandariyyāt* poetry and its countergenre poetics, see Miller, "The Poetics of the Sufi Carnival"; Miller, "The Qalandar King"; de Bruijn, "The *Qalandariyyāt* in Persian Mystical Poetry." On the complicated relationship between actual antinomian spiritual figures in the premodern Islamic world and institutional Sufism, see Karamustafa, *God's Unruly Friends*; Algar, "Impostors"; Watenpaugh, "Deviant Dervishes."

19. I agree with de Bruijn's remarks in his brief study of the *qalandariyyāt* of Sanā'ī where he argues that the "shocking nature" of the imagery of *qalandariyyāt* poetry and its "connotation of disrespectability" is "essential to the effect the author wanted to achieve through the choice of this imagery." It "enhances their effect," as he says. However, we part ways, as I indicate in this chapter and elsewhere, on why the shocking nature of the imagery is so central to its poetics, because he ultimately still sees the imagery of the *qalandariyyāt* primarily in symbolist terms as a "set of symbolic allegories" that are used only in a "figurative sense." See de Bruijn, "The *Qalandariyyāt* in Persian Mystical Poetry," 80, 85–86.

9 The people had pity on him;
around him many were gathering to look upon him.
10 Such a dear master became despised
in the eyes of the people of the world from one drink of wine.
11 Our master had become infamous and quite drunk.
When he sobered up for a bit,
12 he said: "If I have been a rancorous drunk, it is licit,
all must become engaged in this work.
13 It is proper for any who have become brave and a rogue
if they become rambunctious drunks in the city."
14 The people responded: "This beggar should be executed!"
The number of people who were calling for his execution became overwhelming.
15 The master said: "Make haste! Look at this affair!
This Magian [that is, Zoroastrian] beggar has become boastful!
16 May a hundred thousand souls be sacrificed to him whom
the life of sincere ones is given!"
17 He said this and let out a fiery sigh
and then went up the ladder of the gallows.
18 From stranger and fellow city-dweller, man and woman,
rocks were piled upon him from every direction.
19 When he gave up his soul, the master in his heavenly ascent
in truth was initiated into all the secrets.
20 Eternally in the sanctuary of union with the beloved,
he tasted the fruit of the tree of love.
21 The story of the Ḥallājian master of our day
expanded the chests of the spiritual elite.
22 Inside the chest and the fields of the heart,
his story became the guide of ʿAṭṭār.[20]

On a formal level, this poem is an example of what I have elsewhere discussed as a "rogue anecdote."[21] It is a formally ambiguous, twenty-two-line poem that contains a sustained narrative. It is similar in length and structure to a twenty-line rogue anecdote by Sanāʾī, but it is difficult to locate comfortably within the later standard classical *ghazal-qaṣīda* formal binary.[22] The poem is well structured with regard to its internal organization and segmentation. Its internal patterning and the interrelation of its segments are not incidental; these structural features play an important

20. ʿAṭṭār, *Dīvān-i ʿAṭṭār*, 193–95, no. 251.

21. On the different subtypes of *qalandariyyāt*, see Miller, "The Poetics of the Sufi Carnival," 10–16.

22. The term "*ghazal*" and the formal expectations of what constitute a *ghazal* poem develop considerably from the (re)birth of Persian poetry in the tenth century until the emergence of the "classical" *ghazal*, often associated with the *ghazal*s of Saʿdī in the thirteenth century. For discussions of the development of the *ghazal* and its relationship to the *qaṣīda*, see Lewis, "The Transformation of the Persian Ghazal"; Lewis, "Reading, Writing and Recitation," 1–111; Bausani, "G̲h̲azal, II." For the referenced poem by Sanāʾī, see Sanāʾī, *Dīvān-i Sanāʾī*, 666–68.

TABLE 1 Section Summary of ʿAṭṭār's Rogue Anecdote Poem

Section (Lines)	Main Topic	Thematic Foci of Section
1 (1–5)	Portrayal of winehouse world	Mock-*raḥīl* from mosque to winehouse, drinks wine of love which causes certain transgressive acts
2 (6–10)	Portrayal of normative Islamic world	Entrance of drunk master into market bazaar causes uproar among Muslims and provokes certain reactionary responses, including censure
C (11)	Center pivot	Master sobers up enough to respond to normative Muslims
3 (12–16)	Dialogue/debate between worlds	Elements of conflicting worlds of sections 1 (winehouse) and 2 (normative Islamic world, i.e., spiritually uninitiated masses) engage, but fail to reconcile
4 (17–20)	Impossibility of reintegration into normative society performed	Rogue poetic persona driven to death, ascends to heaven (*miʿrāj*), and returns to sanctuary of love (i.e., ultimate winehouse)
X (21–22)	Poetic cap	ʿAṭṭār steps outside of poetic anecdote, asserts importance of the poem and its enlightening effects, and includes his poetic signature (*takhallus*)

role in how it constructs meaning as a poem.[23] The basic structure of the main body of this poem embodies the paradoxically deep interrelation and irreconcilability of the world and ultimate Reality, represented by the winehouse and its earthly appendages.[24] The poem can be divided into four primary sections with a bisecting center line (C) that divides these sections into two larger blocks (1–2, 3–4) and concludes with a "cap" (X).[25] With the exception of section 4, which is only four lines, each section is exactly five lines, and the center line occurs at approximately the midpoint of the poem (11).[26] Table 1 presents a basic breakdown of its divisions.

Section 1 (lines 1–5) opens with the "master" waking up and heading in a mock-*raḥīl* (journey passage) from the "mosque to the vintner," which establishes these two institutions as opposing spaces in the poetic geography of this *qalandariyyāt* in both a spatial and spiritual sense. There is a physical distance between the two

23. On the importance of understanding the structure of poems for elucidating their meaning, see Meisami, *Structure and Meaning*, x, 55–143, 190–243.

24. The poem's narrative structure could also be thought of in terms of what Bauer calls "emotional plots"—i.e., the "arc of feelings" in a text that "lead[s] the listener from one emotional state into another emotional state, achieving an emotional transformation" ("Emotion in the Qur'an," 16–22; see also "Emotions of Conversion."

25. Meisami productively uses the term poetic "cap" throughout her influential work, *Structure and Meaning*.

26. Meisami counts cap lines separately. Parenthetically, I would note, though, that it is also possible to read line 11 as the opening line of section 3, thus giving us two equal ten-line larger sections. For reasons that will become clear, I am more inclined towards the former division. The general thrust of my analysis holds true regardless of which approach one adopts to dividing this poem's lines.

institutions that has to be traversed, but the "waking up" of the master in the first hemistich also gestures to the fact that these two worlds differ in a more fundamental way too—a point that ʿAṭṭār makes abundantly clear in the rest of the poem. In the following lines the master is inducted into the winehouse cult, forsaking the "circles of the men of religion" and binding himself in a mock-investiture with the cincture of non-Islamic minorities (*zunnār*). He then enthusiastically participates in its solemn rite of imbibing the "wine of love" (lines 3–5). The section concludes with him "stumbling like the drunks in the morning," with "a goblet of wine in hand," heading to the city's marketplace. This image transitions us smoothly from section 1 to 2, as the master returns from his mock-*raḥīl* to the bazaar, attempting reintegration into a normative social space.

Section 2 (lines 6–10) is the inverse of section 1. It revolves around the reactions of the "people of Islam" gathered in the marketplace to the master's new, transformed "drunken" self. His appearance immediately engenders an "uproar" among them. As in the translation above, "an uproar" (*ghulghulī*) is the first word of this section in the original Persian (6), foregrounding the absolute incompatibility of the winehouse (section 1) and the normative social spaces of the Islamic world (section 2) (here, the bazaar, but one could include others as well, e.g., the mosque of first line). The outraged Muslim crowd or, as he later calls them, "people of the world," now regard him as a "treacherous" "infidel" who, as these words suggest, has invaded Islamdom. They heap opprobrium on him for his "one drink of wine"—the sacred rite of the winehouse world of section 1. The stark contrasts, harsh language, inverted values, and differentiated poetic geography of this section set up and sharpen the conflict between the worlds of section 1 and 2 that the second half of this poem will seek to resolve.

Line 11 marks a turning point. Whether we consider it as a center line or the opening line of the ten-line larger section, it shifts the poem in an important way. The master, "infamous and quite drunk," "sober[s] up for a bit" and engages the spiritually ignorant masses who are casting blame on him. His "sobering up" in the middle of the poem (11) is crucial because only in this state can he converse with the "people of the world." Here, the poem pivots as it inverts the "waking" that the master does in line 1, which is both a literal and spiritual awakening that leads him into the drunken state that he must "sober up" from in the middle of the poem after he retraces his mock-*raḥīl* and ends up back in a normative social space (i.e., the market). In his sober state, he attempts (lines 12–13) to reconcile the winehouse world of section 1 and normative society (represented by the market and its crowd) of section 2, explaining why this "work" and associated behaviors are "licit" for those who have become "rogues" (*ʿayyār*). The people gathered respond only with demands for his execution (line 14), which he willingly accepts as the wages of the work of the winehouse. Indeed, he encourages them, telling them to "make haste!" and taunting them with a prayer that there be many thousand more like him willing to sacrifice themselves for "him whom the life of sincere ones is given."

The last line of section 3 transitions us to the final section (lines 17–20), where he is sacrificed, meeting his Ḥallājian end on the "gallows" and ascending (*mi ʿrāj*) to the "sanctuary of union with the beloved," where he "part[akes] of the tree of love." The "heavenly ascent" here is really a return to the original primordial state of union, which he tasted (in the form of the "wine of love") in his foray in the winehouse world of section 1. His return in death should be understood as a form of the "reaggregation" or "reintegration" drive that we often see in other forms of Persian and Arabic poetry.[27] By the end of line 20, the master is brought back full circle to the winehouse world. But this time he returns permanently to the eternal, master winehouse, the sanctuary of union, where the tree of love grows and the self has been permanently extinguished by death.[28] This reaggregation of the rogue master is thus not a social or heavenly one in the traditional sense, nor is it an outright rejection of reintegration per se.[29] The *qalandar*, as we see in this poem, desires reaggregation, but with the Beloved in his eternal winehouse of love.[30]

ʿAṭṭār concludes the poem with a cap (lines 21–22) in which he steps outside of the poetic anecdote (lines 1–20) and discusses the poem itself. He tells us that this poem has presented the "story" (*qiṣṣah*) of the "Ḥallājian master" of his day and, passed among the "spiritual elite," it "became the guide of ʿAṭṭār."[31] The reference to al-Ḥallāj in the closing lines makes explicit what an informed reader would have already intuited: the figure of the master and his shocking behavior should be understood as resulting from his self-annihilated state (*fanāʾ*). God is in control of him like the servant in the *ḥadīth qudsī*, al-Nūrī in al-Ghazālī's passage, or the drowned man in Rūmī's anecdote. And God, as we will see, is also in control of the wild imagery of this poem—it is a performance of *fanāʾ*, an imaginal embodiment of the force and power of its experience. God uses poetry to æffect, and thereby instruct, his disciples.

ʿAṭṭār's final image makes this point quite explicitly, claiming that "this story"—that is, the one just presented in this long narrative poem—"expanded the chests of the spiritual elite" and became his guide (*rahbar*). The key word in these lines is *inshirāḥ*. Construed here with the Persian verb *shud* ("to become"), it literally denotes an expansion or opening up of the chest or heart and extends

27. On "reaggregation" or "incorporation" in other Persian and Arabic genres, see J. Stetkevych, *The Zephyrs of Najd*, 26–49; S. Stetkevych, *The Mute Immortals Speak*, 3–83; Meisami, *Structure and Meaning*, 175.

28. The linkage of the end with the opening of the poem, which "imparts a circular movement," is not uncommon in Persian and Arabic poetry. See Meisami, *Structure and Meaning*, 90–99, 106, 193, 196, 282.

29. For examples of the strategic rejection of reaggregation for poetic effect in *ṣuʿlūk* poetry, see S. Stetkevych, *The Mute Immortals Speak*, 87–157.

30. For more on the *qalandar*'s reaggregation in the Sufi carnival with the beloved, see Miller, "The Poetics of the Sufi Carnival," 36.

31. ʿAṭṭār also refers to his famous work *Manṭiq al-ṭayr* as a "guide" (O'Malley, *The Poetics of Spiritual Instruction*, 1–6).

metaphorically to convey the palpable sense of cheerfulness, joy, and relaxation that would naturally be produced from the removal of a constriction or compression inhibiting such an opening or expansion. In the Sufi context, this verb needs to be read as an allusion to Qurʾān 6:125 and 94:1–6.[32] Employing the first form of the same Arabic root (*shīn-rāʾ-ḥāʾ*), these lines portray God "opening" (*yashraḥ, nashraḥ*) the chests of the Prophet Muḥammad and other chosen followers:[33]

Did We not expand for thee [Prophet Muḥammad] thy breast,
and lift from thee thy burden
that weighed heavily upon thy back?
And did We not elevate thy renown?
For truly with hardship comes ease!
Truly with hardship comes ease! (94:1–6)

And:

> Whomsoever God wishes to guide, He expands his breast for submission. And whomsoever He wishes to lead astray, He makes his breast narrow and constricted, as if he were climbing to the sky. Thus does God heap defilement upon those who do not believe (6:125).[34]

These lines from the Qurʾān are clearly metaphoric. They are obviously not claiming God performed some sort of divine thoracic surgery on Prophet Muḥammad and "whomsoever God wishes to guide." But they are also equally clear that God's "expan[sion]" of the "breast" is a deeply felt experience. It produces a feeling of relief or "ease" (Q94:5–6) as it removes the "burden" or "heavy load" (*wizr*) and "hardship" (*ʿusr*) that "weighed heavily" or "pressed upon the back of" the Prophet Muḥammad (*anqaḍa ẓahraka*), making him despondent (Q94:2–3, 5–6). It removes the "defilement" that is felt as a dejected or depressive "suffocation" or "constrict[ion]" (*daiyiqan ḥarajan*) of the disbelievers' "breasts" (Q6:125). These pre-"opening" experiences share a common somato-affective foundation of physical pressure upon the body that is felt as negatively valenced and alleviated only through God's intervention.

In the final lines of his poem, ʿAṭṭār graphs this set of references onto his poem and its audience. He presents his poetic versification of the "Ḥallājian master of our day" in the role of God, with the various antagonists of the master peppered throughout the poem playing the part of personified depressive and oppressive burdens, hardships, and constrictions. Like God in the Qurʾān, his poem æffects an "expansion" of the "chests" and "heart[s]" of the spiritual elite—what we should read as a type of "spiritual expansion" (*basṭ*) that relieves the true Sufi lovers of

32. For another example of "expansion" as a Sufi response to a poem, see Shahid's discussion of an interesting example of *samāʿ* portrayed as effecting a "Divine expansion of [the listener's] breast" ("Saif Al-Mulūk," 246, 255).

33. See footnote 17 in Introduction on the Arabic root system and how words with shared common trilateral roots are formed.

34. Translations from Nasr et al., *The Study Quran*. Arabic text referenced from Ali, *Al-Qurʾān*.

the pervasive sense of "contraction" (*qabḍ*) that they, like the master of the poem, feel in their interaction with the spiritual plebes "among the people of Islam," as we will see in more detail below. This somato-affectively expansionary or opening experience also shares a third key feature that is central to both Q6:125 and ʿAṭṭār's poetic cap: it has a spiritual epistemological dimension. Q6:125 explicitly frames God's *yashraḥ*-ing as what he does when he wants to "guide" someone. It is a prerequisite. The individual's somato-affective body has to be "opened up" into a receptive posture to be guided. A constricted and closed off person cannot be led or directed in either literal or metaphoric senses of these terms. This, ultimately, is the role and function that ʿAṭṭār assigns to his poem—and by extension Sufi poetry more generally—in this closing cap: It opens him up and expands his chest and heart, revealing divine knowledge in the process. It "guide[s]" him by acting on him in a somato-affective manner, by fashioning his felt Sufi subjectivity in a particular way.

"EXPAND[ING] THE CHESTS OF THE SPIRITUAL ELITE": ÆFFECTIVE HERMENEUTICS AND THE FORCE DYNAMICS OF POETIC IMAGERY

Force Dynamics: A Theoretical Bridge Between Jāmī's EMICF and Modern Linguistics

But how does poetry do this? Jāmī's EMICF approach presents a model for how we can read Sufi imagery as conveying somato-affective meaning alongside its more well-studied metaphysical import. We need to look closely at how imagery operates in the broader context of the poem, how individual images interact with others, and how imagery performs somato-affective meaning, drawing on our copious wells of quotidian embodied knowledge of different experiences to convey to the audience glimpses into the felt dimension of the poem's topic.[35] In the case of ʿAṭṭār's poem, we need to analyze its imagery with an eye to how it imaginally, performatively embodies the force of the experience of *fanāʾ* in its poetics.

To help with this analysis, I draw here on the theoretical framework and terminology of force dynamics. First developed by the cognitive linguist Leonard Talmy, force dynamics can be understood as a "semantic category" that provides a framework for understanding and describing "how entities interact with respect to force [in language]. Included here is the exertion of force, resistance to such a force, the overcoming of such a resistance, blockage of the expression of force, removal of such blockage, and the like . . . includ[ing] 'letting,' 'hindering,' 'helping,' and still further notions not normally considered in the same context."[36]

35. The need to analyze how imagery functions in poems—evoking meaning as it unfolds as a "complex structure"—is similar in certain ways to how Abu Deeb argues al-Jurjānī saw imagery producing meaning in his work (*Al-Jurjānī's Theory of Poetic Imagery*, 80–81).

36. Talmy first elaborated the theory of force dynamics in "Force Dynamics in Language and Cognition." He later further developed this theory in *Toward a Cognitive Semantics* (from which this quote

In force dynamics, two primary actors each exert different levels of force upon one another. The "agonist" is the "focal point of attention" in the linguistic interaction between these two entities. In the beginning, the agonist manifests an "intrinsic force tendency" either to stay at rest or do/continue doing a particular action/motion. The second figure is the "antagonist," so named because it is the other entity that interacts with the agonist, either employing or restraining its force in order to influence the intrinsic force tendency of the agonist. While it is easier to see how this model applies to physical imagery ("the child knocked the glass off the table"), Talmy's argument is actually much broader. He maintains that force dynamics is "one of the preeminent conceptual organizing categories in language" more broadly.[37] It is "a fundamental notional system that structures conceptual material pertaining to force interaction in a common way across a linguistic range: the physical, psychological, social, inferential, discourse, and mental-model domains of reference and conception."[38] Force dynamics, in other words, extend beyond the purely physical to include portrayals of psychological and social interactions as well, which are understood as "psychosocial 'pressures'" ("he pushed himself to finish writing the book," "X pressured Y to change Z law").[39] Even deeply psychological concepts such as "will" and "desires" are conceptualized as internal forces that either push the individual to engage in certain actions or, conversely, restrain them from doing so.[40]

In the examples from Jāmī's treatise from the last chapter, wine and love in this framework would be the antagonistic forces that overcome the "intrinsic force tendenc[ies]" of a variety of other agonists. They overpower physical bodies rendering them "unconscious"; they defeat the forces of death and disability preying on the weak human body; their "command" (*ḥukm*) takes control of "all the senses (*quvā*) and faculties (*mashāʾir*) of one who it possesses"; and the æffective states associated with wine/love—such as joy, liberality, and audacity—dispatch their subjects' natural tendencies to anxiety, greed, and cowardice. Wine/love, operating in the social realm, even "throws [arrogant elites] down" from "their high stations of honor and eminence to the threshold of humility and neediness." The human being in force dynamics' system of "naive" or "folk physics" is assumed to be an (agonistic) entity with established æffective states, personal desires, personality traits, physical dispositions, and social status that they intend to maintain (against any efforts to change them). The psychosocial self, the director "I" of the human

was drawn, see 1:409). It is important to point out that the concept of "force" in the study of force dynamics in linguistics should not be confused with the understanding of force in modern physics. Rather, "force" in force dynamics is based on the understanding of force in premodern "folk" or "naive" physics. See Talmy, *Toward a Cognitive Semantics*, 1:410, 1:455–61.

37. Talmy, *Toward a Cognitive Semantics*, 1:461.

38. Talmy, 1:410. He repeats almost the same assertion on page 461 as well.

39. Talmy, 1:409, 1:412–13.

40. Talmy, 1:412–13, 1:430–40.

body, is the entity in control of this situation at the outset—that is, the one exerting different force vectors in the physiological, psychology, and social realms in order to keep this status quo intact (the "intrinsic force tendency"). Wine/love/the force of God in *fanāʾ*, however, have different plans. Functioning in the role of the antagonistic force, they quickly supplant the self and invert every element of their subject's old status quo, definitively demonstrating their superior power.

In the years since Talmy introduced the concept of force dynamics, a range of linguists have adopted it, suggesting a variety of ways in which it influences language and thought more broadly.[41] The details of this large body of literature are not essential here. What they all have shown, though, is that force dynamics pervades language and structures, in fundamental ways, both how we conceptualize events and experiences and construct meaning about them. The framework of force dynamics is a useful lens for analyzing poetic imagery because it foregrounds how imagery operates in relation to other imagery within a specific poetic context, while it also allows us to connect it to broader extratextual dimensions, such as elements of Sufi thought and experience (e.g., mystical union and intoxication, *fanāʾ*). The lines between the domains of pre-textual experience, imaginative formulation, text, and reader reception/response begin to blur in this much more dynamic framework for conceptualizing meaning creation in literature.[42]

Reading the Forceful Imagery of ʿAṭṭār's Poetic Ode to the Ḥallājian Master, Æffectively

As we saw above, ʿAṭṭār's poem on the self-annihilated Ḥallājian master opens with the master's mock-*raḥīl* to the vintner's home and participation in its winehouse rites (lines 1–3). The master of these opening lines, however, is not yet the Ḥallājian master of the final verses of the poem, because his self still exists. His volitional force—not God's—moves him from the mosque and its "circles of men of religion" to the winehouse and its "loops of the (non-Islamic) cincture," where he can "drain a jug of dregs." His director self makes this decision to embrace the "treacherous" life of the "infidel," one of absolute infamy and disrepute in the eyes of normative Islamic society (lines 6–11). Rejecting the mosque and "circles of men of religion" for this antinomian life is, of course, admirable in the eyes of the Beloved. But it is not enough to become the Ḥallājian master of the end of the poem.

41. For example, see Kövecses, *Metaphor and Emotion* (2000) and "Metaphor and Emotion" (2008); de Mulder, "Force Dynamics"; Pinker, *How the Mind Works*.

42. Sells, Keshavarz, and O'Malley have in different ways made a similar point in their studies of Sufi poetry. See citations to their works in this and the previous chapter. Relevant here too is Harb's argument that medieval theorists of Arabic poetry saw poetic interpretation as a "process of discovery" that included "experience of" different (what I would call) æffective states, produced in different ways by the structure of poetic language and "logic of [its] image[ry]." Language prompts this process, but it unfolds in the reader's mind-body, and it will unfold, as Harb points out reading al-Qarṭajannī, according to the "receptive[ness]" of the "soul" of the audience member engaging the poem's imagery—a point that any Sufi would corroborate (*Arabic Poetics*, 123).

It is only in lines 3–4 that we begin to see what is essential for a poem on *fanā*ʾ: the force of God, embodied in this poem in the figure of the wine. This is the sine qua non of *fanā*ʾ, the opposing force that will finally dislodge the master's self and take control of his somato-affective body.

This transformation begins "instantly" after he chugs a "jug of dregs." Wine is ʿAṭṭār's chosen metaphoric agent to represent God's machinations on his Sufi subject, and he joins Jāmī in fusing it with love in line 4 ("wine of love"). Within the context of the poem, this meshing of these images connects the wine and the winehouse of the opening section with the "tree of love" in the "sanctuary of union," where the master ends up after the ultimate self-annihilating experience of being executed (line 20). It establishes a parallelism at both the structural and symbolic levels. The worldly winehouse where he finds the self-dissolving "wine of love" in the beginning of the poem is paralleled by the ultimate place of self-dissolution, the "sanctuary of union" where the "tree of love" originates at the end. The winehouse, in this sense, can be read as a microcosm or earthly analogue for the heavenly sanctuary where self-annihilation is inescapable.[43]

This metaphoric fusion also makes clear the true source of the force of these antagonistic entities, as both wine and love have their origin in God. They can in many cases be understood as metonymic, even ontological, force vectors of God. And, as we have seen throughout this book, they are uniquely powerful intoxicating forces that induce wide-ranging somato-affective transformations in their subjects. As ʿAṭṭār says in an understated way in this poem, they "take[e] [their] æffect on" (*dar vay kār kard*) those who dare imbibe them. Metaphorically embodied as a protean force that transfers and rhizomatically reemerges throughout the imagery of this poem, they move poetic personae into new states of being. They force feelings and actions upon their imaginal subjects.[44]

43. For poems as analogs and microcosms, see Meisami, "The Grand Design"; Meisami, "Poetic Microcosms."

44. Cognitive linguists call this basic patterning a COMPULSION FORCE image schema, and the fact that both love and wine share this foundational schema naturally leads them to also share a range of other similar conceptual or primary metaphors (e.g., CAUSES ARE PHYSICAL FORCES, PRESSURIZED CONTAINER, EVENT STRUCTURE). These similarities, of course, do not mean that all metaphoric realizations of amorous or intoxicant themes will be compatible. It does mean, though, that their metaphoric foundations are structured in similar ways and so they can more easily interoperate and combine to form rich poetic tapestries of mutually reinforcing imagery. Work on the metaphoric framework of emotions has been done most prominently by Zoltán Kövecses, who draws on Leonard Talmy's notion of the "force dynamics" in language. Kövecses argues that emotions in a large number of world languages are structured on the EMOTIONS ARE FORCES "master" or "superordinate metaphor." He argues that the "skeletal schema" of emotion is "Cause→Emotion→Response," which is the simple rendering of what he argues is the full cognitive model for emotion metaphors: Cause→Emotion→Control→Loss of Control→Behavioral Response. See Kövecses, "Metaphor and Emotion" (2008), 51–86. See also his book-length treatment, *Metaphor and Emotion* (2000). For an overview of primary or conceptual metaphors, see Lakoff and Johnson, *Philosophy in the Flesh*, 45–59.

We see this (force) dynamic powerfully in the imagery of this poem. The ingested "wine of love" produces myriad changes in the Ḥallājian master. Some are somato-affective in nature. The first action he takes after imbibing the wine, for example, is to "cry out." The motivating æffect behind this vocal eruption is not specified, but it registers a powerful internal transformation that demands expression, that pushes him to release the pent-up pressure that is wrought by wine's introduction to the closed cavity of his body.

The "wine of love" also begins to exert control over the master's external bodily movement, leading him into a rapidly spiraling series of "out of control" actions that indicate that it has begun supplanting his director self as the prime mover of his body and mind. He begins "stumbling like those drunk from a morning draught" toward the bazaar—an image that recalls al-Nūrī's frantic "wandering" before his plunge into the reed bed and performs the waning ability of the master to exert control over his body. By line 5 he is struggling to even keep himself upright. His continuous "falling and getting up," as it literally reads in Persian, is reflected sonically and orthographically in the rapid alternation of long and short vowels; orthographically, *alefs* ا stand straight up while the other vowels *ū* و and *ī* ی remain at the text line or dip below it. (The full line reads *uftān-khīzān chū mastān-i ṣabūḥ* / اوفتانخیزان چو مستان صبوح).

Like in al-Nūrī's account, the exact point at which the master's self is completely annihilated by God's "wine of love" is not specified. It is never a question, though, of if, but when, his self will be jettisoned. In the Sufi imaginary, once one has tasted the "wine of love"—even just "one drink" (line 10)—there is no going back. It propels the Sufi subject inescapably to search for more. As Jāmī said in more explicit terms (see chapter 4), "However much more they drink, they [still] search for more. However much their drinking increases, they increase the amount of hardship (*ranj*) they expend in search for it."[45] They will keep quaffing it until its intoxication robs them of their volition, consciousness, and self. The master's ultimate lack of agency and power to resist is also reinforced in the active and passive verbs attributed to wine/love-cum-God and him, respectively. While the wine/love "tak[es] its æffect on him" and drives him to engage in increasingly carnivalesque inversions of normative social behavior and belief throughout the remainder of the poem, he can only "bec[ome]" (*shud*) things, as the poetic refrain *shud* reinforces for the reader at the end of each line.[46]

If there is a moment in the poem we can point to as indicating the completion of self-annihilation, it is line 5, when the master heads for the bazaar (a normative social space imagined as the socio-political hub of the Islamic city). The wine has already caused him to "bec[ome] disinterested in the good and bad of the world"

45. Jāmī, "Lavāmiʿ (Afṣaḥ et al.)," 360.

46. I would like to thank Paul Losensky for drawing my attention to this point. For more on the "poetic refrain" (*radīf*) in the Persian tradition, see Lewis, "The Rise and Fall of a Persian Refrain"; Losensky, "'Demand, Ask, Seek.'"

(line 4), but his utterly defiant response to the concerns of the "people of Islam" when he arrives in the bazaar points to the fact that God has by then dispensed with his worldly self and its associated normative tethers of social respectability and superficial piety. He does not temper or control what he does any longer—not even to the extent of keeping his disreputable acts contained in the winehouse. The power of God's force acting in/through/on him is too much to be contained. Its "dominance and predominance" (*ghalabah va istīlā*ʾ), as Jāmī terms it in his discussion of wine/love, "require discovery and manifestation" in the social world. Like al-Nūrī, the overwhelming nature of this disturbing force causes him to engage in such outrageous actions in town that his death warrant is all but assured.

The reaction of the "people of Islam" to his appearance in the bazaar is immediate and fierce. Indeed, as we saw above, the first word of the section is "uproar," underlining the radical irreconcilability of the worlds represented by the master and the "people of Islam." The original Persian of "uproar," *ghulghul*, onomatopoetically performs the revulsion of the normative Islamic world at the introduction of this antinomian radical, breaking the smooth flow of the surrounding verse just as he enters the imaginal space of the Islamic city. The *ghulghul* here registers the crowd's rejection and denunciation of this new Ḥallājian version of their old master. But it is stronger than that. It represents a violent and loud somato-affective reaction to the introduction of a dangerous new element that must be transformed or expelled.

The master is the cause of this imaginal and textual-sonic strife, and the townspeople thus reclassify him as "one of the infidels." Crowning him with the chief pejorative appellation of "infidel" completes a process that began in the opening lines of associating the Ḥallājian master with an array of different non-Islamic symbols and transgressive actions. ʿAṭṭār does this to achieve a certain æffect. He wants the reader first to construct an image of the Ḥallājian master as an extreme embodiment of peripherality and weakness in the Islamic city. He is lower and more outside of the circles of social prestige and power than even the "people of the book" (i.e., monotheistic religious minorities). He is the bearer of the combined socio-religious stigma of a religious minority, social rogue, drunk, and even infidel. However, despite his lowly status, he does not act his station. He defiantly "stumbl[es]" drunk into the middle of the Islamic city with a "goblet of wine in hand"—the rogue lover's mock sword—declaring open rebellion against the established Islamic order. The message this imagery provides the audience is that something powerful must be driving him. He has lost his mind—or, as the Sufis would say, his self has passed away. The irony of the townspeople labeling the Ḥallājian master "one of the infidels" (*kuffār*)—an individual who denies God—is, of course, that not only does he not deny God, but the powerful force animating him to perform these seemingly insane actions *is* God. The Ḥallājian master's practice of piety has moved beyond words and concepts. He embodies it. Or, rather, more accurately, his body performs it as God realizes the most radical implication of the central tenet of Islam, *tawḥīd*, through him.

The townspeople cannot understand this form of piety. They do not perceive the true nature, import, and source of the Ḥallājian master's carnivalesque behavior. They react in horror and surprise at the transformation of their "dear master" into a "treacherous," "pit[iable]," "despised," and "infamous" infidel (lines 7, 9–11)—weighty moral judgments that come with serious material and socio-affective implications for the accused. In the Sufi worldview, the default mode of unawake "people of Islam" is to engage in superficial Islamic piety and the ways of the world. Their actions are guided by their selves—both intellect (*ʿaql*) and lower, carnal self (*nafs*)—and the worldly logic they represent. The self-annihilated Sufi lover, in contrast, attacks the logic of the self and its worldly constructs. The dissolution of their selves does not lead to quiescence; rather, its absence is filled by the intoxicating force of love that compels the self-annihilated individual to engage in a wide range of destructive and disruptive behaviors. Their self-annihilation is not intended only to be a self-transformation; they have a social role to play as well. They become another medium for channeling God's "force" into the world. Their actions are deconstructive performances of the illusory nature of the world, and they are meant to æffect (read: exert force on) their audience members and thereby the world as a whole, as Jāmī pointed to as well in a different way in chapter 4.

The æffects of this encounter, however, are not unidirectional. The "people of Islam" do not just sit back and remain passive, as we see in the remainder of the poem. Although the Ḥallājian master's dramatic fall from being a respected community leader to engaging in shocking transgressive behavior initially overpowers their self-control and composure as they erupt into a stupefied furor (line 6–7), they eventually respond in turn with a countervailing form of psychosocial force: moral advice (*pand*) and ethical judgments (lines 8, 9–11). They pepper him with *pand*, exhorting him to repent and change his behavior before it is too late. This "advice" is not just empty words. By invoking the power of moral frameworks, they seek to constrain and change his behavior by subjecting him to the force of their ethical judgments. Their goal is the opposite of *fanāʾ*. They aim to displace his new self-annihilated self and re-establish his old, traditionally religious psychosocial self as the director of his body.[47]

47. The "breaking repentance" (*tawbah shikastan*) motif, which is rife throughout *qalandariyyāt* poetry, though ʿAṭṭār does not use it in this poem, also illustrates well the power normative frameworks invisibly exert on the somato-affective self in a different way. Being in a state of repentance functions in *qalandarī* poetry as a symbol for the daily assent to the internalized framework of normative socio-religious rules that control the behavior of the traditionally religious Muslim self. To repent means to reaffirm the divided self and subjugate the self to another form of psychosocial sovereignty—not the sovereignty of God, the Beloved, but rather the lordship of the *sharīʿa* (Islamic law), religion (*dīn*), ascetic piety (*zuhd*), etc. This form of social control, as the motif suggest, must be "broken." For more on this motif in *qalandarī* poetry, see Miller, "The Poetics of the Sufi Carnival." While in daily life Sufi lovers such as Sanāʾī, ʿAṭṭār, and ʿIrāqī would not advocate openly renouncing these normative frameworks, at the highest spiritual levels they too must be dispensed with—at least in a spiritual sense—because they affirm a separate self that is subject to their regulations. On this point, recall Rūmī's assertion that even worship and servanthood vis-à-vis God is problematic because they presuppose two existences.

Unsurprisingly, ʿAṭṭār says the Ḥallājian master feels these words as painful "chains" and "thorns" digging into his carnivalized body (line 8). Just as the inspiring *fanāʾ*-fueled story of the Ḥallājian master æffectively expands (with a positive valence) the chests of the spiritually attuned audience members, these verbal assaults on his new selfless self are perceived as painful bodily penetration and constriction. The Ḥallājian master's feeling of being increasingly constricted—"made his chains tighter"—by their moral "advice" is the rogue's equivalent of the feeling of depressive suffocation felt by those individuals who God "allows to go astray," instead of "opening up their chests," in Q6:125. These feelings can be read as an individual somatization of the battle of social wills that is raging in this scene. The Ḥallājian master perceives the townspeople's assertion of their collective normative will as coercive and violent because it conflicts with God's will, which now animates him. He correctly, as we will see later, feels these (verbal) moral force projections as a threat to both his new annihilated self and even bodily integrity.[48]

The argumentative contestation between the master and the "people of Islam"/"people of the world" that begins in section 2 continues in section 3 (lines 12–16). The psychosocial force of the townspeople's warnings cannot overwhelm the wine-fortified master. After "sober[ing] up for a bit" in the center line, he responds not with another shocking carnivalesque bodily performance but rather with corresponding argumentative force. His response parallels the "advice" of the townspeople in a formal sense (verbal persuasion), but its content is mock-*pand*. Against their moral judgments, he defends his drunkenness and roguery as "licit" and "proper" and goes on a proselytizing offensive with his opposing moral framework, exhorting all to "become engaged in this work," this "rambunctious" intoxication (lines 12–13). He does recognize, however, that such "work" is not for the faint of heart. It is only "proper" for those "who have become brave and a rogue (*ʿayyār*)" (line 13). They must be resolute and unwavering in the face of the townspeople's normative verbal and physical onslaughts against them. Luckily, as Jāmī pointed out too, wine provides just such æffective fortification of the will and steeling of the body's nerves.[49]

As expected, it is made abundantly clear in line 14 that his arguments have not moved this crowd at all—in fact, his slightly more "sober" attempt at verbal persuasion seems to have only inflamed them further. They go from making moral judgments (i.e., having "pity on him," "despis[ing]" him, etc.) in the second section to overwhelmingly calling for his bodily "execution" by the end of the third. The calls to execute the master and his enthusiastic acceptance of this sentence

48. ʿAṭṭār's portrayal of the Ḥallājian master's experience of words as forces inflicting violence upon him is resonant with Talmy's discussion of force dynamics in argumentation (*Toward a Cognitive Semantics*, 1:452–54).

49. "Anyone who is drunk from love and drunk on wine is fearless and reckless, free of the characteristics of timidity or fear. In dangerous places they are brave, and in perilous situations they [act as if they] have had their fill of life" ("Lavāmiʿ [Afṣaḥ et al.]," 359). See chapter 4.

mark the shift to the fourth section of the poem as well as another transformation in the poem's force dynamics. The psychosocial force of the arguments between the master and townspeople that play out in sections 2–3 ultimately end in a stalemate that must be resolved by other means in the fourth section. The move is to physical force, as the "people of Islam/the world" string him up on the gallows, and "stranger and fellow city-dweller, man and woman" alike all pelt him with "rocks . . . from every direction." The intense physicality of the force in this image parallels the intensity of the master's physical performance of drunkenness in the first section. From the perspective of the "people of Islam/the world," the master represents a dangerous, rogue, even "infidel" force that threatens the foundations of normative Islamic society if not eliminated in one way or another. Since the force of their arguments have proved ineffective in changing his position, they determine that execution—that final elimination of an animated body—is the only force powerful enough to overcome the master's wine-fueled obstinacy.

The æffect of the execution image in the fourth section is augmented by the master's enthusiastic embrace of it (line 17). He does not just accept it; he spurs the crowd on, telling them to "make haste." He flaunts his antinomian behavior ("Look at this affair / This Magian [that is, Zoroastrian] beggar has become boastful!"), and offers up a closing mock-invocation to his rogue Lord to inflame the crowd further against him (lines 15–16). The image here of the master suddenly giving up the fight he has carried on valiantly throughout the poetic anecdote and excitedly embracing his demise at the hands of the crowd of the "people of Islam/the world" seems strange at first, because the fierce contestation between the two force entities that has structured the poem is suddenly ripped out of the poetic scene. The executioners, of course, believe they have triumphed in their battle with this rogue force, but as the remainder of the poem makes clear, their victory is a mirage. His willing acceptance of this death sentence is itself his final bodily riposte to their resort to physical force and his ultimate *forceful* victory over them. In his embrace of bodily death, he performs *fanā*ʾ's self-less logic in dramatic fashion on a public stage, taking it to its logical conclusion. His lack of resistance (i.e., lack of countervailing force) to the townspeople's push to execute him demonstrates the same lack of self that his earlier behavior reflected and leads back to the same point of origin: the experience of *fanā*ʾ. He comes full circle in the poem: the overpowering experience of wine-fueled *fanā*ʾ in the winehouse (section 1) impels him to engage in a range of antinomian and paradoxical behaviors (sections 2–3), including accepting death, which returns him to that eternal winehouse in the sky, the "sanctuary of union with the Beloved" where the "tree of love" grows and from which the "wine of love" flows (section 4).

The play of forces in this long, narrative-heavy poem reveals several important points about the Sufi carnival of selflessness and the radical—in both senses of the term—force that drives it. *Fanā*ʾ and the self-annihilated Sufi bodies it operates are irreconcilable with normative society. They cannot abide the binds of traditional

Islamic social frameworks (e.g., religious and legal proscriptions, norms of comportment) because their normative strictures are intended to control a self that is ultimately illusory. Indeed, admitting the validity of these norms means affirming the false vision of a separate self. The mandate, then, of the *fanāʾ*-ed Sufi rogue is destruction: they are compelled to destabilize the purportedly pious foundations of social order and transgresses its boundaries, revealing them all to be fundamentally flawed and powerless earthly constructs. But in the end, the ultimate paradox is this: Earthly forces can only control the *fanāʾ*-ed Sufi by destroying their body; however, in destroying the Sufi body, they make the *fanāʾ*-ed Sufi victorious in this epic battle because their body's death enables the final reintegration of their (illusory) self in the eternal selflessness of *tawḥīd* to which we all—them included—will return at death.[50] Their earthly forces are powerless to challenge the ultimate force of God that flows through the servants that "He loves," to return to the *ḥadīth qudsī* with which we began.

CODA: IMAGINAL SIMILITUDES AND SOMATO-AFFECTIVE MEANING EVENTS

Since at least the time of Junayd, the self-annihilation of *fanāʾ* has been the apotheosis of the Sufi spiritual path. While Sufi commentators and modern scholars alike have long linked anacreontic and carnivalesque poetry and *fanāʾ* at the conceptual level, the argument that I make in this chapter is that this connection goes much deeper. In fact, the metaphoric foundations of this poetry are to a large degree structured upon the force dynamics of the somato-affective experience of self-annihilation. This poetry's imagery demonstrates a "complete [imaginal] similitude" with *fanāʾ*, to adapt Jāmī's argument on wine and love discussed in the last chapter. While each metaphoric figuration of it differs throughout this and other similar carnivalesque poems, they dovetail with and reenforce one another because of this shared force-dynamic investment. To put this point in more concrete terms, the overwhelming experience of the destruction of the self in mystical union is not just intellectually referenced or represented in the imagery of the poetry. The rogue beloved and his effortless destruction of all norms and sacred laws are not arbitrarily assigned metaphoric symbols/imagery pointing to the Sufi metaphysical concept of *fanāʾ*. They are textual performances of the truly extraordinary

50. Death, in Sufism, is conceived of as an ultimate release from the "veil" of the phenomenal world and joyous re-union with the divine Beloved. Some Sufis even commemorate the anniversary of a Sufi saint's death as their "wedding day" (*ʿurṣ*) with God. The story of the execution of al-Hallāj at the hands of the spiritually uninitiated certainly exerted a powerful force on the Sufi imaginary. Death in the bodily sense, however, is not a primary focus of Sufi poetry. The psychosocial death of *fanāʾ* does not inspire dark dirges for the transient world or exhortations to repent from its evils, *à la* religious-homiletic poetry. Indeed, nowhere is Persian poetry more alive and lively than when celebrating the carnivalesque and anacreontic adventures of those who have been *fanāʾ*-ed.

nature of the self-annihilating force of God and his earthly embodiments. In these poetic enactments of *fanā*ʾ, the beloved must transgress and destroy the most sacrosanct norms and symbols, because it is only in the unthinkable obliteration of these purportedly unassailable figurative embodiments of psychosocial force that one can hope to portray God's overwhelming power in mere words.

As Jāmī seems to have intuitively recognized in his treatment of wine and love imagery, a fixed dictionary definition of poetic symbols in the manner of the lexicons (*istilāhāt*) or traditional poetic commentaries cannot capture this level of meaning. These poems and their imagery do not *just* represent Sufi thought in versified form (even if they do this too, for some). They are also meaning events, in Sells's words, that seek to "effec[t] a semantic union that re-creates or imitates the mystical union"—a much richer understanding of meaning creation that can only be glimpsed when, as Keshavarz exhorts, we "observe [the poems] 'in action.'"[51] In their "re-creat[ion]" of the force dynamics of *fanā*ʾ, they have another objective: They aim to form a somato-affective spiritual subject by modeling the force-dynamic postures required of a true Sufi lover vis-à-vis God.[52] These poems, in short, want the reader to experience—to *feel*—a self-transforming poetic event that is, as Sells suggests, "structurally analogous" in some way to the Sufi experience of self-dissolution.[53] They aim, as ʿAṭṭār suggests above, to act upon the audience members (or at least, the "spiritual elite" among them), to expand their chests and guide them, in a literary meaning event that is epistemological as much for its somato-affective content as for its intellectual references and symbolic allusions to the supernal. They want to try to provide the audience members a little sense of what it *feels* like to be a truly self-annihilated lover—to try to give them even just a little taste of what *fanā*ʾ means in its somato-affective realization.

51. Keshavarz, *Reading Mystical Lyric*, 77; Sells, *Mystical Languages of Unsaying*, 9–10.

52. Also see O'Malley, *The Poetics of Spiritual Instruction*, especially chapters 3–5, on the perlocutionary aim of Persian Sufi didactic literature. He too sees the meaning of Sufi texts as having both a traditional semantic or intellectual level and a "psycho-somatic" one.

53. Sells, *Mystical Languages of Unsaying*, 10.

Conclusion

Restoring the Sufi Mind-Body

In a different place in his discussion of *samāʿ*, al-Ghazālī recounts another intriguing anecdote of the Sufi master al-Nūrī, the saint whose *fanāʾ*-induced, *wajd*-ifed death was explored in chapter 5. At an earlier point in his life, al-Ghazālī reports, al-Nūrī was in a gathering where the attendees were discussing an "issue in science" or "intellectual matter" (*al-ʿilm*). al-Nūrī remained conspicuously silent during the discussion, only breaking his silence finally to utter this poem:[1]

> Many a dove cooing in the morning,
> sang perched among the branches, full of grief.
> She recalled a lover and a worthy time.
> She cried sorrowfully and excited my sorrow.
> Sometimes my crying would make her sleepless;
> Sometimes her crying would make me sleepless.
> Sometimes I would complain, and I would not understand her (*ʾafhamuhā*);
> Sometimes she would complain, and she would not understand me (*tafhamunī*).
> But through love (*bi-l-jawā*), I understand her (*ʾaʿrifuhā*),
> and through love she understands me (*taʿrifunī*) too.

The impression given to the reader of al-Ghazālī's text here is that this was quite a dramatic moment—a premodern mic drop for al-Nūrī and, by extension, for al-Ghazālī's theoretical argument that this anecdote caps and exemplifies. al-Ghazālī then quickly wraps up the anecdote, reporting that everyone in the gathering arose and "æffected ecstasy" (*tawājada*). "This *wajd* that overcame them," he concludes, "was not from the matter of *ʿilm* in which they were engrossed, even though *ʿilm* is serious and true."

1. al-Ghazālī, *Iḥyāʾ*, 2:295–96.

While al-Ghazālī's framing of this story repeats the now familiar Sufi refrain that *ʿilm* has its limits, it would be a mistake to read an absolute mind/body binary into this Sufi formulation. "Matter[s] of *ʿilm*" are "serious and true," al-Ghazālī cautions, even if they cannot effect the highest epistemological and spiritually formative experience of *wajd* that is the climax of this story. But a product of the mind's faculty of language, a poem—which is the indisputable centerpiece of the anecdote—does have this power. The poem is the final, higher answer that al-Nūrī provides to shut down the *ʿilm*-based debate and subtly, though powerfully, æffect his audience. It communicates to the audience members through the mind's tool of language, but in doing so, it also speaks to them in the embodied language of æffect.

The language of poetry can play this role because it is so closely attuned to the body and its somato-affective states, according to Sufis and medieval Islamic litterateurs more broadly. Poetry provides a bridge between the somato-affective body and the rational or intellectual mind, between language as conveyor of information or intellectual ideas, as discursive agent, or as symbolic pointer *and* as æffect distributor. Poetry can *mean* to people in all these ways. But, as al-Ghazālī's telling of this story of al-Nūrī's poetic rebuttal to the bickering assembly members suggests, what poetry most helps Sufis see is that what they need is not more or better *fahm* or *ʿilm*. These epistemological routes are presented as not able to facilitate "understanding" in the anecdote, much less effect the peak Sufi experience of *wajd*. The attendees need, rather, al-Ghazālī via al-Nūrī suggests, more and better æffective knowledge. They need to learn how to *love* and how to speak love's æffective language—something that simultaneously is both higher and more profound and also so astonishingly simple and basic that even the dove, an animal, can "understand" it at the deeper, experiential level (using variations on the *maʿrifa* verb).[2] "Through love (*bi-l-jawā*), I understand her (*ʾaʿrifuhā*), / and through love she understands me (*taʿrifunī*) too." Slightly rephrased, this could serve as a concise statement of the æffective, *maʿrifa*-based epistemological paradigm of the Sufi Path of Love: "Through love (*ʿishq*), God understands you, / and through love you can understand Him too."

Feeling Like Lovers, in broader terms, has sought to unpack this æffective mode of Sufi piety; to show how Sufis cultivated and practiced love and its associated plethora of æffects; to illustrate how æffects are woven into the Sufi hermeneutic and poetic language; to foreground æffect's foundational role in the formation of Sufi epistemology and subjectivity; and to argue, at the most basic level, that to reach the highest levels of the Path of Love, Sufis must come to know (in the

2. This suggestion that æffect constitutes a form of "language" or mode of communication that transcends the human-animal boundary presents an intriguing potential area of investigation at the intersection of Islamic studies, affect theory, and animality studies. On the intersection of religious and animality studies, see Schaefer, *Religious Affects*. Also, for overview of animality studies more generally, see Lundblad, *Animalities*, especially 1–19. Lange relatedly notes that "human and animal sensation . . . form a continuum in al-Jāḥiẓ's thought" ("Al-Jāḥiẓ on the Senses," 34).

ma ʿrifa sense) in their somato-affective body how it *feels* to be a lover, as much or more than they need to know or understand (in the *fahm* or *ʿilm* senses) the metaphysics of love (or, for that matter, any of the Islamic sciences).

I opened this book with a richly elaborated version of the story of the Sufi lover par excellence, ʿIrāqī, participating in what his biography presents as a legendary *samāʿ* assembly in his Sufi lodge in Tūqāt. This scene contained all the seeds that became this book's subsequent chapters: bodies (those of the Sufi participants and, of course, the beautiful body of Ḥasan), the electrifying ambience, music, and poetry—all producing felt forms of power-meaning-knowledge.

As we saw in chapter 1, bodies can produce powerful vectors of æffective meaning. In the case of *samāʿ*, the singers often doubled too as *shāhid*s—embodiments of human beauty that Sufis would meditate on to evoke the powerful and sacred feelings of love, desire, and longing within themselves. At the minimum, the singer's physical presence in the ritual performance context adds another potential source of fuel to the amorous fire. The presence of another desire-inciting element could even be thought of as an alternative mode of presentation for the ritual's æffective (multimodal) pedagogy, in case, for example, one of the participants' "states" does not "fit" well with the particularities of the recited lines of poetry. Some Sufis even went further to argue that the presence of physical beauty in *samāʿ* sessions is essential for true comprehension of a recited poem's deepest levels of spiritual "meanings," as ʿAyn al-Qużāt Hamadānī maintained: "Know that a singer must be a beautiful *shāhid* [i.e., an exemplar of divine beauty] in order that when they sing these lines of poetry one iota of their spiritual meanings (*ma ʿānī*) may be shown." As I argued in chapter 1, this view sees the love evoked by the beautiful *shāhid*-cum-singer as something akin to a hermeneutic homing or honing device that enables the participants to discovery levels of meaning that would be impossible to ascertain in the absence of the æffective excitation they experience at the sight of such an earthly beauty. Without a co-occurring embodied experience of love, the words alone fall flat. They just do not *mean* the same thing, because the participant does not have the somato-affective experience required to guide their understanding of them—to, that is, *feel* what they really mean in the full embodied sense of Sufi meaning that we see Jāmī advancing in chapter 4.

The bodies are not, however, the only æffectively meaningful nontextual components in the *samāʿ* performance context. The performance ambience and music have a strong claim to this power to impress themselves on and move participants æffectively in positive or negative ways, too. The *samāʿ* performance ambience must be æffectively attuned for the purpose, or the æffective fires of *samāʿ* cannot even be kindled. If the ambience does not *feel* right, if someone kills the mood, so to speak, not even a heroic lover will be able to get the *samāʿ* session's æffective (meaning) engine going. *Samāʿ*'s music also contributes its own somato-affective meaning vector to the ritual. Operating through a nonintellectual form of "impress[ively]" felt meaning (*āthār*), music not only helps modulate the æffective ambience but is itself capable of providing its listeners an "illustration" of the beauty of God and the celestial realm, providing a powerful æffective meaning vector much akin to the æffects that the beautiful bodies of the *shāhid*s of chapter 1 evoke in the somato-affective bodies of those who gaze upon them.

While I have been keen throughout *Feeling Like Lovers* to complicate the predominant focus of many earlier studies of *samāʿ* on its recited poetic text as the only or primary meaning-producing element of the ritual, I have been equally interested to expand our understanding of the diverse ways Sufis make meaning in and from poetry. Chapters 3, 4, and 5 all take up the topic of Sufi poetry, moving from a broader focus on the Sufi hermeneutic process in *samāʿ* in chapter 3 to increasingly focused studies of Sufi poetic imagery in chapters 4 and 5. I want to return at this point to the anecdote of al-Nūrī that opened this chapter and use al-Ghazālī's theoretical framing of it to recap these chapters' important points in different terms.

This al-Nūrī anecdote is the concluding illustration of the "first reason" al-Ghazālī provides in his famous seven-reason-long argument—mentioned several times throughout this book—for why *samāʿ* is superior to Qurʾānic recitation for exciting *wajd* and, by extension, for advancing Sufi aspirants on their path of spiritual development.[3] al-Ghazālī opens this argument with a citation of what must have been the critics of this position's understandable proverbial question (heavily paraphrasing): Why, in the world, would Sufis stubbornly insist on using sung poetry, composed by humans, in *samāʿ* when they could instead be using the words of God Almighty, recited from the Qurʾān?!?!

al-Ghazālī argues that the "first reason" for *samāʿ*'s superiority is the fact that many Qurʾānic verses will not "correspond to" or "be in harmony with" the state (*ḥāl*) of the listeners and thus cannot facilitate the "dispatching" of the Qurʾānic verses to other spiritual "meanings."[4] He proceeds to ask, with what seems almost an incredulous tone, how the state of a person overwhelmed by sadness, desire, or remorse could "correspond to" the Qurʾānic verses "God enjoins upon you concerning your children: unto the male a share equal to that of two females. . . ." (4:11) or "And as for those who accuse chaste women. . . ." (24:4).[5] The implied answer is that they cannot. Or, at least, as he admits in a sizable digression, they can only be made to in truly exceptional cases—the cases of those heroic hermeneuts mentioned in chapter 3—in which the listener is so totally conquered by an æffective state *and* possesses truly extraordinary abilities for deriving meanings that are quite "distant" from the primary topic and literal meaning of the texts.[6] But

3. Although he uses only the term "singing (*al-ghināʾ*)" here, it is clear from the rest of his treatment that what he means is sung poetry in the context of the Sufi ritual of *samāʿ*.

4. al-Ghazālī, *Iḥyāʾ*, 2:295.

5. Translations from Nasr et al., *The Study Quran*.

6. al-Ghazālī gives nearly half a page of examples of these interpreters extraordinaire in *Iḥyāʾ*, 2:295.

these super-hermeneutical skills are not the norm, even seemingly in advanced Sufi circles. This is why "poetic verses and song," and by extension their spiritual use in *samāʿ*, are so important for Sufi spiritual practice. They are, in al-Ghazālī's view, unparalleled in their "affinity with [somato-affective] states" (*munāsiba li-l-aḥwāl*), which makes them capable of "mov[ing] [the heart] in a way not found in any other [means]," as he says in the conclusion to his whole exposition.[7]

The most striking part about this entire passage, which stretches over several densely packed pages, is the degree to which his entire discussion revolves around the central premise that the sung poetry of *samāʿ* is more effective than the Qurʾān in exciting *wajd* because it is fundamentally more *æffective*—a point which remains constant throughout his elaboration of the other six reasons for this as well. What Sufis need for spiritual advancement is for their hearts to be moved—that is, they need to *feel* something. And what does this the best is the powerfully intoxicating elixir of sung poetry in *samāʿ*. There is no means of communication better able to capture one's feelings. It is what we turn to if we have something deeply felt that we need to express to others. It is also what we turn to when we want to be prompted to feel something. It speaks the language of æffect in ways no other modes of communication can, and it does this both in the sense of operating as a mode of expression to pour our æffect into and serving as the go-to when we want to be moved by others' attempts to express their complex assemblages of feeling. This conception of poetry demands a new scholarly approach to analyzing it. Fully understanding Sufi poetry, as I argue through a close look at Jāmī's embodied theory of metaphoric imagery in chapter 4 and my attempt to apply a modern version of it in chapter 5, requires us to probe—even if only imperfectly—the complex ways in which poets marshal poetic form, structure, and imagery to communicate this somato-affective layer of meaning.

We should be careful here, though, not to adopt a reductive Sufi hermeneutics. Poetry and song do convey æffect, but they are not just inert suitcases that transfer specific æffects or emotions between bodies. Their authors do not simply encode certain feelings into verse and song, which their audiences then passively receive and faithfully decode and experience like a computer processing binary code. The hermeneutic process, as al-Ghazālī both in this passage and in other places (see chapter 3) shows, is not that simple and unidirectional. What a particular sung poem comes to *mean* to its audience members is produced in a dynamic process of negotiation between what the song-text literally says and how that "fits" or "corresponds" with their internal state. Different ascendant æffective states in the audience members will guide their hermeneutic compasses to find different "fits." Different "fits" produce different meanings for them from the same song-text—sometimes fundamentally different ones than the original author may have intended. Æffect is central here too: guiding the individual Sufi's hermeneutic

7. al-Ghazālī, *Iḥyāʾ*, 2:295, 2:298

process and determining what the author's sung text means to them, which, can also not be separated from how the text makes them feel.

What is the common thread through all these chapters treating bodies, music, performance ambience, and poetry? It is simple: In Sufism, one cannot draw closer to God, learn His lofty divine realities and secrets of the universe (*ḥaqāʾiq, asrār,* and *maʿānī*), and, ultimately, become a Sufi saint without *feeling* certain things. God forms His Sufi saints to a large degree by working on their somato-affective system—through bodies (theirs and others), music, ambience, and language in the form primarily of poetry—entraining it to move to His/Divine Love's rhythms, and ultimately in the final stage of self-annihilation (*fanāʾ*), fully seizing control of it and their entire body. A Sufi aspirant must learn to *feel like a lover* to become one. They must be made into a certain type of feeling subject to progress on the spiritual path. Æffect is everywhere in this process of spiritual formation, guiding it from these saints' initial conversions to the Sufi path at the hands of an earthly "training" or "toy" beloved to their ongoing ritual practice of æffectively driven *samāʿ* and *shāhid-bāzī* sessions even long after becoming elite Sufi masters. Sufi epistemology and subject formation, in short, are as much æffectively as rationally, intellectually, or discursively formed.

This has a broader implication that I will adumbrate, however briefly, before concluding: The imbrication of feeling/æffect/emotion and Sufi epistemology is *not* likely unique historically in the Islamicate world. I suspect that further investigations into the Islamicate world's other domains of knowledge will likewise show feeling/æffect/emotion enmeshment in their epistemologies and technologies of communication and subject formation. As scholars working in other disciplines, cultural traditions, and time periods have argued in diverse ways, the human body and its feelings/æffects/emotions generally cannot so easily be extricated from humanity's other modes of knowledge and genres of cultural production, even the most self-proclaimed "rationalist" ones. The somato-affective dimensions of embodied experience have varied ways of weaving themselves into human cogitation and its seemingly ratiogenic products and tools, such as philosophy, language, and reason. Language certainly conveys propositional content, philosophical ideas, and discursive constructs, but it is formed by embodied experience in the world and circulates feelings and æffects too. Even the most abstract metaphysical ideas and concepts feel like something and, some argue, are made possible by and built upon embodied experience. Rationality often relies on emotions and feeling states in its unfolding process, even as its partisans boast of it being wholly apart from what they view as the lowly body and its fickle somato-affective system. The boundaries—if they exist—between human æffect/emotion/senses/the body and language/rationality/intellect/the mind seem to be exceedingly porous and readily facilitate bidirectional traffic.[8] I doubt, therefore, that the argument I advance

8. For a sampling of some of the major arguments on these points, see Lakoff and Johnson, *Philosophy in the Flesh*; Scheer, "Are Emotions a Kind of Practice"; Schaefer, *Wild Experiment*.

here about the imbrication of feeling/æffect/emotion and Sufi epistemology is an isolated example in the broader Islamicate world.

I do not say all of this to assert æffect or the body's supremacy over the mind, language, or rationality/intellect. Rather, at the broadest level, *Feeling Like Lovers* is interested in restoring the Sufi mind-body, which makes use of these different tools/modes of perception and meaning and knowledge production as the contexts requires, some more so in certain contexts, some more so in others. This book's focus on æffect/emotion/feeling aims to better illuminate the important and largely unappreciated role these somato-affective forces have played in the co-construction of Sufi epistemology and subject formation—a position which I see as contributing to the growing efforts underway in Sufi studies to reembody Sufism and restore the body side of the tired old Cartesian binary. Sufis are not disembodied intellects nor disintellected bodies. They are minded-embodied lover-saints.

BIBLIOGRAPHY

Abu Deeb, Kamal. *Al-Jurjānī's Theory of Poetic Imagery*. Aris & Phillips LTD, 1979.

Abuali, Eyad. "'I Tasted Sweetness, and I Tasted Affliction': Pleasure, Pain, and Body in Medieval Sufi Food Practices." *The Senses and Society* 17, no. 1 (2022): 52–67.

———. "Visualizing the Soul: Diagrams and the Subtle Body of Light (*Jism Laṭīf*) in Shams al-Dīn al-Daylamī's *The Mirror of Souls (Mirʾāt Al-Arwāḥ)*." *Critical Research on Religion* 9, no. 2 (2021): 157–74.

———. "Words Clothed in Light: *Dhikr* (Recollection), Colour and Synaesthesia in Early Kubrawi Sufism." *Iran* 58, no. 2 (2020): 279–92.

Abu-Lughod, Lila. *Veiled Sentiments: Honor and Poetry in a Bedouin Society*. Thirtieth anniversary edition. University of California Press, 2016.

Afary, Janet. *Sexual Politics in Modern Iran*. Cambridge University Press, 2009.

Ahmed, Sara. "Affective Economies." *Social Text* 22, no. 2 (2004): 117–39.

———. *The Cultural Politics of Emotion*. 2nd ed. Edinburgh University Press, 2014.

———. *Queer Phenomenology: Orientations, Objects, Others*. Duke University Press, 2006.

Ahmed, Shahab. *What Is Islam? The Importance of Being Islamic*. Princeton University Press, 2016.

Alexandrin, Elizabeth R. "Minding the Body: Corporeality in Shams al-Dīn al-Daylamī's Treatises." *Ishrāq* 4 (2013): 526–39.

———. "Witnessing the Lights of the Heavenly Dominion: Dreams, Visions and the Mystical Exegeses of Shams al-Dīn al-Daylamī." In *Dreams and Visions in Islamic Societies*, edited by Özgen Felek and Alexander D. Knysh, 215–31. SUNY Press, 2012.

Algar, Hamid. "Impostors, Antinomians and Pseudo-Sufis: Cataloguing the Miscreants." *Journal of Islamic Studies* 29, no. 1 (2018): 25–47.

———. *Jami*. Oxford University Press, 2013.

Alharthi, Jokha. *The Body in Arabic Love Poetry: The 'Udhri Tradition*. Edinburgh University Press, 2021.

Ali, Ahmed. *Al-Qurʾān*. Princeton University Press, 2001.

Ali, Samer M. *Arabic Literary Salons in the Islamic Middle Ages: Poetry, Public Performance, and the Presentation of the Past*. University of Notre Dame Press, 2010.

Andrews, Walter G., and Mehmet Kalpakli. *The Age of Beloveds: Love and the Beloved in Early-Modern Ottoman and European Culture and Society*. Duke University Press, 2005.

Anonymous. "Muqaddimah-yi dīvān." In *Kulliyyāt-i Shaykh Fakhr al-Dīn Ibrāhīm Hamadānī mutakhallaṣ bih ʿIrāqī*, edited by Saʿīd Nafīsī, 46–65. Kitāb-khānah-yi Ṣanāʾī, 1983–4 (1362).

Arjana, Sophia Rose. *Buying Buddha, Selling Rumi: Orientalism and the Mystical Marketplace*. Oneworld Academic, 2020.

ʿAṭṭār, Farīd al-Dīn. *Dīvān-i ʿAṭṭār*. Edited by Taqī Tafażżulī. Shirkat-i Intishārāt-i ʿIlm va Farhang, 1996–97 [1375].

———. *Manṭiq al-ṭayr-i ʿAṭṭār*. Edited by Muḥammad-Riżā Shafīʿī-Kadkanī. 2nd ed. Sukhan, 2005.

Avery, Kenneth S. *A Psychology of Early Sufi Samāʿ: Listening and Altered States*. Routledge, 2004.

al-Baghdādī, Abū al-Barakāt. *al-Kitāb al-muʿtabar fī al-ḥikma*. Intishārāt-i Dānishgāh-i Iṣfahān, 1995.

———. "Lessons in Wisdom." In van Gelder and Hammond, *Takhyīl*, 70–72.

Bashir, Shahzad. "Narrating Sight: Dreaming as Visual Training in Persianate Sufi Hagiography." In *Dreams and Visions in Islamic Societies*, edited by Özgen Felek and Alexander D. Knysh, 233–47. SUNY Press, 2012.

———. *Sufi Bodies: Religion and Society in Medieval Islam*. Columbia University Press, 2011.

———. "The World as a Hat: Symbolism and Materiality in Safavid Iran." In *Unity in Diversity: Mysticism, Messianism and the Construction of Religious Authority in Islam*, edited by Orkhan Mir-Kasimov, 343–65. Brill, 2014.

Bauer, Karen. "Emotion in the Qur'an: An Overview." *Journal of Qur'anic Studies* 19, no. 2 (2017): 1–30.

———. "The Emotions of Conversion and Kinship in the Qur'an and the Sīra of Ibn Isḥāq." *Cultural History* 8, no. 2 (2019): 137–63.

Bausani, Alessandro. "G̲h̲azal, II. In Persian Literature." In Bearman et al., *Encyclopaedia of Islam, Second Edition*.

Beard, Michael. "Introduction: Minds/Senses." In *Losing Our Minds, Coming to Our Senses: Sensory Readings of Persian Literature and Culture*, edited by M. Mehdi Khorrami and Amir Moosavi, 13–24. Amsterdam University Press, 2021.

Bearman, P., Th. Bianquis, C. E. Bosworth, E. van Donzel, and W. P. Heinrichs, ed. *Encyclopaedia of Islam, Second Edition*. Brill, 2012.

Bell, Joseph Norment. *Love Theory in Later Hanbalite Islam*. SUNY Press, 1979.

Ben-Ami, Ido. "Wonder in Early Modern Ottoman Society: A Case Study in the History of Emotions." *History Compass* 17 (2019): 1–12.

Bergen, Benjamin K. *Louder Than Words: The New Science of How the Mind Makes Meaning*. Basic Books, 2012.

Berlant, Lauren. *Cruel Optimism*. Duke University Press, 2011.

Bigelow, Anna. "Senses of Belonging: Materiality, Embodiment, and Attunement at Sufi Shrines in India." *MAVCOR Journal* 6, no. 2 (2022), https://doi.org/10.22332/mav.ess.2022.4.

Black, Deborah L. "Intentionality in Medieval Arabic Philosophy." *Quaestio* 10 (2010): 65–81.

Blatherwick, Helen. "'And the Light in His Eyes Grew Dark': The Representation of Anger in an Egyptian Popular Epic." *Cultural History* 8, no. 2 (2019): 226–47.

Boer, T. J. de, and F. Rahman. "ʿAḳl." In Bearman et al., *Encyclopaedia of Islam, Second Edition.*

Bray, Julia. "Codes of Emotion in Ninth- and Tenth-Century Baghdad: Slave Concubines in Literature and Life-Writing." *Cultural History* 8, no. 2 (2019): 184–201.

———. "Yaʿqūb b. al-Rabīʿ Read by al-Mutanabbī and al-Mubarrad: A Contribution to an Abbasid History of Emotions." *Journal of Abbasid Studies* 4, no. 1 (2017): 1–34.

Bray, Karen, and Stephen D. Moore. "Introduction: Mappings and Crossings." In *Religion, Emotion, Sensation: Affect Theories and Theologies*, edited by Karen Bray and Stephen D. Moore, 1–18. Fordham University Press, 2020.

Brookshaw, Dominic Parviz. "Palaces, Pavilions, and Pleasure-Gardens: The Context and Setting of the Medieval *Majlis*." *Middle Eastern Literatures* 6 (2003): 199–223.

Bürgel, J. Christopher. *The Feather of Simurgh: The "Licit Magic" of the Arts in Medieval Islam*. New York University Press, 1988.

Burger, Glen D., and Holly A. Crocker. "Introduction." In Burger and Crocker, *Medieval Affect, Feeling, and Emotion*, 1–24.

Burger, Glen D., and Holly A. Crocker, eds. *Medieval Affect, Feeling, and Emotion*. Cambridge University Press, 2019.

Bursi, Adam. "'You Were Not Commanded to Stroke It, But To Pray Nearby It': Debating Touch Within Early Islamic Pilgrimage." *The Senses and Society* 17, no. 1 (2022): 8–21.

Cervone, Cristina Maria. *Poetics of Incarnation: Middle English Writing and the Leap of Love*. University of Pennsylvania Press, 2012.

Chittick, William C. *Divine Love: Islamic Literature and the Path to God*. Yale University Press, 2013.

———. "Jāmī on Divine Love and the Image of Wine." *Studies in Mystical Literature* 1, no. 3 (1981): 193–209.

———. *The Sufi Path of Love: The Spiritual Teachings of Rumi*. SUNY Press, 1983.

Chittick, William C., and Peter Lamborn Wilson. "Introduction." In *Fakhruddin ʿIraqi: Divine Flashes*, edited by William C. Chittick and Peter Lamborn Wilson, 3–66. Paulist Press, 1982.

Cornell, Vincent J. *Realm of the Saint: Power and Authority in Moroccan Sufism*. University of Texas Press, 1998.

Crocker, Holly A. "Medieval Affects Now." *Exemplaria* 29, no. 1 (2017): 82–98.

Culler, Jonathan D. *Structuralist Poetics: Structuralism, Linguistics and the Study of Literature*. Routledge Classics, 2002.

Dagli, Caner K. *Ibn al-ʿArabi and Islamic Intellectual Culture: From Mysticism to Philosophy*. Routledge, 2016.

Daylamī, Abū al-Ḥasan ʿAlī ibn Muḥammad. *A Treatise on Mystical Love*. Translated by Joseph Norment Bell and Hassan Mahmood Abdul Latif Al Shafie. Edinburgh University Press, 2005.

de Bruijn, J. T. P. *Persian Sufi Poetry: An Introduction to the Mystical Use of Classical Persian Poems*. Curzon Press, 1997.

———. "The Ghazal in Medieval Persian Poetry." In *Persian Lyric Poetry in the Classical Era, 800–1500: Ghazals, Panegyrics, and Quatrains*, edited by Ehsan Yarshater, 315–487. I. B. Tauris, 2019.

———. "The *Qalandariyyāt* in Persian Mystical Poetry, From Sanā'i Onwards." In *The Legacy of Mediaeval Persian Sufism*, edited by Leonard Lewisohn, 75–86. Khaniqahi Nimatullah Publications, 1992.

de Mulder, Walter. "Force Dynamics." In *The Oxford Handbook of Cognitive Linguistics*, edited by Dirk Geeraerts and Hubert Cuyckens, 294–317. Oxford University Press, 2007.

During, Jean. "What Is Sufi Music?" In *The Heritage of Sufism, Volume II: The Legacy of Medieval Persian Sufism (1150–1500)*, edited by Leonard Lewisohn, 277–87. Oneworld, 1999.

Elias, Jamal J. *Aisha's Cushion: Religious Art, Perception, and Practice in Islam*. Harvard University Press, 2012.

———. *Alef Is for Allah: Childhood, Emotion, and Visual Culture in Islamic Societies*. University of California Press, 2018.

———. "Mevlevi Sufis and the Representation of Emotion in the Arts of the Ottoman World." In K. Rizvi, *Affect, Emotion, and Subjectivity*, 185–209.

El-Rouayheb, Khaled. *Before Homosexuality in the Arab-Islamic World, 1500–1800*. University of Chicago Press, 2005.

Ernst, Carl W. "Introduction." In *Hallaj: Poems of a Sufi Martyr*, 1–45. Northwestern University Press, 2018.

———. *Teachings of Sufism*. Shambhala, 1999.

———. "The Stages of Love in Early Persian Sufism, from Rābi'a to Rūzbihān." In *The Heritage of Sufism, Volume I: Classical Persian Sufism from Its Origins to Rumi (700–1300)*, edited by Leonard Lewisohn, 435–55. Oneworld, 1999.

———. *Words of Ecstasy in Sufism*. SUNY Press, 1985.

Ernst, Carl W., and Bruce B. Lawrence. *Sufi Martyrs of Love: Chishti Sufism in South Asia and Beyond*. Palgrave Macmillan, 2002.

al-Fārābī, Abū Naṣr Muḥammad. "Jawāmiʿ al-shiʿr li-l-Fārābī." In *Talkhīṣ kitāb Arisṭūṭālīs fī al-shiʿr*, edited by Muḥammad Salīm Sālim, 165–75. Lajnat Iḥyāʾ al-Turāth al-Islāmī, 1971.

———. "Treatise on Poetry." In van Gelder and Hammond, *Takhyīl*, 15–18.

Feuillebois-Pierunek, Ève. *A la croisée des voies célestes, Faxr al-Din 'Erâqi: poésie mystique et expression poétique en Perse médiévale*. Institut Français de Recherche en Iran, 2002.

Franko, Mark, and Annette Richards. "Actualizing Absences: The Pastness of Performance." In *Acting on the Past: Historical Performance Across the Disciplines*, edited by Mark Franko and Annette Richards, 1–9. Wesleyan University Press, 2000.

Gade, Anna M. "Islam." In *The Oxford Handbook of Religion and Emotion*, edited by John Corrigan, 35–50. Oxford University Press, 2008.

———. *Perfection Makes Practice: Learning, Emotion, and the Recited Qur'ān in Indonesia*. University of Hawai'i Press, 2004.

Gannagé, Emma. "Al-Kindī on the *Ḥaqīqa–Majāz* Dichotomy." *Revue d'études Anciennes Et Médiévales* 13 (2015): 173–90.

Gāzargāhī, Kamāl al-Dīn Ḥusayn. *Majālis al-ʿushshāq*. Edited by Ghulām-Riżā Majd Ṭabāṭabāʾī. Intishārāt-i Zarrīn, 1996–7 (1375).

al-Ghazālī, Abū Ḥāmid Muḥammad. *Iḥyāʾ ʿulūm al-dīn*. Edited by Badawī Ṭabāna. Dār Iḥyāʾ al-Kutub al-ʿArabiyya, 1957.

———. *Kīmiyā-yi saʿādat*. Edited by Muḥammad ʿAbbāsī. Intishārāt-i Ṭulūʿ va Intishārāt-i Zarrīn, 1982–3 (1361).

———. *Iḥyāʾ ʿulūm al-dīn*. Maṭbaʿat Būlāq, 1873.

al-Ghazzali, Abu Hamid. *The Alchemy of Happiness*. Translated by Claud Field. M. E. Sharpe Inc., 1991.

———. "Emotional Religion in Islām as Affected by Music and Singing." Translated by Duncan B. MacDonald. *Journal of the Royal Asiatic Society of Great Britain and Ireland* 33, no. 2 (April 1901): 195–252.

———. "Emotional Religion in Islām as Affected by Music and Singing." Translated by Duncan B. Macdonald. *Journal of the Royal Asiatic Society* 33, no. 4 (October 1901): 705–48.

———. "Emotional Religion in Islām as Affected by Music and Singing (Concluded from p. 748, October 1901)." Translated by Duncan B. MacDonald. *Journal of the Royal Asiatic Society of Great Britain and Ireland* 34, no. 1 (January 1902): 1–28.

Ghazālī, Aḥmad. "Savānah." In *Risālah-yi savānah va risālah dar maw'iẓah*, edited by Javād Nūrbakhsh, 13–61. Intishārāt-i Khānigāh-i Ni'mat Allāhī, 1973–4 (1352).

Ghazzal, Zouhair. "From Anger on Behalf of God to 'Forbearance' in Islamic Medieval Literature." In *Anger's Past: The Social Uses of an Emotion in the Middle Ages*, edited by Barbara H. Rosenwein, 203–30. Cornell University Press, 2018.

Giffen, Lois Anita. *Theory of Profane Love Among the Arabs: The Development of the Genre*. New York University Press, 1971.

Gill, Denise. *Melancholic Modalities: Affect, Islam, and Turkish Classical Musicians*. Oxford University Press, 2017.

Golchin-Ma'ānī, Aḥmad. *Tazkirah-yi paymānah: Dar zikr-i sāqi-nāmah-hā va aḥvāl va āsār-i sāqi-nāmah-sarāyān*. Kitāb-khānah-yi Sanā'ī, 1989–90 (1368).

Gondos, Andrea. "Seekers of Love: The Phenomenology of Emotion in Jewish, Christian, and Sufi Mystical Sources." In *Esoteric Transfers and Constructions. Palgrave Studies in New Religions and Alternative Spiritualities*, edited by M. Sedgwick and F. Piraino, 21–41. Palgrave Macmillan, 2021.

Graham, William. *Divine Word and Prophetic Word in Early Islam: A Reconsideration of the Sources, with Special Reference to the Divine Saying or Ḥadîth Qudsî*. Mouton, 1977.

Green, Nile. *Sufism: A Global History*. Wiley-Blackwell, 2012.

Gribetz, Arthur. "The Samā' Controversy: Sufi vs. Legalist." *Studia Islamica* 74 (1991): 43–62.

Griffel, Frank. *Al-Ghazali's Philosophical Theology*. Oxford University Press, 2009.

Gruber, Christiane. "In Defense and Devotion: Affective Practices in Early Modern Turco-Persian Manuscript Paintings." In K. Rizvi, *Affect, Emotion, and Subjectivity*, 95–123.

Ḥallāj, al-Ḥusayn ibn Manṣūr. *Hallaj: Poems of a Sufi Martyr*. Translated by Carl W. Ernst. Northwestern University Press, 2018.

Hamadānī, 'Ayn al-Quẓāt. "Tamhīdāt." In *Muṣannafāt*, edited by 'Afīf 'Ussayrān, 1–354. Intishārāt-i Dānishgāh-i Tihrān, 1962–3 (1341).

Harb, Lara. *Arabic Poetics: Aesthetic Experience in Classical Arabic Literature*. Cambridge University Press, 2020.

Heinrichs, Wolfhart. "Contacts Between Scriptural Hermeneutics and Literary Theory in Islam: The Case of *Majāz*." *Zeitschrift Fur Geschichte Der Arabisch-Islamischen Wissenshaften* 7 (1991/1992): 253–84.

———. "Literary Theory: The Problem of Its Efficiency." In *Arabic Poetry: Theory and Development*, 19–69. Harrassowitz, 1973.

———. "On the Genesis of the Ḥaqîqa-Majâz Dichotomy." *Studia Islamica*, no. 59 (1984): 111–40.

———. *The Hand of the Northwind: Opinions on Metaphor and the Early Meaning of Istiʿāra in Arabic Poetics*. 1. Aufl. Abhandlungen für Die Kunde Des Morgenlandes, Bd. 44, 2. Deutsche Morgenländische Gesellschaft, 1977.

———. "On the Figurative (*Majāz*) in Muslim Interpretation and Legal Hermeneutics." In *Interpreting Scriptures in Judaism, Christianity and Islam: Overlapping Inquiries*, edited by Adele Berlin and Mordechai Z. Cohen, 249–65. Cambridge University Press, 2016.

Heinrichs, Wolfhart, and Alexander Knysh. "Ramz." In Bearman et al., *Encyclopaedia of Islam, Second Edition*.

Hermansen, Marcia K. "Religious Literature and the Inscription of Identity: The Sufi Tazkira Tradition in Muslim South Asia." *Muslim World* 87 (1997): 315–29.

Hermansen, Marcia K., and Bruce B. Lawrence. "Indo-Persian Tazkiras as Memorative Communications." In *Beyond Turk and Hindu: Rethinking Religious Identities in Islamicate South Asia*, edited by David Gilmartin and Bruce B. Lawrence, 176–98. University Press of Florida, 2000.

Hirschkind, Charles. *The Ethical Soundscape: Cassette Sermons and Islamic Counterpublics*. Columbia University Press, 2006.

Hofer, Nathan. "On the Material and Social Conditions of Khalwa in Medieval Sufism." *MAVCOR Journal* 6, no. 2 (2022). https://mavcor.yale.edu/mavcor-journal/essays/material-and-social-conditions-khalwa-medieval-sufism.

Hoffmann, Alexandra. "Angry Men: On Emotions and Masculinities in Samarqandī's Sindbād-nāmeh." *Narrative Culture* 7, no. 2 (2020).

Hoffmann, Thomas. "Taste My Punishment and My Warnings (Q. 54:39): On the Torments of Tantalus and Other Painful Metaphors of Taste in the Qur'an." *Journal of Qur'anic Studies* 21, no. 1 (2019): 1–20.

Homerin, Th. Emil. *The Wine of Love and Life: Ibn al-Fāriḍ al-Khamrīyah and al-Qayṣarī's Quest for Meaning*. Middle East Documentation Center, 2005.

Hotham, Matthew. "Affect, Animality, and Islamophobia: Human-Animal Relations in the Production of Muslim Difference in America." *Bulletin for the Study of Religion* 46, no. 3–4 (2017): 25–38.

———. "Sensing the Ascent: Embodied Elements of Muhammad's Heavenly Journey in Nizami Ganjavi's *Treasury of Mysteries*." In *Transformational Embodiment in Asian Religions: Subtle Bodies, Spatial Bodies*, edited by George Pati and Katherine Zubko, 145–67. Routledge, 2020.

Houghteling, Sylvia. "Sentiment in Silks: Safavid Figural Textiles in Mughal Courtly Culture." In K. Rizvi, *Affect, Emotion, and Subjectivity*, 124–47.

Hubert, Thibaut d', and Alexandre Papas, eds. *Jāmī in Regional Contexts: The Reception of ʿAbd Al-Raḥmān Jāmī's Works in the Islamicate World, Ca. 9th/15th-14th/20th Century*. Brill, 2019.

Huda, Qamar-ul. *Striving for Divine Union: Spiritual Exercises for Suhrawardī Sūfīs*. Routledge Curzon, 2003.

Hunsberger, Alice C. "'On the Steed of Speech': A Philosophical Poem by Nāsir-i Khusraw." In *Pearls of Persia: The Philosophical Poetry of Nāsir-i Khusraw*, edited by Alice C. Hunsberger, 147–90. I. B. Tauris in Association with the Institute of Ismaili Studies, 2012.

Hussain, Ali. "Dāwūd al-Qayṣarī." In *Encyclopaedia of Islam, Third Edition*, edited by Kate Fleet, Gudrun Krämer, Denis Matringe, John Nawas, and Devin J. Stewart. Brill, 2015.

Ibn al-Fāriḍ, ʿUmar. "Wine Ode." In *ʿUmar ibn al-Fāriḍ: Sufi Verse, Saintly Life*, translated by Th. Emil Homerin, 41–66. Paulist Press, 2001.

Ibn Sīnā, Abū ʿAlī al-Ḥusayn. *al-Ishārāt wa al-tanbīhāt*. Edited by Sulaymān Dunyā. Dār al-Maʿārif, 1983.

———. *Kitāb al-majmūʿ, aw al-ḥikmah al-ʿarūḍīyyah fī maʿānī kitāb al-shiʿr*. Edited by Muḥammad Salīm Sālim. Maṭbaʿat Dār al-Kutub, 1969.

———. "Remarks and Admonitions." In van Gelder and Hammond, *Takhyīl*, 25.

———. "The Compendium, or Wisdom for al-ʿArūḍī." In van Gelder and Hammond, *Takhyīl*, 26–28.

Ilahi-Ghomshei, Ḥusayn. "The Principles of the Religion of Love in Classical Persian Poetry." In *Hafiz and the Religion of Love in Classical Persian Poetry*, edited and translated by Leonard Lewisohn, 77–106. I. B. Tauris, 2010.

Ingenito, Domenico. *Beholding Beauty: Saʿdi of Shiraz and the Aesthetics of Desire in Medieval Persian Poetry*. Brill, 2021.

———. "'Tabrizis in Shiraz Are Worth Less Than a Dog': Saʿdī and Humām, a Lyrical Encounter." In *Politics, Patronage and the Transmission of Knowledge in 13th–15th Century Tabriz*, edited by Judith Pfeiffer, 77–128. Brill, 2014.

ʿIraqi, Fakhruddin. *Fakhruddin ʿIraqi: Divine Flashes*. Translated by William C. Chittick and Peter Lamborn Wilson. Paulist Press, 1982.

———. *Kulliyyāt-i Fakhr al-Dīn ʿIrāqī (majmūʿah-yi āsār-i Fakhr al-Dīn ʿIrāqī)*. Edited by Nasrīn Muḥtasham (Khuzāʾī). Intishārāt-i Zavvār, 2003–4 (1382).

———. *Kulliyyāt-i Shaykh Fakhr al-Dīn Ibrāhīm Hamadānī Mutakhallaṣ bih ʿIrāqī*. Edited by Saʿīd Nafīsī. Kitāb-khānah-yi Ṣanāʾī, 1983–4 (1362).

Jāmī, Nūr al-Dīn ʿAbd al-Raḥmān. "Lavāmiʿ: fī sharḥ-i qaṣidah-yi mīmiyyah-yi khamriyyah-yi Fāriḍiyyah." In *Bahāristān va rasāʾil-i Jāmī*, edited by Aʿlākhān Afṣaḥ, Muḥammad Jān ʿUmarʾuf, and Abū Bakr Ẓuhūr al-Dīn, 343–406. Mīrās-i Maktūb, 2000–1 (1379).

———. *Lavāmiʿ-i Jāmī: Sharḥ-i qaṣidah-yi khamriyyah-yi Ibn Fāriḍ*. Edited by Ḥikmat Āl-i Āqā. Bunyād-i Mihr, 1962.

———. *Lavāmiʿ-i Jāmī: yaʿnī, sharḥ-i qaṣīdah-yi mīmiyyah-yi tāʾiyyah-yi Fāriḍiyyah*. Edited by Muḥammad ʿAbd al-Aḥad. Mujtabāʾī, 1902.

———. *Nafaḥāt al-uns min ḥażarāt al-quds*. Edited by Mahdī Tawḥīdīpūr. Intishārāt-i ʿIlmī, 1996–7 (1375).

———. *Nafaḥāt al-uns min ḥażarāt al-quds*. Edited by Maḥmūd ʿĀbidī. Sukhān, 2007–8 (1386).

Johnson, Mark. *The Meaning of the Body: Aesthetic of Human Understanding*. The University of Chicago Press, 2007.

Junayd ibn Muḥammad, Abū al-Qāsim. *The Life, Personality and Writings of Al-Junayd: A Study of a Third/Ninth Century Mystic, with an Edition and Translation of His Writings*. Edited by ʿAlī Ḥasan ʿAbd al-Qādir. Luzac and Gibb Memorial Trust, 1976.

al-Jurjānī, ʿAbd al-Qāhir ibn ʿAbd al-Raḥmān. *Asrār al-balāgha*. Edited by Helmut Ritter. Govt. Press, 1954.

———. "The Secrets of Eloquence." In van Gelder and Hammond, *Takhyīl*, 30–69.

Karamustafa, Ahmet T. *God's Unruly Friends: Dervish Groups in the Islamic Later Middle Period, 1200–1550*. University of Utah Press, 1994.

———. *Sufism: The Formative Period*. University of California Press, 2007.

Kāshifī Shīrāzī, Kamāl al-Dīn Ḥusayn Vāʿiẓ. *Badāʾiʿ al-afkār fī sanāʾiʿ al-ashʿār*. Edited by Mīr Jalāl al-Dīn Kazzāzī. Nashr-i Markaz, 1990–91 [1369].

Katz, Marion Holmes. "Beyond *Ḥalāl* and *Ḥarām*: *Ghayra* ('Jealousy') as a Masculine Virtue in the Work of Ibn Qayyim al-Jawziyya." *Cultural History* 8, no. 2 (2019): 202–25.

Kemal, Salim. *The Philosophical Poetics of Alfarabi, Avicenna and Averroës: The Aristotelian Reception*. Routledge, 2003.

Keshavarz, Fatemeh. *Reading Mystical Lyric: The Case of Jalal Al-Din Rumi*. University of South Carolina Press, 1998.

Keshavmurthy, Prashant. "Translating Rāma as a Proto-Muḥammadan Prophet: Masīḥ's *Masn avī-i Rām va Sītā*." *Numen* 65 (2018): 1–27.

Key, Alexander. *Language Between God and the Poets: Maʿnā in the Eleventh Century*. University of California Press, 2018.

Khalek, Nancy. "Al-Dāraquṭnī's (d. 385 AH) *Faḍāʾil Al-Ṣaḥāba*: Mild Anger and the History of Emotions in Religious Merits Literature." *Bulletin of the School of Oriental and African Studies* 83, no. 3 (2020): 415–36.

Khalil, Atif. "Ḥāl in Ṣūfism." In *Encyclopaedia of Islam, Third Edition*, edited by Kate Fleet, Gudrun Krämer, Denis Matringe, John Nawas, and Devin J. Stewart. Brill, 2022.

Khoja-Moolji, Shenila. *Sovereign Attachments: Masculinity, Muslimness, and Affective Politics in Pakistan*. University of California Press, 2021.

Khorrami, M. Mehdi, and Amir Moosavi, eds. *Losing Our Minds, Coming to Our Senses: Sensory Readings of Persian Literature and Culture*. Leiden University Press, 2021.

King, Anya. "Medieval Islamicate Aromatherapy: Medical Perspectives on Aromatics and Perfumes." *The Senses and Society* 17, no. 1 (2022): 37–51.

———. *Scent from the Garden of Paradise: Musk and the Medieval Islamic World*. Brill, 2017.

Klein, Yaron. "Music, Rapture and Pragmatics: Ghazālī on *Samāʿ* and *Wajd*." In *No Tapping Around Philology: A Festschrift in Honor of Wheeler McIntosh Thackston Jr.'s 70th Birthday*, edited by Alireza Korangy and Daniel Sheffield, 215–42. Harrassowitz Verlag, 2014.

———. "Musical Instruments in Samāʿ Literature: al-Udfuwī's *Kitāb al-Imtāʿ bi-aḥkām as-Samāʿ*." *Oriens* 51, no. 1–2 (2023): 14–37.

Knight, Michael Muhammad. *Muhammad's Body: Baraka Networks and the Prophetic Assemblage*. University of North Carolina Press, 2020.

Knysh, Alexander. "Tasting, Drinking and Quenching Thirst: From Mystical Experience to Mystical Gnoseology." *Manuscripta Orientalia: International Journal for Oriental Manuscript Research* 26, no. 2 (2020): 37–43.

Kövecses, Zoltán. "Metaphor and Emotion." In *Cambridge Handbook of Metaphor and Thought*, edited by Raymond W. Gibbs Jr., 380–96. Cambridge University Press, 2008.

———. *Metaphor and Emotion: Language, Culture, and Body in Human Feeling*. Cambridge University Press, 2000.

Kueny, Kathryn. "Tasting Fire: Affective Turn in Qur'anic Depictions of Divine Punishment." *Body and Religion* 3, no. 1 (2019): 5–26.

Kugle, Scott. "Caps, Heads, and Hearts." In *Islam Through Objects*, edited by Anna Bigelow. Bloomsbury Academic, 2021.

———. *Homosexuality in Islam: Critical Reflection on Gay, Lesbian, and Transgender Muslims*. Oneworld, 2010.

———. *Sufis and Saints' Bodies: Mysticism, Corporeality, & Sacred Power*. University of North Carolina Press, 2007.

———. "Sultan Mahmud's Makeover: Colonial Homophobia and the Persian-Urdu Literary Tradition." In *Queering India: Same-Sex Love and Eroticism in Indian Culture and Society*, edited by Ruth Vanita, 30–46. Routledge, 2001.

Kukkonen, Taneli. "Al-Ghazālī on the Emotions." In *Islam and Rationality: The Impact of al-Ghazālī*, edited by Georges Tamer, 1:138–64. Brill, 2015.

Lakoff, George. "The Neural Theory of Metaphor." In *The Cambridge Handbook of Metaphor and Thought*, edited by Raymond W. Gibbs Jr., 17–38. Cambridge University Press, 2008.

Lakoff, George, and Mark Johnson. *Metaphors We Live By*. University of Chicago Press, 1980.

———. *Philosophy in the Flesh: The Embodied Mind and Its Challenge to Western Thought*. Basic Books, 1999.

Landau, Justine. "Nasīr al-Dīn Ṭūsī and Poetic Imagination in the Arabic and Persian Philosophical Tradition." In *Metaphor and Imagery in Persian Poetry*, edited by Ali Asghar Seyed-Gohrab, 15–65. Brill, 2012.

———. *De rythme et de raison: lecture croisée de deux traités de poétique persans du XVIIIe siècle*. PSN—Presses Sorbonne Nouvelle, 2013.

Lane, Edward William, and Stanley Lane-Poole. *An Arabic-English Lexicon*. Librairie du Liban, 1968.

Lange, Christian. "Al-Jāḥiẓ on the Senses: Sensory Moderation and Muslim Synesthesia." *The Senses and Society* 17, no. 1 (2022): 22–36.

———. "Introduction: The Sensory History of the Islamic World." *The Senses and Society* 17, no. 1 (2022): 1–7.

Larkin, Margaret. "Abū l-ʿAlāʾ al-Maʿarrī's *Muʿjiz Aḥmad* and the Limits of Poetic Commentary." *Oriens* 41, no. 3–4 (2013): 479–97.

Lawrence, Bruce B. "The Early Chishtī Approach to *Samāʿ*." In *Islamic Society and Culture: Essays in Honour of Professor Aziz Ahmad*, edited by Milton Israel and N. K. Wagle, 69–93. Manohar, 1983.

Leaman, Oliver. "Poetry and the Emotions in Islamic Philosophy." In *Classic Issues in Islamic Philosophy and Theology Today*, edited by A-T. Tymieniecka and Nazif Muhtaroglu, 139–50. Springer Netherlands, 2010.

Lewis, Franklin D. "Reading, Writing and Recitation: Sana'i and the Origins of the Persian Ghazal." PhD thesis, University of Chicago, 1995.

———. "The Rise and Fall of a Persian Refrain: The *Radīf 'Ātash u Āb'*." In *Reorientations: Arabic and Persian Poetry*, edited by Suzanne Pinckney Stetkevych, 199–226. Indiana University Press, 1994.

———. "The Transformation of the Persian Ghazal: From Amatory Mood to Fixed Form." In *Ghazal as World Literature II: From a Literary Genre to a Great Tradition; The Ottoman Gazel in Context*, edited by Angelika Neuwirth, Michael Hess, Judith Pfeiffer, and Borte Sagaster, 121–39. Ergon Verlag, 2006.

Lewisohn, Leonard. *Beyond Faith and Infidelity: The Sufi Poetry and Teachings of Mahmud Shabistari*. Curzon Press, 1995.

———. "Prolegomenon to the Study of Hafiz." In *Hafiz and the Religion of Love in Classical Persian Poetry*, edited by Leonard Lewisohn, 3–73. I. B. Tauris, 2010.

———. "Sufi Symbolism in the Persian Hermeneutic Tradition: Reconstructing the Pagoda of 'Attar's Esoteric Poetics." In *'Attar and the Persian Sufi Tradition: The Art of Spiritual Flight*, edited by Leonard Lewisohn, 255–308. I. B. Tauris, 2006.

———. "Sufism's Religion of Love, from Rābi'a to Ibn 'Arabī." In *The Cambridge Companion to Sufism*, edited by Lloyd Ridgeon, 150–80. Cambridge University Press, 2015.

———. "The Sacred Music of Islam: *Samā'* in the Persian Sufi Tradition." *British Journal of Ethnomusicology* 6 (1997): 1–33.

Losensky, Paul E. "'Demand, Ask, Seek': The Semantics and Rhetoric of the *Radīf Ṭalab* in the Persian Ghazal." *The Turkish Studies Association Bulletin* 21 (1997): 19–40.

———. "Saqi-Nameh: Song of the Cupbearer." In *The Layered Heart: Essays on Persian Poetry*, edited by A. A. Seyed-Gohrab, 173–96. Mage Publishers, 2019.

———. "Vintages of the Sāqī-nāma: Fermenting and Blending the Cupbearer's Song in the Sixteenth Century." *Iranian Studies* 47 (2014): 131–57.

Lumbard, Joseph E. B. *Aḥmad al-Ghazālī, Remembrance, and the Metaphysics of Love*. SUNY Press, 2016.

———. "From *Hubb* to *'Ishq*: The Development of Love in Early Sufism." *Journal of Islamic Studies* 18 (2007): 345–85.

Lundblad, Michael. *Animalities: Literary and Cultural Studies Beyond the Human*. Edinburgh University Press, 2017.

Lunn, David, and Katherine Butler Schofield. "Delight, Devotion and the Music of the Monsoon at the Court of Emperor Shah 'Alam II." In Rajamani, Pernau, and Butler, *Monsoon Feelings*, 219–54.

Maḥjūb, Muḥammad Ja'far. "Sāqī-nāmah—Mughannī-nāmah." *Sukhan* 11 (1960): 69–79.

Mahmood, Saba. *Politics of Piety: The Islamic Revival and the Feminist Subject*. Princeton University Press, 2005.

Marranci, Gabriele. *The Anthropology of Islam*. Berg, 2008.

Massignon, Louis. *The Passion of al-Hallāj: Mystic and Martyr of Islam*. Translated by Herbert Mason. Princeton University Press, 1982.

Matthee, Rudolph P. *Angels Tapping at the Wine-Shop's Door: A History of Alcohol in the Islamic World*. Oxford University Press, 2023.

———. *The Pursuit of Pleasure: Drugs and Stimulants in Iranian History, 1500–1900*. Princeton University Press, 2005.

McGregor, Richard J. A. *Islam and the Devotional Object: Seeing Religion in Egypt and Syria*. Cambridge University Press, 2020.

McNamer, Sarah. *Affective Meditation and the Invention of Medieval Compassion*. University of Pennsylvania Press, 2010.

———. "Feeling." In *Middle English*, edited by Paul Strohm, 241–57. Oxford University Press, 2007.

———. "The Literariness of Literature and the History of Emotion." *PMLA* 130, no. 5 (2015): 1433–42.

Meier, Fritz. "Dervish Dance: An Attempt at an Overview." In *Essays on Islamic Piety and Mysticism*, edited by Bernd Radtke, translated by John O'Kane, 23–48. Brill, 1999.

Meisami, Julie Scott. "A Life in Poetry: Hāfiz's First Ghazal." In *The Necklace of the Pleiades: 24 Essays on Persian Literature, Culture and Religion*, edited by Franklin D. Lewis and Sunil Sharma, 163–81. Leiden University Press, 2010.

———. "Allegorical Techniques in the *Ghazals* of Hāfez." *Edebiyât* 4 (1979): 1–40.

———. "Este'āra." Edited by Ehsan Yarshater. *Encyclopædia Iranica, Online Edition*, 1998. http://www.iranicaonline.org/articles/esteara.

———. "Imagery as Argument: Khāqānī's *Qasīda* to the Sharvānshāh on the Occasion of 'Īd al-Fiṭr." *Edebiyât* 9 (1998): 35–59.

———. *Medieval Persian Court Poetry*. Princeton University Press, 1987.

———. "Nāsir-i Khusraw: A Poet Lost in Thought?" In *Pearls of Persia: The Philosophical Poetry of Nāsir-i Khusraw*, edited by Alice C. Hunsberger, 223–55. I. B. Tauris in Association with the Institute of Ismaili Studies, 2012.

———. "Poetic Microcosms: The Persian Qasida to the End of the Twelfth Century." In *Qasida Poetry in Islamic Asia and Africa (Vol. I): Classical Traditions & Modern Meanings*, edited by Stefan Sperl and Christopher Shackle, 137–82. E. J. Brill, 1996.

———. *Structure and Meaning in Medieval Arabic and Persian Poetry: Orient Pearls*. Routledge, 2003.

———. "The Grand Design: Medieval Persian Poetic Microcosms." In *Proceedings of the XIIth Congress of the International Comparative Literature Association*, 458–63. Judicium, 1990.

Melchert, Christopher. "Exaggerated Fear in the Early Islamic Renunciant Tradition." *Journal of the Royal Asiatic Society* 21, no. 3 (2011): 283–300.

Mian, Ali Altaf. "Muslim Political Philosophy and the Affective Turn: Farabi on Language, Affect, and Reason." *Journal of Shi'a Islamic Studies* 4, no. 1 (2011): 47–70.

Michon, Jean-Louis. "Sacred Music and Dance in Islam." In *Islamic Spirituality: Manifestations*, edited by Seyyed Hossein Nasr, 469–505. Crossroad Publishing, 1991.

Mikkelson, Jane. "Flights of Imagination: Avicenna's Phoenix (*ʿAnqā*) and Bedil's Figuration for the Lyric Self." *Journal of South Asian Intellectual History* 2, no. 1 (2020): 28–72.

Miller, Matthew Thomas. "Embodying the Beloved: Embodiment, (Homo)eroticism, and the Straightening of Desire in the Hagiographic Tradition of Fakhr al-Dīn ʿIrāqī." *Journal of Middle Eastern Literatures* 21, no. 1 (2018): 1–27.

———. "The Ocean of the Persians: Fakhr al-Din ʿIrâqi, Poet and Mystic." In *Mystical Landscapes: Voices and Themes in Medieval Persian Literature*, edited by Fatemeh Keshavarz and Ahmet T. Karamustafa, 243–86. Edinburgh University Press, 2025.

———, trans. *God's Wild Lovers: The Ecstatic Lyrics of Sufism's Rogue Poets*. University of California Press, forthcoming.

———. "'In the Winehouse with Our Fellow Rascals': The Poetics, Textual Transmission, and Reception of Fakhr al-Din ʿIraqi's Wine Ode (Saqi-Namah)." In *Medieval and Early Modern Persian Poetry: Welcoming New Directions and Forgotten Geographies*, edited by Domenico Ingenito and Matthew Thomas Miller. Edinburgh University Press, forthcoming.

———. "The Poetics of the Sufi Carnival: The Rogue Lyrics (Qalandariyyāt) as Heterotopic Countergenre(s)." *Al-ʿUsur Al-Wusta* 30 (2022): 1–46.

———. "The Qalandar King: Early Development of the *Qalandariyyāt* and Saljuq Conceptions of Kingship in Amir Moʿezzi's Panegyric for Sharafshāh Jaʿfari." *Iranian Studies* 55, no. 2 (2022): 521–49.

Mojaddedi, Jawid A. "Getting Drunk with Abū Yazīd or Staying Sober with Junayd: The Creation of a Popular Typology of Sufism." *Bulletin of the School of Oriental and African Studies, University of London* 66, no. 1 (2003): 1–13.

———. "Ḥallāj, Abu'l-Moḡit Ḥosayn." Edited by Ehsan Yarshater. *Encyclopaedia Iranica*, 2003. http://www.iranicaonline.org/articles/hallaj-1.

———. *The Biographical Tradition in Sufism: The Tabaqāt Genre from al-Sulamī to Jāmī*. Curzon Press, 2001.

Morris, James Winston. "Ibn ʿArabi and His Interpreters Part II (Conclusion): Influences and Interpretations." *Journal of the American Oriental Society* 107, no. 1 (1987): 101–19.

———. "Ibn ʿArabi and His Interpreters Part II: Influences and Interpretations." *Journal of the American Oriental Society* 106, no. 4 (1986): 733–56.

Moukheiber, Karen. "Gendering Emotions: *Ṭarab*, Women and Musical Performance in Three Biographical Narratives from 'The Book of Songs.'" *Cultural History* 8, no. 2 (2019): 164–83.

Murata, Kazuyo. *Beauty in Sufism: The Teachings of Rūzbihān Baqlī*. SUNY Press, 2017.

Myrne, Pernilla. "Discussing *Ghayra* in Abbasid Literature: Jealousy as a Manly Virtue or Sign of Mutual Affection." *Journal of Abbasid Studies* 1, no. 1 (2014): 46–65.

Najmabadi, Afsaneh. "Re-Membering *Amrads* and *Amradnumās*: Re-Inventing the (Sedgwickian) Wheel." In *The Necklace of the Pleiades*, edited by Franklin D. Lewis and Sunil Sharma, 295–308. Leiden University Press, 2010.

———. *Women with Mustaches and Men Without Beards: Gender and Sexual Anxieties of Iranian Modernity*. University of California Press, 2005.

Nasr, Seyyed Hossein, Caner K. Dagli, Maria Massi Dakake, Joseph E. B. Lumbard, and Mohammed Rustom, eds. *The Study Quran: A New Translation and Commentary*. HarperOne, 2015.

Nelson, Kristina. *The Art of Reciting the Qur'an*. University of Texas Press, 1985.

Ngai, Sianne. *Ugly Feelings*. Harvard University Press, 2005.

Nizami, K. A. "Bahāʾ al-Dīn Zakariyyā." In Bearman, et al., *Encyclopaedia of Islam, Second Edition*.

Niẓāmī ʿArūżī Samarqandī, Abū al-Ḥasan. *Chahār maqālah va taʿlīqāt*. Edited by Allāmah Muḥammad Qazvīnī and Muḥammad Muʾīn. Revised. Nashr-i Muʾīn, 2009–10 (1388).

Nurbakhsh, Javad. *Sufi Symbolism (I–XVI)*. Khaniqahi Nimatullahi, 2007.

O'Malley, Austin. *The Poetics of Spiritual Instruction: Farid al-Din 'Attar and Persian Sufi Didacticism*. Edinburgh University Press, 2023.

Ohlander, Erik S. "Between Historiography, Hagiography and Polemic: The 'Relationship' Between Abū Hafs 'Umar al-Suhrawardī and Ibn 'Arabī." *Journal of the Muhyiddin Ibn 'Arabi Society* 34 (2003): 59–82.

———. "Fear of God (*Taqwā*) in the Qur'ān: Some Notes on Semantic Shift and Thematic Context." *Journal of Semitic Studies* 50, no. 1 (2005): 137–52.

———. *Sufism in an Age of Transition: 'Umar al-Suhrawardī and the Rise of the Islamic Mystical Brotherhoods*. Brill, 2008.

Osborne, Lauren E. "Aural Epistemology: Hearing and Listening in the Text of the Qur'an." *Body and Religion* 3, no. 1 (2019): 71–93.

———. "Feeling the Words: Sayyid Qutb's Affective Engagement with the Qur'an in *al-Taswir al-Fanni fi al-Qur'an*." *Religion Compass* 13, no. 10 (2019): 1–9.

———. "The Experience of the Recited Qurʾan." *International Journal of Middle East Studies* 48, no. 1 (2016): 124–28.

———. "The Qur'an and Affect: Introduction to Special Issue." *Body and Religion* 3, no. 1 (2019): 1–4.

Papan-Matin, Firoozeh. *Beyond Death: The Mystical Teachings of 'Ayn al-Quḍāt Al-Hamadhānī*. Brill, 2010.

Papas, Alexandre. "Creating a Sufi Soundscape: Recitation (*Dhikr*) and Audition (*Samā'*) According to Ahmad Kāsānī Dahbīdī (d. 1542)." *Performing Islam* 3, no. 1 (2014): 25–43.

Patel, Youshaa. "'Their Fires Shall Not Be Visible': The Sense of Muslim Difference." *Material Religion* 14, no. 1 (2018): 1–29.

Pinker, Steven. *How the Mind Works*. W. W. Norton & Company, 1997.

Pourjavady, Nasrollah. *Bādah-yi ʿishq: Pazhuhishī dar maʿnā-yi bādah dar shiʿr-i Fārsī*. Nashr-i Kārnāmah, 2008–9 (1387).

———. "Dow asar-i kuhan dar samāʿ." *Maʿārif* 5 (1988–9/1367): 3–78.

———. "Stories of Ahmad Al-Ghazālī 'Playing the Witness' in Tabriz (Shams-i Tabrīzī's Interest in *Shāhid-bāzī*)." In *Reason and Inspiration in Islam*, edited by Todd Lawson, 200–20. I. B. Tauris in Association with the Institute of Ismaili Studies, 2005.

———. "The Concept of Love in ʿErāqi and Ahmad Ghazzāli." *Persica* 21 (2007): 51–62.

———. *Zabān-i ḥāl dar ʿirfān va adabiyyāt-i Pārsī*. Intishārāt-i Hirmis, 2006–7 (1385).

al-Qarṭājannī, Ḥāzim. "The Path of the Eloquent and the Lamp of the Lettered." In van Gelder and Hammond, *Takhyīl*, 85–113.

———. *Minhāj al-bulaghāʾ wa sirāj al-udabāʾ*. Edited by Muḥammad al-Ḥabīb ibn al-Khawjah. Dār al-Gharb al-Islāmī, 1986.

Qays al-Rāzī, Shams al-dīn Muḥammad. *Al-Muʿjam fī maʿāyir ashʿār al-ʿajam*. Edited by ʿAllāmah Muḥammad bin ʿAbd al-Waḥḥābb Qazvīnī, Mudarris Rażavī, and Sīrūs Shamīsā. Nashr-i ʿIlm, 2009–10 (1388).

al-Qayṣarī, Dāwūd. "The Commentary on Ibn Al-Fāriḍ's Wine Ode." In *The Wine of Love and Life: Ibn al-Fāriḍ Al-Khamrīyah and al-Qayṣarī's Quest for Meaning*, translated by Th. Emil Homerin. Middle East Documentation Center, 2005.

Qazvīnī, ʿAbd al-Nabī Fakhr al-Zamān. *Tażkirah-yi may-khānah*. Edited by Aḥmad Gulchīn-i Maʿānī. Iqbāl, 2011–12 [1390].

Qureshi, Regula Burckhardt. "Listening to Words Through Music: The Sufi *Samāʿ*." *Edebiyât* 2 (1988): 219–45.

Rahman, F., and William C. Chittick. "ʿAql." Edited by Ehsan Yarshater. *Encyclopaedia Iranica*, 2011. https://www.iranicaonline.org/articles/aql-intellect-intelligence-reason.

Rajamani, Imke, Margrit Pernau, and Katherine Butler Schofield, eds. *Monsoon Feelings: A History of Emotions in the Rain*. Niyogi Books, 2018.

Reddy, William M. "The Unavoidable Intentionality of Affect: The History of Emotions and the Neurosciences of the Present Day." *Emotion Review* 12, no. 3 (2020): 168–78.

Ridgeon, Lloyd. "Shaggy or Shaved? The Symbolism of Hair Among Persian Qalandar Sufis." *Iran and the Caucasus* 14 (2010): 233–64.

———. "The Controversy of Shaykh Awhad al-Dīn Kirmānī and Handsome, Moon-Faced Youths: A Case Study of *Shāhid-Bāzī* in Medieval Sufism." *Journal of Sufi Studies* 1 (2012): 3–30.

Ritter, Hellmut. *The Ocean of the Soul: Man, the World and God in the Stories of Farīd al-Dīn ʿAttār*. Brill, 2003.

Riżāʾī, Ihtirām. *Sāqī-nāmah dar shiʿr-i Fārsī*. Amīr Kabīr, 2008–9 (1387).

Rizvi, Kishwar. "Introduction: Affect, Emotion, and Subjectivity in the Early Modern Period." In K. Rizvi, *Affect, Emotion, and Subjectivity*, 1–20.

Rizvi, Kishwar, ed. *Affect, Emotion, and Subjectivity in Early Modern Muslim Empires: New Studies in Ottoman, Safavid, and Mughal Art and Culture*. Brill, 2017.

Rizvi, M. Sajjad Alam. "Music, Emotions and Reform in South Asian Islam: Perspectives from the Eighteenth to the Twentieth Century." *South Asian History and Culture* 9, no. 3 (2018): 340–63.

Robinson, Francis. "The Great Mughals: Relationships, Emotions, and Monuments." In *Turks in the Indian Subcontinent, Central and West Asia: The Turkish Presence in the Islamic World*, edited by Ismail Poonawala, 191–226. Oxford University Press, 2017.

Robson, James. "Introduction." In *Tracts on Listening to Music, Being Dhamm Al-Malāhī*, 1–13. Royal Asiatic Society, 1938.

Ruffle, Karen G. *Gender, Sainthood, & Everyday Practice in South Asian Shi'ism*. University of North Carolina Press, 2011.

Rūmī, Jalāl al-Dīn. *Fīhī mā fīhī*. Edited by Tawfīq Subḥānī. Kitāb-i Pārsah, 2011–12 (1390).

———. *Kulliyyāt-i Shams (Dīvān-i kabīr)*. Edited by Badīʿ al-Zamān Furūzānfar. Dānishgāh-i Tihrān, 1984–85 [1363].

———. *Signs of the Unseen: The Discourses of Jalaluddin Rumi*. Edited and translated by W. M. Thackston. Shambhala, 1994.

Rustom, Mohammed. *Inrushes of the Heart: The Sufi Philosophy of ʿAyn al-Quḍāt*. SUNY Press, 2023.

Safi, Omid. *The Politics of Knowledge in Premodern Islam: Negotiating Ideology and Religious Inquiry*. University of North Carolina Press, 2006.

Salamah-Qudsi, Arin. "Yūsuf ibn al-Ḥusayn al-Rāzī (d. 304/916–917) and Malāmatī-oriented Sufi Piety During the Third/Ninth Century." *Orientalia Suecana* 70 (2021): 74–88.

Sanāʾī, Abū al-Majd Majdūd ibn Ādam. *Dīvān-i Ḥakīm Abū al-Majd Majdūd ibn Ādam Sanāʾī Ghaznavī*. Edited by Muḥammad Taqī Mudarris Rażavī. Sanāʾī, 2009–10 (1388).

Sattārī, Jalāl. *ʿIshq-i Sūfīyānah*. Tihrān: Nashr-i Markaz, 1995–6 (1374).

Schaefer, Donovan O. *Religious Affects: Animality, Evolution, and Power*. Duke University Press, 2015.

———. *The Evolution of Affect Theory*. Cambridge University Press, 2019.

———. "The Promise of Affect: The Politics of the Event in Ahmed's *The Promise of Happiness* and Berlant's *Cruel Optimism*." *Theory & Event* 16, no. 2 (2013).

———. *Wild Experiment: Feeling Science and Secularism After Darwin*. Duke University Press, 2022.

Scheer, Monique. "Are Emotions a Kind of Practice (And Is That What Makes Them Have a History?): A Bourdieuian Approach to Understanding Emotion." *History and Theory* 51, no. 2 (2012): 193–220.

Schimmel, Annemarie. *A Two-Colored Brocade: The Imagery of Persian Poetry*. University of North Carolina Press, 1992.

Schofield, Katherine Butler. "Emotions in Indian Music History: Anxiety in Late Mughal Hindustan." *South Asian History and Culture* 12, no. 2 (2021): 182–205.

———. "Learning to Taste the Emotions: The Mughal Rasika." In *Tellings and Texts: Music, Literature and Performance in North India*, edited by Katherine Butler Schofield and Francesca Orsini, 407–22. Open Book Publishers, 2015.

———. "Music, Art and Power in 'Adil Shahi Bijapur, c. 1570–1630." In *Scent Upon a Southern Breeze: The Synaesthetic Arts of the Deccan*, edited by Kavita Singh, 68–87. Marg Foundation, 2018.

Sells, Michael A. "Guises of the Ghūl: Dissembling Simile and Semantic Overflow in the Classical Arabic *Nasīb*." In *Reorientations: Arabic and Persian Poetry*, edited by Suzanne Pinckney Stetkevych, 130–64. Indiana University Press, 1994.

———. *Mystical Languages of Unsaying*. University of Chicago Press, 1994.

Seyed-Gohrab, A. A. *Laylī and Majnūn: Love, Madness, and Mystic Longing in Niẓāmī's Epic Romance*. Brill, 2003.

———. "Magic in Classical Persian Amatory Literature." *Iranian Studies* 32, no. 1 (1999): 71–97.

———. "Beyond Senses: Rumi's Mystical Philosophy of Sense Perceptions." In *Losing Our Minds, Coming to Our Senses: Sensory Readings of Persian Literature and Culture*, edited by M. Mehdi Khorrami and Amir Moosavi, 49–70. Amsterdam University Press, 2021.

Shafīʿī-Kadkanī, Muḥammad Riżā. *Suvar-i khiyāl dar shiʿr-i Fārsī: Taḥqīq-i intiqādī dar taṭavvur-i īmāzh-hā-yi shiʿr-i Pārsī va siyar-i naẓariyyah-yi balāghat dar Islām va Īrān*. Āgāh, 1971 (1350).

Shahid, Taimoor. "*Saif Al-Mulūk*, The Quest for Love: Islam, Travel, and the Ethics of Cosmopolitanism in the Indian Ocean World." PhD thesis, University of Chicago, 2023.

Shah-Kazemi, R. "The Notion and Significance of *Maʿrifa* in Sufism." *Journal Of Islamic Studies* 13, no. 2 (2002): 155–81.

Shaikh, Sa'diyya. *Sufi Narratives of Intimacy: Ibn ʿArabī, Gender, and Sexuality*. University of North Carolina Press, 2012.

Shamīsā, Sīrūs. *Shāhid-bāzī dar adabiyyāt-i Fārsī*. Intishārāt-i Firdaws, 2002–3 (1381).

Sharma, Sunil. "Ḥāfiz's *Sāqīnāmah*: The Genesis and Transformation of a Classical Poetic Genre." *Persica* XVIII (2002): 75–83.

Sobieroj, F. "Suhrawardiyya." In Bearman et al., *Encyclopaedia of Islam, Second Edition*.

Somerset, Fiona. *Feeling Like Saints: Lollard Writings After Wyclif*. Cornell University Press, 2014.

Steinfels, Amina. "His Master's Voice: The Genre of *Malfūzāt* in South Asian Sufism." *History of Religions* 44 (2004): 56–69.

Stetkevych, Jaroslav. "Arabic Poetry and Assorted Poetics." In *Islamic Studies: A Tradition and Its Problems*, edited by Malcolm H. Kerr, 103–23. Undena, 1980.

———. *The Zephyrs of Najd: The Poetics of Nostalgia in the Classical Arabic Nasīb*. University of Chicago Press, 1993.

Stetkevych, Suzanne Pinckney. *The Mute Immortals Speak: Pre-Islamic Poetry and the Poetics of Ritual*. Cornell University Press, 1993.

Stewart, Tony. "The Subject and the Ostensible Subject: Mapping the Genre of Hagiography Among South Asian Chistis." In *Rethinking Islamic Studies: From Orientalism to Cosmopolitanism*, edited by Carl W. Ernst and Richard C. Martin, 227–44. University of South Carolina Press, 2010.

al-Suhrawardī, Abū Ḥafṣ ʿUmar. *ʿAwārif al-Maʿārif*. Edited by Aḥmad ʿAbd al-Raḥīm Sāyiḥ and Tawfīq ʿAlī Wahbah. Maktabat al-Taqāfah al-Dīniyyah, 2006.

Sviri, Sara. *Perspectives on Early Islamic Mysticism: The World of al-Ḥakīm al-Tirmidhī and His Contemporaries*. Routledge, 2020.

Takacs, Axel Marc Oaks. "Transposing Metaphors and Poetics from Text to World: The Theo-Poetics of Lāhūrī's 'Mystical Commentary' on Ḥāfiẓ's Love Lyrics." *Journal of Sufi Studies* 9 (2020): 106–44.

Talmy, Leonard. "Force Dynamics in Language and Cognition." *Cognitive Science* 12 (1988): 49–100.

———. *Toward a Cognitive Semantics*. MIT Press, 2000.

Tourage, Mahdi. "Affective Entanglements with the Sexual Imagery of Paradise in the Qur'an." *Body and Religion* 3, no. 1 (2019): 52–70.

———. *Rūmī and the Hermeneutics of Eroticism*. Brill, 2007.
Treiger, Alexander. *Inspired Knowledge in Islamic Thought: Al-Ghazālī's Theory of Mystical Cognition and Its Avicennian Foundation*. Routledge, 2012.
Trigg, Stephanie. "Introduction: Emotional Histories—Beyond the Personalization of the Past and the Abstraction of Affect Theory." *Exemplaria* 26, no. 1 (2014): 3–15.
van Gelder, Geert Jan, and Marlé Hammond, trans. *Takhyīl: The Imaginary in Classical Arabic Poetics*. Gibb Memorial Trust, 2009.
van Lit, L. W. Cornelis. "Ibn ʿArabī's School of Thought: Philosophical Commentaries on Fuṣūṣ Al-Ḥikam, Not a Sufi Order." *Journal of Islamic Philosophy* 14 (2023): 162–87.
van Ruymbeke, Christine. "Iskandar's Bibulous Business: Wine, Drunkenness and the Calls to the Sāqī in Nizāmī Ganjavī's Sharaf-Nāma." *Iranian Studies* 46 (2013): 251–72.
Vignone, Joseph. "Fear and Learning in Medieval Islam: Dread as an Affective Marker of the Scholarly Class." *Body and Religion* 3, no. 1 (2019): 27–51.
Watenpaugh, Heghnar Zeitlian. "Deviant Dervishes: Space, Gender, and the Construction of Antinomian Piety in Ottoman Aleppo." *International Journal of Middle East Studies* 37 (2005): 535–65.
Wehr, Hans, and J. Milton Cowan. *A Dictionary of Modern Written Arabic*. 4th ed. Harrassowitz, 1979.
Weinrich, Ines. "Sensing Sound: Aesthetic and Religious Experience According to al-Ghazālī." *Entangled Religions* 10 (2019). https://doi.org/10.46586/er.10.2019.8437.
Werbner, Pnina. "The Abstraction of Love: Personal Emotion and Mystical Spirituality in the Life Narrative of a Sufi Devotee." In *Cultural Fusion of Sufi Islam: Alternative Paths to Mystical Faith*, edited by Sarwar Alam, 161–77. Routledge, 2020.
Wilcox, Andrew. "The Dual Mystical Concepts of *Fanā'* and *Baqā'* in Early Sūfism." *British Journal of Middle Eastern Studies* 38, no. 1 (2011): 95–118.
Wolf, Richard K. *The Voice in the Drum: Music, Language, and Emotion in Islamicate South Asia*. University of Illinois Press, 2014.
Wolper, Ethel Sara. *Cities and Saints: Sufism and the Transformation of Urban Space in Medieval Anatolia*. Pennsylvania State University Press, 2003.
Wynn, Mark. "Metaphysics and Emotional Experience: Some Themes Drawn from John of the Cross." In *Feeling Religion*, edited by John Corrigan, 53–68. Duke University Press, 2017.
Yaghoobi, Claudia. *Subjectivity in ʿAṭṭār, Persian Sufism, and European Mysticism*. Purdue University Press, 2017.
———. "Yusuf's 'Queer' Beauty in Persian Cultural Productions." *The Comparatist* 40, no. 1 (2016): 245–66.
Yarshater, Ehsan. "Ḡazal II. Characteristics and Conventions." Edited by Ehsan Yarshater. *Encyclopædia Iranica, Online Edition*, 2006. https://www.iranicaonline.org/articles/gazal-2.
———. "The Theme of Wine-Drinking and the Concept of the Beloved in Early Persian Poetry." *Studia Islamica* 13 (1960): 43–53.
Yep, Stephanie. "Emotion and Islamic Hagiology: A Post-Taxonomic Approach." *Method & Theory in the Study of Religion* 1 (2022): 1–31.
Zangī Bukhārī, Muḥammad. "Nuzhat al-ʿāshiqīn." In *Zangī-nāmah*, edited by Īraj Afshār, 121–65. Chāp-khānah-yi Khwājah, 1993–94 [1372].
Zargar, Cyrus Ali. *Sufi Aesthetics: Beauty, Love, and the Human Form in the Writings of Ibn ʿArabi and ʿIraqi*. University of South Carolina Press, 2011.

INDEX

Abu-Lughod, Lila, 62n48
adab (rules), 55, 111
addiction, 148
æffects
in general, 23–24, 34–35, 37, 73, 190–92
as bridges, 69–70
as impressions, 93
knowledge and, 49, 109, 120, 190
love and, 52–53, 62–63
music and, 45, 94, 96–97, 99
nonintellectual forms of, 43–44, 46–47, 49
in Path of Love, 35, 46, 73, 108
poetry / literature and
in general, 26–27, 29, 33, 43, 190
ʿAyn al-Qużāt on, 63–64, 73
bodies, human, 69–70, 73
in commentaries, 144–45n43
al-Ghazālī on, 189–90
Jāmī on, 36–37, 141, 157–58
love, 41
metaphoric imagery, 27–28, 47, 131–32
not æffective enough, 64
reembodying meaning, 25–29
wine / love. *See* wine / love
religion and, 21–22
samāʿ sessions and
in general, 36, 76, 79–80
al-Ghazālī on, 83–85, 86–87, 91, 94, 119–22, 128–29
states and, 107–9, 119–22, 128–29
use of word, 16–17, 20
See also emotions / feelings
affect theory
Burger and Crocker on, 17–18
Deleuzian branch of, 18
feeling / knowledge and, 22–24
focus on literature in, 24–25
on history-of-emotion approach, 18
on how religion feels, 21–22
intersectional approach to, 20
mind in, 21
Ngai on, 19
phenomenological branch of, 18–19
power / knowledge and, 22–24
practice approach to, 19–20
Schaefer on, 18
Scheer on, 19–20
See also æffects; history of emotion
agitation. *See* turmoil / agitation
Ahmed, Sara, 24, 90n46, 148–49n55
Ahmed, Shahab, 15n34, 69n69
Ahrar, Shaykh, 64n55
aḥwāl / *ḥālāt*. *See* states
Akbarian Sufism, 133, 134, 137n15
amatory piety, 55–56
ambience, 81–85, 112–13, 191–92
amorous training
in general, 12–13, 35
ʿAyn al-Qużāt on, 48–49
God's role in process of, 14–15, 51–52

amorous training (*continued*)
of ʿIrāqī, 53
Rūmī on, 12, 13–15
winehouse's role in. *See* winehouses
Zangī Bukhārī on, 50–53
See also embodied love; love play; Path of Love; *samāʿ* sessions; *shāhid-bāzī*
anecdotes
about al-Nūrī, 189–90, 192
about Ḥasan the singer. *See* Ḥasan the singer, tale of
rogue, 162, 171–75, 179–86
See also love poetry / stories
animals, 91n51, 103, 190
ʿaql (intellect), 7, 46, 97–98, 183
ʿaql- ʿishq paradigm, 46
āthār. *See* impressions
ʿAṭṭār, Farīd al-Dīn, 80, 162–63
See also under qalandariyyāt
ʿAyn al-Qużāt Hamadānī, 48–49, 63–64, 73, 191

Bahāʾ al-Dīn Zakariyyāʾ, 53–57
Bashir, Shahzad, 5n9, 16, 33n99, 34, 39–40n3, 49n23, 64n55
bāṭin (inner meanings), 134
Bauer, Karen, 173n24
Beard, Michael, 9
beauty. *See* divine beauty; physical / earthly beauty
biographies
as important genre, 33–34
of ʿIrāqī. *See Kulliyyāt*
of Sufi lovers. *See Kulliyyāt*; love poetry / stories
bī-ṭāqat, 43–44, 166
bodies, human
actions and, 54, 122–23, 124
æffects and, 69–70, 73
central role in Path of Love, 68, 194
in force dynamics, 178–79
vs. mind, 20–21, 193–94
nondiscursive meaning of, 64
See also movements; *under specific body parts*
Bray, Julia, 33n100
Bray, Karen, 25
Burger, Glen D., 17–18

Cairo, 71
celestial world, 86–88, 89
Chahār maqālah (Niẓāmī ʿArūżī), 26
chests
opening up of, 172, 175–77
of Prophet, 118, 119, 176
See also hearts
Chishtīyya order, 55
Chittick, William C., 1n1, 5n9, 137n19
"click" moments / "fit" moments, 47, 64, 74, 109, 111, 114, 121, 193–94
command (*ḥukm*), 146–47, 178
commentaries
æffect of poetry in, 144–45n43
diversity in, 138
on Ibn al-Fāriḍ's wine ode
by Jāmī, 61, 138–42, 144–59
by al-Qayṣarī, 133–36
mode of interpretation in, 136–38
company (*al-ikhwān*), in *samāʿ* sessions, 81–82, 83–84
compulsion force image schema, 180n44
conquer / conquering (*ghālib / ghalaba*), 48, 87, 95, 103, 106, 116, 125–26, 146, 147
consciousness
heightened, 78n16, 102n5
loss of, 123, 124
contemplation (*tafakkur*), 90n43, 93, 103, 109–10, 159
creation accounts, 96–98, 100
crescent, as metaphor, 132, 134, 141n31
Crocker, Holly A., 17–18, 26
crying / tears
during ecstasy, 54, 122–23, 124
al-Ghazālī on, 107, 122–23
importance of, 73
when reciting the Qurʾān, 129
The Cultural Politics of Emotions (Sara Ahmed), 24

dānistan (knowing), 66
de Bruijn, J. T. P, 171n19
desire / longing (*shawq*)
al-Ghazālī on, 86, 89–90, 92, 94, 95, 96n63, 107, 111, 113, 116–17
of ʿIrāqī, 42, 45, 48
dīn (religion), 7–9, 21–22
dispatching (*tanzīl*) process, 101, 104–5, 106–8, 109, 114, 121, 141
distractions, *samāʿ* and, 82–83
divine beauty
in love-evoking earthly bodies
in general, 3n5, 12, 14, 26, 58, 60–61, 98–99
*shāhid*s and, 62–65
See also embodied love; physical / earthly beauty
divine love (*ḥaqīqī*)
in general, 4–5

embodied love as training for. *See* amorous training
underpinning existence, 65–66
Zangī on, 51–52
divine meanings / realties
in general, 36, 61
achievability of, 63–65
al-Ghazālī on, 159
Jāmī on
in general, 159–60
EMICF. *See* expressing meanings
poetic symbols and, 77, 134
in *samā'* sessions, 77–78, 103, 104–5, 106, 110, 121–22
dominance and predominance (*ghalabah va istīlā'*), 146, 182
dominant (*ghāliba*) states, 121
drowning, process of, 168–69
During, Jean, 93n58

ecstasy (*wajd / vajd*)
in general, 76, 79
acting like, 128–29, 167
bodily actions and, 54, 122–23, 124
See also movements
'Irāqī's experience of, 54, 113
Lewisohn on, 78n16
Muḥammad's experience of, 118–19, 122
Qur'ān and *ḥadīth* on, 118–19
Qur'ānic recitation and, 121, 122
in *samā'* sessions
in general, 111
crying / tears during, 54, 122–23, 124
as experiential realization of *samā'*'s first stage, 113–14
al-Ghazālī on, 88–89, 101, 111, 113–15, 117–18, 121–25, 189
intellectual knowledge and, 115
irresistible force of, 125–26
self-composed approach to, 123–27
from singing / poetry, 121–22
two types of, 115, 123–24, 128
See also samā' sessions; self-annihilation
embodied (*majāz / majāzī*) love
'Irāqī and, 11–12, 50, 71–73
as lifelong practice, 70–72
lover's suffering and, 52–53, 69–70
in poems by 'Irāqī, 12–13, 35, 66, 68, 69
Rūmī on, 12–14, 73
as training stage. *See* amorous training
translation issues, 67–69
triviality of, 12–13
See also divine beauty
EMICF. *See* expressing meanings
emotions / feelings
in general, 10, 16, 34–35, 180n44, 194–95
heart as site of, 120–21n60
literature and, 24–25, 144n41, 173n24
samā' sessions and, 79–80
soul and, 159
states and, 90–92, 109, 116, 119–20
See also æffects; affect theory; history of emotion; *under specific emotions*
entrainment, 14–15, 73, 100, 120, 127, 154, 194
experiential (*ma'rifat / ma'rifa*) knowledge, 7, 8, 11, 13–14, 66, 116–17, 155, 156, 157, 190
expressing meanings (*ma'ānī*) in the clothing of forms (EMICF)
in general, 141, 152–55, 161–62
force dynamics and, 178–79
reasons for, 156–60

fahm. *See* understanding
fahm-tanzīl stage, 101, 103–5, 106–8, 109–10, 114, 121, 141
fanā'. *See* self-annihilation
al-Fārābī, Abū Naṣr Muḥammad, 142
fear, 117–19, 149–50
felt experiences
in general, 11, 18, 49
bī-ṭāqat and, 43–44
of "clicking" into place, 64, 74
knowledge and, 22–24, 46, 66, 153–54, 158
of opening up of chest, 176
of self-annihilation, 164, 165–66, 169, 176
See also emotions / feeling
fermentation, 145–46
Fīhī mā fīhī (Rūmī), 168–69
"fits." *See* "click" moments / "fit" moments
force dynamics, 177–79
forms
bodily and imaginal, 153–60
of knowledge. *See* knowledge, forms of
See also expressing meanings; transformations
Foucault, Michel, 22, 73

Gannagé, Emma, 67
Gāzargāhī, Kamāl al-Dīn Husayn, 39–40
gazing at beautiful youths (*shāhid-bāzī*), 35, 55, 61n46, 62n49, 71–73, 75, 154–55
ghalabah va istīlā' (dominance and predominance), 146, 182

ghālib / ghalaba (conquer / conquering), 48, 87, 95, 103, 106, 116, 125–26, 146, 147
ghāliba (dominant) states, 121
ghayn-lām-bā' root, 106
al-Ghazālī, Abū Ḥāmid
  adopting Sufism, 6
  anecdote about al-Nūrī, 189–90, 192
  on bodily experiences of love, 40
  on impressions, 89–93, 95, 116, 123, 159
  on Junayd, 125–27
  on knowledge, 189–90
  on love poetry, 6–7, 102–4, 106–7 114
  on *samā'* sessions
    æffects. *See under* æffects
    ambiance of, 81–85
    body of Sufi lover in, 78
    crying / tears, 107, 122–23
    desire in, 86, 89–90, 92, 94, 95, 96n63, 107, 111, 113, 116–17
    distractions and, 82–83
    ecstasy (*wadj*) stage, 88–89, 101, 111, 113–15, 117–18, 121–25, 189
    fahm-tanzīl stage, 101, 103–5, 106–11, 114, 121, 141
    music in, 86–98
    reasons for engaging in, 129
    self-annihilation and, 164–67
    states in, 101, 106–11, 115–22
    superior to Qur'ān recitations, 75, 121, 122
  on *tawājud*, 128–29, 167
  on turmoil, 117, 165, 167
  on wine / love, 6–8
  on winehouses, 7–8
  works of
    Iḥyā' 'ulūm al-dīn, 36, 81n24, 88–89, 92, 102–3, 115, 117–18, 123, 164–65, 189, 192
    Kīmiyā al-sa'ādat, 6–7, 36, 81n24, 86–88, 92, 95, 102, 108, 116, 157n79
Ghazālī, Aḥmad, 8–9
ghazals, 42, 65, 74–75, 85, 172n22
ghulghul (uproar), 174, 182
God
  beauty of. *See* divine beauty
  fear of, 117–19
  "lassos and traps" of. *See* "lassos and traps"
  is love, 4–5, 14, 50
    See also divine love; Path of Love
  as musician, 96–97
  opening up of chest by, 176–77
  power of, in self-annihilation process, 166, 168, 169, 171, 180
  reaggregation with, 175
  role in amorous training, 14–15, 51–52
  "tresses" of, 3, 4–5, 12, 58–60, 72, 156
  unity with, 66, 163, 165, 169, 170–71, 182, 185–86
  way to. *See* Path of Love
grabbing, 60, 72

habitus
  of love-naive Muslim, 48
  of Sufi lovers, 35, 49, 70, 129
ḥadīṣ (talk / discussion), 7
ḥadīth, on ecstacy, 118–19
ḥadīth qudsī, 163–64, 166, 168, 169, 175
hagiographies. *See* biographies
al-Ḥallāj, Manṣūr, 169, 170, 171, 175
Hamadān, 41–42
'(ḥamza)-thā'-rā' root, 92
happiness (*inbisāṭ*), 150–51
ḥaqīqa-majāz dichotomy, 67
ḥarakat. *See* movements
Harb, Lara, 144, 179n42
Ḥasan the singer
  in general, 57–58
  as active force, 62–65
  beauty of, 1–2, 12, 26
  performance skills of, 1–2, 29
  performing 1st poem of 'Irāqī, 2–3, 11–12, 58–59
  performing 2nd poem of 'Irāqī, 59
  performing 3rd poem of 'Irāqī, 65, 96–97
  See also Ḥasan the singer, tale of; *qalandars*; *samā'* sessions
Ḥasan the singer, tale of
  Ḥasan the singer in. *See* Ḥasan the singer
  'Irāqī's poetry in
    1st in in tale of Ḥasan the singer, 2–5, 11–12, 58–59
    2nd in tale of Ḥasan the singer, 59
    3rd in tale of Ḥasan the singer, 65–68, 96–97
  poetry in
    of 'Irāqī, 2–5, 11–12, 58–59, 65–68, 96–97
    love in, 2–3, 4–5, 11–12, 58–59, 65–66, 69–70
    "tresses" / "lassos and traps" in, 3, 4–5, 12, 58–60
    "whiffs" in, 60–62
    winehouses in, 42, 59–60, 74–75
  qalandars (rogues) in
    entrance of, 80–81, 85
    'Irāqī following lover, 49–50
    'Irāqī leaving lover, 53
    'Irāqī travelling with, 53–54
    musical skills of, 42, 43, 45

physical beauty of, 42, 43, 45
samā' sessions of, 1–3, 11–12, 42, 44–45, 112–13
samā' session in
in general, 191
beauty of singers in, 61–65
hearing (*samā'*), 103–4, 117–18, 164, 166
hearts, 86–89, 95, 106–9, 120n60, 127, 193
See also chests
Heinrichs, Wolfhart, 67
ḥiss (tools of sense), 153–54
history of emotions
in general, 17, 20, 30, 33n100, 40
vs. affect theory, 18
focus on literature in, 24–25
on how religion feels, 21–22
mind in, 21
See also æffects; affect theory
homoeroticism, 40n4, 51, 68
ḥukm (command), 146–47, 178

Ibn al-'Arabī, Muḥyī al-Dīn, 57, 133, 136n14
Ibn al-Fāriḍ, Umar. *See under* wine odes
Ibn Mas'ūd, 118
Ibn Sīnā, Abū 'Alī al-Ḥusayn, 78n15
iḍṭirāb. *See* turmoil / agitation
Iḥyā' 'ulūm al-dīn (al-Ghazālī), 36, 81n24, 88–89, 92, 102–3, 115, 117–18, 123, 164–65, 189, 192
al-ikhwān (company), in *samā'* sessions, 81–82, 83–84
'ilm. *See* knowledge
'Imād al-Dīn, 54, 55, 57
imagination (*khiyāl*), 153–54
imitation, in poetic imagery, 142–44
impressions (*āthār*)
in general, 93, 191–92
al-Ghazālī on, 89–93, 95, 116, 123, 159
See also divine meanings / realties
imprinting (*tu'aththir*), 90
inbisāṭ (happiness), 150–51
inclinations (*mayl*), 154–55
infidels (*kuffār*), 171, 174, 179, 182–83, 185
Ingenito, Domenico, 2n3, 3n5, 62n49, 66n62, 67n65, 78, 102n5, 105, 106, 155–56n76
inner meanings (*bāṭin*), 43–44, 134
inshirāḥ, use of term, 175–76
intellect (*'aql*), 7, 46, 97–98, 183
intuitive discovery (*istinbāṭ*), 109
'Irāqī, Fakhr al-Dīn
in general, 1–3, 130
embodied love and, 11–12, 50, 71–73
life of
in general, 39, 40
amatory piety of, 55–56
at Bahā' al-Dīn's lodge (Multān), 54–57
experiencing ecstasy, 54, 113
following lover, 49–50
Ḥasan the singer and. *See* Ḥasan the singer
internal turmoil of, 42, 45, 47, 74, 75, 83–84, 85–86, 88
Islamic sciences and, 41
leaving lover, 53
marked as Sufi from birth, 41
move to Cairo, 71
as *mujarradvār*, 42, 50
passionate desire of, 45, 48
Path of Love, conversion to, 35, 41–48, 74, 112–13
practicing amorous arts, 50, 70–72
Qur'ān recitations by, 43–44
samā' sessions in, 1–3, 11–12, 42, 44–45, 112–13
sensitivity of, 43–44
spiritual experiences of, 54–55
throwing away his books, 42, 45–46
travelling with *qalandars*, 53–54
on love, 4, 15–16, 50, 70
poetry of
1st in tale of Ḥasan the singer, 2–5, 11–12, 58–59
2nd in tale of Ḥasan the singer, 59
3rd in tale of Ḥasan the singer, 65–68, 96–97
creation account in, 96–97
embodied love in, 12–13, 35, 66, 68, 69
love in, 2–3, 4–5, 11–12, 58–59, 65–66, 69–70
pardah in, 65–66, 96, 98
tarjī'-bands of, 59–60, 72
works of
creation account in, 100
Kulliyyāt, 1n1, 29–30
Lama'āt, 4, 15, 50, 57, 70, 100
ishārāt (signs / pointers), 61, 77, 104, 134, 152, 156, 157, 159, 161
Islam
philosophy and. *See* philosophy
See also religion; Sufism
istinbāṭ (intuitive discovery), 109
iżṭirābī. *See* turmoil / agitation

Jāmī, 'Abd al-Raḥmān
in general, 140
on poetry

Jāmī (*continued*)
commentary on wine ode, 36, 61, 138–42, 144–52
EMICF approach, 141, 152–62
metaphoric imagery, 27–28, 36, 138–42, 144–52
somato-affective meaning, 27–28, 131–32, 177
"whiffs," 61
on self-annihilation, 151–52, 163, 181
on singers, 63n53
works of
Lavāmiʿ, 36, 61, 138–42, 144–62
Nafaḥāt al-uns, 63n53
Junayd b. Muḥammad, Abū al-Qāsim, 82, 125–27, 163–64
al-Jurjānī, ʿAbd al-Qāhir, 143n37

Kāfūr (Qurʾānic spring), 135–36
Karamustafa, Ahmet T., 163
Keshavarz, Fatemeh, 139n23, 162, 187
Key, Alexander, 67n66, 139n23, 159n82
khāʾ-rāʾ-bāʾ root, 130n1
kharābāts (winehouses). *See* winehouses
khiyāl (imagination), 153–54
khwush (sweet / merry), 85–86, 87–88, 97
Kīmiyā al-saʿādat (al-Ghazālī), 6–7, 36, 81n24, 86–88, 92, 95, 102, 108, 116, 157n79
Klein, Yaron, 88–89n40, 109n28, 122n65, 127n81
knowing (*dānistan* / *shinākhtan*), 66, 155
knowledge (*ʿilm*)
æffects and, 49, 109, 120, 190
forms of
experiential, 7, 8, 11, 13–14, 66, 116–17, 155, 156, 157, 190
intellected, 6, 7, 8–9, 13, 41, 46, 66, 98, 153–54, 158
sensed / felt, 22–24, 46, 66
sensed vs. intellected, 153–54, 158
transmitted, 7, 13, 41, 98
See also expressing meanings; forms
al-Ghazālī on, 189–90
Jāmī on, 152–55
love and, 15n34
power and, 22–24
See also meaning (*maʿānī*) production
Knysh, Alexander, 119n57
Konya, 57
Kövecses, Zoltán, 180n44
kuffār (infidels), 171, 174, 179, 182–83, 185
Kulliyyāt (ʿIrāqī), 1n1, 29–30

Lamaʿāt (ʿIrāqī), 4, 15, 50, 57, 70, 100
lām-dhāl-dhāl root, 87n37
language
in general, 194
as bodily tool, 139
force dynamics and, 177–79
See also metaphoric imagery; poetic imagery
"lassos and traps," 3, 4–5, 12, 58–60
Lavāmiʿ (Jāmī), 36, 61, 138–42, 144–62
Lewisohn, Leonard, 3n5, 77n8, 78, 84n31, 102n5, 110, 137
liberated man (*mujarradvār*), 42, 50
linguistic fallacy, 24–25, 31
lips, 71–72
listeners / participants
in general, 160
distractions and, 82–83
al-Fārābī on, 142–43
al-Ghazālī on
fahm-tanzīl stage and, 101, 103–5, 106–11, 121
wadj stage and, 114–17
Jāmī on, 157–58
music and, 91n52, 93n58
See also transformations
literature (Persian), 9
literature (Sufi)
actualization of absences in, 29–32
emotions and, 24–25, 144n41, 173n24
genres in
in general, 32–33
biographies, 33–34
See also Kulliyyāt; love poetry / stories
poetry. *See* poetry
logocentrism and, 9
not æffective enough, 64
sensory aspects of, 9–10
longing. *See* desire / longing
love (*ʿishq*)
æffects and, 52–53, 62–63
bodily experience of, 5–6, 16, 40–41, 49
compulsion force image schema and, 180n44
different modalities of, 16
divine (*ḥaqīqī*). *See* divine love
embodied (*majāzī*). *See* embodied love
God is, 4–5, 14, 50
ʿIrāqī on, 4, 15–16, 50, 70
Jāmī's EMICF and, 141, 152–62, 178–79
knowledge and, 15n34
music and, 95
power of, 39–40

in Sufism. *See* Path of Love
in tale of Ḥasan the singer, 2–3, 4–5, 11–12, 58–59, 65–66, 69–70
terminology of, 15–16
wine and. *See* wine / love
See also amorous training
love play (*ʿishq-bāzī*), 13–14, 35, 51–52, 53, 57–58, 61
love poetry / stories
in general, 39–40
al-Ghazālī on
in defence of, 102–3
licit / illicit use if, 104, 106, 114
on wine and love, 6–7
homoeroticism in, 40n4, 51, 68
khwush in, 86
"lassos and traps" in. *See* "lassos and traps"
"tresses" in. *See* "tresses"
"whiffs" in. *See* "whiffs"
winehouses in. *See* winehouses
See also samāʿ sessions

maʿānī. *See* divine meanings / realities
madrasas, 6, 41
maḥsūsāt (sensed) knowledge, 22–24, 46, 66, 153
Majālis al-ʿushshāq (Gāzargāhī), 39–40
majāz / majāzī. *See* embodied (*majāz / majāzī*) love
manqūl (transmitted) knowledge, 7, 13, 41, 98
maʿqūl (rational) knowledge, 7, 13, 41, 98, 153–54, 158
maʿrifat / maʿrifa (experiental) knowledge, 7, 8, 11, 13–14, 66, 116–17, 155, 156, 157, 190
mayl (inclinations), 154–55
McNamer, Sarah, 25–26, 30–31, 47
meaning (*maʿānī*) production
in general, 6–7
bodily experiences and, 143–44
al-Ghazālī on, 115
in *samāʿ* sessions, 34–37, 78–80, 99, 102–4, 109–10, 115, 128
See also stages in *samāʿ* sessions
meanings (*maʿānī*)
divine. *See* divine meanings / realities
emotional, 89, 91–92, 116
inner, 134
reembodying of, 24–29
somato effective. *See* somato-affective meaning
symbolic, 9
textual absences and, 29–32
See also expressing meanings; meaning (*maʿānī*) production
meditation (*tafakkur*), 90n43, 93, 103, 109–10, 159
ménage à trois, 59
merriment (*ṭarab*), 97
metaphoric imagery
in general, 29, 47, 186–87, 193
æffects and, 27–28, 47, 131–32
drowning as, 168–69
emotions and, 180n44
imitation in, 142–44
Jāmī on, 27–28, 36, 138–42, 144–52
moon as, 134–35, 141n31
self-annihilation and, 37
strangulation as, 93–94
sun as, 141n31
symbols as, 133–37
*tanzīl*ing and, 104
wine as. *See* wine / love
See also poetic imagery; symbols
mind, vs body, 20–21, 193–94
mock-*raḥīl* (journey passage), 173, 174
moon, 134–35, 141n31
moral advice (*pand*), 183–84
mouths, 72
movements (*ḥarakat*)
in general, 92, 117
al-Ghazālī on, 95–96, 101, 123, 125, 127
Junayd on, 125, 126–27
Muḥammad, Prophet
chest of, 118, 119, 176
ecstasy and, 118–19, 122
muhla (reflection), 103, 109
mujarradvār (liberated man), 42, 50
mukāshafāt (unveilings), 63, 66, 113, 114, 115, 117–18, 123–24
Multān, 53–57
mushāhadāt (witnessings), 115, 123
music
æffects and, 45, 94, 96–97, 99
beauty and, 86, 87–89
in *samāʿ* sessions
in general, 76–77
al-Ghazālī on, 86–98
poetry and, 100–101
power of, 96–97
role of, 95–96
See also musical skills
musical skills, 42, 43, 45
See also music

Nafaḥāt al-uns (Jāmī), 63n53
nafs. *See* soul / self

Najmabadi, Afsaneh, 40
Neoplatonism, 3–4, 136
Ngai, Sianne, 19, 20
Niẓām al-Mulk, Saljūq vizier, 6
Niẓāmī ʿArūżī Samarqandī, Abū al-Ḥasan, 26, 145n43
Niẓāmiyya Madrasa (Baghdad), 6
al-Nūrī, Abū Ḥusayn, 165–66, 167–68, 171, 189–90, 192
Nuzhat al-ʿāshiqīn (Zangī Bukhārī), 51

Osborne, Lauren E., 152n67
outsiders, *qalandars* as, 43, 80–81

pand (moral advice), 183–84
pardah (veil or tune), 65–66, 96, 98
Parvānah, Amīr, 1–2, 57, 71
passionate desire (*shawq*), 7, 35, 45, 48, 113
Path of Love (*rāh-i ʿishq*)
  in general, 3–6, 73, 99, 108, 190–91
  æffects in, 35, 46, 73, 108
  amorous training and. *See* amorous training
  bodies central role in, 68, 194
  ʿIrāqī's conversion to, 35, 41–48, 74, 112–13
  wine imagery as metaphor for. *See* wine / love
  See also love play; Sufi lovers
people of Islam, in ʿAṭṭār's *qalandariyyāt*, 171, 174, 181–85
performance studies, 30–31
philosophy
  in general, 6, 78n15
  poetry and, 26–27, 32–33, 142
  shāhid-bāzī and, 61
  theory of metaphor, 143–44
  See also expressing meanings
physical / earthly beauty
  in general, 1, 43, 58, 61–65, 191
  of Ḥasan the singer, 1–2, 12, 26
  music and, 86, 87–89
  pedagogical potential of, 35
  of *qalandars*, 42, 43, 45
  See also divine beauty
piety, amatory, 55–56
poetic imagery
  in general, 36
  æffects and. *See under* æffects, poetry / literature and
  diversity in, 139
  in *fahm-tanzīl* stage, 104, 109
  force dynamics and, 177–79
  al-Ghazālī on, 103–4, 107–8
  imitation in, 142–44
  of ʿIrāqī, 65–66, 72
  Jāmī's EMICF, 141, 152–62, 178–79
  metaphor-as-imaginal-embodiment, 138–42
  metaphor-as-symbol, 133–37
  metaphoric. *See* metaphoric imagery
  as representational, 137
  textual authority and, 136–37
  wine as. *See* wine / love
poetry
  æffects and. *See under* æffects, poetry / literature and
  by Aḥmad Ghazālī, 8–9
  ghazals, 42, 65, 74–75, 85, 172n22
  by ʿIrāqī. *See under* ʿIrāqī, Fakhr al-Dīn
  Jāmī on. *See under* Jāmī, ʿAbd al-Raḥmān
  listeners and. *See* listeners
  lived reality of author and, 139
  love in. *See under* love
  as meaning event, 162
  meanings in. *See* meanings
  performance of
    centrality of context in, 62n48
    See also Ḥasan the singer; *samāʿ* sessions
  philosophy and, 26–27, 32–33, 142
  qalandariyyāt. See qalandariyyāt
  by Rūmī, 12–13, 14–15
  superior to Qurʾān recitations, 156, 157–58, 162
  wine odes. *See* wine odes
  See also love poetry / stories
pointers. *See* signs / pointers
power / knowledge theory, 22–23, 73
proportionality, 86, 88, 98

qalandariyyāt (rogue) poems
  in general, 80–81, 171
  by ʿAṭṭār
    in general, 37, 162
    æffective reading of, 179–86
    section summery, 173–75, 173*t*
    structure of, 172–73
    text of, 171–72
  breaking repentance motif in, 183n47
qalandars (rogues)
  in general, 130
  missionary goal of, 81
  as outsiders, 43, 80–81
  samāʿ's ambience and, 85
  See also Ḥasan the singer, tale of
al-Qarṭājannī, Ḥāzim, 143
qavvāls (singers), 62n47, 63, 94n59, 191
al-Qayṣarī, Dāwūd, 133–36, 141n31

Qūnawī, Ṣadr al-Dīn, 57, 133
Qurʾān
  æffective mode of reading, 152n67
  creation account in, 97–98
  on ecstasy, 118–19
  recitations
    in general, 44
    æffects and, 45
    crying during, 129
    inferior to poetry, 156, 157–58, 162
    inferior to *samāʿ*, 75, 121, 122, 192–93
    by ʿIrāqī, 43–44
  springs mentioned in, 135–36
  Sura Hūd, 118–19
  verses
    4:11, 192
    4:41, 118
    5:83, 118
    6:125, 176–77, 184
    8:2, 118
    13:28, 117
    19:52, 48
    24:4, 192
    27:88, 126
    39:23, 117
    59:21, 118
    73:12–13, 118
    76:5–6, 135
    76:17–18, 135
    83:25–28, 136
    94:1–6, 176
  wine drinking in, 130–31
Qureshi, Regula Burckhardt, 77
Qutb, Sayyid, 152n67

ranj (hardship), 148, 181
rational (*maʿqūl*) knowledge, 7, 13, 41, 98, 153–54, 158
al-Rāzī, Yūsuf b. al-Ḥusayn, 157, 158
reaggregation, with Beloved, 175
reflection (*muhla*), 103, 109
religion. *See* Islam
religion (*dīn*), 7–9, 21–22
Rūmī, Jalāl al-Dīn
  in defense of al-Ḥallāj, 170
  on embodied love, 12–14, 73
  on *samāʿ* singers, 94n59
  on self-annihilation, 168–69, 170
  on training to become a lover, 12, 13–15
  works of
    Fīhī mā fīhī, 168–69
    poetry, 12–13, 14–15
rumūz / *ramz*. *See* symbols
Rūzbihān Baqlī, 63n53

Saʿdī, 3n5, 66n62, 78, 155–56n76
Salsabīl (Qurʾānic spring), 135–36
samāʿ (hearing), 103–4, 117–18, 164, 166
samāʿ sessions (spiritual concert)
  in general, 55, 75–76
  æffects and. *See* æffects
  ambiance of, 81–85, 112–13, 1910192
  bodies in, 35, 55, 56, 61–65, 73–74, 75, 154–55, 191
    See also embodied love
  company in, 81–82, 83–84
  divine meanings / realties in, 77–78, 103, 104–5, 106, 110, 121–22
  emotions in, 79–80
    See also ecstasy; states
  existing scholarship on, 76–79
  al-Ghazālī on. *See* al-Ghazālī, Abū Ḥāmid
  listeners and. *See* listeners
  meaning production in, 34–37, 78–80, 99, 102–4, 109–10, 115, 128
  music in. *See under* music
  necessary conditions for, 82
  opposition to, 55
  participants in. *See* listeners / participants
  physical beauty in, 1, 43, 61–65, 191
  rationality and, 77–78
  reasons for engaging in, 129
  stages in. *See* stages in *samāʿ* sessions
  superior to Qurʾān recitations, 75, 121, 122, 192–93
  in tale of Ḥasan the singer. *See* Ḥasan the singer, tale of
  textual features in, 76–77
Sanāʾī, Abū al-Majd, 80, 171n19, 172
Savānah (Aḥmad Ghazālī), 8–9
Schaefer, Donovan O., 18, 21, 23, 25, 139
Scheer, Monique, 19–20, 22, 23, 128
self-annihilation (*fanāʾ*)
  in general, 7, 37, 170, 186–87
  ʿAṭṭār on, 162–63
  in ʿAṭṭār's *qalandariyyāt*, 180–83, 187
  death and, 167, 185–86
  as drowning, 168–69
  fahm-tanzīl stage and, 104–5n16
  felt experience of, 164, 165–66, 169, 176
  al-Ghazālī on, 164–67
  ḥadīth qudsī and, 163–64
  Jāmī on, 151–52, 163, 181
  Junayd on, 163–64

self-annihilation (*continued*)
al-Nūrī's, 165–66, 167–68
power of God in process of, 166, 168, 169, 171, 180
Rūmī on, 168–69, 170
See also unity; wine / love
self-control, 126–27, 183
Sells, Michael A., 162, 187
sensed (*maḥsūsāt*) knowledge, 22–24, 46, 66, 153
sensory aspects, 9–11
shāhid-bāzī (gazing at beautiful youths), 35, 55, 61n46, 62n49, 71–73, 75, 154–55
shāhids, 56, 61–65, 191
Shahristān Madrasa (Hamadān), 41
Sharḥ khamriyyat Ibn al-Fāriḍ (al-Qayṣarī), 133–36, 141n31
shaving, of hair, 50
shawq. *See* desire / longing
shinākhtan (knowing), 66, 155
shīn-ghayn-lām root, 83
shīn-rāʾ-ḥāʾ root, 176
signs / pointers (*ishārāt*), 61, 77, 104, 134, 152, 156, 157, 159, 161
singers (*qavvāls*), 62n47, 63, 94n59, 191
See also Ḥasan the singer, tale of; *shāhids*
social behavior, 149–50
somatic sequelae, 117
somato-affective body, definition of, 23
somato-affective meaning
in general, 28–29, 35, 49, 122
bī-ṭāqat and, 43–44, 166
al-Ghazālī on, 141
Jāmīʾ on, 27–28, 131–32, 177
metaphors and, 27–28, 142
soul / self (*nafs*)
emotion and, 159
music and, 89–90, 91, 116–17
See also self-annihilation
stages in *samāʿ* sessions
in general, 101
fahm-tanzīl stage, 101, 103–5, 106–8, 109–10, 114, 121, 141
ḥaraka stage. *See* movements
scholarly elision of, 111
wajd stage. *See* ecstasy
states (*aḥwāl* / *ḥālāt*)
in general, 76
æffects and. *See under* æffects
agreeing with poetic imagery, 109, 111, 114, 121, 193–94
dominant, 121
emotions and, 116, 119
al-Ghazālī on, 101, 106–11, 115–22
meaning production in, 115
music and, 90, 91, 116–17
somatic sequelae, 117
strange, 89, 91, 116, 117
unfamiliar, 107, 111, 114
See also ecstasy (*wajd* / *vajd*)
strange states (*aḥwāl gharība*), 89, 91, 116, 117
See also states
strangulation, 93–94
suffering, of Sufi lovers, 52–53, 69–70
Sufi lodges, 53
Sufi lovers
in general, 190–91, 194
body of, 78
habitus of, 23, 35, 49, 70, 129
learning to become, 127
social behavior of, 149–50
suffering of, 52–53, 69–70
uniting with Beloved. *See* self-annihilation
See also Path of Love (*rāh-i ʿishq*)
Sufism
æffect's role in. *See* æffects
Akbarian, 133, 134, 137n15
amorous training in. *See* amorous training
knowledge. *See* knowledge
as lived mode of piety, 32–33
Neoplatonism and, 3–4, 136
Path of Love in. *See* Path of Love
philosophy and. *See* philosophy
poetic tradition of. *See* poetry
samāʿ sessions. *See samāʿ* sessions
self-annihilation in. *See* self-annihilation
al-Suhrawardī, Abū Ḥafṣ ʿUmar, 55, 130
Suhrawardiyya lodge (Multān), 54–57
Suhrawardiyya order, 55, 56
sun, 141n31
sweet / merry (*khwush*), 85–86, 87–88, 97
symbols (*rumūz* / *ramz*)
in general, 161, 186–87
linked to textual authorities, 136–37
poetic imagery and, 58, 61–62, 64, 134–37
al-Qayṣarī on, 134–36
sun as, 142n31
wine as, 152
See also wine / love; wine / wine drinking

taʿallum (learning), 7
tafakkur (contemplation / meditation), 90n43, 93, 103, 109–10, 159
Takacs, Axel Mark Oaks, 138
talk / discussion (*ḥadīs̱*), 7

Talmy, Leonard, 37, 177–79
tanzīl. See dispatching (*tanzīl*) process; *fahm-tanzīl* stage
ṭarab (merriment), 97
tarjīʿ-bands (strophic poems), 59–60, 72
Tasnīm (Qurʾānic spring), 136
tasting (*ẕawq*), 7, 8, 156, 157
tawājud (forced *wadj*), 128–29, 167
ṭāʾ-wāw-qāf root, 166
tawḥīd (unity), 66, 163, 165, 169, 170–71, 185–86
teeth, 72
tools of sense (*ḥiss*), 153–54
transformations
- in general, 46
- not by Quran but by poetry / sama
  - al-Ghazālī on, 75, 121, 122
  - Jāmī on, 156, 157–58, 162
- wine drinking and, 148–50, 180–83
- *See also samāʿ* sessions; self-annihilation

transmitted (*manqūl*) knowledge, 7, 13, 41, 98
Treiger, Alexander, 78n15, 120nn60–61
"tresses," 3, 4–5, 12, 58–60, 72, 156
Tūqāt, 1–2, 39, 57, 191
turmoil / agitation (*iḍṭirāb* / *iżṭirābī*)
- al-Ghazālī on, 117, 165, 167
- ʿIrāqī's experience of, 42, 45, 47, 74, 75, 83, 84, 85–86, 88

ʿumūm-i sarayān (all-embracing penetration and spread), 146–47
understanding (*fahm*)
- Jāmī on, 153
- as stage in *samāʿ* sessions. *See fahm-tanzīl* stage

unfamiliar states (*aḥwāl mukhālifa li-ʿādatihi*), 107, 111, 113, 114
- *See also* states

unity (*tawḥīd*), 66, 163, 165, 169, 170–71, 182, 185–86
unveilings (*mukāshafāt*), 63, 66, 113, 114, 115, 117–18, 123–24
uproar (*ghulghul*), 174, 182

wadj / vadj. See ecstasy
Weinrich, Ines, 86n35, 92n57
"whiffs," 60–62
Wilson, Peter L., 1n1
wine / love
- in general, 130–31
- in ʿAṭṭār's *qalandariyyāt*, 180–83
- force dynamics and, 178–79
- al-Ghazālī on, 6–8
- God as origin of, 180
- Jāmī on, 181, 187
- Jāmī's EMICF and, 141, 152–62, 178–79
- similitude, 138, 142, 144–52, 161
- *See also* wine / wine drinking; wine odes; winehouses

wine / wine drinking
- compulsion force image schema and, 180n44
- fermentation process, 146
- *ḥukm* and, 147–48
- love and. *See* wine / love
- normative society's ideas on, 171, 174, 179, 181–85
- personal transformation and, 148–50, 180–83
- physical craving and, 148
- self-annihilation and, 151
- social impact of transformation, 149–50
- *ʿumūm-i sarayān* and, 146–47
- *See also* wine odes; winehouses

wine odes (*khamriyyas*)
- in general, 130–31
- of ʿUmar ibn al-Fāriḍ
  - in general, 131, 132–33
  - Jāmī's commentary on, 36, 61, 138–42, 144–52
  - Jāmī's EMICF approach, 141, 152–62
  - al-Qayṣarī commentary on, 133–36, 141n31
- *See also* wine / love; wine / wine drinking; winehouses

winehouses (*kharābāts*)
- in general, 43, 130
- in 1st poem in tale of Ḥasan the singer, 42, 74–75
- in 2nd poem in tale of Ḥasan the singer, 59–60
- in ʿAṭṭār's *qalandariyyāt*, 173–75, 179
- al-Ghazālī on, 7–8
- ʿIrāqī's poetry performed at, 55
- Zangī Bukhārī on, 51
- *See also* wine / love; wine / wine drinking; wine odes

witnessings (*mushāhadāt*), 115, 123

Zangī Bukhārī, Muḥammad, 51–52, 53
Zargar, Cyrus I., 34, 61n46, 138, 139n23
ẕawq (tasting), 7, 8, 156, 157

Founded in 1893,
UNIVERSITY OF CALIFORNIA PRESS
publishes bold, progressive books and journals on topics in the arts, humanities, social sciences, and natural sciences—with a focus on social justice issues—that inspire thought and action among readers worldwide.

The UC PRESS FOUNDATION
raises funds to uphold the press's vital role as an independent, nonprofit publisher, and receives philanthropic support from a wide range of individuals and institutions—and from committed readers like you. To learn more, visit ucpress.edu/supportus.

www.ingramcontent.com/pod-product-compliance
Lightning Source LLC
Chambersburg PA
CBHW030646230426
43665CB00011B/977
9780520426344